AGE OF AUSTERITY

AGE OF
AUSTERITY

EDITED BY

MICHAEL SISSONS
AND
PHILIP FRENCH

GREENWOOD PRESS, PUBLISHERS
WESTPORT, CONNECTICUT

Library of Congress Cataloging in Publication Data

Sissons, Michael, ed.
    Age of austerity.

    Includes index.
    Reprint of the ed. published by Hodder and
Stoughton, London.
        1.   Great Britain--History--George VI, 1936-1952--
Addresses, essays, lectures.   I.   French, Philip.
II.   Title.
DA588.S5   1976   941.084   75-45350
ISBN 0-8371-8732-X

ll 11-9

CONTENTS

LIST OF ILLUSTRATIONS

Quotation from Noël Coward's song *Don't Make Fun of the Fair* (see page 322) printed by permission of Chappell & Company Limited.

The Gallup Poll findings in Michael Frayn's essay *Festival* (see page 326) are reproduced by permission of Social Surveys (Gallup Poll) Limited.

INTRODUCTION

"Austerity" was a word as current after 1945 as "affluence" has been since 1958. Sir Stafford Cripps presented it to the right-wing critics of the Labour Government, just as Professor Galbraith provided "affluence" for the critical vocabulary of the left in the late Fifties. The years between the election of the first majority Labour Government and the strange ritual of the Festival of Britain which immediately preceded its downfall afford enough examples of austerity amply to justify the title of this book. Yet the word retains an ambivalence in relation to those years. "Affluence" and "austerity" are both words now too loaded for use in any neutral, descriptive sense. So "austerity" in the title of this book (it has rarely been allowed to appear in the text) has a different meaning for different people, as a justification of the period or as a criticism.

However, the dates which we have taken to mark the Age of Austerity are not arbitrary: increasingly 1951 seems a political and social landmark. Little has been written on these years so far, beyond the inevitably partisan memoirs of the political protagonists. In the growing prosperity of the Fifties there was perhaps a conscious turning away from memories of the days of rationing and shortages. And in many ways the atmosphere of the post-war years is incredibly remote. It is difficult to recall a time when so much idealism was in the air . . . when T.V. was only a metropolitan toy, ball-point pens a source of wonder, and long-playing records a transatlantic rumour.

Nevertheless, for all the talk of austerity, this was an exciting time, with a strong flavour of its own. As a period it is much of a piece . . . from the spiv and the squatter to the New Look and the Lynskey Tribunal. Politically it is hardly the age of anyone in particular, but some magnetic figures did strut the national stage and belong essentially to these years. The great social experiment that was being conducted gave rise to a sense of crusading idealism, and to virtually all a feeling of involvement in national affairs which was to become muffled in the following decade.

We have tried to give the essence of these six years by concentrating on certain key incidents and personalities as seen today by fifteen writers, who have in common an interest in the period and the fact that they were too young to vote in 1945.

This is not a definitive history of the times. There is no more than passing reference to the Korean War, the Berlin air-lift, the atom spies, the new towns, and other political and social events which would require attention in such a history. It is an attempt to give a fresh perspective by examining in detail some aspects which seem significant in shaping the character of the period.

Four of the essays explore different aspects of domestic politics. Anthony Howard tells the story of the 1945 election and the ensuing honeymoon period which ended abruptly with the food and fuel crises of the second post-war winter. As criticism of the Government's handling of the economic situation mounted in 1947 and 1948, no member of the Cabinet came under heavier fire than Sir Stafford Cripps. David Marquand describes the devaluation crisis, and gives a picture of Cripps's personality and political development which has a wider relevance to the nature of the Labour Party in the years leading up to 1945. The legislative achievement of this Parliament is dealt with by Peter Jenkins, whose account of the rearguard action fought by the doctors against the implementation of Aneurin Bevan's National Health Service brings into relief the nature and vehemence of the reaction in some quarters against nationalisation. But, as Mr. Jenkins also shows, many of the measures of public ownership on Labour's programme had surprisingly smooth passages through Parliament, backed, as Zec's cartoon on page 239 suggests, by overwhelming popular support. This could hardly be said of the Iron and Steel Nationalisation Bill of 1948. Godfrey Hodgson, with a reconstruction of the steel debates, conveys the atmosphere of intense partisanship in both Houses which is very much a part of this time. The Conservative Party, dragging itself up under Woolton and Butler out of the wreckage of 1945, gathered strength from the success of its tactics in opposition, and a coda to the story of the steel debates is the internal reorganisation and electoral resurgence of the Conservatives which bore fruit in 1950 and 1951.

The chapters involving the foreign policy of the Labour Government concentrate on the issues which had the most immediate repercussions in Britain rather than others equally significant in a world context. The growth of terrorism in Palestine, Ernest Bevin's measures to solve this problem, and the events leading up to the creation of the State of Israel are analysed by David Leitch, and Bevin's qualities as Foreign Secretary are also discussed by David Watt in his essay on the British decision to withdraw from Greece in 1947, with the far-reaching implications of this decision on American foreign policy. This was one of two momentous steps taken by the Government in the sphere of foreign policy, and it proved to be a crucial factor in determining the character of the Cold War. We believe that this story, rather than that of the Berlin air-lift, the fall of Czechoslovakia, the growth of U.N.O., or even the Korean War, is integral to the role of Britain in the early stages of East-West tension. The second great step was the granting of independence to India, and John Higgins traces the rise of the independence movement in India and the part which the Labour Government played in bringing it to fruition.

Shortages and crime are recurrent themes in the social history of the period. Susan Cooper recalls the trappings of austerity, the tribulations of the housewives who for the first time became a coherent national force, with the pent-up irritation at rationing and the bureaucracy that existed to enforce it coming to a head in the grim winter of 1946–7. But, if whalemeat steaks, groundnuts, and bread units are very much of this period, so too is the mood which Pearson Phillips has found expressed in the rapturous reception accorded to the New Look . . . "interpreting hopes for the future, but at the same time gazing nostalgically back to the past . . . interpreting hopes for the unknown in terms of memories of the known." A different shortage is suggested in David Pryce-Jones's survey of post-war writing—a shortage of talent and an overall artistic failure to adjust to the profound social revolution which was taking place. A shortage of talent was also apparent in the world of sport, on which, with life drab and restricted in other respects, the public focused so much attention. In Britain to a unique extent concern over sporting success is linked with more fundamental complexes about national prestige. Brian Glanville examines the illusions of athletic supremacy to which the British public clung in the shadow of the country's declining status as a world power. If sport was one form of escapism, the cinema was another and quite as significant, and Peter Forster follows in the career and personality of J. Arthur Rank the fortunes of the British film industry in decline, with at the end of the period television looming up to threaten its very existence.

The post-war crime wave had important long- and short-term effects on Britain. David Hughes, in his evocation of the spiv, and John Gross, on the Lynskey Tribunal, concentrate on different aspects of this. The spiv was a totem, someone who by his wits became a successful symbol of rebellion against authority, but there was in the long run a heavy price to be paid for the tolerance, even sympathy, shown to the fiddling and petty crime of the spiv . . . what Mr. Hughes calls "a form of civil dis-obedience that millions found endearing." If the spiv was an everyday figure, universally recognised, the colourful tales unearthed by the Lynskey Tribunal with its whiffs of spivvery on the grand scale and in high places, cast serious yet ultimately exaggerated aspersions on the integrity of public life, and on the calibre of a Government which by the end of 1948 was under constant and well-directed fire from its critics.

But it would be wrong to end on that note. As its political fortunes sank ever lower, the Labour Government was still responsible for an event which in an important respect brings the period to an end on a note of confidence and optimism. Like most of the Government's proposals, the Festival of Britain became a burning political issue and the subject of much effective abuse and ridicule. But Michael Frayn sees reflected in the Festival of Britain most of what was best in these years . . . "a brilliant sign riding the tail of the storm and promising fairer weather."

One strong thread ran through most of the essays, and, to avoid repetition, has necessarily been somewhat lost in editing. Nearly every contributor stressed the importance of the grim winter of 1946-7, not only because of its severity and its crises, but as a turning-point in the political fortunes of the Government. Thereafter the *élan* and energy of 1945 and 1946 were never recaptured. The climatic and economic misfortunes of 1947 came so thick and fast that Mr. Attlee appears in retrospect cast in the role of Job. From 1947 onwards the Tories, with increasing confidence and voice, castigated the Government for mis-management – of the economy, of rationing, of Britain's part in the Cold War, of the dissolution of the Empire – in a sustained campaign of extraordinarily effective parliamentary opposition. Yet in 1963 it is difficult not to feel that, whatever else contributed to the fall of the Labour Government, merciless outside pressures – economic, physical, inter-national – played an uncontrollable part. For Labour the high hopes of 1945 ended on a sour note of frustration and discord. But the legislation and social evolution for which the Attlee administration was responsible proved to be an immensely strong formative influence on the years that followed, an influence which, in the subsequent spectacular decline in the electoral fortunes of Labour, was often overlooked.

MICHAEL SISSONS
PHILIP FRENCH

London,
March 1963

I

"WE ARE THE MASTERS NOW"
The General Election of July 5th, 1945

ANTHONY HOWARD

Anthony Howard was born in 1934, and educated at
Westminster and Christ Church, Oxford, where he was
President of the Union. He was called to the Bar in 1956,
joined *Reynolds News* in 1958, worked for *The Guardian*—
as a reporter—and *Sunday Pictorial*—as political columnist
—before becoming political correspondent of the *New
Statesman* in 1961. He contributed to *The Baldwin Age*
(Eyre and Spottiswoode 1960).

"WE ARE THE MASTERS NOW"

Anthony Howard

OCCASIONALLY late at night at a Labour Party conference – or in the small hours of the morning at the more strenuous gatherings of the T.U.C. – the cry can still be heard. "Where," a plaintive, maudlin voice will ask, "did it go wrong?" Reverie will soon take over from reproach; the glorious hour will once again be summoned back; and across the years will come wafting the atmosphere of July 26th, 1945.

Mr. and Mrs. Attlee driving up to the Palace in their Standard 10 fifteen minutes after Churchill had left in his chauffeur-driven Rolls, the crowds of Labour supporters surging up the Mall and chanting not "We want the King" but (astonishingly) "We want Attlee", even Mr. Herbert Morrison and Professor Laski overreaching themselves in fulsome tribute to the new Prime Minister at the packed Victory celebration that night in the Central Hall – in the full flush of nostalgia only the dedicated masochist will recall that within five years power was to be lost and eighteen months after that office as well.

For British Socialism it was, of course, its one great historic moment. The election result (announced on July 26th but decided on July 5th) came – and we have it in the pained words of the reigning monarch – "as a great surprise to one and all." Only, indeed, the Duke of Devonshire, Lord Templewood, Mr. Aneurin Bevan and Mr. Emanuel Shinwell (in a splendidly comprehensive democratic quartet) were later to be given credit for having foreseen it. For the rest, Mr. Ernest Bevin, accosted by reporters in the foyer of Transport House, was, for once, "speechless," Mr. Attlee (as King George VI never tired of recalling) turned up to kiss hands "looking very surprised indeed," and in the Savoy Hotel a lady diner was reduced to gasping "But this is terrible – they've elected a Labour Government, and the country will never stand for that."

For years the mystery has, of course, been why no one saw it coming. The Conservatives, after all, had suffered rebuff after rebuff at wartime by-elections (after 1942 Mr. Attlee was even prevailed upon to send messages of support to Conservative coalition candidates in a vain effort to stop the rot), the official reaction to the Beveridge Report had been so badly bungled that the Liberals were, throughout the election, content

15

to rely on that political-museum-piece slogan "Let Beveridge Take the Helm," and the Labour Party, in its turn, enjoyed the unique advantage of being an opposition denunciatory party and of having five years' experience of national administration behind it as well. At the time the importance of this tremendous (and almost unfair) asset seems to have been widely overlooked. The businessman who remarked to a Labour M.P. in 1942, "I do admire the way you Socialists are getting in everywhere: you've got control of the Navy, the Police, and Scotland – and now you've worked one of your men in as Archbishop of Canterbury too" certainly showed a much greater political prescience than did Mr. Churchill himself in his notorious election broadcasts. Even the totally uncommitted voter found it impossible to believe that it was these people – the trustworthy Attlee, the perkily patriotic Morrison, the rock-quarried Bevin – who were going to have to fall back "on some form of Gestapo."

But the Conservatives did not – as is often suggested – merely misjudge their electoral tactics. They also seem to have based their whole vote-getting strategy on a fundamental misreading of the nation's mood. The task which faced them was not one of having to ask for a vote of confidence in the continued War Effort ("Help Him Finish the Job, Vote National"); it was rather having to plead for a vote of forgiveness for the years that the locusts had eaten before the war.

The 1945 voter was not so much casting his ballot in judgement of the past five years as in denunciation of the ten before that. The dole queue was more evocative than El Alamein, the lack of roofs at home more important than any "national" non-party edifice, the peace that might be lost far more influential than the war that had been nearly won. And by refusing to come to grips with these problems at all the Conservatives signed and sealed their defeat.

Instead they had taken refuge behind one thing – or rather person. The Conservative Party's election managers no doubt knew very well that a whole host of factors pointed to a Conservative reverse. But they took their comfort and their confidence from the fact that it was to them starkly inconceivable that the nation should reject "the man who won the war." There is even some evidence that their opposite numbers in the Labour Party shared this view. The one point at which the wartime coalition nearly fell victim to political jealousy and personal suspicion was when, in the aftermath of V.E. Day, Mr. Churchill decided to go on a two-day triumphal tour throughout London. Herbert Morrison, with the natural apprehension of the born political manager, referred to this episode as "all this circus riding" — adding darkly that he had heard that people felt that the Prime Minister had pushed the King right into the background. And Ernest Bevin, in his turn, seems to have had his worst suspicions confirmed when Churchill frankly confessed to him about the Conservatives "They know they can't win without me."

As it turned out, Labour's fears were by no means entirely solidly based. Among the middle and professional classes Churchill's ascendancy was certainly absolute. But in the munitions factories, the ordnance depots, the barrack rooms, and even in the aircraft hangars the allegiance was much more conditional.

What perhaps had been forgotten was that even historic broadcasts can sound very different when heard above the communal raucousness of the Naafi and the works-canteen than when listened to reverently around the family fireside with the black-out curtains drawn. Moreover, even the victory sign itself — accepted in all innocence by a middle-class citizenry — had from the beginning (at least in the Nissen huts) rather different connotations. When "Bomber" Harris told Churchill that eighty per cent of the Royal Air Force would vote against him, and (as the unkindest cut) that the other twenty per cent wouldn't bother to vote at all, he was not speaking of a necessarily vindictive attitude. He was simply describing a reflex reaction to national reverence.

At home, at least on the surface, the Churchill writ did indeed seem to run everywhere. It is hard today to recapture the mood. Perhaps, though, it is best preserved in the telegram sent by the Conservative candidate for Jarrow (of all places) to the Prime Minister five days before polling. "Tyneside," it read simply, "would like to touch the hem of your garment on Monday, Tuesday, or Wednesday of next week." And, more extraordinarily, the press echoed that melody — with the exceptions of the *Mirror*, the *Herald*, and the *Manchester Guardian*, it persisted in seeing the election as some kind of Roman triumph for a conquering hero. "We are Winning," cried the *Daily Express* on polling day, "Churchill Flays Morrison for Cowardly Speech" countered the *Daily Mail* — while even from such restrained quarters as the *Glasgow Herald*, the *Liverpool Daily Post* and the *Financial Times* came estimates of a Conservative majority ranging from forty to one hundred.

By midday of July 26th, however, such forecasts already ranked among the political howlers of the century. From the beginning — which was roughly when Mr. Macmillan's head rolled at Stockton-on-Tees at 10.25 a.m. — it was clear that the carnage was going to be virtually complete. One after another — partly, no doubt, as the price of middle-class evacuation to rural refuges – even the most respectable residential citadels fell: Dover, Winchester, Buckingham, St. Albans, even lawn tennis's national home at Wimbledon. Nor did the electorate show itself to be any respecter of persons – twenty-nine Conservative Ministers of the "Caretaker" Government were defeated, including L. S. Amery (Secretary of State for India), Brendan Bracken (First Lord of the Admiralty), Sir James Grigg (Secretary of State for War), Leslie Hore-Belisha (Minister of National Insurance), and Duncan Sandys (Minister of Works). Ten thousand votes were cast for an Independent at Woodford against Mr. Churchill himself, and among the 136 former Conservative M.P.s who rode to defeat were most of the young men of promise in the party. In Transport House Mr. Attlee characteristically sat throughout the day almost *incommunicado*: but in the London streets his supporters showed no such inhibitions. They sang, they danced, they lit bonfires – and even in India a red flag went up outside an officers' mess.

What, of course, they were celebrating was the greatest British political earth tremor since 1906. The Conservatives and their allies had lost 203 seats, Labour had gained 227, and the Liberals – for whom even the *New Statesman* had been predicting great things – found themselves on the way to the tomb with a bare dozen. The Communist Party had two representatives: Willie Gallacher in West Fife and Phil Piratin in Mile End. Perhaps most significant of all – since men are more interesting than statistics – were the 393 Labour M.P.s. When the Parliamentary party assembled in the City's Beaver Hall (a defiant stone's throw from the Mansion House) the gathering included no less than 253 people who had never sat in Parliament before except in the public gallery. Most of them, far from knowing each other, were not even on nodding-acquaintance terms with the leaders of the party.

But, whatever its personal inconvenience, the size and dimension of the Labour majority did at least mean one very important political thing. Overnight the party had ceased to look like a faction or a sect – representing, as it were, just one estate of the nation – and had come instead to look like a truly national party commanding the support of the whole people. Some of the new M.P.s, like Hugh Gaitskell and Richard Crossman, had admittedly been apprenticed to Labour's cause since long before the war; but others, like Woodrow Wyatt or Aidan Crawley, had simply travelled to selection conferences, found themselves nominated, and then, to their astonishment, a couple of months later, elected. And this meant, as was noted in some sophisticated quarters, that for the first time the Labour parliamentary party looked something like a national microcosm. Years before, Hugh Dalton had once remarked to Professor G. D. H. Cole that Labour could only win power with "the votes of the football crowds" – Cole had "shuddered and turned away." It had now done exactly that: and the fears of the purists found absolutely no echo among the constituency activists.

For the moment, however, attention naturally centred on the men who were going to govern the realm. Mr. Attlee, who was due to return to the Potsdam conference after the week-end (from now on as of right rather than out of courtesy), acted quickly and decisively. Within twenty-four hours of taking office he had appointed his six most important Ministers – Ernest Bevin to the Foreign Office, Hugh Dalton to the Exchequer, Herbert Morrison to the Leadership of the House, Sir Stafford Cripps to the Board of Trade, Arthur Greenwood to the co-ordinating sinecure of Lord Privy Seal, and Jowitt to the Lord Chancellorship. There could hardly have been a sharper contrast with the appalling dither and delay which had attended Ramsay MacDonald's formation of the Labour Government of 1929: but then Attlee, lacking completely the histrionic gift, was not the kind of man to dramatise the situation with such a confession as "It has been terrible – I've had people in here weeping and even fainting."

On this occasion there was no evidence that anyone – except possibly Dalton in disappointment at losing the prospect of the Foreign Office which Attlee had held out to him – was given the chance to shed the slightest tear. The deed had been done so quickly that the nation hardly realised that it had happened. And it had some reason for not doing so. In the rush of getting back to Potsdam with Bevin, his new Foreign Secretary, Attlee spared a moment to request all Conservative "Caretaker" Ministers who had not yet been replaced to stay at their posts so that "the King's government might be carried on." It scarcely seemed like the age of "the gauleiters" which Churchill had forecast.

But at least some elements within the nation insisted on having their fears confirmed – and they were soon to get their chance. The first meeting of the new Parliament – held on August 1st to elect a Speaker – was necessarily something of an eerie occasion. The Conservatives greeting each other like fortunate survivors of some great bomb disaster, the Labour members crowding in past the, for once, wholly defeated Commons policemen, the lack of seats on the Government side of the House, the embarrassment at having only four Ministers on the Treasury bench – the whole situation was, from the beginning, strained to the point of disbelief. And it was, of course, in this atmosphere that the first, and almost the last shock of Labour rule was administered. Twenty-one years before, Ramsay MacDonald had assured King George V that, had not the "unfortunate incident" of the singing of *The Red Flag* taken place at the Albert Hall, it might even have happened on the floor of the House of Commons. This time, however, it really did – and all the self-appointed "defenders of the constitution" throughout the land massaged the bruise in communal gratification. They had not, they told each other wisely, been wrong after all. When one of the Royal Palaces was desecrated in this way, the revolution had surely begun; and, at least in Club-land, they looked anxiously at the lamp-posts.

In retrospect, there can be little doubt that this incident was greatly blown up and exaggerated. The scattered remnant of the Conservatives (joined eccentrically by Ellen Wilkinson) had to some degree at least provoked it by getting up and gallantly singing *For He's a Jolly Good Fellow* when Churchill entered the chamber; and the Labour Party's reply was a spontaneous back-bench demonstration – made perhaps less than alarming by the obvious inability of a number of Labour M.P.s to remember the words. It was, in any case, tradition's victory in the end. When the re-elected Speaker, Colonel Clifton-Brown, had finally been formally dragged to his chair he remarked – with the wry humour that Speakers are always meant to show – that he hoped he had been elected Speaker of the House of Commons and not director of some musical chorus. In face of such *sang-froid* it was surely impossible to believe that revolution was round the corner.

That it was a good deal further down the road still Mr. Attlee proved the very next week. Only perhaps in Britain could a social revolution intended to introduce "a new age" be consummated by the appointment of a Cabinet with an average age of well over sixty. Yet when on August 4th the Cabinet was announced it was found to contain practically all of Labour's veterans – and very little else. Naturally enough it received, if not a cordial, then at least a relieved welcome. There was a slight sniff at Emanuel Shinwell's appointment to the Ministry of Fuel and Power, an air of faint surprise at the readiness with which Mr. Attlee had forgiven Miss Ellen Wilkinson for her pro-Morrison activities in placing her at the Ministry of Education – but for the rest, those in high and traditional places clearly felt that they had been given a reprieve.

There was, however, one exception. Nothing is more indicative of the growing feeling among the far-seeing that the Labour Party had already been tamed than the way in which they chose to greet Mr. Bevan's appointment to the Ministry of Health. *The Times*, in particular, surpassed itself. "Mr. Aneurin Bevan at the Ministry of Health," it wrote, "is conspicuously the poacher turned gamekeeper. If his powers of administrative contrivance and ministerial negotiation are comparable with his striking talents, devoted so often and so effectively to destructive criticism, he may at the comparatively early age of forty-seven be at the beginning of a distinguished career." Not, one would have thought, the words of genuinely frightened men – any more than was the wonderfully magisterial comment of the *Spectator* that Mr. Bevan's appointment was "something of an adventure."

But the Labour Party, too, was by now in a remarkably passive mood. By and large, the new members – most of whom were probably not yet fully acclimatised to the idea of being M.P.s, much less to the notion of being possible prospective Ministers – no doubt felt that to criticise Mr. Attlee was nothing very far short of *lèse majesté*. Indeed, the only evidence of any disappointment at the astonishingly Baldwinesque choices that Mr. Attlee had made comes from a dinner party which Hugh Dalton gave four days after the results had been announced. Both Hugh Gaitskell and Evan Durbin (others present included Harold Wilson, George Brown, and Raymond Blackburn) are reported to have spoken up there and urged that new and younger men should be "blooded" quickly. Nor did either of them speak in vain – within two years one (Gaitskell) was a full Minister and the other (Evan Durbin – to be tragically drowned in 1948) was a very promising Under-Secretary.

But for the most part modesty and awe was still the proper mental dress within the Parliamentary Labour Party. Attlee, of course, had bought off criticism by making it almost threateningly clear at the original Beaver Hall meeting that the Ministers whom he selected would be very much "on trial": it would – and, as it turned out, it looked like it – be very much "a provisional government." With that everyone for the moment seemed to rest content – though some were more cruel about it than others with remarks about "the triers being given their Second XI Colours." Even when the Ministry was finally completed on August 11th – and found to contain only three new M.P.s as junior ministers (Hilary Marquand, George Lindgren, and Harold Wilson) – there was no ground-swell of revolt from the new men who now controlled the Parliamentary Labour Party. In place of "the weepings" and "faintings" that Ramsay MacDonald had complained of in 1929 there is only one recorded case of a protest being made. And that came from Ivor Thomas, who had sat for Keighley since 1942 and who therefore, as it appeared to him, having qualified for office, could not understand why he was now being overlooked. Not altogether surprisingly he immediately got an Under-Secretary's job. (Later he was to hyphenate his name, become a Conservative candidate, and chairman of the Historic Churches Preservation Trust.)

One other factor probably had something to do with the extraordinarily peaceful transfer of power that took place in August 1945. Throughout the period in which the Government was being formed, world events consistently over-shadowed the domestic political scene. On the day on which Mr. Attlee completed his Cabinet, the appointments were almost buried underneath the mushroom cloud that rose over Hiroshima. And even when Parliament met on August 15th to hear the King's Speech in Westminster Hall a good deal of its time and energy was taken up in tramping to St. Margaret's and back to give thanks for the victory over Japan.

In such an atmosphere, domestic political combat necessarily seemed to be something of "a phoney war." In the short nine-day session which took place after August 15th only one member succeeded in striking a really firm and challenging note. "We have before us," declared Major John Freeman (M.P. for Watford) in moving the address in reply to the King's Speech, "a battle for peace no less arduous and no less momentous than the battle we have lived through in the past six years. Today the strategy begins to unfold itself. Today we go into action. Today may rightly be regarded as D-Day in the battle for the New Britain." Everyone agreed that it was "an admirable speech," "a model parliamentary performance": it does not appear to have occurred to anyone that it was seriously meant.

Indeed, on the day it was delivered at least one Labour member could be found loitering in the lobbies afterwards and waiting respectfully to speak to the deputy leader of the Conservative Party. His purpose was at once revealing and pathetic. It was to find out whether arrangements could possibly be made for him to have "a few words" with Mr. Churchill so that he might convey to him that despite all that had happened the British people still felt about him in exactly the same way as they had done in the dark days of the war. In such a mood – almost of guilt and certainly of dazed shock – was Labour's social revolution launched.

It was, in its way, understandable enough. For the world then was a very strange one. A distribution of bananas to children under fourteen in selected provincial centres took precedence as a news item over a junior political appointment. Indeed, so far had the wartime belt-tightening process gone that the first stern words addressed even by the *New States-*

man to the Government arose out of an obviously long pent-up feeling of frustration. "Mr. Shinwell," its London Diarist announced (scarcely, one would have thought, entering into the full spirit of the Socialist experiment), "would do well to tell us more about the petrol situation. The small increase in the petrol ration announced for the next three months seems to take all too little into account the ending of the Far East War."

So against a background of vocal but conventional grievances – many of them arising at the beginning out of the new Government's steadfastly maintained principle of "First in, First out" over demobilisation – the "honeymoon period" began. It was exactly that at first. Even the urgency of building a New Britain was not allowed to interfere with the Parliamentary recess: away for six weeks went the whole House of Commons, leaving only the new Ministers to sort out their departments with their civil servants. The effect of this enforced absence was, not surprisingly, to make for a certain restlessness. And it was during the recess that the first considered attack on the new Government came – not from any Conservative but from the newly-elected youthful Labour member for Aston, Major Woodrow Wyatt.

Wyatt was, in his way, the symbol of the new type of Labour member. The son of a prep-school headmaster in Esher, the product of a minor South Coast public school, a creditable war record which had enabled him to meet another Labour member at a court-martial and thereby gain his introduction to the Labour Party headquarters – he had come into the House at the age of twenty-seven. And with all the impetuousness of youth he was already, by September 1945, puzzled and perplexed. Remarking sternly that "At present the country is far to the left of Labour ministers," he went on to put the simple query "What is the use of having an orderly revolution if it turns out not to be a revolution at all?" There is little sign that the Government was rocked to its foundations by this question. But Wyatt's point was at least taken to this extent: Attlee shortly afterwards had a P.R.O. (Francis Williams) appointed in Downing Street. Once the whole thing was properly explained it was clearly felt that the chaps would all understand.

And yet Wyatt's question refused ever quite to lie down and die. It certainly provided the main impetus behind all the restiveness with Bevin's foreign policy. Labour members sat throughout most of the early Foreign Affairs statements by the Foreign Secretary in glum silence at least partly because these gloomy sentences would have sounded far more natural on Conservative lips. It was almost as if here the millennium had had no impact – and that was the hardest thing of all to forgive, especially as Bevin himself had spoken openly before the election of "Left under-standing Left" while Sir Stafford Cripps had actually urged the electors of Bristol to "return a government that would have the broad sympathy of the Russian people."

There was something of the same disenchantment with the first Labour nationalisation proposals. Sir Herbert Williams – defeated at Croydon

Among those present . . .

in the election but throughout these years the vocal spokesman of the ultra-Conservative right – may have complained about there not having been "a single meeting in the City to protest at the nationalisation of the Bank" and have suggested that the reason lay in the presence of "quislings in Threadneedle Street"; but his indignation might have been a little reduced had he known of the frustration felt by the least militant Labour members at the vision of Labour's first great measure of public ownership eventually ending up with a cosy glass of sherry for the reappointed Governor and Deputy Governor of the Bank at Number 11 Downing Street. It was not quite the dawn of Socialism that some had looked for; and the jobs on this occasion – despite the later slogan – hardly went to the boys.

But although in the minds of some members it was taking an un-conscionable time for Labour's revolution to get moving, some changes at least become visible immediately. There was first of all the capitulation of the House of Commons itself as an exclusive club. Its dining-rooms surrendered unconditionally to the spirit of the age by introducing two-shilling dinners and one-and-six lunches (the first of these – soup, venison,

Vicky
News Chronicle
26.9.45

and plum pie – was reported by the apparently slightly surprised M.P.-Editor of the *Spectator* to be "excellent"). And democracy reached out even beyond the Commons' walls. One of the earliest quarrels of the session concerned "Demob Shirts." A Labour member complained that soldiers on demobilisation were being fobbed off with button-down collar shirts, "not now considered in the fashion by the outfitting trade." He called for a wide range of choice to be available: and although predictably the odd supercilious eyebrow was raised at this new socialist regard for sartorial distinction, he got his way – all the more impressive an achieve-ment, as the King himself was to complain in vain a month later to Mr. Attlee: "We must *all* have new clothes – my family is down to the lowest ebb."

Until Christmas, in fact, Labour – even if it had not chosen to push its cause home dramatically – was making modest gains everywhere. At the first two by-elections of the new parliament it increased its majorities even beyond those of the high tide of the general election (at the third the Conservative candidate quit in disgust, obligingly complaining that there was now no room for reformers in a Conservative Party dominated by Bracken and Beaverbrook). The story was the same at the local elections held in November; far from suffering from any understandable reaction on the part of the electorate at the enormity of what it had done, the Labour Party virtually swept the board, even electing Labour councillors in Westminster for the first time for forty years. Potential critics found themselves silenced by present success, and when an ex-president of the Railwaymen sailed away to become (of all things) Governor of Bengal, the "new era" seemed to have found its symbol.

It is always difficult, long after the event, to decide at what exact point a high-water mark was reached. But the Labour Government of 1945 was never to look quite as invulnerable as it did when Parliament broke up for its Christmas recess. Even the American Loan debate on the eve of the adjournment – concerning which there had been a good deal of apprehension – had ended up by throwing the Conservatives into far greater disarray than the Labour Party. And although much later the original Labour dissidents on this issue (there were twenty-three of them) might look back and claim it as the moment when the wrong turning was taken, it scarcely appears to have ranked at the time as anything more than a massive illustration of unity through strength. Far more important for Labour's immediate future than any doctrinal dispute about the advantages of "a siege economy" was a starkly simple headline that appeared on the day that Parliament broke up. It read "Corned Beef for 7,000 People Stolen."

Sooner or later the Labour Government was clearly going to have to fight the battle of shortages with an increasingly restive public opinion. Nonetheless, when the battle really opened the Government was taken badly by surprise. It could not, of course, have predicted that the first ministerial resignation would raise the issue. But that, in however muddled a way, was what happened. When on January 9th the news broke of Mr. Ellis Smith's resignation from the Parliamentary Secretary-ship of the Board of Trade "owing to differences with the President", the temptation – except in the most loaded propagandist newspaper reports (which naturally enough detected "an inevitable rift" in Labour's ranks) – was not to take it very seriously. The President of the Board of Trade,

Sir Stafford Cripps, did not have the reputation for being the most tolerant of mortals; and Mr. Ellis Smith – a trade union M.P. – was suspected of being more warm-hearted than clear-headed.

But, setting a famous precedent for six years later, Mr. Ellis Smith went on later "to widen" what had been supposed to be "the area of disagreement." Speaking in his constituency (Stoke-on-Trent) he announced that, as well as being in favour of more planning than was the President of the Board of Trade (the particular bone of contention seems to have been the Cotton Industry), he had also taken the view that there was "too much austerity" and that Cripps had refused the relaxations that he had suggested. For the already embattled ranks of the Housewives' League, it was enough. The headlines of the next month had had their curtain-raiser.

When these came they were grim enough – "Food Shortages for Some Time," "Coal Position Very Grave," "Ministerial Warning on Food: Possibilities of Still Future Sacrifices," even (prophetically) "No Coal Next Winter?" For the first time on the opposition benches, behind the looks of high national seriousness, there began to lurk the smiles of partisan satisfaction. Labour's original Food Minister, Sir Ben Smith, a sixty-seven-year-old trade union veteran who sat for Rotherhithe, was given a very rough passage. A bluff merchant of *bonhomie*, his attitude hardly seemed appropriate to the atmosphere; an abrupt ending of the supply of dried eggs, a reduction in the fat ration, a crisis over animal foodstuffs, all combined to produce a sudden change of mood from the high optimism of the preceding months. But the Labour Party for the moment – though there were to be sacrificial victims later – refused to be worried. "The future," remarked the *New Statesman* (neatly combining the euphoria of victory with an intimation of mortality), "may not be plain sailing, but the rocks are not yet clearly in sight."

And so far as Parliament was concerned it was certainly right. Here at least the tide now began to flow strongly. In the three months between January and April 1946, bills were brought in to nationalise the mines, to set up a national insurance scheme, to repeal the Trade Disputes Act of 1927, to establish a National Health Service. Outside the voting lobbies at the end of debates Labour members began to queue up early to get a good place in the scrum that preceded divisions; the Conservatives by the sheer massiveness and monotony of defeat began to look progressively more ineffective; and on the members of White's Club the truth slowly dawned that the kingdom was in reality "under enemy occupation."

If they wanted the proof they were provided with it on April 2nd, 1946.

For it was then, on the Third Reading of the Government's Trade Disputes and Trade Unions Bill, that the words were uttered that for two elections at least were to haunt the Labour Party's election managers. "We," announced Sir Hartley Shawcross, "are the masters at the moment—and not only for the moment, but for a very long time to come." The odd thing, however, was that at the time the Attorney-General's words were hardly reported. From such an obvious statement of fact—and estimate of future prospects—no one thought it was wise to dissent. And even the emotional atmosphere of the time, despite the difficulties of the winter, scarcely lent itself to any libertarian hands being thrown up in horror.

On the surface, indeed, the spring of 1946 looked very much like another Labour peak. The fog of distrust in February—caused by trouble on the food and fuel front—had been cleared away by Dalton's buoyant first April budget. And when just after the Recess Attlee announced the first minor reshuffle of his Government, it looked far more like a promise of confidence than a confession of failure.

Unmourned and unsung, the first major casualty, Sir Ben Smith, departed—leaving behind him the plaintive remark, "It's been a very difficult and exhausting time. I am sorry I have not been able to do more to improve our diet, and I hope my successor will have better fortune." That successor turned out to be Mr. John Strachey—who had been a highly successful Under-Secretary for Air. *The Spectator* may well have stretched a point a little by remarking that, as a junior minister, Mr. Strachey had been "in a class of his own" (if only because, as was nastily pointed out at the time, he also happened to be the only junior minister with a share-holding in the paper); but initially, anyway, his appointment was generally well received, as were those of three new members, Mr. Hugh Gaitskell, Mr. Arthur Bottomley and Mr. Arthur Blenkinsop, to junior offices. (The right-wing commentator who remarked at the time that "Mr. Gaitskell is probably the most promising of the many promising young men on the Labour benches" surely deserved a small prize for political foresight.)

Mr. Attlee—or so it seemed in the light of a May morning—had simply taken some remedial action to solve early teething troubles. But in retrospect it is possible to think that there was slightly more to this incident than was recognised. The luckless Sir Ben Smith—later to receive his consolation prize on a regional coal board—was, after all, the first Labour minister to become generally unpopular; and his summary departure—together with his personal admission of regret at not having pleased the nation – seemed to prove that Labour was still determined above all to be loved. The social revolution would, of course, go through – but it would be best for everyone if it did so without causing too much offence or provoking unnecessary prejudice.

Such, anyway, was the lesson brutally spelt out by Mr. Herbert Morrison to that summer's Labour Party conference. At Bournemouth

"*Make Way!*"

Low, *Evening Standard*, 27.7.45

in June the architect of Labour's electoral victory (which was still less than a year old) decided that the time had come for some plain speaking. "The Government," he warned the delegates (in a remarkably thin-blooded, socialist phrase), "has gone as far Left as is consistent with sound reason and the national interest." And the conference – for once almost as docile and well-behaved as a Conservative one – placidly accepted his judgement.

And yet, as it turned out, that remark was virtually the epitaph of

Labour's revolution. Certainly the solid electoral achievements of Labour's first year were never to be matched again. The "victory parade" at Bournemouth had, in fact, come only just in time: ahead lay the fiasco of bread rationing, the shock of the Bexley by-election (with a twelve-month-old Labour majority tumbling by 10,000 votes), even the first serious break in the party's unity over Mr. Bevin's foreign policy. And from these shocks the party's confidence and resolution never really recovered.

Why was this confidence so vulnerable? The answer surely lies in these first months – the months when pride in popularity and a sense of permanence first went to the party's head. Nostalgia is an outstandingly bad political counsellor, but always afterwards there was the memory of the atmosphere which had once prevailed and a determination at all costs to restore it. In the party's folk-lore the year went down as an *annus mirabilis*; and in the minds of its electoral managers it assumed the proportions of a golden age of political perfection.

Even on the surface it was hardly that – most of the clouds that were later to over-shadow Labour's record had already made ominous appearances by 1946. The Labour Government, after all, must have known that its first year would be its period of maximum opportunity – if only because then at least it was assured of overwhelming popular support. And yet it chose to use its first year of power as essentially one of reassurance and acclimatisation.

It was not just that its most controversial and antagonising proposals, like the nationalisation of Road Transport and the Steel Industry, were carefully left out of its first year's legislative programme (allowing even the *Economist* to say "A Socialist Government with a clear parliamentary majority might well have been expected to go several steps further"). Far more significant for the future was the fact that while Labour, as the electoral *victor ludorum*, was collecting its long-coveted trophies – the nationalisation of the Bank of England, of the Coal Mines, even its revenge for the vindictive aftermath of the General Strike of 1926 – the Conservatives were waging what turned out to be a decisive second front.

For 1945 was not merely a political watershed: it had at least the potentiality for being a social one too. The war had not only buried the dinner jacket – it had reduced famous public schools to pale, evacuated shadows, it had destroyed the caste system in the Civil Service, it had eroded practically every traditional social barrier in Britain. And while the Labour Government (to this extent at least a victim of Marxist orthodoxy) painstakingly set about taking over the citadels of economic power, the Conservatives, with a livelier appreciation of reality, went assiduously to work to restore and recreate the environment in which alone they could flourish.

It is, no doubt, easy to be wise – and indeed unduly suspicious – after the event. But it remains, surely, a strange irony that while Labour was winning every public political battle, the only war that really mattered for the future was being fought and won almost unnoticed. The public schools made a genuflection in the direction of Fleming and "guinea pigs" (the Fleming Report of 1944 had suggested the voluntary association of public schools with state-aided schools), and quietly set about building up their fee-paying waiting lists, the ancient universities made use of their war-time convalescence to develop a stronger power and prestige than ever, and even the House of Lords (who ever heard of their debates in the war?) devoted itself to peaceful recuperation until, with impunity, it could in a single year strike down both the nationalisation of steel and the abolition of capital punishment. Far from introducing a "social revolution" the overwhelming Labour victory of 1945 brought about the greatest restoration of traditional social values since 1660.

It may, of course, have been inevitable. The whole complex pattern of social behaviour – or, to be frank about it, class distinction – is an inappropriate one for legislation. But the doubt remains that in its first year – and certainly its naturally most fruitful one – Labour was fighting the symbolic battles and not the real ones. Its slogan in the election had been "Let us Face the Future"; its practice in Parliament was to correct the outstanding arrears of the past. And for that – since there is a continuity in all things (and especially in the shape and mould of a society) – it eventually paid the price.

Where, then, did it go wrong? To claim that it was from the very beginning might appear to be the most damaging answer of all. But, in fact, it merely indicates the difficulties which lay in wait to ambush the 1945 Socialist electoral dream. They may not have been insuperable, but they certainly were not overcome.

The electoral triumph of 1945 was one of men over institutions; the victory of Parliament in the years that followed was one of institutions over men. From the choice of Mr. Attlee's first Labour Cabinet right the way through to the passive acquiescence of the 1946 Labour Party conference, the lesson was clear: the old bottles had won and the new wine had lost. It may well have been the only way to preserve democratic government, as it had always been understood, in Britain; it was not, however, a means by which "a social revolution" could possibly be introduced. No one, of course, ever said "We are the masters *now*." It might have been better if someone had. And it might even have been important had he really meant it.

2

SNOEK PIQUANTE

The trials and tribulations of the British housewife

SUSAN COOPER

Susan Cooper was born in 1935, went from Slough High School to Somerville College, Oxford, where she edited *Cherwell*. She is a feature-writer on the *Sunday Times*, which she joined in 1956. Her first novel, entitled *Mandrake*, is to be published by Hodder and Stoughton in 1964. Her children's book *Over Sea, Under Stone* is being published in 1963, by Jonathan Cape.

SNOEK PIQUANTE

Susan Cooper

THERE was a great bonfire in our street that day, with fireworks, and all of us wearing red-white-and-blue ribbons pinned V-shaped to our lapels. Afterwards, we wandered through the dusk with lighted stubs of candle, ten-year-olds in solemn procession, to show that there was no black-out any more. "The war's over . . ."

But afterwards, after the war and the victory, where was the transformation scene? We still bathed in water that wouldn't come over your knees unless you flattened them; we still wore clothes with the ugly "Utility" half-moons on the label. Chewing carrots for sweets, we still said avidly to our parents: "Tell us about pre-war days," and wondered at stories of chocolate cigars and real pineapple that didn't come out of tins. For years after the war a faint aura of the miraculous seemed to hover round shops piled with oranges, lemons, grapes, bananas: all the routine-exotic fruits unknown to an island enclosed by war, and the aftermath of war. Austerity, like poverty, leaves its children with a lingering appreciation of the treat.

Of the generation in Britain which remembered vanished pre-war treats, perhaps no one in 1945 was expecting a sudden magical return of prosperity. All the same, hope was burgeoning. It was, after all, the hope of release from the long grinding privations of wartime life which had done much to put the Labour Government so resoundingly in power; release from the small, dull, makeshift meals, from darkness and drabness and making do, from the depressing, nerve-aching, never-ending need to be *careful*. For a great many people, war had meant the same kind of food, clothes, and living conditions as the Thirties; now, the vitality of Labour would whisk them out of both. The housewife knew she would have to be patient a little longer, whipping up her mock cream from cornflour and margarine; but there was a good time coming soon. Well, fairly soon.

Into this atmosphere, on the fourth day of 1946, the *Daily Mirror* injected an editorial headed "The Old Firm Gets Going." As well as political triumph, the man in the street might perhaps have found, in its guarded optimism, a kind of foreboding. "The process of turning over from war to peace," said the *Mirror*, "is proceeding smoothly and quickly. It will mean a certain slackening of 'austerity' at home, but for the present it would be unwise to expect a large flow of goods for individual consumption in this country . . . The first and essential task which faces this nation is to get on its feet by means of the export trade. To live, to pay our way and to regain our position in the world, we must sell our goods abroad. This we are enabled to do at a much earlier date than at one time seemed possible. As industry develops there will be more and more things available for the consumer at home . . ."

But the post-war housewife, in her strait-jacket of austerity, had only very vague ideas about the export trade. She was more concerned with keeping a beady eye on the greengrocer, who might with a great deal of luck produce a pound of bananas for each blue and green ration book. She was reading, while the darns rubbed blisters on her lisle-clad heel, about the "stockings of the future", seamless nylons. She was absorbing instructions on How to Make Dried Milk Delicious: "Put two teaspoonsful of dried milk, one of sugar, one of cocoa into a cup . . . result is nourishing, chocolatey, economical."

Advertising is an excellent barometer. The advertisements from the years after the war reflected poignantly the tentative optimism, the frustration, and the sense of good things just out of reach – with inevitable bathos in the final lurch back to reality, as if the supply ran out just as the housewife reached the head of her queue:

"Won't it be nice when we have lovely lingerie, *and* Lux to look after our pretty things? Remember how pure, safe Lux preserved the beauty of delicate fabrics? . . . And how easily it rinsed out! But while there is still no Lux, and you have to wash treasured things with the soap or flakes available, do take extra care . . ."

The maddening titillation of memory was typical of the irritations of those years. Our milk chocolate is wonderful, said the advertisements: "unfortunately, Cadbury's are only allowed the milk to make an extremely small quantity, so if you are lucky enough to get some, do save it for the children . . ."

The children, of course, had the best of it all round. Unable to remember a time without shortages, they were not haunted by the ghosts of freedom and bulging shops and real cream. They were a large and healthy generation, guarded by regulation orange juice, halibut liver oil and milk, It was the older generations which suffered physically from niggling privation. Although the nation as a whole was healthier by 1951 than it had ever been, due to the even distribution of basic foods, the average adult's resistance to infection was often, like his spirits, low. Recording the post-war years in her autobiography, Phyllis Bentley quotes an oculist's laconic observation in 1947 that attacks of conjunctivitis among his patients, "normally despatched in five days, were lingering for six weeks."

The adult world continued to be one of queues and shortages: where the Ministry of Health was advising women to book a maternity bed not as soon as they were pregnant, but as soon as they were married; where the first concern of the new British international cross-country team was to find the 1,816 clothing coupons needed for all their shorts, vests, and track suits. It seemed sometimes as if no one could go anywhere or do anything without producing some kind of permit or coupon (or, as Sir Stafford Cripps would have it, "coupong").

Food rationing, after five years, was a familiar routine. Milk, eggs and oranges were distributed according to supply, with one tin (four pints) of dried milk per person every eight weeks. Of the basic foods, the weekly ration during the war had varied from a shilling to 2s. 2d. worth of meat; four to eight ounces of bacon; one to eight ounces of cheese; two to four ounces of tea and eight ounces to a pound of sugar. Nearly every other comestible had a value in "points", of which the monthly allocation had varied from sixteen to twenty-four. "Personal points", governing chocolate and sweets, fluctuated between three and four ounces. Soap was limited to four coupons a month, and a twelve-ounce packet of good quality soap powder took two coupons.

By 1948, rations had fallen well below the wartime average. In one week, the average man's allowance was thirteen ounces of meat, one and a half ounces of cheese, six ounces of butter and margarine, one ounce of cooking fat, eight ounces of sugar, two pints of milk and one egg. It sounds depressing; it looked even worse. In the three years after the war every kind of external pressure tended to diminish Britain's food supply; in 1946 the housewife felt the first prickling premonition of what was to come when she found herself suddenly deprived of a food which had itself been born of austerity.

During the war, dried egg had become a household staple in Britain. It was baked in cakes, to which it gave a curious flavour and dryness, and as a lurid, leathery pancake it played substitute for the golden, white-floating eye of a real fried egg. All at once, in February 1946, it vanished from the shops; a casualty of the teething troubles of the post-war American loan which Maynard Keynes, in a splendid final burst, was anxiously negotiating to replace Lend Lease. Sir Ben Smith, Labour's first Minister of Food, was attacked in the Commons:

Mr. Lipson (Ind., Cheltenham): Will you not reconsider the supply of dried egg until the American Congress has given its decision on the loan, and review the situation then?

Sir Ben Smith: You assume that I have the dried egg in the country. I have not.

A member: You ought to have.

Sir Ben (heatedly): Of course I ought to have, but I have not the means of getting it.

Poor Sir Ben; Ministerial popularity in the late forties was even more elusive than usual. The shortage of food was looming large, not least in the mind of a nation which had been mildly hungry for five years and now saw itself getting hungrier still. The *Daily Mirror* asked its readers to choose the dollar imports in which they would most readily accept a cut: cheese, dried egg, films, fruit, grain, meat, tinned and powdered milk, or tobacco. They voted overwhelmingly for a cut in films, with tobacco, fruit and milk next on the list. Anything to keep the versatile egg. Every newspaper sang the same indignant song. The Government, breathing heavily, brought dried egg back to the shops.

But, even as dried egg began to reappear, the Battle of Bread began. The cumulative dislocation of war, and the droughts and bad harvests of 1945, had brought to every part of the world a food crisis which, Mr. Bevin grimly told the United Nations, was "really alarming". For the British, "shortage" was by now such a familiar word that the looming threat of world famine during the past six months had merged into the general grey background of life. This time, it struck home.

The Minister of Food announced on February 5th, 1946, that the world wheat shortage would mean a cut in bacon, poultry and eggs. Rice, what there was of it, would vanish from the shops. The whaling season had been as poor as the harvest, so the fat ration would be reduced by an ounce. The Government appealed to farmers to sow grain, promising them prisoner-of-war labour (there were still 400,000 Germans in British camps) to help with the ploughing. Households were encouraged to go on digging their allotments; few had stopped anyway, and the patchwork fields of little family plots were still providing battered crops of broccoli and winter greens to reinforce the erratic supplies from greengrocers' shops.

Much of the countryside was scattered with the jetsam of war: anti-aircraft posts in cornfields, banked with dribbling sandbags; concrete tank-traps lining the roads, like idols left by some gloomy, extinct race; minefields and pill-boxes lurking in the coastal dunes. At Taplow, in Buckinghamshire, the national output of barbed wire rusted gently into an orange mountain. But, of all this military litter, it became most urgent now that the airfields should be cleared. At the height of the war they had covered 240,000 acres of land (not counting the concrete), and this now meant a vital addition to farming resources. A hundred airfields had already been cleared, and part of fifty more; but this amounted only to 75,000 acres, and of that only 30,000 arable. And, for the period from January to July 1946, Europe was short of eight million tons of wheat.

An emergency conference on European cereal supplies met in London. By now many people in former enemy-occupied countries were dangerously near starvation level; rationing there amounted to a uniform thousand calories a day — the level, in normal times, of a stringent slimming diet. The Prime Minister trod firmly on little Quixotic peaks in the unexcitement of British life; people might feel impelled to send food parcels to Europe, he said, but they would do more good simply by eating less. He backed this with a grand gesture by announcing that Britain was willing to ration bread.

Summed up in the abortive story of bread rationing there is all the frustration and worry and fiddling fuss of life in post-war Britain. Bread, as Mr. Churchill resonantly pointed out, had never been rationed even in the darkest days of submarine warfare. One great support for morale had been the fact that while most of us were under-nourished, few of us were ever acutely hungry. Starch was the great filler-up. "Rations go twice as far this way," said the soup advertisements. "Start with platefuls of piping hot, thick, appetising soup, and plenty of bread. It's filling and satisfying and you can make do with smaller servings of the rationed foods . . ."

But now even the staff of life was wobbling. Campaigns against waste were concentrated on bread; Hammersmith Borough Council sorted out all the thrown-away bread from a single day's dustbin collection, and thoughtful Londoners gazed at a mound of stale half-loaves weighing almost a ton. Mrs. Jean Mann observed tartly in the Commons that much waste might be stopped by bringing back wrapped bread: the bread that she threw away consisted of the dirty bits which had to be chopped off the crust.

The housewife had grown used to grimy loaves; complaints seemed pointless, in a world where the retort "Don't you know there's a war on?" had been swiftly replaced by "Well, you know how difficult things are . . ." Now, however, she found that the British loaf was not only grubby but shrinking. In April, 1946 the Ministry of Food reduced the size of two-pound and one-pound loaves to twenty-eight and fourteen ounces, lopping off the equivalent of two thickish slices from a large loaf. Never very shrewd psychologists, they hoped the public would be bamboozled into buying the same number of loaves as before, so saving the country

Giles, *Daily Express*, 4.7.46

"Now don't forget—anyone hanging around with a wistful look in their eye —let 'em have it—bang, bang!"

300,000 tons of wheat a year. They were, of course, wrong. The man-œuvre might have worked if the new loaves had been the same size as the old; bakers had suggested putting more air in the dough. But in proposing to sell bread in units other than pounds, the Ministry found themselves up against the Weights and Measures Act. To evade it, they were forced to seek a special Cabinet dispensation, and the cat was out of the bag. The public ate no less bread than before.

Three months later, after much havering, the new Minister of Food, Mr. Strachey, announced that bread was to be rationed. The size of the coming Canadian harvest was uncertain, and there had been a cut in grain supplies from America (a nation much attacked in the Press for hoarding, profiteering and various other iniquities – charges prompted largely by the suspicion of the hungry for the well-fed). So rationing of bread, flour and "flour confectionery" was added to the rest, introducing yet another small symbol of austerity: the Bread Unit. "That we should have had to do such an unpopular thing," wrote Dalton enigmatically fifteen years later, "illustrates vividly the urgent shortages of the post-war years, and the inescapable reasons for our gradual loss of backing in the country."

The Bread Unit represented seven ounces of bread – half a small loaf. A large loaf, now weighing one and three-quarter pounds, would require four Units, one pound of flour three Units, one pound of "flour confectionery" two Units. The weekly ration equalled two new large loaves a week for adults, and one for children under six; twelve million people, mainly manual workers, had a higher ration ranging up to three and three-quarter pounds. But the complexities of controlling the nation's flour consumption were so enormous, especially with the inadequate machinery set up by the Ministry, that the scheme had, as the official history of rationing points out in a happy phrase, "no teeth in it." Given three weeks' warning, housewives and bakers stashed away large hoards of flour, throwing the national supply out of balance. In the week before rationing began, on July 21st, 1946, there was a further rush for bread. "Shops were besieged," reported *The Times*, "by customers asking for six, seven, even ten loaves each – twice or thrice as much bread as their families could eat at the week-end. 'The women have gone mad,' said a baker."

In restaurants, bread was made one of the maximum number of three dishes allowed at any one meal. Served as bread and cheese, or as the ground floor of Welsh rarebit or sardines on toast, it didn't count as a separate dish. But any customer who now demanded bread with his soup would find, by the end of the meal, that he had forfeited his right to a pudding. The irritation was small, but to a public pricked by regulations at every turn it brought an increasing despondency.

The bakers, faced with quantities of form-filling and extra controls, were furious at the whole idea of rationing. "I shall go to jail rather than collect Bread Units from housewives," said one master baker. "This country is getting worse than Germany under the Nazis." Another observed bitterly that the quality of most British bread – greyish-coloured, with a low fat and high chalk content lingering from the war – was so bad that it hardly needed rationing at all. "It will ration itself. We have never used worse flour. It is thirty-five per cent cattle food."

In fact, there was never a bread shortage. The first day of rationing was quiet, and by the end of it bakers had loaves and cakes still unsold. And the public found themselves made unexpectedly better off – and the Government alarmed – by the one aspect of the scheme which particularly showed its toothlessness. Bread Units were exchangeable for points. By eking out their hastily hoarded flour, housewives were able to save Bread Units to obtain the precious points foods which could brighten the dreariness of rationed meals. Sultanas, for instance, were now eight points a pound; English tinned fruit twelve points for a two and a half pound tin; suet, recently transferred to the points system from its place in the fat ration, eight points a pound. ("This," said the Ministry, announcing the transfer in bleak, Job-comforting tones, "will be appreciated by housewives now that the cooking fat ration is down, because of the world shortage, from two ounces to one ounce a week.")

As a result, the consumption of points foods shot upwards: by 106 per cent in the first bread rationing period, 116 in the second and 111 in the third. Alarmed, the Ministry halved the points value of Bread Units; five months after rationing had begun they abolished the exchange entirely. Bread rationing itself went on. It was not finally abolished until July 21st, 1948. The ration, in practice, proved adequate, no one went hungry and there were no shortages – but nor was there any great saving of grain. "The most that could be said," observes the official history, "was that consumption had not gone up." Instead, something else went up: the number of civil servants occupied with controls. By March 1948 seven hundred and fifty Food Officers and other staff in Food Offices throughout the country were dealing full-time with bread rationing alone. And for two years the public juggled irritably with the pieces of paper that meant bread or flour or buns; beginning for the first time to blame their frustrations and sense of gloom not only on externals like war or famine, but squarely on their Government. It was, perhaps, a sign that we were properly back at peace.

Few bonfires were lit on the first anniversary of V.E. Day: May 8th, 1946. Although it was declared a public holiday, the mood of the British was one not of festivity but of bleak resignation, with a faint rebelliousness at the restrictions and looming crises that hung over them like a fog. Coal was already short; by the beginning of winter, Mr. Shinwell warned, the country would be five million tons understocked. Everyone still looked – and what was worse, felt – drab; though it had seemed hopefully symbolic that the restrictions on the height of women's heels had been removed, clothes were neither gay nor abundant, and no one had yet seen what the Board of Trade unromantically called "the new non-austerity trimmings." There was no soft fruit in the shops; the Ministry had taken it all to make jam. Even beer was weaker, and whisky had become a dim, golden dream. "Please continue to show forbearance with your supplier," pleaded one firm of distillers, without much conviction. "Better times will come, when there'll be more White Horse and we shall all be glad." The irrepressible *Daily Mirror* printed a helpful feature called "Wine from Weeds."

By the autumn of 1946, the forbearance of one group of people wore thin. The housing shortage, in all parts of the country, was desperate. Demobilisation was moving quickly; some two million men and women were already out of the Forces, and more flooding back home every day – not to mention the 160,000 Poles who had asked to stay in Britain rather than go back to Poland. Councils in London, Bristol, Portsmouth, Coventry and all the worst-bombed cities were struggling to clear the shambles left by the war, and estates of "prefabs" had sprung up everywhere like a matchbox rash. But although 60,452 houses (two-thirds of them prefabricated) had been built since the end of the war, and 100,000 others repaired, only 210,000 families had been rehoused. Thousands of others remained homeless, living cramped in rented or borrowed rooms, often with small children. Despair, rootlessness, and the strain of over-crowding had brought them to a state where their patience was ready to snap.

The English are an obedient race, as the clichés jostling in the language prove. In time of adversity they pull in their belts, put their shoulders to the wheel, grin and bear it, make the best of a bad job, keep chins and peckers up and upper lips stiff. But there are limits. The homeless families of 1946 saw round them the rapidly emptying camps which soldiers and airmen had occupied during the war: walls, roofs, shelter going to waste while they themselves hunted in vain for somewhere to live. In the stresses of post-war life, the mental jump was inevitable. The war was over, wasn't it? These camps had been built for wartime, hadn't they? It wasn't as if they belonged to anyone – only to the Government, who ought to be providing homes in any case. It wasn't like pinching another family's house. It was only an extension of that accepted tradition of Service life, the scrounge: a weakness on which the spivs and black marketeers already pressed gently, to lure people round the edges of restriction.

There was no explicit restriction here, no actual law that you couldn't commandeer an old Army camp. Suddenly, in the summer of 1946, the squatters came. Groups of families, in defiant relief, carried their children and belongings into empty, still-camouflaged Nissen huts, and set up house. Local councils and police forces argued, were rebuffed and scratched their heads. The idea spread like smallpox, and by the middle of August some twenty thousand people had moved into derelict camps. Some hardly even waited for dereliction; at Prestwick, one August night, urgent messages summoned airmen back from dance halls and cinemas as dozens of determined squatters, working by candlelight, invaded the airport, and carried their own furniture and bedding into seventeen "luxury" R.A.F. huts.

As the egg-and-stocking-starved housewife was vulnerable to the spiv, so the homeless, especially in an atmosphere of mild defiance, were easy meat for political agitators. London had no service camps, but it did contain quantities of empty houses and flats. Some were privately-owned, but untenanted because prohibitive rents were asked, and some were requisitioned; in the whole country, twenty thousand requisitioned houses still stood empty. In London, eyeing these tantalising roofs, there was an extremely active Communist Party.

Early in September 1946 Londoners were startled by what was christened the Great Sunday Squat. Quietly and deliberately, directed by Communist organisers, several hundred squatters converged on Duchess of Bedford House, an empty block of flats in Kensington. They carried furniture, bedding and baskets of food. They came from Stepney, Hammersmith, Westminster, Wembley, Hendon, Wandsworth, Croydon, every part of London to which the news of the impending squat had travelled, through that curiously effective grapevine which links those who have a strong and particular grouse. By no means all of them were Communists; most were simply people who badly wanted homes and who, seeing the chance of acquiring one temporarily, were not going to be left out. They were not much interested in the political implications; the Communists, for them, were little more than the means of at least drawing attention to their plight.

In houses all over Central London, the squatters settled like winter seagulls. A retired brigadier, in the process of buying a house in Kensington (3 bed., 7 recep.), arrived one morning to find it full of strangers. The young mother of one of the squatting families met him on the stairs; their exchange crystallises all the hesitant defiance, with its overtones of outraged self-respect, which sometimes broke through the safety-valves of the restricted post-war years.

Brigadier: This is my house. May I come in?

Squatter: I'm very sorry I can't let you in. Especially as it is your property.

Brigadier: Well, I've just been demobbed and I want this place for myself and my wife. Er . . . I called to have a look. Er . . . Have you done any damage?

Squatter: (indignantly) What kind of people do you think we are?

This house was relinquished within days; the police were in close but tactful attendance, closing in after every invasion to keep later arrivals away. But short of guarding every empty house in London, they couldn't keep the squatters down. On the morning after the Great Sunday Squat, the advance guard of a group independent of the Communists slipped past a Ministry of Works caretaker into an eight-storey block of flats in Westminster, and locked themselves in. They chose flats for their families and sat for five hours watching other hopefuls gather outside, opening the doors only when some began climbing through the windows. The pattern was much the same elsewhere.

Once installed, the London squatters were easily made helpless. They had no water, electricity or gas, and policemen besieged each block so that no food could be taken in. But the Communists took advantage of this treatment to draw still more attention to the spreading squat. To do them justice, they used civil disobedience methods of a maddeningly calm and orderly nature. At Abbey Lodge, a block in Regent's Park, fifty squatter families had moved into empty flats for which rents of up to £24 a week were being asked. A moot of policemen took up guard outside, and crowds gathered in an attempt to send food and water in through the cordon. At dusk, emergency rations of bread and milk were allowed through. But the crowds, toured by an agile loudspeaker van, remained, and sat down five deep in the middle of the road. The police, as yet unfamiliar with this gambit, arrested nobody, and at length a voice announced from the Communist van: "There is no need to hold the traffic up any longer." Next day the whole process was repeated. A crowd of two thousand people surrounded the police-beset block of squatters; again they sat down, again the Communist van directed their movements. It was all very controlled and – fairly – unemotional. The Communists boldly wrote to the Minister of Health asking that the squatting families should be allowed to take over the empty property.

But the Government took "a serious view" of the whole affair. They issued writs against the leading Communists concerned, arrested five of them, and served eviction orders on all the London squatters. Within a few days most of the families had been moved to hostels. They went willingly, feeling not without reason that they had achieved a considerable success.

Elsewhere, however, the squatters remained. There was no simple way of ejecting some twenty thousand homeless people from several hundred Army camps. In any case the public, only too familiar with the sensation of shortage, were particularly sympathetic towards these localised groups. Slowly, through the creaking intuition of authority, the Ministry began to realise that on all counts the squatted-in camps were really rather a useful temporary stop-gap for the housing problem.

Some camps were needed for prisoners-of-war, or for builders employed on major housing projects; the squatters there were persuaded to move. Local authorities were asked to provide lighting and sanitary arrangements in the habitable camps, and eventually, after – of course – regional committees had submitted reports to the Ministry, five hundred and sixty-three camps, all full of squatters, were offered to local authority control. They held, in all, about six thousand families. Washing flapped triumphantly outside each sergeants' mess; flowers and vegetables began to sprout on soil that had held nothing for five years but bleak Army grass. The squatters had won, even though some of them were to find themselves still in the same makeshift villages four or five years later. The Government launched a new housing drive, and with it an attack on the building "black market" which diverted labour for inessential repairs. For many people the whole affair had momentarily brightened the austere face of Britain, a bright spot in a grey sky; it had been a small rebellion, against shortage and restriction and gloom-breeding circumstance. And it had worked.

At the end of 1946 such small encouragements were precious enough. There were few more coming. A large murky cloud was creeping up towards Britain, full of industrial unrest and impending shortages and – in larger quantities than either – snow. As winter approached, the Ministry of Fuel warned that the coal situation was grave; the country was still half a million tons short. America was already gripped by the coldest winter for years; on December 16 it struck Britain, and the paralysis of transport brought industry an even worse shortage of coal. Just before Christmas, Austins were forced to give notice to 14,500 men; a week later twelve cotton mills in Blackburn did the same. Coal supplies were rushed to both areas, and the dismissals avoided, but industry all over the country was holding on to production only by its teeth. The standard of living had been kept down, and the shops half-empty, in a great effort to maintain dollar exports which now seemed to be dwindling as well. Morale dropped; the miners, in their newly nationalised industry, seemed unable to pull out the stops as they had done during the war years, and in the docks a rash of strikes began. On Merseyside, 27,000 men were unemployed. On January 23rd, 1947, the main headline in the *Daily Telegraph* showed the encouraging note on which the new year was being launched:

Bread Ration May Be Cut
Peers Hear Review of 1947 Food Outlook
Less Bacon and Home Meat
Beer Supplies to be Halved Immediately

But there was most significance in a small headline tucked far down the page. "Snow Falls in London," it said.

The snow fell, and fell, and went on falling. By January 29th the entire country was paralysed by the appalling freak winter of 1947: the worst winter of the century, which chose the worst possible year in which to arrive.

All over Britain the wind howled snow down to block roads and railways; heavy snow fell even in the Scillies and the Channel Isles. Off the south-east coasts, all shipping was immobilised by a twelve-hour blizzard. Not only the remoter villages and farms were cut off by snowdrifts; in Essex the drifts were fourteen feet deep, and half the London commuters in Surrey and Middlesex woke on January 29th to find themselves unable to reach the city for several days. London itself had sixteen degrees of frost that night, and long gas and electricity cuts during the day. Freak disasters all over the railways brought transport to a complete standstill even where the lines were free of heavy drifts; at Purley, for instance, eight inches of snow short-circuited the electric railway, and the fuses exploded, leaving twenty-five yards of rail to glow red-hot before the current was cut off.

Everyone who remembers 1947 has his own winter story. At Beaumont, in Essex, the local postmaster walked sixteen miles through head-high drifts to the nearest town, to collect rations for his hungry village. On the morning of January 29th, the fireman of the 6.23 a.m. train from Huddersfield to Bradford glanced out of his cab and was knocked unconscious by a large icicle hanging from a bridge. On a national scale, the story was one of unrelieved disaster. By the end of the first week in February two million men were out of work, and there was no electricity at all for industry in the South, the Midlands and the North-West. Several power-stations closed for lack of coal; a hundred and twenty-five colliers were stormbound in the Tyne. Parsnips were being dug out of the ground with pneumatic drills. To every small trial so far there was now added that of the cold.

In the severe framework of the Defence Regulations, domestic power was restricted all over Britain; no family was allowed to switch on an electric fire between 9 a.m. and midday, or between 2 p.m. and 4 p.m. The Prime Minister banned greyhound racing, suspended television and the B.B.C. Third Programme, and cut transport in London, where snow-ploughs were clearing the streets. Everywhere, people walked hunched against the cold; there were few fur-lined boots in the 1947 shops, and no new heavy coats for those who had spent all their clothing coupons. And most people's shoes leaked.

In one wry sense, perhaps it was not after all the worst possible year for such a winter to descend. The morale of the British tends always to flourish perversely in time of war or disaster, blossoming through the communal grumbles and groans into a kind of cheerful fortitude. It's the national hubris perhaps, a Goliath complex; a deliberate waiting for impossible odds. At any rate it was this quality, rather than simple, uncomplicated patriotism, which Churchill had understood and exploited during the war ("I have nothing to offer but blood, toil . . ."). The day-to-day tribulations of austerity had roused it as well, to some extent, but it couldn't properly survive all the endless petty deprivations as year succeeded bleak year. It sagged. Now, the appalling winter of 1947 tautened it again. People shook themselves out of gloom to help one another. Railway staff worked with manic speed to keep coal supplies moving, and by the middle of February industry picked up a little.

But the winter was by no means over yet; nor was the fuel crisis. At Crewe, Rolls-Royce were using their car engines to generate local power. A slight thaw covered the country in fog; then, at the beginning of March, the snow came back. Ice-floes were seen off the Norfolk coast; ten-foot drifts of snow muffled most of Britain as the Commons stormily debated fuel. Labour were having a dismal time of it, doggedly pushing their complex nationalisation Bills through Parliament whilst wrathful Tories attacked them for paying too little attention to food and fuel, and for employing three times as many civil servants as miners. The winter, cried the Opposition, was being made unendurable by the effects of "control without planning." They found a new slogan: "Starve with

Strachey, and Shiver with Shinwell." To many people, it seemed only too accurate.

By the middle of March, when Britain was listening cheerlessly to its first party political broadcast from the Prime Minister and from Anthony Eden, three hundred main roads were still impassable, with houses, trains and trees buried in thirty-foot drifts of snow. Scotland was completely cut off by the worst storm in living memory. Everywhere the farmers were desperate; thousands of sheep lay dead under the snow in the hills, and more than 20,000 acres of winter corn had already been destroyed by frost. People trudged through the snow wondering dismally if the spring would ever come. Instead, in a final, brutal thwack at the country's teetering food supplies, the floods came.

A single, cataclysmic storm on March 16th, 1947, hurled the flood-waters loose all over Britain. Forty miles of the Severn spilled over, completely isolating the town of Shrewsbury; the Thames swelled to a width of three miles below Chertsey, and in London (where a million people, by the nice irony of such disasters, were left without water supplies) part of the Underground had to be closed. All over the Fens, brown water washed away grain and gutted potato clamps; when Easter came, with snow, rain and seventy miles an hour squalls, troops were battling to control the floodwaters of the Trent. Floods hit thirty-one counties, and the nation which had cheered round its victorious bonfires eighteen months before stood clutching its ration-books, still shivering from the worst winter since 1880; gazing at peeling wallpaper and flood-soaked carpets while the river-water trickled triumphantly out of its front doors. The Government poured money into distress funds, housing drives, farming subsidies, but the food and fuel prospects were worse than ever. In all, 600,000 acres of arable land had been flooded, the water destroying 80,000 tons of potatoes and a further 70,000 acres of wheat; thirty-two per cent of all the hill sheep had died, and 30,000 cattle. On the Welsh hills, the farmers were burning great mounds of dead sheep; you could smell the smoke miles away, and it wasn't at all like roast mutton.

When the 1947 summer, as freakish as the winter had been, poured over the country like white-hot lead, the muttering thunderstorms seemed symbolic. Britain's dollar deficit was by now alarming; within a year it was expected to reach £475,000,000. As first Hugh Dalton, and then Sir Stafford Cripps chanted doom from the Treasury, people began, for the first time, to feel a real sense of national crisis. "We're up against it," intoned the Government posters, £400,000 worth of them, all over the country: "We Work or Want." It was not simply shortage now, or natural

disaster; it was restriction. Whilst appeals for higher production rang
in their ears, the public found, in Dalton's autumn budget of 1947,
cigarettes rising from 2s. 4d. to 3s. 4d. for twenty, and pipe tobacco by
1s. 2d. an ounce, in a deliberate Government drive to cut smoking by a
quarter. "And smoke your cigarettes to the butts," said the Chancellor,
"it may even be good for your health." American films stopped arriving
in Britain when a seventy-five per cent import duty was imposed, and
cinemas began to empty. Timber and petrol imports were cut, so newspapers shrank back to four pages and the basic petrol ration was abolished,
although anyone living more than two miles from public transport could
draw a supplementary allowance. Foreign travel was suspended and public
dinners dwindled into silence. Clothing coupons were cut, and there
seemed to be less food than there had ever been since the beginning of the
war. It became a criminal offence to switch a fire on during the summer
months.

The only good thing was the sunshine, and there was too much even
of that, in a refrigerator-less country where ice was as scarce as oranges
and where children were kept away from swimming-baths after a polio
scare. Less than six months after the floods, drought came to the Welsh
hills, and Manchester's water supply nearly gave out. Struggling over a
desert of crisis, the Government hunted wildly for ideas which might
catch the public imagination. They looked for help through a period which,
although it might, with luck, prove to be the end of the beginning, was
the blackest they had yet faced. Famine, frost and flood had pinned them
firmly in austerity since the war ended; a new impetus was needed now
to help the long slow haul out of it.

They had already made a mistake with the Groundnut Scheme in East
Africa: no good done for morale there. Instead they turned to food, to
schemes for relieving shortage and brightening the dismal British diet. In
doing so, they accidentally touched a spring of absurdity revealing perhaps more than anything else the strength which had resisted the series
of catastrophes that had gone before. The only defence against austerity
is good humour, and in their flounderings with food the Government,
without intending it, worked the spell which brought this forth when it
was most needed. A rabbit was produced out of the hat, to provide food;
but the public didn't eat it. They sat back, looked at it, and laughed and
laughed.

In fact, there were two rabbits: the first was whalemeat, and the second
was snoek. Of the two, whalemeat caused the smaller stir. Introduced in

1947, when disagreements with the Argentine were making it difficult to augment the dwindling home meat supplies, it was accepted at first in the spirit of hopeful, try-anything-once daring which had already driven some housewives back to Grandmother's recipes for salads of dandelion leaves. Whalemeat was a curious, powdery-textured substance resembling a meaty biscuit, with overtones of oil. But it had a fair success. By September 1947 Lyons were serving six hundred whale steaks a day at one London Corner House, and the Caterers' Association were observing, with enthusiasm and some relief, that "the public will take all we can give them, especially now the meat ration is cut."

Since a single blue whale weighs about ninety tons, the Ministry of Food found this joyful news. Vast refrigerated ships were despatched to the Antarctic, and whalemeat became familiar on butchers' slabs. By 1949 it was arriving in tins; described by the shippers as "rich and tasty – just like beef steak." But no one was really wedded to whale. The house-wife made her attempt at novelty, but without changing her basic allegiances; back she went, eventually, to tins of Spam and the bursting bread-filled sausage. Early in 1950, four thousand tons of whalemeat lay unwanted for months in warehouses on Tyneside; then it was taken to Norway, to lie all the summer in its refrigerated ship alongside the Tonsberg quay. But nobody wanted it there either, and the shippers had to bring it back: to find still no buyer in Britain, even though further rows with the Argentine had reduced the meat ration to a shilling a week. The Government took no hand; they had diverted their attention, by then, to a fish.

In October 1947, with the butter and meat rations newly cut, the bacon ration halved, restaurants' food supplies dwindling, and potato rationing on the way, the hungry British first heard the word "snoek". Ten million tins of it from South Africa were to replace Portuguese sardines, whose import was restricted by exchange troubles; the new fish, said Mr. Strachey, would go on points. "I have never met a snoek," he added, with the Ministerial waggishness that always holds a faint sense of doom, "so I cannot tell you much about it. It is long and slender, weighing up to eighteen pounds."

The name, of course, was a gift. Before it even arrived in the shops this unfortunate fish was seized with cries of delight by cartoonists, sub-editors, music-hall comedians, and Members of Parliament; not least when one early consignment was found to be packed in salt, and inedible except as fish paste. Research revealed that the snoek was a large, ferocious, tropical fish, like a barracuda; that it was dangerous to bathers, had rows of fearsome teeth, and when displeased hissed like a snake and barked like a dog. A Lieutenant-Colonel (retd.) wrote a long letter to *The Times* about snoek fishing, ending: "I have the greatest respect for this notable fighter as an article of diet. It tastes like a mackerel, only more so." *The Times*, infected by the gentle delirium, headed his letter: "Hunting the Snoek".

Wholesalers did not welcome snoek; they had already imported a number of tins, off points, and these had not been a success. "People didn't like it," said one. "Tasteless and unpalatable," said another. "Abominable stuff." The Minister, however, had not only spent £857,000 on snoek, but had eaten it: at a picnic, in sandwiches. It was, he said with rash honesty, "good, palatable, but rather dull."

In May 1948, when the first large consignment arrived, Dr. Edith Summerskill presided at a snoek-tasting party at the Ministry; the Government put up quantities of snoek posters (even, as an Opposition member pointed out, in fishing ports) and published eight remarkable recipes.

Snoek piquante: 4 spring onions, chopped; liquid from snoek; 4 tablespoons vinegar; ½ can snoek, mashed; 2 teaspoons syrup; salt to taste; ½ teaspoon pepper. Cook the onions in the fish liquor and vinegar for five minutes. Add the snoek, syrup and seasoning and mix well; serve cold with salad . . .

It cost 1s. 4½d. for a half-pound tin, and took only one point – thirteen points less than red salmon, five points less than household salmon, and much cheaper than either. But nobody seemed quite clear whether it was being eaten. The crescendo of music-hall jokes rose. "We can sell every tin," said Mr. Strachey, in October 1948, and arranged to import some more. The *Daily Express* chose twenty-five Mrs. Smiths from the telephone directory, rang them all up and asked if they had bought any snoek yet. "The name frightened me," said one Mrs. Smith. "Well, if I were *very* hard pushed," said another. Only two, reported the *Express*, had actually bought a tin: one said it tasted terrible, and the other gave it to the cat. Grocers and distributors alike reported guardedly that snoek was "not going well."

The fact was that the housewife, conditioned by shortage, had learnt during the war years to regard any food publicised by the Ministry with fatalistic suspicion. She knew that its quality would probably be low, due to the austerity principle of selecting foods primarily for their capacity to "go round," and, without the incentive of wartime effort, she was not now disposed to play ball. Also, she disliked the taste of snoek. By the summer of 1949, more than a third of the snoek imported since 1947 was still unsold: 3,270,000 half-pound tins, out of a total of 11,110,400 – with 1,209,000 still to come under existing contracts. The Ministry hopefully put out more recipes: snoek sandwich spread, snoek pasties, snoek with salad. Their leaflets were still going the rounds when in August 1949 two thousand more tons of tinned fish, in 8,960,000 half-pound tins, arrived from Australia to be sold at a shilling a tin. They called it barracuda, but it still tasted like snoek.

The Ministry began to wilt. In September 1949 they reduced the price of their South African snoek from 1s. 4½d. to 1s. 3d. a tin. By December the Minister, on a note of affectionate farewell, was referring to it as "dear old snoek," and claiming that every tin bought from South Africa had been sold without loss. His honest incredulity was even more apparent this time. "It was eaten, believe it or not. I ate it myself. I must say, I thought it was one of the dullest fish I have ever eaten."

Three weeks later snoek, with tinned tomatoes and various tinned meats, came off points. The worst privations of austerity were over by then, and decently obscure mists closed round the piles of tins; there were new jokes, this one wasn't needed any more. But eighteen months later, quiet among the junketings of the Festival of Britain, a mysterious quantity of tinned fish came onto the market, labelled: "Selected fish food for cats and kittens." It cost tenpence a tin, and its origins were left muffled in tact. One of the distributors admitted that it might be either snoek or barracuda. "Cats," he said, "are very fond of both."

Wars end tidily in the history books, with the moment of signing a document. But there was no single finishing line for the shortages of food, clothes and fuel, and all the aspects of austerity which gave a dull grey tinge to post-war life. They slackened, gradually. When clothes rationing ended in March 1949, and the lights went up in London for the first time since the war began, the weekly meat ration was lower than it had ever been. When points rationing was abolished in May 1950 the Korean War arms programme was advancing to cut the rising supplies of cars and television sets.

Throughout 1950 controls were steadily eased; in January milk rationing was suspended, in May hotels and restaurants were freed of the five-shilling meal limit and the restriction on the number of courses they might serve. In the autumn, flour, eggs and soap were removed from control. But the process was slow, and perhaps that very slowness is one reason for the gulf which exists now between the generations of the young and the middle-aged.

For those who remembered the years between the wars, the gradual climb back to prosperity was a long, dispiriting haul, echoing with pre-war memories of better days. For the wartime children, it was different. Those years were not a return, but a revelation. They were lit by surprises; between 1945 and 1951 we saw not only the first pineapples and bananas of our lives, but the first washing-machine, the first fountain, the first television set. The world opening before us was not a pale imitation of one we had lost, but a lucky dip of extraordinary things we had never seen before. If, later, we seemed to snarl with baffled rage at the disillusionment and apathy of our elders, perhaps this is why. They treated it all as a dreary mess; they forgot that for us it could have been a brave new world.

3

EXPLOSION AT THE KING DAVID HOTEL
Britain and the problem of Palestine

DAVID LEITCH

David Leitch was born in 1937 and educated at Merchant Taylors' and St. John's College, Cambridge. Lived in Europe, mainly Rome, for a year after going down and then worked in Manchester as a reporter on *The Guardian*. Left to join *The Times* in London (as a reporter for nearly three years), and has published literary and political articles in various British and American periodicals. Now on the staff of the *Sunday Times*.

EXPLOSION AT THE KING DAVID HOTEL

David Leitch

A FEW minutes after noon on July 22nd, 1946, a battered Chrysler truck stopped outside the best hotel in Jerusalem – the King David. A group of apparently quite ordinary youths dressed in the flowing robes of Arab hotel workers unloaded some milk churns from the back of the Chrysler and carried them into the luxurious, seven-storey building. No one paid them the slightest attention, and there was no reason why anyone should have done. In a matter of hours, as it turned out, the Arabs with their churns were to achieve that sudden, short-lived, and almost universal fame reserved for those who figure in the most spectacular news stories: but there was no hint of this as they walked through the hotel doors. Someone recalled afterwards that the Chrysler's number was M.7022, and it is surprising that anyone noticed even that much.

The King David Hotel was one of the few institutions deriving any benefit from the ill wind afflicting Palestine and, on the morning when the milkmen arrived, it had been full to capacity for some time. Its entire south wing was given over to housing the secretariat of the British Mandatory Administration, and the British Army in Palestine, with about 100,000 men on its strength, was paying £1,000 a month for the privilege of having its headquarters in the north wing. Foreign journalists, paying a comparatively modest £25 a week, formed a fair proportion of the hotel's private guests, and the troubles in Palestine were providing plenty of good copy. The most recent big story had been the arrest, just three weeks before, of nearly all the leaders of the Jewish Agency. This was the governmental body of the *Yishuv*, the community of 600,000 Jews living in Palestine. The King David boasted the best informed bar in the country and foreign journalists spent a good deal of time moving between it and La Régence, an unsuitably named basement restaurant in Tudor style, talking to soldiers and civil servants, and trying to assess what the unpredictable British administration might be going to do next.

The milkmen followed a parallel course, and made for La Régence, which was directly beneath the secretariat offices. At this point came the first indication that something was wrong. A Captain Mackintosh of the

Royal Signals looked hard at the churns and called to the Arabs to stop
—the noise they made pushing the churns had brought him out of the
military telephone exchange. The Arabs ignored his order, but one
produced a revolver from under his robes and shot the captain twice in
the stomach. Mackintosh, who died two days later, thus narrowly failed
to avert a disaster and became, in the process, the first casualty on a day
that abounded in them. He had noticed that one of the churns had a fuse
sticking out of its top.

The men planted their churns in the kitchens next to La Régence,
after holding up the staff, and in a matter of minutes, as soon as their
job was done, made rapidly for the exit. Simultaneously a diversionary
bomb exploded under a tree one hundred yards away, and a party of men,
later identified, like the supposed Arabs, as an assault party of *Irgun Zvei
Leumi*, the Jewish terrorist or resistance organisation, opened fire on the
guarded entrance to the secretariat. Although one was fatally wounded
by a sentry, all the first party reached the exit and succeeded in escaping
northwards in a taxi that had been parked with its engine running. The
second group ceased their covering fire, and escaped south.

There are discrepancies of detail in the different versions of how the
Irgun men entered and escaped from the hotel, but the various stories
of what happened in the twenty or so confused minutes after their
departure contain flat contradictions. There is no doubt that the French
Consulate General, opposite the King David, received a telephone
warning. "There will be an explosion. Open your windows before the
blast." And while consulate staff were hurrying round the building to
obey these instructions, the offices of the *Palestine Post* and the manage-
ment of the King David also received anonymous warnings. One story
says that the King David received a message to evacuate within a minute
of the milkmen leaving the building. According to another version, a very
senior British official, who was passed a similar warning, refused to take
any action and said: "We aren't here to take orders from Jews. We give
them orders." The official British communiqué admitted that a warning
arrived, but claimed it came too late for evacuation.

In this case it seems most likely that the official story is the true one.
There can be no argument about the fact that the churns, marked
"Mines—do not touch", remained in the basement for something like
twenty minutes after Mackintosh was shot. They contained a mixture of
gelignite and T.N.T. specially designed for the purpose by a man called
Gideon, the *Irgun* bomb specialist who personally led the assault group.
He had done his job well.

When the churns exploded at 12.37 the effect was as though a 1,000 pound bomb had scored a direct hit on the building from above; one seven-storey wing was sliced completely away; the blast uprooted huge marble slabs from the hotel lobby and threw them sixty feet, and wounded A.T.S. girls lay moaning in the gutters of King David Street outside. Passers-by heard the thud made by a man's body as the blast flung it against the side of a Y.M.C.A. recreation hall on the side of the street opposite the hotel, and the body left a red patch on the white wall. *The Times* correspondent reported that a British official in a small government building next to the south wing saw the face of a clerk next to him cut almost in two by a sheet of flying glass.

Inside the shattered building Sir John Shaw, the Acting High Commissioner, fought his way with a sledge-hammer out of an office reduced to rubble, and began to direct rescue operations, which continued well into the next day. More than twenty-four hours later a corporal leading a squad digging in the ruins heard a faint voice. He knelt down and shouted: "Is that a wog down there?" The reply came back: "Yes, a wog named Thompson, assistant secretary." When he was finally released, Mr. D. C. Thompson had been under the wreckage thirty-one hours. He died in hospital ten days later, one of the last casualties in a list that had by then stretched to nearly 100 killed and half as many injured. They included some very senior British and Jewish officials, as well as many private individuals, including Arabs, who had the misfortune to be on the premises.

By the time Thompson was dug out the world knew about the biggest single act of violence in the twenty-nine years that Britain had controlled the Holy Land. Menahem Beigin, the *Irgun* leader, had admitted responsibility for the explosion, and David Ben-Gurion, speaking for the Jewish Agency, had condemned it as a "dastardly crime committed by a gang of desperadoes." Ben-Gurion himself was not connected with the affair, but his statement would have carried more weight had there not been collusion between *Irgun* and the *Palmach*, the commando force of the Jewish defence army which had for some time worked closely with the Agency itself. A dusk to dawn curfew was imposed on central Jerusalem and in a three-day swoop on Tel Aviv security forces interrogated 120,000 Jews. They arrested several hundreds, but found no terrorists, and though troops entered the house where Beigin was staying they failed to find him concealed behind a false wall. Despite the price on his head of £2,000, the *Irgun* leader was never betrayed, and the architect of violence, a bespectacled, rather ordinary-looking little man approaching middle-age, outlasted the British to form an extremist and unsuccessful political party in the new state.

The day after the explosion, people in Britain woke up to find eye-witness reports under banner headlines across the front of their papers, and it was not the only bad news of the day: John Strachey had announced the start of bread rationing, and beer was to be ten per cent weaker from August 1st. That morning also brought news of violence nearer home than Palestine – at Harringay Stadium. Here several hundred spectators wrecked the track, smashed a restaurant, and invaded the tote office after a greyhound called Ballymack Border had been disqualified in an evening race. (The *Daily Mirror* rather oddly decided this was the most important story of the day, and ran it above its Jerusalem report.)

The tenor of editorial comment on the explosion was unanimous. To *The Times* it was "A Senseless Outrage," the product of "insensate fanaticism and perverted propaganda," executed by men who were "dupes of an education which has taught them to rate nationalist ambition above justice and mercy." The *Daily Telegraph* headed its leading article "Plain Murder," emphasised the harm terrorism was doing the Jewish cause, and said: "We have no longer to deal with the Jewish Agency in its former character, but with a new and nameless organisation which believes its aims can be achieved by violence." (In the event, this belief unhappily turned out to be true.) The *Daily Express* adopted a fighting stance, as was its habit over Palestine, and said: "The immediate duty is plain – to uproot and destroy terrorism." Despite 100,000 troops, not counting police, this task proved impossible short of total war against the *Yishuv*, a course that had its champions among senior officers but was never carried into operation. Two days later the *Daily Express*, as ever with its thumb tight against the contemporary pulse, gave a hint of how public opinion was reacting. The *Express* reproduced a recruiting poster issued for the Palestine Police Force, which bore the heading: "HOW TO JOIN A CRACK FORCE. £20 a month and all found!" Since the increase in terrorism, the *Express* pointed out, the flow of volunteers had increased by half.

Jewish leaders in Britain had condemned earlier acts of terrorism, knowing it was a short step from shock and indignation to a desire for reprisal and ultimately general anti-Semitism. Events confirmed their fears; the King David explosion, and later – perhaps even more effectively – the murder of two British sergeants, neutralised much of the sympathy in Britain for the plight of European Jewry. And in the same way politicians who had long held pro-Zionist leanings became noticeably more discreet about the advantages of a Jewish National Home. But on the Continent and in America it was a different story. Many felt that the British Army deserved all it got and did not hesitate to say so.

In Palestine the explosion marked a turning-point in Anglo-Jewish relations. The breach was too deep to be plastered over by diplomacy, and this marked the beginning of the final phase of British rule in

Vicky, *News Chronicle*, 6.1.47

The Ultimate Winner

Palestine – or, put another way, in the creation of the sovereign state of Israel. Either way, twenty-two months later the British had withdrawn, in a rather unedifying way, and Zionism had finally triumphed.

It had not been an easily won victory, for Zionism, the creation of a people exiled from their homeland, had existed in one form or another since the Babylonian captivity. There had been a Zionist renaissance towards the end of the nineteenth century, and Theodor Herzl, a Viennese journalist, had founded the Zionist Organisation in 1897 soon after the upsurge of anti-Semitism that preceded the trial of Dreyfus in France.

By 1917, Chaim Weizmann, a Russian Jew born in the province of Grodno in 1874, who had become a chemistry lecturer at Manchester University, had used his singular diplomatic gifts, and his ability for impressing and influencing British politicians, to lay the ground for the Balfour Declaration. With certain clauses reiterated in the British Mandate of 1922, this formed the basis of Zionist claims from that time until independence.

In ebullient vein, A. J. Balfour once described the concept of the Jewish National Home as the most significant outcome of the First World War; particularly when expounded by Weizmann, the ideal of the National Home fired the imaginations of many leading British politicians. There was an element of the magnanimous in the Declaration, conceived in the depths of 1917 as one of the desperate appeals to all possible nationalisms; but besides moral satisfaction it had political advantages to offer. A Jewish Palestine, dependent on the British for protection, and indebted to Britain for its creation, was an excellent means of consolidating the territorial gains that General Allenby's army had gained from the Turks after the "Arab revolt" led by Hussein, Sherif of Mecca. Here was an excellent base for protecting British interests; the shorter route to India had long been an Imperial preoccupation, Middle East oil was becoming increasingly important and, in 1917, any step calculated to impress American Jewry was worth considering.

In combination, these factors led to a letter from A. J. Balfour to Lord Rothschild: "His Majesty's Government view with favour the establishment of a National Home for the Jewish people, and will use their best endeavours to facilitate the achievement of this object, *it being clearly understood that nothing shall be done which may prejudice the civil and religious rights of existing non-Jewish communities in Palestine . . .*" (my italics).

The Zionists pinned their hopes on this, but as the Emir Feisal and his supporter Colonel Lawrence pointed out at Versailles, there was a community of nearly half a million Arabs in Palestine, and it had been there uninterruptedly for at least 1,300 years. However, Feisal was prepared to make territorial concessions to the Jews so long as sovereignty rested with the Arabs. He wrote to Felix Frankfurter, a leading member of American Jewry: "We will wish the Jews a most hearty welcome home. The Jewish movement is national and not imperialist; our movement is national and not imperialist; there is room in Syria for us both." Such good-will became an increasingly rare commodity as the years passed; mass Jewish immigration to the Holy Land as foreseen by Weizmann did not materialise, mainly because the Russian source of supply was cut off by the Bolsheviks. Only 100,000 Jews arrived in Palestine between 1920 and 1930, and in 1928 the immigration figure was as low as 2,200. Arab hostility towards the Jews came increasingly to include the Palestine Administration; in 1936 there was open rebellion.

It was Hitler who became the most efficient recruiting officer for Zionism, and after 1933 the immigration rate soared. British attempts to placate Arab nationalist feeling failed, and for the Jews the tide was turning against them in Palestine as well as Europe. The British Government White Paper of May 1939 was their Munich; apart from nullifying their hopes of an independent state, it restricted immigration to 10,000 a year (one-sixth of the number who had entered Palestine in 1936) and so largely removed Palestine as a refuge at the time European Jewry most desperately needed one. The White Paper failed to please the Arabs; Winston Churchill called it "a base petition in moral bankruptcy" and Herbert Morrison, speaking for the Labour Party, described it as "a breach of British honour" and said, with some irony as it turned out, that future Governments might not feel themselves bound by it.

To the Jews, coming when it did, the White Paper was a death sentence. After the Jewish Agency had aided refugees to arrive illegally – 35,000 arrived in the twelve months beginning in September 1938 against the 10,150 officially allowed for – Malcolm MacDonald, the Colonial Secretary, suspended all immigration for ten months. It is impossible to calculate how many Jews died in the gas chambers because the British Government would not grant entry permits; even after the era of the coffin ships like the *Struma*, which sank with 763 drowned after waiting eight weeks for visas off Istanbul, the Government refused to regard immigration as a humanitarian and not a political matter. The gates to Palestine were not opened, and when the help they had waited for did not arrive, the European Jews went to the gas chambers.

The extent of the Nazi horror was so great as to strain credulity, but the complaisance of the Jewish people is almost as amazing. Their leaders connived with the German bureaucrats of extermination, and the Jews took their orders. They died in queues, sometimes having prepared their own graves. They accepted the role of universal scapegoat as if it were ordained, an inevitable part of the pattern of natural events. The only explanation is the pervading inheritance of the ghetto, which repeatedly emerges in unexpected forms in the history of the Jewish people. (An odd example is the attitude of the influential British Jews who sided with pro-Arab politicians during the discussions and manœuvres that preceded

the Balfour Declaration. They withheld their support from the National
Home, fearing that it would arouse latent anti-Semitism if it came into
existence.) After nearly 300,000 Jews had perished in the Warsaw ghetto,
70,000 more turned on the Nazis in April, 1943 and fought until they
were wiped out. The Warsaw uprising introduced a new phenomenon into
modern history – that of the fighting Jew, previously unknown since Bar
Kochba's revolt eighteen centuries before: or at least almost unknown,
because Jews had been fighting in Palestine for some years.

On the *kibbutzim*, colonies of Jews had been working since the beginning
of the century, toiling to make fertile land that had lain fallow since
antiquity. To protect themselves against attacks from Arab marauders
they founded a defence army, called *Haganah*. It was a loose-knit, ill-
armed organisation, manned mainly from *kibbutzim*. Sometimes the
Administration tried to wipe it out; at other times they tried to make use
of it, according to the policy in force at the time. For some time after the
Arab rebellion in 1936 there was open co-operation, but although Captain
Orde Wingate trained "special night sections" in guerrilla tactics,
Haganah remained an essentially defensive organisation. In 1936, Haj
Amin, Mufti of Jerusalem, who was later to appear at Himmler's side in
Berlin, was pursuing a policy of atrocities against Jewish and Arab
opponents alike. In order to carry out reprisals, an organisation called
Irgun Zvei Leumi came into being under Jacov Zabotinski. *Irgun* operated
against British as well as Arabs, but declared a truce on the outbreak
of war, whereupon many of its members joined the British forces. David
Raziel, by then leader, was killed on a sabotage mission for the British
during the Iraqi revolt in 1941. Abraham Stern opposed the truce, and
left *Irgun* to form a group of his own with a policy of war to the death
with the mandatory Government. This continued after Stern himself was
shot in the back while trying to escape from members of the Palestine
Police Force, and the Stern Gang was responsible for the murder of Lord
Moyne, Minister resident in Cairo, in November 1944: with equal
pointlessness, Sternists murdered the United Nations mediator, Count
Bernadotte, in 1948. Membership probably never numbered more than
200, but they were dangerous fanatics, prepared to do anything to revenge
themselves on the British. One of them has described, probably with
some embroidery, how he came to London in 1948 on a mission to murder
Ernest Bevin. He claims that he used a three-pronged fish hook to fasten
a book bomb under the Foreign Secretary's seat on the Government
front bench in the course of a guided tour. It remained there for the month
of December, 1948, but failed to go off.

Irgun itself ended the truce in 1943, and by the end of 1944 the Government was spending £4½ million on maintaining law and order in Palestine – nine times the sum budgeted for health, six times the sum spent on education. Many of the terrorists had been brought up in Eastern Europe and had acquired their know-how, as well as their faith in the efficacy of violence, from the Nazis and the Russian police. (Some had also been taught sabotage methods by the British.) Their indifference to the traditional tenets of Judaism appalled religious leaders and moderates alike, and *Ha-aretz*, a middle of the road Palestine paper, spoke for many of these when it asked its readers after the King David explosion: "Even if murder can get us a state – which is more than doubtful – what would such a state be worth?" Martin Buber was only one of the religious thinkers, bred on the ancient Zionist concept of a holy marriage of land and people, who recalled the words of Isaiah: "Israel can only be built with justice."

Unfortunately this was not the case, and the state was founded on violence – in the first instance terrorism, and ultimately war. The I.R.A. had learnt that it was possible to get away with outrages like "Bloody Sunday" without losing the sympathy that the Western world in the twentieth century had come to feel for national determination. *Irgun* and the Stern Gang pointed to this precedent; the homeland could only be won, they said, if the Jews were prepared to fight for it. The *Irgun* badge showed an outline of Palestine and Transjordan joined together, with a fist clenching a rifle superimposed. Their motto was "Only Thus." One of the many tragic by-products of post-war events in Palestine was that they convinced many Jews who were temperamentally antipathetic to all forms of violence that *Irgun* was right.

But this is moving ahead too fast, and when, on May 8th, 1945, the bonfires blazed in Britain to celebrate V.E. Day, the mood was more optimistic. The full extent of the Nazi extermination of European Jewry was only just becoming realised by people in Britain and America: but at least it was over. And the first priority was to aid the 600,000 Jews who had managed to survive, the majority of them in the hopeless squalor of refugee camps. Delegations and individuals from Britain and America visited these camps, and established that most of the survivors, probably influenced to some extent by Zionist propaganda, wished to make their future in Palestine among their own people. If they were to return, the restrictions on immigration imposed by the 1939 White Paper would have to be lifted, or at least modified. The Jewish Agency wasted no time in applying to the British Government for 100,000 permits. They found support from Harry S. Truman, who had been President of the United

5

States for less than three months when he proposed to Churchill that Palestine should be one of the subjects discussed at the Potsdam Conference. The President added a hope that "the British Government may find it possible without delay to lift the restrictions . . . on Jewish immigration."

But Churchill had other things besides Palestine on his mind, and, before he could reply to Truman, a General Election intervened, leaving him leader of the Opposition. For the first time Britain had a Labour Government backed by a large Parliamentary majority – 187 in the lobbies. The Zionists were naturally pleased at the result: although Churchill had a reputation for being sympathetic to the Jewish cause – in 1939 he had mounted a contemptuous attack on the White Paper – the Zionist ardour that had flourished in opposition had diminished somewhat while he was in office. (This was a syndrome the Zionists were shortly to meet again.) And after the assassination of his old friend, Lord Moyne, Churchill had hinted that "If our dreams of Zionism are to end in the smoke of assassins' pistols, and our labours for its future to produce only a new set of gangsters worthy of Nazi Germany . . ." British supporters of Zionism might come to reconsider their position.

The Labour Party, on the other hand, had no reservations – Jewish resettlement in Palestine had been a major plank in its foreign policy for more than a quarter of a century. Successive annual conferences had pledged the party to do its utmost to create a new Jewish state, and the conference of December 1944 was no exception. Hugh Dalton had drafted a statement, and Labour fought the General Election with this as its official view on Palestine: "There is surely neither hope nor meaning in a 'Jewish National Home' unless we are prepared to let the Jews, if they wish, enter this tiny land in such numbers as to become a majority. There was a strong case for this before the war. There is an irresistible case now, after the unspeakable atrocities of the cold and calculated German Nazi plan to kill all the Jews in Europe." Dalton wrote in the third volume of his autobiography, *High Tide and After*: "It was inherent in our Declaration of 1944 that there should henceforth be no such thing as a Jewish 'Illegal immigrant'."

This policy was stated clearly enough, and the Zionists apparently had cause for nothing but jubilation at the election result. But from the beginning things went awry for them. When the Cabinet was announced, Ernest Bevin, not Dalton, was Foreign Secretary. This was contrary to general expectation and to Clement Attlee's original decision, which is described in Wheeler-Bennett's biography of George VI. As he later wrote, in the foreword to Francis Williams' biography of Bevin: "Britain was facing a difficult decision, as a great power which had temporarily been gravely weakened. It needed a very strong personality to counter-balance this as far as possible." Whether Attlee's change of heart was the result of pressure from King George (at Churchill's suggestion) or not, the man who had drafted the pro-Zionist statement gleefully gave himself over to preparing a budget and planning to nationalise the Bank of England. It is pointless to speculate on the course of events in Palestine had the appointments gone the other way (as both men had wished), but Bevin's qualities were ill-suited to the problems posed by the Middle East, and Palestine was his greatest single failure. He proved himself to be a strong man — indeed at times a ferocious one — but his implacable quality, the lack of flexibility, aggravated a difficult situation to the extreme.

When Truman finally received a reply to his Palestine proposals, it came from Attlee, who, had he ever any predilection for Zionism, kept it well camouflaged. The reply stated with characteristic terseness that the President's memorandum would receive attention. It soon became evident that the Government had no intention of being influenced by humanitarian sentiment in America or in the United Nations, and that the 100,000 permits would not be forthcoming. From the beginning the Government stalled, and with a brutal insensitivity that Bevin was to make his personal trademark in dealings with Palestine, the Foreign Secretary remarked that as the Jews had already waited 1,900 years an additional twelve months would make little difference. He unwisely assured the Commons that he would stake his personal reputation on solving the Palestine problem, and, when his efforts at arbitrating between Jews and Arabs failed, he intemperately accused the Americans of being the culprits. When the Anglo-American Inquiry which he had set up recommended, in effect (on May 1st, 1946), the abrogation of the White Paper and the establishment of a state under international guarantees dominated neither by Arabs nor Jews, he reacted as if it were a personal slight, accepted none of its points, and later claimed that he had accepted them all. Here was an opportunity for a settlement — *Irgun* announced it would suspend operations if the permits were granted — but the Government frittered the chance away, and clamped down even more severely on illegal immigration. Six weeks after the Inquiry's report, what the official phrase called "operations to restore law and order" were in full swing.

On June 30th, security forces broke into the headquarters of various Jewish organisations in Jerusalem, including the Jewish Agency. As it was the Sabbath they were deserted, and the troops later arrested almost all the leaders of the Agency at their homes. These included Rabbi Jehuda Fischman, the seventy-three-year-old acting chairman, who was forced to break his religious prohibitions about travelling on the Sabbath, and was dragged into a car by British soldiers. He later went on hunger strike, and had to be transferred to hospital. At the same time 2,000 Jews were detained throughout the country, and the Government statement praised the troops for having "exercised great restraint in the face of considerable provocation." The casualty list for this operation was three Jews killed, thirteen admitted to hospital, and a number of others slightly injured. (One British soldier was accidentally killed by the same bullet that killed one of the Jews.) British policy was hardening, and although the High Commissioner, Sir Alan Cunningham, had stressed in a statement on June 29th that operations were directed only against the terrorists, and not the community as a whole, it became apparent after the King David explosion on July 22nd that British policy was then aiming to teach the Jews a lesson – all the Jews.

Four days after the explosion, General Sir Evelyn Barker, the G.O.C. in Palestine, circulated a letter marked "Restricted" to all his officers. It began:

"The Jewish community in Palestine cannot be absolved from the long series of outrages culminating in the blowing up of a large part of the Government offices in the King David Hotel, causing grievous loss of life . . .

"I am determined that they shall suffer punishment and be made aware of the contempt and loathing with which we regard their conduct. We must not allow ourselves to be deceived by the hypocritical sympathy shown by their leaders and representative bodies, nor by their protests that they are in no way responsible for these acts as they are unable to control the terrorists . . .

"Consequently I have decided with effect on receipt of this letter you will put out of bounds to all ranks all Jewish places of entertainment, cafés, restaurants, shops, and private dwellings. No British soldier is to have any intercourse with any Jew, and any intercourse in the way of duty should be as brief as possible and kept strictly to the business in hand.

"I appreciate that these measures will inflict some hardship on the troops, but I am certain that if my reasons are fully explained to them they will understand their propriety, and they will be punishing the Jews in a way the race dislikes as much as any – by striking at their pockets and showing our contempt for them."

General Barker made one other point in the letter – that the terrorist gangs could not evade capture "without the support, actual and passive, of the general Jewish public," and he went on to describe "the Jews in this country" as accomplices of the terrorists. This was undoubtedly true in part, and the Jewish Agency, through *Haganah*, was an accomplice in the explosion, although they had intended it to take place after a warning that would have given the occupants time to evacuate. But when the Agency and the Jewish community, appalled by the explosion, were more violently opposed to terrorism than at any time since the murder of Lord Moyne (after which the Agency had furnished the security forces with a list of leading members of *Irgun* and the Stern Gang), Barker's letter had an unfortunate effect. *Irgun* copied it on a poster that was widely displayed in Palestine, and a chance to unite Jews against the terrorists was lost – *Irgun*'s membership sharply increased.

The anti-Semitic gibe in the last sentence of the letter was so blatant that Herbert Morrison dissociated the Government from it in a speech made to the Commons on July 31st. In the course of a long debate on Palestine, in which the so-called "Morrison Plan" for a federal state was put forward, the Labour member for Wednesbury, Mr. Stanley Evans, made a small but significant contribution. For the first time in his experience, he said, ordinary, decent working-men were talking in their pubs and clubs, at the barber's and at work, about the loss to which British troops had been subjected in Palestine. It was the irony of ironies and the epitome of ingratitude that it was the men of the Normandy beaches and Arnhem who were facing these murderous attacks.

In General Barker's letter, indignation at the wickedness of a single act, the King David explosion, had provoked an expression of general anti-Semitism, containing the traditional Shylock sneer, levelled against the Jewish community as a whole. An identical reaction came in Britain, only more slowly. As Mr. Evans pointed out, ordinary people were discussing the explosion with disgust and passion. It had thrust events in a remote country the size of Wales into the forefront of the public imagination, and sown a seed of hostility against the Jewish community in Britain, the Jew next door, which took twelve months almost to the day to bring forth its fruit. In the interim it required nourishment – and this was provided by a year's press reports of violence against British troops who had the misfortune to be doing a job that no one should be required to do. When the casualty list for 1946 was published it showed that seventy-three of them had been killed and 130 wounded; over 300 civilians, British, Jewish and Arab, were also killed or wounded in the same period. 1946 ended with *Irgun* challenging the Administration's policy of caning captured terrorists by kidnapping and flogging a group of British soldiers, including a major in the 6th Airborne Division, probably the least popular unit in Palestine. The caning policy was dropped early in 1947, but a new chain of violence started when Dov Gruner, a young *Irgun* member, was sentenced to death for his part in a raid on Ramat Gan police station the previous April. Inevitably *Irgun* retaliated – by kidnapping Judge Ralph Windham on January 27th, in the Tel Aviv district court of which he was president. The authorities stayed Gruner's execution, and three days later the judge was released. He announced that the terrorists had treated him in a gentlemanly way – "My guards talked about art and religion, and gave me a copy of *Thieves in the Night* (Arthur Koestler's novel of the *kibbutzim*) to read," the judge told a reporter. And he added that he was annoyed because they had insisted on keeping his wig as a souvenir – "It was the only one I had."

But there were few light touches in the history of Palestine in 1947. Gruner was finally hanged on April 16th with three other *Irgun* members. A few hours earlier emergency regulations had been gazetted suspending normal prison rules before an execution. They also suspended all right of appeal against any sentence passed either by the G.O.C. or a military court. Three weeks later, on May 4th, Acre Prison, where Gruner had been executed, was attacked by about a hundred *Irgun* members in military uniform. They blew a hole in the ancient wall, enabling about 180 Arab and 33 Jewish prisoners in the exercise yard to escape. Three of the raiders who were captured in the attack were shortly afterwards sentenced to death. Despite an appeal for clemency from the United Nations Committee touring Palestine – on June 22nd they warned the Government through the Secretary-General, Mr. Trygve Lie, of "unfortunate repercussions" – these sentences were confirmed on July 8th. One week later two sergeants in an intelligence unit, Clifford Martin of Coventry and Mervyn Paice from Bristol, were kidnapped in Nathanya. Begin announced that, if the raiders were executed, the sergeants would be hanged at the same time.

Despite extensive and unremitting searches for them in the Nathanya area, no trace could be found. When the three raiders, aged twenty, twenty-one and twenty-three, were hanged on July 29th in the same prison that they had attacked, Nathanya was full of rumours that the sergeants had also been killed. Security troops continued their search even more feverishly, and finally found the sergeants on July 31st; their bodies, with notes pinned to them, were hanging in a eucalyptus grove near Nathanya. When a Royal Engineers captain began to cut the first down a booby trap exploded, injuring him in the face. One body was blown to pieces, and the other thrown twenty yards.

The news, in all its gruesome detail, reached Britain at the start of the holiday week-end, shocking public opinion as it had not been shocked since the King David explosion a year and a week before. On its front page the *Daily Express* used a picture of the sergeants hanging, and a wave of revulsion against the Jews swept the country. That Bank Holiday week-end has earned a squalid niche in post-war history for the events which followed.

In Liverpool, a crowd numbering several hundreds rioted in Myrtle Street, smashing and looting shops belonging to Jews. Similar mob demonstrations took place in Manchester, and a crowd of seven hundred in the Lancashire town of Eccles also attacked Jewish shops. Police at Bethnal Green in London were forced to order a Jewish Ex-Servicemen's meeting to disperse after it had been threatened by a large, hostile crowd. And events of the same kind were repeated in miniature throughout the country – several synagogues suffered from acts of idiotic hooliganism, a harmless portable land mine was found in the door of a shop in Devonport containing the message: "Only because English lives are involved this is empty. Down with The Jews." At Stanley Abattoir in Liverpool eighty slaughtermen refused to process meat intended for Jewish consumption. They passed a resolution stating that all Jews were as much responsible for the hanging of the sergeants as the actual murderers, and *The Times* quoted them as saying that they would continue their embargo on the meat "until organised terrorism in Palestine ceased and the leaders are given the same taste of British justice as were the German gangsters in the war." When Merseyside dockers returned to work after the holidays they found someone had painted a slogan across the entrance to Canada Dock: "Death To All Jews."

On August 6th, when a number of people arrested during incidents of this kind were receiving stiff sentences for what an Eccles magistrate called "un-British and unpatriotic acts," an obscure local newspaper in the north-west of England published a leading article which in due course received a wider circulation than its author could have anticipated. The newspaper in question was the *Morecambe and Heysham Visitor*, an independent weekly with a pegged circulation of 17,800 in its immediate area. Extracts from the editorial were read in court when its author, James Caunt, who was also proprietor of the paper, was charged with writing and publishing a seditious libel concerning people of the Jewish faith and race resident in Great Britain. The article began:

"There is very little about which to rejoice greatly except the pleasant fact that only a handful of Jews bespoil the population of our borough. The foregoing sentence may be regarded as an outburst of anti-Semitism. It is intended to be, and we make no apologies, neither do we shirk any responsibilities or repercussions."

The writer continued by complimenting the *Daily Express* on its decision to publish the photograph of the sergeants, and referred to a twenty-one-year-old boy from Blackpool who had been shot in Palestine. It described protests against terrorism from various sections of British Jewry as "blatant hypocrisy" and "face-saving propaganda". It became clear as the article continued that the *Morecambe and Heysham Visitor*, at least, had not been blinded to the truth by these Hebrew manœuvres.

"It is not sufficient for British Jews, who have proved to be the worst black market offenders, to rush into print with howls of horror and sudden wreaths at cenotaphs. They should use their ill-gotten wealth in trying to dissuade their brothers in the United States from pouring out dollars to facilitate the entrance into Palestine of European Jewish scum, a proportion of whom will swell the ranks of the terrorist organisation and thus carry on the murderous work which British Jewry professes to abhor . . .

"There is a growing feeling that Britain is in the grip of the Jews. There are more Jewish M.P.s than at any time in British history, and, for the purpose of emphasis, we repeat that if any analysis could be made of the people convicted for black market offences the Jewish community in Britain would come out an easy first.

"The Jews, indeed, are a plague on Britain. . . . Violence may be the only way to bring them to the sense of their responsibility to the country in which they live."

So ended the first editorial, but a week later the *Visitor* returned to the subject again. Mr. Caunt then referred to a visit he had made to America a year before, and described anti-British propaganda which he had seen displayed on hoardings and elsewhere. The article continued (in what was largely an attempt to justify the earlier editorial):

"We considered the time was overdue when the inactivity of British Jewry to what is happening to Britishers in Palestine should be commented on without mincing words. We took our courage in both hands and decided that if a thing is worth doing at all, it is worth doing properly."

When Mr. Caunt appeared at Liverpool Assizes on November 17th, counsel for the prosecution said the material point was whether the article had been published with the intention of stirring race violence by promoting feelings of hostility and ill-will between different classes of the

King's subjects. He submitted that Mr. Caunt had quite designedly set about creating such hostility. In evidence Mr. Caunt denied that his intention had been to incite anyone to violence; he was simply warning the Jews what would happen to them if they did not mend their ways. Addressing the jury his counsel said it would be "a black day for the liberty of the subject and the people of this country" if his client were convicted; and he called the prosecution an attempt to put the clock back by at least a hundred and fifty years. The judge, Mr. Justice Birkett, said in the course of an extraordinary summing-up:

"Two matters would seem to emerge over all others in this case. It is in the highest degree essential – and I cannot over-emphasise the importance of it to you – that nothing should be done in this court to destroy or weaken the liberty of the Press; and secondly, remember at all times that it is the duty of the prosecution to prove the case beyond all reasonable doubt."

The judge's direction was plain enough, and it took the all male jury only thirteen minutes to decide: "It is our unanimous decision that he is *Not Guilty*."

So, in this rather odd way, the freedom of the Press was defended, and the *Visitor* once more faded away into the obscurity it so richly deserved.

It would be doing the "ordinary, decent working-men" that Mr. Evans had talked about a great injustice to suggest they shared Mr. Caunt's picture of the world, but his views indicate that the Palestine neurosis, a product of twelve months' almost permanent crisis, had spread as far as England. After the hangings, the view that British troops must be withdrawn, whatever the cost, became common coinage throughout the country. Opinion on the left and the right, politicians who had concerned themselves with the National Home for decades, as well as men in the street who could not have indicated Palestine on a map, found themselves brought together in brief unanimity – it is time, they said, we packed our bags. The signal for departure was not long in coming, but the decision had already been taken out of British hands.

Bevin had paved the way for this decision six months before, in the course of that grim February when nothing went right for Government or country. Fuel cuts had put 2½ million people out of work; fog, frost, and snow followed each other daily, as though the weather were determined to provide a counterpoint to disturbances in the body politic with Shakespearean appropriateness. In the gloom of the Foreign Office, Bevin devoted three days to surrendering control of the Indian Empire, arranging the withdrawal from Greece, and putting the Palestine problem in the lap of the United Nations. This operation was accompanied by his well-known joke about there being no need for candles "as we have Israel*lites* here," a pleasantry which in those circumstances probably raised few laughs. Despite the evacuation of women and children from Palestine – the first plane load of departing British had taken off from Lydda airport on February 2nd – the Government was not thinking of a general withdrawal. Its view was that neither Jews nor Arabs, nor the two together, had the faintest hope of making a state without the British there to administer it. Under pressure in the Commons debate from Mr. Churchill, who wanted to know why, if it was right to call in the United Nations then, it had not been equally right twelve months earlier, Mr. Bevin said: "It would be a fatal policy for Great Britain, with all the leadership she has done in the world in all her history, to have gone to the United Nations without attempting to exhaust every possibility."

Quite apart from British strategic interests in the Middle East, Bevin was still thinking in terms of British responsibility. He believed that the United Nations would in due course throw the ball back where it had come from, and that Britain, using the techniques of ruling and administration evolved in the course of her long Imperial experience, would succeed in clearing up the mess. There were good reasons for thinking that once the United Nations had tried its hand at the problem – and failed – Britain's own position would be strengthened. America had been notably free with her criticism. It was thought that she might be more restrained after being faced with the prospect of expending her own money, and blood, to enforce a United Nations settlement. A good way of ending the noise that she made in the gallery was to bring her on to the stage itself.

But, by autumn, events proved that the Foreign Office had once more misjudged the situation badly. When the u.n. Special Committee reported on August 31st, 1947, its first recommendation – that the mandate should end at the earliest possible date – was hardly a compliment to Britain. The other main recommendations were firstly political partition (although the country was to remain an economic entity), and secondly early independence. Rather optimistically the Committee suggested that Britain should shoulder the responsibility of putting this scheme into operation, helped by one or more members of the United Nations "if so desired." But responsibility without advantage, and the prospect of being associated with a scheme so violently opposed by the Arab states, failed to appeal to the Foreign Office. It was decided to withdraw the army as soon as possible, salvaging as much equipment as could be taken. The mandate administration would also withdraw, and in such a way that nothing of value would be left for the new state. British policy in the interim would be "strictly neutral"; this involved non-co-operation with the U.N. and blatant attempts to ensure that, when war broke out after the British left, as was inevitable, the Arabs would fulfil their reiterated threats to sweep the Jews into the sea.

The Government refused to comply with a recommendation made at Lake Success, the temporary H.Q. of the General Assembly, that they should open a major port to the Jews; on the contrary, it operated a blockade to ensure that neither immigrants nor arms entered Palestine from Europe. Meanwhile, British arms flowed into the Arab states "under existing treaty obligations," and in Damascus Jamil Mardam Bey, the Syrian Prime Minister, happily watched recruits joining the Arab Liberation Army for a holy war against the Jews. "The world will soon see the Arabs rise as one man," he told the foreign press in January 1948. "The people's army will soon be able to teach the treacherous Jews a lesson." Britain so effectively refused to co-operate with the Five Power Commission, entrusted with making the transition between mandate and partition as peaceful as possible, that only four of its members ever reached the Holy Land, and they were to all intents and purposes confined in the military area of Jerusalem.

British delegates to the United Nations continued to deny that His Majesty's Government was behaving in anything but a strictly disinterested way: Ernest Bevin was franker, particularly when speaking off the cuff and not restricted by an official brief. Question time in the House of Commons on April 28th was such an occasion. Three Labour members, Messrs. Cocks, Levy, and Janner, wanted to know whether the Government would stop sending arms to Arab countries, some of whom had announced that they would invade Palestine after the British left on May 15th. Alternatively, would the Government let the Jews have arms with which to defend themselves? Bevin said that the Governments concerned naturally expected their contracts to be fulfilled as speedily as was technically possible. He added: "I warned both Jews and Arabs. I appealed to them in London, and warned them that we would leave Palestine. And you must remember the British sergeants were hanged to the tree – not by Arabs." Later he allowed himself a dig at Jewish M.P.s: "I say to the Jews and Arabs – the Arabs are not in this House – (loud cheers) the way for both of you to settle this is to stop fighting."

But Bevin had put his money on the wrong horse. Far from sweeping the Jews into the sea, the Arab states and their regular armies were badly mauled in the war which they so exuberantly began on May 14th, 1948, the day that Israel came into being. In the fighting which followed, the new state considerably extended her borders beyond those that had been laid down in the partition scheme (and created in the process a refugee problem as acute as that of European Jewry, when her armies drove more than three-quarters of the Arab population out of the country). The failure of the Foreign Office was complete. British policies were so illogical that some critics, particularly Americans, have tried to explain them in terms of a basic irrationality in the Foreign Secretary himself, and have accused Bevin of being motivated by anti-Semitism.

"His bitterness against Truman was almost pathological. It found its match only in his blazing hatred for his other scapegoats – the Jews, the Israelis, the Israeli Government." This was how Bevin impressed James G. McDonald, first American envoy to Israel, who left the Foreign Office after a stormy interview in the summer of 1948 reflecting: "Bevin had taken all the worst of his bullying nature from Transport House . . . and installed it in the uncongenial atmosphere of the Foreign Office." Certainly Bevin's belief that the Jews were only a religious group, not a national one, had been conditioned by those whom he had met in the Transport Union; this may have been an insular view, but it was shared by Bevin's expert advisers, the men called by Truman with a healthy overtone of scepticism "the striped pants boys." But, whatever Bevin thought when he first became Foreign Secretary, a flow of briefs from the Foreign Office, the Colonial Office, the Middle East Office in Cairo, and the Palestine Government were unanimous in assuring him of two points – the Jews were not a nation, and it would be fatal for British interests in the Middle East and the future of the Arab alliances if they were ever allowed to become one. The pro-Arab bias that Churchill had noted in nine-tenths of the Palestine officials who first administered the mandate was equally evident in the generation that succeeded them. One reason was that the Arabs were more susceptible than the Jews to methods that many of these officials had learned in the Indian Empire; another was the extraordinary appeal that the Arab aristocracy and the Bedouin (but not the urban Arabs) always had for the British. This highly charged, almost mystical feeling of kinship (which notably failed to stand up under political stress) affected down-to-earth men as well as visionaries like T. E. Lawrence. And their cumulative view of realities in the Middle East soon convinced the Labour Cabinet, contrary to all expectations, that the letter and spirit of the 1939 White Paper must be preserved. Any concessions to the Jews, they were assured, meant political disaster.

One of the most unfortunate by-products of the policy recommended by the men on the spot was its effect on relations with America. The bluntness that had served Bevin well elsewhere consistently aggravated a difficult situation. His decision to arrest the Jewish Agency leaders in June 1946 was timed to coincide with the long congressional debate in which the decision whether or not to replace discontinued Lend-Lease by a loan to Britain hung in the balance. Truman eventually got the loan through Congress, but Bevin's action did not help to ease the process. Eventually Bevin flatly accused the Americans of being responsible for the breakdown in the Palestine negotiations. This came during the Commons debate on the decision to pass the mandate to the U.N. (February 5th, 1947), when Bevin referred to the meeting with Jewish leaders the previous October:

"There was a feeling, I do not think I overestimated it, when they (the Jewish delegation) left me in the Foreign Office that day, that I had the right approach at last. (Cheers.) But what happened? I went back to the Paris Peace Conference the next day—I believe it was the Day of Atonement or a special day of the Jewish religion, I forget which—the Prime Minister telephoned me at midnight, and told me the President of the United States was going to issue another statement on the 100,000 (immigration permits). I think the country ought to know about this. (Cheers.)

"I went next morning to Mr. Byrnes, and told him how far I had got the day before. I believed we were on the road if only they would leave us alone. I begged that the statement be not issued, but I was told that if it was not issued by Mr. Truman a counter statement would be issued by Mr. Dewey. In international affairs I cannot settle things if my problem is made the subject of local elections."

Later in the debate Bevin was cheered by a House as hopelessly optimistic as he was himself, when he said: "I hope I am not saying anything to cause bad feeling with the United States, but I feel so intensely about this." Truman was outraged by this statement, which he later described as "undiplomatic" and "almost hostile." The State Department issued a denial that United States interest in a Palestine settlement was motivated by partisan local elections, and Representative Emanuel Celler of New York said that Bevin's accusation was "a damned lie." It was not, not entirely at least, but neither was it good diplomacy nor good sense for a Foreign Secretary to make such a statement about the head of an allied state. The impression which Bevin made on American opinion was such that on one occasion when he arrived in New York the dockers refused to handle his luggage; a sad reception for the greatest trade union leader Britain had produced in the century, the man who had fought for the "dockers' tanner". Bevin grew increasingly petulant as the Palestine situation deteriorated, illuminating the extent of his own failure. R. H. S. Crossman, who watched the process, later wrote: "By 1947 British policy in Palestine was largely motivated by one man's determination at almost any cost to teach the Jews a lesson." But Bevin's anger was not the product of anti-Semitism: as James McDonald indicated, he had equally bitter feelings about the Americans. He had staked his personal reputation on finding a settlement, and many of his off-the-cuff statements indicate that he regarded the Jews' refusal to accept less than the mandate promised as a personal slight. "In international affairs *I* cannot settle things if *my* problem . . .": this is the voice of egotism. And it was the voice of egotism gone mad that initiated the fiasco of the British departure, with its deliberate aim of creating chaos.

Mr. Caunt and the Foreign Secretary were not the only ones who felt angry with both Jews and Americans. The Palestine affair produced a widespread sense of national *pique*, and a hypersensitivity to all criticism from outside was particularly evident among the middle income groups, exacerbated by the economic pressure which they were facing. Hit by inflation, at the mercy of the depredations – as they were regarded – of Dalton and Cripps, most of them were experiencing for the first time the unpleasantness of living through an economic crisis governed by a party primarily committed to the interests of another group.

British frustration was frequently expressed in a widespread and largely unreasoned hostility to America and all things American. Some of this resentment was justified; for instance when Ben Hecht, the Hollywood scriptwriter, sent an open letter to the terrorists in May 1947 saying "We are out to raise funds for you." And again, when he made his stupid remark about there being a song in his heart every time a British soldier was killed. But much of the antipathy to America, based largely on jealousy and a conviction that she was meddling where she had no business, was unjustified and vitiating. If one post-war characteristic more than any other is illuminated by the story of Palestine it is the widespread belief that the rest of the world, and particularly Europe and America, was insufficiently grateful for the British war effort. And the kind of jingoism so often purveyed by the *Daily Express* was never more clouded with prejudice and misinformation. People had no idea what was happening in Palestine, and the Press was responsible for consistently falsifying the issues, almost always by omission. When a soldier during a security check on civilians said: "Hitler killed six million Jews, the 6th Airborne will kill sixty million if you don't bloody well behave," the British papers kept quiet.

But the French and American newspapers did not. Mr. Caunt was not the only British visitor to America appalled by what he read. Some of the reports were Zionist propaganda, but many were simply factual accounts of what was happening, accounts that never stood a chance of appearing in the British press. Britons abroad who read them were frequently so indignant that they wrote to papers at home, saying in effect: "The Americans and the French are convinced that we are running an imperialistic and oppressive régime in Palestine. How can we educate them?" This reaction was a common one, and as good an example as any occurs in a *Times* report of the House of Lords debate shortly after the hanging of the sergeants. "Lord Altrincham (formerly Sir Edward Grigg: created 1st Baron Altrincham in 1945) said it was a terrible tragedy that the world did not seem to agree with us about the horror of what was happening in Palestine. Civilised countries were taking these things for granted and as if we deserved what we were getting . . ." These countries included France, where most of the illegal immigrations were mounted with the connivance of successive French Governments. Opposition to Britain's policy brought America and Russia into a temporary and unexpected alliance. Finally, even the faithful Dominions withdrew their support from Britain at the United Nations.

A delegate at the Labour Party conference in 1946 accused Bevin of pursuing a traditional Conservative policy of power politics in Palestine. The criticism was entirely justified, as the affair of the five R.A.F. planes shot down by the Israelis on the Egyptian border, and shown to have been flying with the Egyptian air force, later demonstrated, to the Foreign Secretary's considerable embarrassment. The delegate might have gone on to say that the main disadvantage of such policies was that they no longer worked. British dealings in Palestine indicated with great clarity one way that the country was out of step with the post-war world. Somewhere the empirical gift that had played such a large part in Britain's greatness had been lost, the flexibility in the face of changing conditions had disappeared. Unfortunately the lesson of Palestine was not learnt. The same loss of touch and timing recurred in dealings with many emergent nations, but it was left to one of Bevin's successors to make the final mistake that the Labour Foreign Secretary avoided. Bevin was prepared to hover on the brink of war in the Middle East, but at least he knew that it would be fatal to go over the edge.

4

THE SPIVS

DAVID HUGHES

David Hughes was born in 1930. He took a degree in English at Oxford, then worked for the *London Magazine*. He has been Features Editor and Editor of *Town*. He has had three novels published by Rupert Hart-Davis, the latest being *The Horsehair Sofa* (1961). He has also written a critical study of J. B. Priestley, and has just finished a travel book on Sweden. He has made documentary films on Provence and Lapland with his wife, Mai Zetterling.

THE SPIVS

David Hughes

NOBODY knew how Stanley Setty had spent the war. He entered it without assets, as unprepared as England, and in the late forties he popped up miraculously rich, like Germany. In pre-war days he had always lived on his wits, gambling at the fringes of a basically honest society and mostly losing. But in 1949, four years after the war, when that same society had learned that only a touch of dishonesty gave any spark to life at all, Setty was reckoned to have a capital of fifty thousand behind him and always paid for his triple-price double-whiskies from a roll of two hundred fivers.

Most days he stood on the corner of Warren Street, that cracked axle of the used-car trade, where he waited for business to come his way. He worked alone, his bank in his pocket, his brain furnished as slickly as an office. His only premises, a garage in a dead-end mews off Albany Street, were concealed close at hand, and he lived evasively in that flashy, decrepit half-world of sloppy pubs and steamed-up caffs, linked by bomb-sites (for violence) and railway stations (for quick thefts), which described a crooked circle from Aldgate round the Euston Road to Hammersmith and on round to the Elephant. This was an area where crime, or the half-operatic post-war version of it, was hard to disentangle from decent enterprise.

Much of his traffic in the second-hand car business was shrewd and legal; he would buy sedate monsters with a high petrol consumption against the time when rationing ended. But a lot of it was deep under the counter – necessarily so, for he was an ambitious dealer and the times were against him. Neither he nor anyone else was permitted to resell new cars for a twelvemonth even if he could obtain them. Petrol was so short that a man could be (indeed, was) prosecuted for riding home on the trickle of petrol left in the motor-bike he had just bought. To men like Setty breaking – or rather outwitting – a law that got tied up in such ridiculous knots offered a sense of triumph, if not of dubious virtue; people under pressure needed his services, the game was worth playing financially, and, thanks to a police force depleted by sluggish demobilisation, he courted only a nominal risk.

His activities were an exercise of skill. They also provided a means of paying for what money alone could not buy: silk shirts, a range of fifty-guinea suits, and that sleek and weighty air of prosperity, very rare in those days, that implied a meat ration of far more than the permitted shilling a week. And it was this obvious aura of success, associated then with a knavery that only the middle-class really deplored, which drew Setty into uneasy friendship, one night at the Hollywood Club early in 1949, with a man called Donald Hume.

Ingenious, pettily self-centred, Hume belonged to one type of spiv; Setty to another, more grand. Neither had much in common with the character in soft hat, whip-striped suit, and burnt-cork moustache whom Osbert Lancaster had pinned down like a butterfly on the front page of the *Express*. The weekly chronicling of the spivs' tricks by Arthur Helliwell in *The People* made Helliwell's column the most widely read in the country. But the definition, worked out in the cramped correspondence columns during the summer of 1947, covered them all. Sid Field, whose most popular variety act was his take-off of a spiv, and Arthur English, "Prince of the Wide Boys", made the spiv a radio and music-hall cliché. A spiv, it was agreed, was a relentless opportunist who earned his living by not working, preferably within the law. In fact they were not averse to a touch of crime, provided it looked (and perhaps felt) like something else, just as they didn't mind driving lorries as long as their clothing vividly proclaimed that they weren't lorry-drivers. They never planned their opportunities, as criminals did; they merely took them, snatched and improvised, inventing as they went along.

Thus the definition not only fitted the boys who slyly gadded their barrows about a London that cried out for such patches of colour. It applied equally well, though no one realised it at the time, to the back-room hordes of layabouts who, convinced that all their scrounges and rackets were too widespread to be reprehensible, poached on crime when no one happened to be looking. So it was hardly criminal, merely spivvish, to waylay a lorryload of whisky, and, by breaking a crate of bottles over a filter and soaking the lorry in neat alcohol, enable the deprived publican to claim against the distributor. Nor, for a trio of ex-submarine officers, was it criminal to buy an old motor-boat and ferry quantities of liquor from Cherbourg to a remote marshy spot on the Hampshire coast. After all, people wanted the stuff; and they, quick off the mark (unlike the Government), had the guts to provide it.

A few detectives, keeping their ears to the ground at race meetings, had picked up the word spiv as early as the twenties. Now, like the long drape-cut that took a couple of decades to cross the Atlantic, the word passed belatedly into public usage, fired off in radio cross-talk, peppering the newspapers, exchanged between friends almost as an endearment. Such a word was needed at that time, as much to define the attitude, which was universal, as to describe the showy character who had earned his racketeering right to it.

The spiv got rave notices that summer. He became the fashionable entertainment for social observers. Correspondents delved into that fund of useless knowledge that is always available to confuse public issues: some said the word came from *spilav* (Welsh gypsy, to push), others that the type was a direct copy of the wide-boys who had riveted suburban Detroit in the twenties. Even the sheepish Establishment, who in 1947 had never had it so bad, shepherded the spiv into formal existence. Lord Rosebery and Peterborough of the *Daily Telegraph* crossed ornamental swords over the derivation of the word. A retired racecourse detective, Mr. W. Bebbington, supported Lord Rosebery, describing the spiv as "one who makes a living on the racecourse without having to work for it." The essence of the spiv, it was again agreed, was that he had no visible means of support. (Like England herself, no one added.)

This certainly applied to Stanley Setty, who was at the top of his lack of profession, though he conceded to the public image of spivvery only a taste for rash ties. And it was equally true of Donald Hume, though by 1949 in a somewhat ironic sense: for at that time he had no means of support at all, visible or otherwise.

If Setty wore the super-suave outfit of the aristocratic spiv, Hume belonged to the middle ranks. In check sports-coat and flannels he preferred the raffish manners that averted suspicion, not by flamboyance in public places, but by cheating people gently off their feet. Rebecca West later described him as having "the air of self-conscious impudence that is the spiv's hallmark," and this had served him well.

Early in the war the R.A.F. threw him out for medical reasons. So, as if to create the dream-world he missed, in an officer's uniform that cost him a fiver, he peddled his bogus charm round airfields for two months, leaving behind, in his own phrase, "a paper-chain of forged dud cheques," before they pinched him. Again, his was the brain behind a product called Finlinson's Old English Gin, composed of surgical spirit parsimoniously laced with the genuine article, that fetched him three pounds a bottle in the blacked-out dives of the West End. The foundations for peace were laid in a war that had disappointed and rejected him.

Even so, when the fighting packed up, Hume, like countless others, some of whom would later slide back almost despairingly into crime, responded to the hour of supposed challenge by going straight. He worked hard. He patented an electric toaster (the Little Atom, grimly topical) and converted surplus landing-lights into bowl-fires. His towel-rails were snapped up by a country dying for the silliest luxury-goods. He squeezed a huge legitimate profit out of the business boom. Yet he found, as the novelty of honest work wore thin, that he wanted something more than plenty of hard-earned tosheroons to lash out in night-clubs. He became as restless as the country itself and as impotent, hungry for easier solutions to what had become not peacetime but a state of armistice, a bewildering anticlimax. He pined for the kicks that would knock to hell the dreary official demands which, daily shocking the papers into tantrums, cast such despondency over those first halting years of peace.

In the beginning, as if limbering up, he toyed with quite unnecessary crime. He had a hand in snatching a vanload of eggs outside a transport café in Barnet; he took his cut from a chocolate haul in Kentish Town. He began to allow his own situation to deteriorate in the general sad slackening of tension and tightening of belts. Taxes crippled his business as his private spending hysterically grew. He had a few strokes of bad luck. And then he met Setty.

His luck turned at once. In the disorganised forties, when linen sheets or whisky surpassed the Crown Jewels in rarity value, crime couldn't help paying. At the rear of Setty's garage forged petrol coupons changed hands at half a crown a time, and Hume was soon netting forty pounds a week from picking out likely customers on his beat of drinking-clubs. But this was child's play compared with their next collaboration. From derelict cars, which he had bought for a song and destroyed, Setty possessed a number of log-books, and Hume's task was to steal vehicles that roughly corresponded with them. Hume received £300 for each car, which was then hastily resprayed to match the log-book and flogged in whispers on the corner of Warren Street.

One racket led fast to another, and Hume was soon involved in activities which even more surely titillated his sense of adventure; and again, as with all true spivvery, other people got the benefits, the common man was served at the expense of governments. Aerial smuggling, of goods or human beings or currency, had already seduced many ex-pilots irked by the squalors of peacetime, and Hume was soon busy ferrying Dakotas to Palestine, illegal immigrants to Europe, money for sweepstake tickets to Eire. "I suppose I could be called a racketeer," he said later, "though I don't like the word myself. The plain fact is that wartime shortages encouraged the so-called rackets . . ." and somehow, the war over, almost justified them. Perhaps he would have preferred the word spiv.

But then, on October 4th, 1949, Setty had occasion to visit Hume's flat in the Finchley Road. Whatever happened in that room remains a mystery. Hume later claimed that he killed Setty with a German s.s. knife, so surrendering whatever sympathy the public might have felt for him in his eager search for compensations; and that later he cut Setty into suitable pieces (placing his head in a baked-beans carton) and dropped him from a plane over the North Sea.

That was late in the day, when spivs were commonplace. Much earlier, in the summer of 1946, another murderer, whose crime was exclusively the product of his own contorted nature, had emerged from the half-light where spivs had started their long, nagging campaign against the lean times. Neville George Clevely Heath was a slippery customer, plainly one of their number; the fact that he was recognised as a known type, and peculiarly topical, accounts in some measure for the stir caused by the case. The public response to Heath was uneasy and exceptional. His trial cast a long shadow.

It matters little to the history of those years that Neville Heath frenziedly lashed and ripped and crushed two women to death. It matters more that at various times, having deserted or jumped a ship or been cashiered, he assumed the names (and possibly in his own mind the superior identities) of Captain Selway, Group Captain Rupert Brooke, Captain Armstrong, and Lord Dudley. He had manipulated a pair of paybooks, flaunted false decorations, forged a banker's order, stolen jewellery, dishonoured cheques, and worn a colonel's uniform. All these frauds and posturings, never very serious and hardly worth honouring with the name of crime, formed a standard background for the kind of spiv who worked at Hume's level.

For Heath had all the equipment to build around himself the bright, meretricious structure of life, only half real, as gaudy as a nude on a necktie, that suited the mood and conditions of those post-war years. Perhaps his personality attracted so much grim attention, not just from a perverse delight in his perversions, but because he was accepted and studied as a quite normal manifestation of that time, all too plausible, which made his vicious sallies into madness at Notting Hill and Bournemouth all the more snakishly repellent. According to the verdict, Heath was sane.

Sooner or later, but for the hangman, his temperament would have drawn him into a web of rackets. All his attitudes obeyed the first rule of spivvery: pretending to be something other than he was. He was a dab-hand at small talk, and, by flashing around the slang, he could turn any bar into an officers' mess, imitation, rather garish, but excitable, and could flatter any company, however staid, into accepting his charm. Even if you saw through the airs of fake grandeur which he could assume (and cast off) at a moment's notice, he managed it so convivially that nobody minded. He lacked the staying power that got you nowhere in those years, and his vanity quickened his brain into a kind of sharp, wary intelligence. He was particularly well fitted for a life of spivvery.

But his hand slipped, and his mind. He forgot, as a good spiv never did, which side his bread was – at thirty shillings a pound on the black market – buttered.

They say that outcrops of spivvery have bothered Europe at all times, and this was nothing new. History tosses up wide boys as a face erupts boils, to force out the poison in the body politic. The *yass* terrorised Budapest. *Voyous* and *oisifs* played hell with Paris. Even Hitler had his difficulties with the *stenz*. But these rattier boys never belonged in spirit to any part of the societies they roughed up and exploited. And the spiv did; he was the caricature of us all. He tricked authority with a grin. He talked fast and laughed himself out of tight corners. He got away with it.

When the war finished Britain expected, not perhaps the lap of luxury, but at least bananas, a few more cigarettes, a range of cloths to choose suits from, a car maybe or a trip abroad, the odd bottle of whisky to celebrate the expanding horizons that had already started closing in. No arguments from the front bench ever quite persuaded people that they could not be given these things; somewhere, sadists were at work, or puritans. Almost unwillingly and half-guiltily, the public looked to the spiv to correct the balance. Even if no whisky materialised, the snook had to be cocked. Thus, when the look-out bawled at the glimpse of a policeman and the barrow-boys scarpered out of the forbidden streets, sympathies were apt to turn against the law. And no wonder they stayed against it, when the papers reported, for example, that a costermonger with a licence for vegetables had been hauled up for selling rhubarb, which might legally be interpreted as fruit; or that a restaurant was in trouble for serving asparagus, not lawfully on the same plate as the meat-balls, but as a separate course. Everyone waited for something to be done about such follies. Nothing was, officially.

The spivs descended on the wreckage of central London during 1946, as if by magic, to fill the gap left by the exodus of the toffs. The West

End has never been abandoned for long without an élite, a carefree cynosural focus for the tired eyes of sightseers, a brand image for the idea of a great, gay capital. Before the war, the upper crust, still residential, attended functions in full drag; now, patriotic to the last clothing-coupon, they dressed dowdily and the spivs had assumed their plumage as well as their habitat. Even during the black-out, bizarre touches of colour kept the centre of town alive, when soldiers of all nations packed the clubs and were billeted in the grander homes. But now, all foreigners dispersed, it was the spiv who stood for London, set the tone of her recovery from war, and was regarded with that blend of affection and mistrust which the English reserve for anyone who seems to symbolise the way things are going.

However, the barrow-boys – as flashy as neon, as exaggerated as the cut of their suits – were only the façade that stuck out with such vitality against the scarred hungry background of a city down on its uppers. They over-compensated for the drabness, becoming almost feminine in the process, tricked out in the patterns and shades of cheap bulls-eyes, all their tough swagger just a device to conceal a soggy cowardice beneath. For such pansy braggadoccio surely meant that these characters only flirted with crime, never embraced it; and this was largely true. The front-line spivs merely tagged on, like sycophants, to the tail-end of rackets.

Take a boy like Joe, who had left school at fourteen for a milk-round during the blitz. He longed for a taste of war and was dead keen on joining the Army. But, with a discipline that struck him as petty in such a crisis, liberating rather than breaking his spirit, they soon cheesed him off to the point where he deserted: only mugs worked, he said. By the time the war had whimpered out, he was spending Sundays down Petticoat Lane, where he could sell enough dresses in one day to spend his entire week in idleness; but his boss was pinched for dabbling in the black market. So he skidded out into the gadget trade, bits of radios for home mechanics, and, when the money didn't roll, Joe, like plenty of others whom the war had prevented from taking the natural step from school into trade, started keeping his eyes open for a place in the fancy chorus of dealers and wide-boys. This, so overt that it almost seemed like a performance put on for the public benefit, started at the dockside, pirouetted through a routine of Soho pubs and murky basements in Paddington, and eventually danced into the lap of an ordinary customer too long thwarted by the spastic efforts of the country to get back on her feet.

Between the end of the war and 1948, when the fruit market turned rotten on him, the street spiv could pick up a tax-free ten or twelve pounds a week from plying his trade hard; he bargained niftily at Covent Garden, he barked at risky corners from dawn to sunset, with a few pairs of nylons ("They fell off a lorry," was the stock defence) under some sacking on his stall. But this was never enough. It satisfied neither the yen for easy money nor the urge to be admired and envied in his own circle. (This partly accounted for the big splash of his appearance: lemon-yellow shoes, the full drapes down from shoulders as wide as a yoke, the spectacular tie that resembled a giant tongue poked vulgarly out at life.) A gangsterish dream hung vaguely in his mind, though he wanted no truck with the reality which might involve prison. He required only freedom, to spread his wings, and size, bigger wings than anyone else. Into the cinemas he poured money, scattered it round dance-halls like a squire at a garden party, sent it chasing in fistfuls after the greyhounds, and covered his body with a smooth, camel-hair boast of it. He was top people, and he knew it.

Wherever the spiv met up with his mates – down Old Compton Street, outside the Forum in Kentish Town, anywhere – there was always a caff round the corner, less sinister than it seemed, where deals were struck. Rings flashed on middle fingers, hats were crushed rakishly down on ducks-arse haircuts, and the mood, as if sustained from the war, was one of tough casual humour in the face of grave hardships: such as how to dispose at high speed of a hot lorryload of socks, twelve and a tanner in the stores, four bob to you. Luckily for the spiv, a surprisingly large number of people were soon wearing the socks (or drinking the Scotch or luxuriating in the sheets), and keeping mum about it.

This, then, was the spiv the public saw and sneakingly liked. He was divided by the narrowest of lines – a distinction unacceptable to the police – from that darker world where the same attitudes prevailed but the stakes were higher. For even in the more serious, planned crimes, crimes which in normal days strike us as stark and crafty and untoothsome, there was sometimes a nice element of abandon that bore the stamp of spivvery, almost as if no one cared but it was fun trying.

In December 1947 a gang of thieves filched a huge quantity of spirits from a bonded warehouse in Portsmouth. Despite the grandeur of the operation, involving a couple of lorries and several men and the speed necessary to accomplish it, they took the trouble – a glint of humour, perhaps of art – to supply their own padlocks in place of those they had destroyed. There were no clues. The owners then installed a steel grid within the warehouse, which was torn open in a flash when the same thieves struck again a month later. Again they left no clues.

Osbert Lancaster, *Daily Express*, 24.6.47

"Don't be so stuffy, Henry! I'm sure that if you asked him nicely the young man would be only too pleased to give you the name of a really GOOD *tailor who doesn't worry about coupons!"*

So it seemed at least. In fact they had dropped in their wake a paper chase of errors which would have shocked a keen professional. To begin with, their greed had drawn them back to the scene of their first crime. Next, descending on Portsmouth a shade early, they had paused for refreshments at a wayside café, and, although the boss (with a dramatic streak common to spivs) kept darkly to his car, the boy who brought out his tea treated the regulars in the café to a line of flashy bantering show-off that thoroughly aroused their suspicions; they took the number of the car. The gang had also brought with them a mechanic ignorant of the crime, an idiotic risk; they kept having to invent unlikely pretexts that would get rid of him at crucial moments. And finally the lorry owner, ill-content with keeping his mechanic in the dark and perhaps sweetening him with a bonus, unwisely sacked the man as too dangerous to have around.

Thus, when the police launched their inquiries, the mechanic was only too glad to help, and they soon tracked down the stolen goods to a pub in Coulsdon. The landlord was hit badly all round. Not only was he sent down for a year, but it emerged that the thieves, after selling him the first batch of spirits, instantly stole them back and then blackmailed him into receiving the second haul. This was an enchanting touch that only the middle forties, with crime geared very closely to the national frame of mind, could have provided.

That was just it; crime was so close to the people. Like the spivs. Unlike, with all their vaunted ideals, the Government. Nobody after the war wanted ideals. They wanted change and movement and life.

The mass of people saw glimpses of life – the nice rich capers others seemed to be cutting – but at first only under counters, behind scenes. So long as crime stayed underground, the shady business of a tight pro-fessional class, people could stomach the uncontrolled riot of controls. But very soon, even as early as 1945, the various small fiddles began to appear quite respectably before the public, with decent and even noble names attached to them. And the rot set in. Sacrifice was no longer necessary or fashionable, said the *Spectator* in December 1945, and lawlessness was in the air.

First of all it was currency. The papers reported a man stationed in Germany who bought a camera for fifty cigarettes (then valued at 6s. 8d. apiece on the German black market). He sold the camera in London for £75, converted it unofficially into Belgian francs (thus making it £100) and bought enough watches in Brussels to sell immediately in London for £175. At the same time it was recorded that in a single year our army of occupation on the Continent had cheated the Treasury of sixty million pounds by dealing illicitly in currency and goods. All this qualified as crime, fair enough.

But then, rather shockedly, a knight's name figured in court. A northern industrialist was questioned about cheques for £3,500 he had made out. Two notable daughters, both the offspring of Dukes, were heavily fined in successive years for buying francs from unauthorised dealers in France. Although the magistrate said that Lady Elizabeth Clyde was quite genuinely satisfied in her own mind that she was able to do a perfectly legal evasion of the Defence (Finance) Regulations, this side-stepping leniency cut very little ice with the middle-class thousands who had ached for hot sunlight and appetisers for the better part of a decade. Quite suddenly breaking the law had become anybody's game.

Who was behind all this? A flood of such prosecutions had followed the exposure, in April 1947, of a figure who shot out from behind the scenes like the grisly attractive ogre of pantomime, and then, being the high-tension spiv he was, vanished almost at once in a cosmopolitan puff of smoke. His name was Max Intrator, and he became a public figure overnight. Faced with the gaunt pronouncements of Cripps and with Attlee's pale gentility, the country craved for characters like Black Max, a bald, shifty personage lapped in self-indulgence, villainous to perfection, all ravaged Europe at his command. He was pictured with his arm round a veiled woman at a café table in Paris, and on horseback in Cairo wearing robes and a tarbush. Champagne was incessantly linked with his name. His shadowy minions came straight from the pages of a spine-chiller: Frederic Nemnich, the man from Panama, an unnamed Hungarian, a Pole called Krol Bitter who represented a family firm in Tel-Aviv. To a country starved of romance, Max Intrator was the suave guerrilla who smoked and smuggled away behind the backs of tottering governments, who "did business only with prominent visitors to Paris," at whose command ships loaded with illegal Jewish immigrants left remote Mediterranean ports for Palestine, whose rooms at the Lincoln Hotel off the Champs-Elysées yielded twenty-four thousand pounds in notes and ten thousand in Egyptian bonds, who was living big and rich and legendary. Too bad he was arrested.

The myth was perhaps invented, but only because it was needed. Names on Intrator's files included foreign royalty and diplomats, the public was told. Sixty people a day trooped to his bedroom (it was this procession that caught the eye of the police) to cash their cheques advantageously. His assets in London were instantly frozen by a panicking

Government. Agents in New York and Geneva were watched; names standing high in French finance were no longer above suspicion. The Quai d'Orsay suspected legations of abusing the diplomatic bag for currency purposes and having a spree on the black bourse. Meanwhile, from prison, protected by the high integrity of Maître André Klotz, Max Intrator granted the briefest of interviews. His words seemed as dignified as his smile, and were probably just as false: "I am a financier," he said, "not a swindler, and all my transactions are paper ones. I never peddled pound notes like a vulgar black market man . . ."

The master-spiv disappeared from sight, into prison, ill-health, thin air. Soon, it was felt, he would be plotting again, in a dozen sly and luxurious alcoves of Europe. Meanwhile he had made his point. It was the idiocy, not the dire necessity, of the law that stuck in people's minds. Their imaginations were stirred, not by the prospect of an ordered society, but by those who undermined it: spivs.

"I've taken things from work – that's not really stealing though, is it?"

In 1949 Mass-Observation published a report on delinquency which inquired into the personal honesty of people whose lives seemed as proud and irreproachable as a semi-detached villa.

"I only tip them because I feel like doing so. I don't expect anything in return, although I wouldn't say no if it was offered. Lots of people do give tips to shopkeepers to get extra rations – you won't get them to admit it, though."

Questions were asked of men and women who for four years had suffered an existence stricter than wartime, and apparently – for they had never been spurred by eloquent leadership to understand it – quite senseless.

"I've taken toilet paper from women's lavatories I've been to. There was a shortage of it a little while ago. When I was working in a pub part-time, I used occasionally to take packets of cigarettes – I gave them to my husband. Everyone else used to take them so I thought I might as well."

A thousand novels had vanished from the shelves when a London public library checked the stock. Loot from the railways in 1948 amounted to almost three million pounds, much of it in pilfered cups and towels. Currency offences, which "brought many hitherto worthy people into a merited notoriety" (*The Times*, needless to say), jumped from 322 in 1946 to 4,583 in 1948. There were frequent cases of lorry-drivers who had, by request, left their laden vehicles unattended for a few moments and returned to find a fiver on a seat and a gaping interior. Property to the value of thirteen million pounds disappeared during 1947; in 1938 the figure was two and a half million pounds.

Had the nation lost all respect for law and order? If so, it was not surprising, for every day the prissy futility of that law made an ass of itself in the courts and newspapers. The Ministry of Food prosecuted a green-grocer for selling a few extra pounds of potatoes, while admitting that they were frostbitten and would be thrown away if not cooked at once. The Ministry clamped down on a farmer's wife who served the Ministry snooper with Devonshire cream for his tea. A shopkeeper was fined £5 for selling home-made sweets that contained his own ration of sugar. Ludicrous penalties were imposed on farmers who had not kept strictly to the letter of licences to slaughter pigs; in one case, the permitted building was used, the authorised butcher employed, but the job had to be done the day before it was permitted; in another case the butcher and the timing coincided, but the pig met its end in the wrong building. Never had a bureaucracy so absurdly flaunted its total failure to comprehend the spirit of the times, which was low and resentful, or to indulge, even in small measures, the desperate moods and requirements of the people.

So, really, almost everyone participated; it was a sort of pale hangdog spivvery in back kitchens and at the rear of shops. Farmers retired to their candle-lit barns with shotguns and murdered the animal which they could later swop at local stores for tea and sugar. Delicious hens, requiring only a wrung neck and a good plucking, appeared openly in the markets as "stock cockerels" or "laying birds". Managers of shops sold off to their pals the left-over rations of butter, bacon and cheese belonging to customers too poor to claim them; they would even square the local food authorities by causing hampers to be delivered to their homes on dark nights. Men in saloon bars would always listen to the voice that whispered temptation in their ears: petrol coupons, a few nice sheets, a box of chocolates for the wife. Wholesale clothiers, living substantially in the outer suburbs, often turned out quite by chance to have warehouses only a stone's throw from a genial banana distributor who liked to be well-dressed. There was always someone, in everyone's acquaintance, with tabs on something. By no means all succumbed. But many did. In 1947 the Magistrates' Association took a count: thirty thousand prosecutions, for just this kind of breach, passed through the courts every year. Most people, like good spivs, were never found out. They merely felt, in some obscure way, that they had struck a blow: like spivs, by flirting with crime.

Sometimes an otherwise commendable citizen would go too far.

"Between the person who lightheartedly takes advantage of an easily evaded regulation," wrote *The Times* in January 1948, "and the person who is a determined black-market operator, there is a whole range of dishonest and anti-social practice . . ." Into that range fell headlong two men in South London, one a parcels clerk at Clapham Junction, the other an outfitter in Clapham High Street. A parcel of clothes left the shop addressed to a customer, entered the station, and there received another label which delivered it back to the shop. The outfitter then irritably claimed against the railway for the loss of his goods in transit, the money was shared, and the goods crept into a state of prosperous non-existence until required for barter.

No wonder, then, that the Recorder of London referred to "this distemper of dishonesty which has swept over the country in the last few years until people have lost sight of the difference between right and wrong." No wonder Lord Goddard cried: "It appals me!" No wonder that a boy of thirteen, infected by that distemper and caught in skilful burglary at Birmingham, said to his partner of eight: "Now you keep your bloody mouth shut. I'll do the talking." It was possible to feel, as never before, that the entire country had dipped a finger in the criminal pie, that all were spivs. And no wonder.

The explanations? Most people, for convenience, called it a crime wave. The Home Secretary had announced that stealing was easier than ever before, and shortages had made simple things expensive enough to be worth stealing. There was a shrug in these words, a bowing to the inevitable. In France they accepted the situation with total cynicism; the *gendarmerie* could be seen leaning against the very stalls that offered butter and steaks at fancy prices. And here the mood was cautiously similar; except that you rarely saw a policeman, because no campaign for seductive recruiting had so far been launched. For the first time in history the law was openly mocked on its own ground; on one occasion three spivs in court blandly claimed that they netted a clear profit of £1,250 in five weeks from the sale of roasted chestnuts and toffee-apples. Such men did not care whether they were believed or not. The old shame in the face of justice had been eaten away, partly by the demoralised climate of opinion, partly by the crude fact that worse crimes, far worse, had raced into the forefront of the courts.

Violence was afoot. And with it, sex. Neville Heath was not alone at that time, and nor was Donald Hume. The real criminals, pushed back by the amateurs, had thrown off their pre-war reluctance to use guns and coshes.

In 1945 the *Spectator* drew attention to the case of a butcher who had to sleep in his shop with a loaded revolver for two weeks before Christmas because he had managed to get a few turkeys in stock. In 1948 *The Times* deplored the failure to search positively for the 20,000 deserters, without the right to a ration book, as yet unpardoned, who formed a pool of law-breakers. They had been taught the techniques of violence in wartime and were bitter enough to exercise them now; indeed, London in 1946 attributed nine per cent of all crimes to them. By 1950 a legal paper had stated that the ordinary citizen no longer felt safe in his own home, and the Lord Chief Justice had earlier cited cases of old people trembling, often with good reason, when they heard a knock on the door at night. The statistics showed that every large school in the country could hope to have on the register a couple of active criminals who had no fear of the police. A small boy sneered on arrest: "You can't touch me, mate. I'm under eight." If care wasn't taken, such lads could mean a terrorised future. The highest ratio of offenders to the population occurred at the age of fourteen. Someone coined the mouthful "juvenile delinquency," and, as the forties creaked out, the horrid fear arose that the crime wave would not just recede as a matter of course, but might swill back and forth with mounting fury over the ruins of the nation. When in 1950 the Bishop of Croydon insisted, somewhat unfashionably, that the causes of post-war crime had been (and he tempted Providence by using the past tense) lone-liness, a sense of inferiority, frustration and lack of purpose, he was really, without knowing it, casting a prophetic eye over the facts of the fifties.

If only to explain the official concern, the figures are worth noting. Whereas in 1937 only 266,265 indictable offences were recorded, the figure had jumped to 415,010 in 1944, to 498,576 in 1947 and to 522,684 in 1948. The most popular single item (which dropped after 1951) was larceny; to break and enter in those years was as childishly easy as fiddling a money-box. In 1951, cases of violence against the person, which had soared steadily since the war, were two and a half times more than in 1938, and criminals, it seemed, were three times more vilely sexual. Figures seem to be no guide whatever to post-war crime, which eludes calculation as cunningly as a spiv. Trivial breaches of the controls blocked the courts, while large-scale operators like Stanley Setty went scot-free for years. When so many amateurs had turned to the fringes of crime, and justice was easy to evade, what counted was the atmosphere, the feeling in the country which no politician had the gifts or inclination to assess. It was a grim, aggressive feeling, which would have turned sentimental at the smallest sign of luxury, or relaxation.

In revolutionary times it is man's nature to loot, pillage, and rape, explosively, first as a revenge against the past, then lest the unknowable future should let him down or pin him to an irksome responsibility. Riot goes to his head. The post-war social revolution, though it proceeded more slowly than the bloody type and therefore reduced the violence of the outbreak, had much the same effect of creating a vacuum, of stopping time. No one – least of all the voters – fully anticipated it. People behaved against their natures, or perhaps allowed their natures full savage scope. Crime became something that, on a small scale, even men of probity could rationalise as their proper defence against the turbulent forces around them. All these offences, not just the serious ones, were monstrous. They undermined the economy at a difficult time. They delayed our recovery from war. Yet they could seem, to those who quietly committed them, to be somehow a justifiable way of righting the balance, of re-asserting the power (if not the dignity) of the individual.

The welfare state, apart from sounding the note of revolution, was responsible in another sense for the drop in morals. The Government unluckily projected its forthcoming policies, not as a vision of living for which the country would need to work hard, but, naïvely, as the first great chance to get something for nothing. At all levels, but especially at those where crime was likely to fester, there was a touching faith in an administration too overworked to pay subtle attention to the side-effects of its measures. Parents sat back, waiting for their children to be taken off their hands by the state. Youngsters, snatched by national service, broke away from home as early as they could. Religion, which requires society to jog along in an ordered, predictable way, began to lose its grip; and the flagging community spirit, which the war had whacked to a jelly, turned the country into a vast, unfriendly suburb where people preferred to live in ignorance of their fellows. All these drops of poison were distilled in wartime and frequently served a good purpose. Now, at leisure, they were destroying the fibres of England.

The Government, committed to an enlightened policy even for crime, badly mistimed their legislation. In 1948, the worst year yet for crime, they launched the Criminal Justice Bill. Hard labour and penal servitude, twin ogres of the assize courts, were abolished. Whipping was out. An elaborate system of probation was prepared like a rest cure for the young offender. For the accent, quite rightly, was on remedy, not punishment. The prisoner must be won back to decency. But the timing was unhappy for two reasons. First, on a purely practical level, much of the proposed reform had to wait for better times. Prison buildings were dilapidated, understaffed, overstuffed; in one case there was so little accommodation that four prison officers were forced to sleep in the condemned cell. And, secondly, even if displays of brute force were scarcely in order, the climate was wrong for a show of leniency. Like so many of Labour's reforms in those days, we had to wait for the solid benefits until the country – by good luck – was stable enough to bear them.

Do people ever want peace? Even as the fireworks flashed skywards and someone on ten pairs of shoulders swayed near Eros with a policeman's helmet, the sense of anticlimax was already worrying the triumph which people were supposed to feel. The trouble was that people expected the benefits of peace, whatever they were, to be immediate. Nobody quite wanted to settle down, to pick up the threads of their life hastily dropped five years back; nor, of course, did they want to be shot or bombed or invaded. There should have been an intermediate state – a promise, an exuberance – which sustained the excitement of war without carrying the risks. There wasn't – and this produced tensions which some people released in a volley of blanks over weekend territorial landscapes, some poured into the spate of war-books and barbaric films, and others got rid of, rather more satisfactorily, in crime. Crime indeed reproduced the conditions of war at minimal risk and with substantial promise of benefit. Crime in those years – though not subsequently, in a society of more measured routines – removed tensions and doubts and insecurities that everyone felt.

Just so. The spivs were tense, dubious, insecure. Yet the essence of spivvery was deeply English, a small boyish lust for life, an eagerness to play practical jokes on the clumsy, long-winded motions of a bureaucracy. While many people were putting up with the hardships in the name of a social revolution that would pay off handsomely later, the spivs – and their countless accomplices among ordinary people – by-passed the House of Commons and contrived a revolution of their own. A crime wave? Perhaps. But, though everyone expected to see the figures wobble down to normal after a few years, this did not happen. The spivs, in fact, were not merely the harbingers and outward sign of a crime wave, which the law would stamp out in due time, but a much more disturbing indication that times in England had finally changed.

They were, more than trade union leaders, more than the politicians, the voice of the working-class – busy undermining (oh, the irony) the future of their own people. The spivs, flashily displaying all the suppressed energies of the back streets, were an unconscious, dramatic protest, a form of civil disobedience that millions of English people found endearing and which, since the Government found no affable or challenging way of dealing with it, survived beyond that Government.

Indeed, they spread their attitudes so effectively that, many years after the last barrow was trundled away from the damp pavements of Oxford Street, the country was still living on the slightly bruised fruits of that revolution. Expense accounts conceal a complex of spivvery in high places. Behind many industrial disputes, lumped in with wage-claims, class feelings, and a perfectly fair desire to improve conditions, there still skulks an ingenuous belief—true now, but not true in any progressive state—that work has no virtue or purpose, that money should be easy-come easy-go, and that the individual must look after himself, if necessary at the expense of others.

This is the legacy of the spiv, which no Government has plumbed, or tried to correct, or even admitted.

5

WITHDRAWAL FROM GREECE

The end of balance-of-power diplomacy: the beginning of the
Cold War

DAVID WATT

David Watt was born in 1932, and educated at Marlborough and Hertford College, Oxford. From 1956–8 he
was Dramatic Critic of *The Spectator*, and from 1958–61
Diplomatic Correspondent of *The Scotsman*. From 1961–3
he was Common Market Correspondent and leader-writer
on the *Daily Herald*. He is now political correspondent of
The Spectator.

WITHDRAWAL FROM GREECE

David Watt

THE first two months of 1947 were the lowest point plumbed by the Attlee Government. Everything began to go wrong at once. Chuter Ede, the Home Secretary, had a thrombosis; Ernest Bevin's heart, long suspect, first gave serious trouble; Ellen Wilkinson, the Minister of Education, died on February 6th. The snow and frost of that terrible spring went on and on, depressing and undermining the confidence of the whole country, bringing in its wake the fuel crisis and prophecies from the Attorney-General, Sir Hartley Shawcross, of "the end of Socialism in our time."

It was not a good moment to be taking decisions of high policy in international affairs. The Cabinet bickered so endlessly about the relative priority to be given to armies and factories, welfare and a workable foreign policy that Hugh Dalton, the Chancellor of the Exchequer, nearly resigned. And out of this bickering came two of the most important decisions of the Labour Government — the withdrawal of economic aid from Greece and the final departure from India. They were first announced within twenty-four hours of each other when the unemployment caused by the fuel shortages was running at more than two million.

On a day in mid-February Bevin had arrived at a Cabinet Committee meeting in Great George Street, his vast frame heaving from the exertions of walking with a weak heart up two flights of stairs. The electricity was cut off and the lifts were not working. He found Dalton determined to bring to a head the long-standing question of Britain's expenditure in Greece. Bevin had been told by his officials that a withdrawal would mean disaster in the Balkans, and had fought a rearguard action since the previous autumn. Now, suddenly, he gave way to Dalton's demand that the Americans should be told that Britain was definitely determined to leave. Dalton was puzzled, and wondered whether Bevin quite realised what he was agreeing to; but at any rate the Chancellor got his way.

Accordingly, on February 21st, 1947, the British Ambassador in Washington telephoned to the State Department for an appointment with the new Secretary of State, General George Marshall. Marshall himself turned out to be at Princeton, where he was receiving an honorary degree and ushering in his term of office with a painstakingly philosophical public speech. However, his Under-Secretary, Mr. Dean Acheson, learning that the matter was important, arranged that the notes which he was told Lord Inverchapel wished to deliver should be brought round privately at once, so that they could be studied over the week-end by his officials before they were formally delivered by the Ambassador on the Monday. This diplomatic fiction had its results, for by the time Marshall returned from Princeton, Acheson had already mapped out with his staff the answer to the problem with which he was faced. Marshall was new to the job, and by Monday the State Department had the bit between its teeth.

The British notes had been drafted in terse terms by the Treasury. They stated that, after March 31st, Britain could no longer be responsible for further economic aid to Greece and Turkey. They pointed out that the Greek economy was on the verge of collapse, that the Turkish army was disastrously under-equipped, and that if either of these countries fell to Communist aggression, the strategic results for the West would be catastrophic. All that was needed was the expenditure of between £60 million and £70 million in 1947 in economic aid to Greece, complete re-equipment of the Turkish army, and economic subvention to both countries for an indefinite period. Joseph M. Jones, the State Department publicist, who has chronicled these events, remarks that the First Secretary of the British Embassy, a Mr. Sichel, handed over his messages with such insouciance that their recipient wondered whether he really knew what he was doing. Mr. Jones knows better – "his blandness of manner came from his training in the British diplomatic service."

It was three weeks before Britain knew precisely what the result of this démarche would be. Britain has sometimes been accused of engineering the exact terms of the President's reply, but the subsequent protestations of Hector McNeil, the British Foreign Under-Secretary, that Britain knew nothing of the text, are probably correct. Had Lord Halifax, the previous Ambassador in Washington, still been at his post things might have been different. Lord Inverchapel had only recently arrived in Washington, and was never in fact much in the confidence of either the British or American Governments. He was an amiable extrovert with all the theoretical qualities of the ideal Ambassador to the United States except that of intellectual capacity. One of his subordinates has described him to me as the ideal chief: "he always signed anything you put in front of him."

Exchanges between Britain and the United States during the vital three weeks were on a fairly formal if not actually chilly basis. Inverchapel was told on March 1st that America would try to maintain Greece and Turkey and would seek the necessary authority from Congress. Meanwhile, the Americans wanted to know how long Britain would be prepared to keep her troops in Greece in order to ride the country over the period before American aid could arrive. But these were, relatively speaking, technicalities, and President Truman, when he finally appeared in person before Congress on March 12th, had left technicalities behind.

The President's request was that Congress should authorise a grant of 400 million dollars to Greece and Turkey. His argument was not based on the fact that Greece might starve if aid were not forthcoming, but on the fact that "Greece must have assistance if it is to become a self-respecting democracy."

"At the present moment in world history," said Mr. Truman, "nearly every nation must choose between alternative ways of life. The choice is too often not a free one. One way of life is based on the will of the majority, and is distinguished by free institutions, representative Government, free elections, guarantees of individual liberty, freedom of speech and religion and freedom from political oppression. The second way of life is based upon the will of a minority forcibly imposed upon the majority. It relies upon terror and oppression, a controlled press and radio, fixed elections, and suppression of personal freedoms.

"I believe that it must be the policy of the United States to support free peoples who are resisting attempted subjugation by armed minorities or by outside pressures.

"I believe that we must assist free peoples to work out their destiny in their own way.

"I believe that our help should be primarily through economic and financial aid, which is essential to economic stability and orderly political processes."

It was immediately clear to the world, when these words were pronounced, that something exceedingly important had been said. In the first place, any expansion of Soviet Communism was to be resisted by American dollars wherever it appeared in the world. Secondly, America was publicly committed to moving with military and economic aid into an area which had for centuries been regarded as a British preserve — the Eastern Mediterranean. It required very little exercise in journalistic imagination to maintain, as practically every newspaper did next day, that by this speech Truman had taken over the endless burdens and tribulations of world leadership.

It was, as James Reston of the *New York Times* reported, a "grim and resentful Congress" which contemplated this prospect. "The tendency today," he informed his readers, "is to blame the British and the Administration – the British for going broke and passing the baton to us, and the Administration for asking Congress so suddenly to assume such tremendous responsibilities by March 1st."

Truman was well aware of it. The Republicans, who were in a majority in Congress, had been in no mood for giving the President anything he wanted, and for several weeks had been busy trying to lop six billion dollars off his budget. Senator Arthur Vandenburg is reported to have told Truman that if he wanted his money for Greece he would have to "scare the hell out of the country." Truman had taken his advice.

Congressional leaders had been summoned on February 27th to the White House. There they had been read a short but ineffective lecture from Marshall on the British withdrawal, and, when that produced no reaction, a long and hair-raising one from Acheson. There was, he said, an "unbridgeable chasm" between Russia and the United States which set them apart from each other as no great powers had ever been since Rome and Carthage. If, said Acheson, the Communists were allowed to capture Greece, which would inevitably occur unless American aid was forthcoming, their possibilities of penetrating Southern Asia and Africa were limitless. These arguments, which were repeated in various form in the Congressional hearing which followed the President's speech, had their effect, especially in combating what was to the right-wing Republican the chief drawback to the Bill (apart from its cost) – the fact that America would be pulling British chestnuts out of the fire.

The following exchange which took place in the House of Representatives' hearing on March 20th is typical of the anxious patriotism with which Congressmen considered the matter.

Q.: Is the State Department making it clear to Americans and the world that the U.S. does not propose to step into the shoes of Great Britain but has shoes of its own?

Acheson: My present ordeal is part of that process.

The American public at large was no easier to convince. For the Truman Doctrine, as the President's speech rapidly came to be called, received a thoroughly bad press. It was widely thought, and not only by the liberals, that the speech amounted to a declaration of war by America on Russia and that it would inevitably lead to shooting sooner or later. Genuine belief in the Russian wartime alliance joined forces with the remnants of isolationism and instinctive distrust of Britain. A

Southern Democrat Senator spoke with the people's voice when he declared: "I am for giving aid to the people of Greece, but as to money for maintaining British soldiers in Greece, I would say nix. It is poppy-cock this fear that Russia would move in. There are a lot of nations crying wolf against the Russians to get us in."

Criticism made by more liberal citizens was the absence of any mention of the United Nations in the Truman speech. This omission created a considerable stir, and even the Republican Senator Arthur Vandenburg endorsed the criticism by moving an Amendment to the Truman Bill which gave the U.N. the power to end the programme if asked to do so by a procedural vote in the Security Council or a majority in the General Assembly.

The Administration's defence of the omission was that the U.N. was powerless to administer this kind of scheme, since it would almost certainly be vetoed by the Russians. But there was clearly substance in the suspicions of Truman's critics that there were other reasons why the U.N. had been left out. At least sixty per cent of the aid was to be used for military purposes, and Truman refused to contemplate American cash being administered by someone else. The American pressure which had resulted in the winding up of U.N.R.R.A. (United Nations Relief and Rehabilitation Administration) the previous December had been based on just such reasoning.

In Britain reactions were even more equivocal. The Opposition took its lead from Mr. Churchill, who was understandably jubilant that his efforts to produce a firm Anglo-American alliance appeared to be bearing fruit. But the Government's supporters had their doubts. The *Daily Herald*, which only deserted its father-figure, Ernest Bevin, under great stress, was in the van.

"The question," it said, "is to what extent the American people as a whole will accept the thesis that the well-being of the world rests mainly on the might of the United States as a counter-force to the might of Russia. If that belief takes hold – and is matched, as it will be, by increasing anti-American reaction in Russia – the prospect of an armed clash between the two greatest powers on earth becomes frighteningly clear." For almost the first time, the cry of the Fifties was heard in its next sentence: "Although Great Britain's financial resources have shrunk, her right to exert moral leadership has in no way declined . . . She must become ever more active in her endeavour to bring about a real comradeship and understanding between her two great allies."

Left wing critics of the Government were in some difficulty, since they had been urging for months that Britain should reduce expenditure on overseas commitments, and especially that it should cease to shore up the corrupt reactionaries in Greece. Nevertheless, the Co-operative Party which met in April condemned the Truman Doctrine as a menace to world peace, and Tom Driberg asked Hector McNeil, Bevin's Under-Secretary, in the House of Commons whether "he could really view with equanimity the invasion of South-East Europe by dollar imperialism?" Harold Laski wrote that President Truman's action was a "threat to peace greater than any since the rise of Hitler."

But the issue only began to provoke general fervour with the appearance in Britain in April 1947 of Henry Wallace, the former American Vice-President, at the invitation of the *New Statesman and Nation*. Bearing the dying lamp of New Deal liberalism across the Atlantic, he was a romantic figure and his pronouncements over here produced a storm of abuse and counter-abuse. Kingsley Martin gave him a cocktail party at the Savoy, at which he replied genially to the hopes expressed by the editor of the *New Statesman* that the American and Russian eagles might be persuaded to mate. He addressed a big and enthusiastic audience in the Central Hall, Westminster, and exhorted Britain to stand firm between American free enterprise and Soviet Communism, and informed his hearers that the Truman policy was "sown with the seeds of war." The B.B.C. was denounced by the *Sunday Times* for allowing him a quarter of an hour on the air. The *New Statesman* was perhaps a little flattered to hear that back in America he was threatened with impeachment under the antique Logan Act, for "treating with a foreign power."

Amid this uproar the Government maintained a virtuous silence. The Foreign Office had given the Americans its initial blessing and its "great appreciation for the President's wise recognition of the wider issues involved." Thereafter it took refuge in the usual News Department formula that it would be improper to comment while the U.S. Congress was discussing the matter. A British diplomat in the Middle East was indiscreet enough to remark to Stewart Alsop, the American columnist, that he thought the Americans had done the right thing "but my God, what a way to do it." There spoke the voice of officialdom. But Attlee and Bevin and Dalton as politicians had much more sympathy with Truman's difficulties with Congress, and held their peace.

On May 22nd the final processes of democracy were completed and Truman signed the Bill.

Everyone agrees that something changed on that day, but exactly how and why did it change? The incident has by now been hallowed by tradition on each side of the Atlantic. To Americans this seemed the moment at which the United States shook off the diffidence of her formative years and strode unashamedly into the rodeo as the leader of the West. Britain had let fall the reins from her aged fingers, and there was nothing for it but for America to accept her destiny and pick them up.

The British account of these events is naturally less picturesque, but Attlee and the apologists for Ernest Bevin have still managed to snatch victory from retreat in exemplary British fashion. The case is most elaborately set out in *Cards on the Table*, a pamphlet in which the Government tried to answer its Left wing critics in the summer of 1947.

It argued that our straitened circumstances forced on us the necessity of reducing our foreign commitments as fast as possible, consistent with our security, and trying to adjust our policy to our diminished resources. Yet this reduction must be carried out in an orderly way so that at no point would we lose our power of initiative and our ability to control the process. The United States had been unable and unwilling to shoulder the responsibility of her immense power, and her public opinion was opposed to foreign commitments.

In other words, the chief danger was Russia, but the next danger was American isolationism in the pattern of 1919. Britain had to hold the fort until America was ready to come in. Bevin chose his moment, assessing the current of American opinion, and presented America with his ultimatum at the precise moment at which she was bound to respond as he wanted. This was an act of shrewd and subtle statesmanship, or, as Attlee pithily put it later, "a big step."

It was admitted in *Cards on the Table* that the Americans had taken their decision entirely in the interests of American defence — but this was claimed as a positive advantage. "There is," said the pamphlet, "no case therefore where Britain had been required in return to assist in protecting anything which is primarily an American interest. Indeed, we refused point-blank even to retain our troops a day longer in Greece because of the proposed American loan to the Greek Government, but we can only be grateful if America is prepared in any way to make it easier for us to defend our security. So the gibe that America provides the money while we provide the men is simply answered — for that suits us better than providing both the men and the money!"

The fact that at American insistence British troops were still sitting in Greece (though in reduced numbers) in the middle of 1948 shows that this argument was not without its flaws of detail. But it is the main contention which needs analysis. In other words, was Bevin really in control of events? To answer this question, it is necessary to review the Greek affair from the beginning.

Britain's presence in Greece was the result of the somewhat dubious deal contracted in May 1944 between Stalin and Winston Churchill. Churchill, to do him credit, clearly believed that he was saving at least something from an inevitable wreckage when he tossed across the table to Stalin a piece of paper which guaranteed Britain a seventy-five per cent influence in Greece in return for a guaranteed seventy-five per cent Russian influence in Rumania, Hungary and Bulgaria. (Stalin presumably chuckled to himself over the fifty-fifty partition of influence in Yugoslavia.)

Throughout the ensuing bloodshed and complications in Greece, Britain's influence had been maintained with the acquiescence of her allies. Stalin gave Churchill *carte blanche* as British troops rounded up the Communist guerrillas (E.A.M. and E.L.A.S. fought under the same banner) after their abortive attempt to seize power in Athens on December 4th, 1944. Roosevelt and Truman were glad enough to be rid of an intractable problem which could, moreover, be used, as the necessities of Washington politics or international affairs arose, as a moral stick with which to beat the British.

When Labour came to power, the issue seemed perfectly simple to its own supporters – and to the American Government. (What the Russians thought we shall never know.) Was the Labour Government going to support the return of the corrupt right wing politicians who were alleged to surround the Greek king (still in exile in London) or was it prepared to support democracy and the gallant people of Greece who had fought in the resistance against the Fascists?

The Labour Party's war-time vision of the future was of a Europe in which widespread revolution would sweep away Fascism. The Resistance movements which were naturally in the van of this progress were history's heroes, transfigured by martyrdom. The fact that many of them were Communists was perfectly well known, but that seemed to many people a positive advantage at that stage. *Tribune*, then under Bevan's influence, had actually argued in December 1944 that Communist leadership in Greece was essential as a condition of successful revolution, and scouted the old liberal idea that free elections in the framework of law and order would be enough. "The first condition of democracy in Europe," it said, "is the revolutionary overthrow of anti-democratic ruling groups." Tom Driberg was not being particularly eccentric when he said in the

House of Commons during the Athens crisis of December 1944 that what was occurring was a "war between the bulk of the Greek population on the one side and a few quislings and royalists on the other, backed by British bayonets."

From the beginning the Labour leadership had been highly suspect with the extreme left in Britain on this issue, since most of its members had taken part in, and had voted in support of, Mr. Churchill's policy in December 1944. The exceptions were Philip Noel-Baker, Emanuel Shinwell, John Strachey, and James Griffiths, who had abstained, and Aneurin Bevan and Hector McNeil, who had opposed. But though it is probable that in Cabinet Bevan and Shinwell made their views felt throughout 1947, both carried the principles of Cabinet secrecy to a pitch which infuriated their friends and astonished their colleagues.

Nevertheless, in September 1945 the new Government went some way towards implementing the Party's wishes by revoking the Varkiza agreement, made in February between the Greek Government and E.A.M.–E.L.A.S., which had laid down that a plebiscite on the issue of the return of the Greek king would precede elections for a Greek Government. Under the new scheme, the plebiscite was postponed until "tranquillity has been restored" by a new revisionary assembly. On paper this appeared to give the people a better chance of throwing out the monarchy. But the ironies of the situation were at once made clear, for no sooner was this declaration made than the reasonably effective, though admittedly thoroughly illiberal government of Admiral Voulgaris fell amid almost inconceivable confusion and intrigue, and Hector McNeil was forced to descend upon Athens and install the less competent, even more corrupt, and not much less reactionary government of the octogenarian Mr. Sophoulis. The final result was that the Communists decided to boycott the elections when they were finally held in April 1946, and, in spite of an Anglo-American commission set up to observe the polls, it was thereafter impossible to persuade the Left wing of the Labour Party in Britain that the Government was not determined to support black reactionaries in office and force the brave partisans to take once more to the hills.

When Russia arraigned Bevin at the first meeting of the Security Council at the beginning of 1946 on the grounds that the presence of British troops in Greece constituted a threat to world peace, Bevin's understandably truculent replies were criticised on the left as being too aggressive. The *New Statesman* took a characteristic line in claiming first that Bevin was in the wrong, and secondly that even if he were not he should have modified his approach to meet Soviet suspicions, since it was certain that Russia desired only peace, and nothing could be gained by attacking her in public.

After the elections in April 1946 Greece receded a little as a political issue in Britain, though it was never far from the consciousness of the Government supporters. Britain continued to pour economic aid into the country at a rate which brought the total expended between 1944 and 1947 to £87 million, not counting £46 million of war debts which were forgiven, and a sizeable contribution via U.N.R.R.A. Some idea of the eager generosity with which this largesse was distributed may be gathered from the following exchange which took place when these figures were announced by Dalton in the House of Commons on March 6th, 1947.

> *Mr. Zilliacus:* Is it correct, as stated by the U.S. Secretary of State, that Greece is now on the verge of economic collapse?
> *Col. Gomme-Duncan:* So are we!
> *Mr. Dalton:* The only comment I will allow myself on this topic at the moment is that both the British soldier and the British taxpayer have done a good deal more than their fair share for both (Greece and Palestine).
> *Mr. Tiffany:* Will my Right Honourable friend ensure that gifts from New Zealand and Australia are not poured into this Greek sink of iniquity?
> *Mr. Dalton:* Those gifts will not be diverted in either of those two directions.

At the same time, the British military garrisons in Greece were rapidly reduced during 1946, and strict instructions were given to their commanders to make themselves as unobtrusive as possible. Greatly to the annoyance and alarm of the Greek Government, it was made plain that the British troops would not be available for fighting the Communist guerrillas, nor, strictly speaking, were British staff officers even allowed to give their advice in the crucial campaign against the Communists in 1947.

On the political side the forceful Sir Reginald Leeper, the British Ambassador in Athens, who had had no hesitation since 1944 in trying as best he could to manipulate the Greek political kaleidoscope, was replaced in March 1946 by Sir Clifford Norton, a career diplomat with no special pretensions to either force or finesse. Leeper had become the *bête noir* of the left, although he himself had socialist leanings. Norton, with more conventional political views, found greater favour by steering clear of Greek politics and by ostentatiously disclaiming knowledge of anything that had happened under his predecessor's reign.

The result of this policy of non-intervention in the internal affairs of Greece was to get the worst of both worlds. Britain had set the stage for a non-Communist government in Greece by force of arms and by propping up the tottering economic structure of the country with piecemeal aid. But since the British Government refused to give this régime effective support either militarily or economically, it was not surprising that it was attacked by the right for weakness, and by the left for imperialism. Hector McNeil was clear-sighted enough to remark once that "Greece is an Egypt waiting for its Cromer." The trouble was that Bevin's instincts on Greece were split. He told Dalton in 1946 that he was sorry the plebiscite he had arranged should have resulted in a victory for the Greek King George II rather than a republic, yet he clung tenaciously to the notion that, if Greece went Communist, Turkey would follow, and that Russia would simply move down on Britain's oil supplies in the Middle East. Bevin's position on this issue was pure Palmerston. "We cannot," he told the Labour Party Conference in 1947, "afford to lose our position in the Middle East; our navy, our shipping, a great deal of our motive power for our industry, in the shape of oil, are there ... The standard of life and the wages of the workmen of this country are dependent upon these things, as indeed they are upon other things. Why should Great Britain be the only country to hand over?"

The main advocate of withdrawing entirely from the Middle East and the Mediterranean was, strangely enough, Attlee. He was, it seems, in the habit of constantly circulating small pieces of paper to his colleagues arguing that we could never hope to keep open the Mediterranean route in time of war, nor could we hope to defend Turkey, Iraq, and Persia against "a steady pressure of the Russian land masses." Dalton even recorded that in 1945 Attlee was pressing for a withdrawal to a line from Lagos to Kenya so that we should put "a wide glacis of desert and Arabs between ourselves and the Russians." Bevin was evidently impressed by the notion to some extent, for Lord Strang, his Permanent Under-Secretary, noted that "the word Mombasa was constantly on his lips." These policies lost their attractions, however, as the Palestine situation deteriorated, and as hopes rose that the United States would come into the gap left by an eventual British withdrawal.

Until the end of 1946 this possibility was still very uncertain. Ever since the early war years, there had been strong suspicions in America that Britain was using the Atlantic alliance to bolster up and even extend her imperial position. Constant friction was caused by the fear of Roosevelt and his chiefs of staff that, whenever Churchill proposed operations in the Mediterranean, his concealed imperialist objectives were more important to him than winning the war. The "Spheres of Influence" agreement with Stalin confirmed the worst suspicions of Cordell Hull, and the British intervention in Athens in December 1944 was greeted with a storm of abuse from the American public and chilly disapproval from the Administration. If Stalin had not kept his part of the bargain, the British action might have been fatally undermined. But, as Churchill noted with satisfaction afterwards, "during all the long weeks of fighting the Communists in the streets of Athens, not one word of reproach came from *Pravda* or *Izvestia*."

That was not the end of American caution. In May 1945, Walter Lippmann, not a notably anti-British commentator, was mourning the fact that, since Roosevelt's death, America was being drawn as a partisan into the real quarrel which lay between Moscow and London. "Anglo-Soviet difficulties," he said, "extend in a wide arc through the Balkans to the Middle East and Persia. If ever there was a moment when a wise reserve was called for on our part, it is now." And again in January 1946, when Bevin and Vyshinsky were exchanging their pleasantries over Greece at the first meeting of the Security Council, Edward R. Stettinius, who was acting as the leader of the American delegation, remained studiously non-committal.

It was only after Russia referred to withdrawing her troops from Persia in March 1946 that Truman plucked up courage to counter Russia's propaganda against Turkey, and her demands for an internationalised Dardanelles, by the bizarre gesture of returning the body of the Turkish Ambassador, who had died in Washington, to his countrymen in the u.s.s. *Missouri*, the largest battleship afloat.

In August 1946 several developments combined to increase American involvement. Alarming reports were received of preparations for renewed Civil War in Greece, with provisions for the training of Communist guerrilla bands in Yugoslavia and Southern Bulgaria. Then Tito, on August 9th, made the enormous error of shooting down an American transport plane flying from Austria to Italy, and keeping the few survivors from communicating with the American Embassy. Finally, Moscow chose this moment to send formal proposals to Turkey, the United States, and Britain, under which Russia would not only have had a part in the control of the Black Sea Straits, but would have leased strategic naval and military bases there for "joint defence purposes." The American reaction was formidable. Her new aircraft carrier, the u.s.s. *Franklin D. Roosevelt*, and two destroyers were despatched to the Eastern Mediterranean, and on August 15th we hear of the first of these slightly farcical but effective meetings at the White House, at which President Truman was wont to lecture his senior advisers on the strategic importance of the Middle East from Genghis Khan to the present day.

Another factor in the situation, much alluded to by Communist commentators, but not necessarily invalid on that account, was the agreement reached in December 1946, with approval of the British and American Governments, between the Anglo-Iranian Oil Company and Standard Oil, and Socony Vacuum, for co-operation in the Middle East, including joint investigation of the possibility of building a pipeline from the Persian Gulf to the Mediterranean.

Bevin noted the trend towards American involvement with relief and some time in the autumn of 1946 decided to make what he could of it. Both the Greek and the American Governments were told that Britain could not continue to hold the line in Greece indefinitely. It would be interesting to know the exact extent and forcefulness of this warning, but there is some evidence that it was taken a good deal more seriously than was later made out. In the certainty that u.n.r.r.a. aid would run out at the end of March 1947, the Greek Prime Minister, Constantin Tsaldaris, approached the United States Secretary of State, James Byrnes, to discover what military and economic aid the Americans could supply instead. He had presumably been told already that he was unlikely to get much from the British. Further investigation by the Americans showed that the Greek Government had not the faintest intention nor possibility of repaying any loan that might be made, and that under American law no help could be offered by the Import Export Bank.

This discovery raised the problem to very serious proportions, for it meant that Congress would have to be approached, and Congress – and the Administration – were still recovering from the nervous prostration of passing the British loan. Truman temporised by sending an Economic Mission to Greece in January 1947 under Paul Porter, while Mark Ethridge, the American member of the U.N. Committee for observing the Balkans, and Lincoln McVeagh, the extremely experienced American Ambassador in Athens, watched with interest and alarm the rapid disintegration of the Greek political and economic scene.

Throughout February 1947 Porter, Ethridge, and McVeagh were sending a crescendo of warnings to Truman; first, the British were getting out, and, second, the Communists were preparing a take-over. Guerrilla activity in the North was increasing steadily, and there was soaring inflation. The two Populist governments of Messrs. Tsaldaris and Maximos, which had been born of the famous elections in April 1946, had proved as totally incompetent as any that had been imposed by the British, yet, as the Foreign Office had pointed out to Bevin in February 1947, if the Maximos government fell there was no other to replace it. The British Embassy were sufficiently alarmed to draw up a plan for the evacuation of all British women and children in Athens.

The Athenians, with their habitual political sensitivity, did not fail to notice which way the wind was blowing, and, as C. M. Woodhouse remarked: "Those who had devoted years to proving that they were practically natives of Claridges now turned their energies to proving that they were practically indistinguishable from Southern Democrat Senators."

The pattern of these events casts serious doubt on the genuineness of the Truman Administration's reactions to the British notes of February 21st, 1947. Truman and his advisers knew very well what was coming and were making their preparations for it. The elaborate expressions of stunned surprise in Washington, the febrile running hither and thither, had some foundation in the excitement of the State Department at being allowed to shake off the shackles it had worn up to a few weeks previously under the glum James Byrnes. But it was mostly a question of "scaring the hell" out of the country. Truman, as so often, had to play politics, and like everything else he did, he played it hard.

It is, of course, possible to maintain that nothing justified the outright declaration of Cold War which Truman's speech implied. Indeed, this was the main line on which his Left wing critics approached the question. Marshall Aid, which followed the Truman Doctrine in two months, was admitted to be an imaginative and beneficent initiative, but, it was claimed, after the Truman Doctrine it was impossible that the Communist bloc could accept it, for it appeared to be linked irrevocably with a capitalist system. It is difficult not to agree that the way in which Truman was forced to get Congress over the hurdle was very unfortunate. Even if opposition between America and Russia was now inevitable, his statement lacked the touch of conciliatory hypocrisy which is essential to public diplomacy because it leaves one's opponent a face-saving way out.

How much blame should attach to the British Government depends on whether one accepts the *Cards on the Table* view of Bevin's foreign policy.

Illingworth, *Punch*, 30.3.49

Jonathan's Leap

Bringing the Americans into Europe was bound to challenge Russia, and if, as is claimed for him, Bevin was actively responsible, then he must bear whatever moral consequences history heaps upon the act.

Bevin's Left wing critics in Britain, who, throughout his first two years of office, amounted, in varying shades of discontent, to about one hundred back-bench Labour M.P.S, had little doubt about the matter. Bevin, they maintained, had failed to sustain a Socialist foreign policy, and was continuing in the most craven fashion along the bellicose lines marked out by Churchill. When Bevin failed to repudiate Anthony Eden's claim in the first foreign affairs debate after the installation of the new Government, that he and Bevin had never differed on any major aspect of foreign policy, the Left drew this not unjustifiable conclusion: that the attack on the Tories in *Let Us Face The Future*, Labour's 1945 election manifesto, for not having made friends with Russia before the war, had not amounted to much in reality.

There was the usual element of pacifism on the one hand and fellow-travelling on the other in the attack which rapidly developed on the Labour back benches. But there was an irreducible core of opponents who could not be written off on either of these grounds, and, though the pacifists and fellow-travellers frequently joined forces with them, this band had a well-defined and reasonably consistent line of its own.

The first premise was that Russia was exhausted by the war, and was only concerned to build up her own strength within the borders of the Soviet Union. She had therefore no economic inducement to expand. This was an argument most frequently seen in the *New Statesman*, where it was maintained long after it had been abandoned by *Tribune*. It survived the initial shocks of Soviet behaviour in the Balkans and Persia, because, with suitable modifications, it could be used to show that Russia would not have needed to consolidate her position in this way had it not been for aggressive acts by the West.

The second strand in the argument was that Europe must be rebuilt on Social Democrat lines, and that anything which was tinged with the remaining infection of Fascism must be swept away at all costs. Much could be forgiven "progressive governments." Even Major Denis Healey had warned the Labour Party Conference in 1945 that "if the Labour movement in Europe finds it necessary to introduce a greater degree of police supervision and more immediate and drastic punishment for their opponents than we in this country are prepared to tolerate, we must be prepared to understand their point of view." Thus Bevin's complaints about the undemocratic activities of the Bulgarian and Rumanian

Governments were dubbed by the *New Statesman* as "political formalism", and his failure to impose an economic boycott on the Franco Government was a sell-out to Fascism. Greece, where Bevin actually seemed to have the power to impose a progressive solution, was the most disappointing case of all.

As it became clear that some Russian actions really could not be explained by fear alone, and that Bevin had no choice but to resist them in certain areas, the attack turned on the Americans and Bevin's close relations with them. It became particularly strident after Churchill's speech at Fulton, Missouri, on March 5th, 1946, which proposed a close Anglo-American alliance to resist aggression. The speech was correctly interpreted by the Left as being anti-Russian by implication, and, when the Government failed to repudiate it, they opened themselves to the charge of "ganging up" on the Soviet Union. Bevin, it was said, was trying to maintain the British Empire with American dollars, and had, as one would expect, been forced to toe the capitalist line.

These notions received a heavy emotional boost from the easily-observed fact that the Government's policy was perfectly acceptable on the other side of the House. Lester Hutchinson put the point frankly when he told the Commons in February 1946: "It is felt that when our policy meets with such hearty approval from the opposition there must be something wrong with it. It is felt that if the Tories applaud it cannot be a Socialist foreign policy."

All this was very puzzling and disappointing to the Left. They could not understand how Bevin, a trade union leader, who it was impossible to suppose had not got the interests of the working-class at heart, should repudiate these criticisms with devastating rudeness and disregard for the democratic methods of the Labour Party. The *New Statesman* started a popular hare, therefore, when it suggested, early in 1946, that Bevin was being run by Right wing officials in the Foreign Office. This feeling gradually gained momentum until, at the 1946 Labour Conference, a bizarre resolution was moved enjoining the Government to "ensure that the execution of the Socialist foreign policy is not entrusted to those whose whole background and tradition have rendered them incapable of understanding the first principles of such a policy" and to "make the fullest use of its powers of retirement on generous terms, without stigma, of public servants whose capacity for useful service is exhausted and their replacement by persons in accord with the progressive attitude of the British public as shown in their decision at the last General Election."

The alternatives to Bevin's policy, as set out on the left, lacked definition for some time. One solution would no doubt have been that proposed during the war by G. D. H. Cole in *Europe, Russia, and the Future*, in which he asked whether it might not be better to allow Germany as well as Eastern Europe to be included in an enlarged Russia. This would at least have removed Russian fears of encirclement, but it was rather strong meat. However, there gradually emerged an "official Left wing alternative" to Bevin's policy, much of it originating in the fertile brains of Richard Crossman and Michael Foot. It was first stated by Crossman in his rebel speech in the debate on the King's Speech in November 1946 – the so-called "stab in the back" perpetrated while Bevin was in Washington. The main argument was expanded in the pamphlet *Keep Left* which Foot, Crossman, and some others produced in the spring of 1947.

Britain's socialist policy at home, said the pamphlet, was threatened by the vast sums we were spending abroad. By reducing our commitments in the Middle East and Germany, we could save money and also end our present policy of supporting American expansion with British resources. At the same time, we should build up a strong progressive force in Europe, based on an Anglo-French alliance. The goal would be a federation which "binds together the nations now under Eastern domination with the peoples of Western Europe." This new bloc would renounce the manufacture of atom bombs, and thus live in friendship and "equal terms" with America and "Socialist rivalry" with the U.S.S.R.

With the best will in the world, it is difficult to see this policy as a realistic alternative to what was in fact going on.

In the first place the question of Russian intentions was far more complicated than the Left made out. Bevin was often accused of having a phobia about Communism, and although, as he often pointed out, he had had a hand in organising the Committee of Action which opposed the Allied intervention in Russia in 1918, his subsequent experiences with Communists in his beloved Transport Union had given him a tough antipathy to them. He also had a strong personal dislike of Molotov, whom he could never meet, he said, without thinking of the hundreds of thousands of peasants he had liquidated. He once told Dalton that Molotov was like a Communist in a local Labour Party – if you treated him badly he made the most of the grievance, and if you treated him well he only put the price up and abused you next day.

Yet until 1947 he seemed genuinely to believe that it might be possible to reach some kind of agreement with the Russians. At the 1945 Labour Party Conference, it was he who coined the slogan "Left understands

Left." This pious thought had rapidly to be abandoned. But in general Bevin's line with the Russians appears to have been conceived on three levels. At the day-to-day level he took the attitude of a trades unionist talking to a difficult manager. He gave and expected some hard blows. It was he who bore the brunt of the Soviet attack in the interminable peace conferences, and it was British positions that were the principal objects of Soviet propaganda. But, though he sometimes lost his temper – he once called Molotov "another Hitler" – the endless wrangles over Germany, Poland, Italy, and Austria were the kind of sparring matches that, because they involved a strict balance of great power interest, could hardly have ended otherwise than they did. Bevin's bluntness made little difference.

In the medium range of his policies, he was an optimist. He was constantly telling his subordinates that an agreement with Russia was possible, and it only needed a slight slackening of international tension to convince him that it was just round the corner. He did not want what he called "a line-up", and when he told the 1946 Party Conference "I am not going to be a party, as long as I hold this office, to any design, any strategy, any alignment of forces, any arrangement of defence, to attack Russia," he was certainly sincere. His efforts in 1946 to get the twenty years' Anglo-Soviet treaty extended to fifty years failed only because Stalin would never disclose his terms. What Bevin seems to have envisaged is the kind of "realistic" armed truce which sometimes exists between a trade union boss and an industrialist. Their interests clearly differ, but at least the industrialist knows where he stands, and that any nonsense will cause more trouble than it is worth.

In the long run, of course, Bevin clearly had his doubts. The obsession of the entire British Cabinet with the possibility that America might stand aloof from Europe, as she had done after the First World War, could only really be explained on the basis of a calculation that, unless America filled the gap, Russia would. Bevin may, in his optimistic moments, have thought that there was room in Europe for co-operation between both the great powers; but, if so, this hope was shattered when Russia and her satellites refused Marshall Aid. That was the turning point for Labour. In May 1947, he was trying to teach Molotov to sing "The More We are Together" on the platform of Moscow railway station, even though the Moscow Conference of Foreign Ministers had proved abortive. Three months later, all this was impossible. Looking back on it, even members of the "Keep Left" Group now admit that an amicable agreement with Russia was probably outside the bounds of possibility.

And yet, if it was not to be Russia, it had to be America. The "Keep Left" thesis was that Europe should cut itself off from America, and yet stand on equal terms with the two major powers. Bevin may be forgiven for regarding this as economic nonsense. The abrupt termination of Lend Lease in August 1945 had convinced the British Cabinet that nothing could be done without more American money, and Maynard Keynes produced a paper of the utmost brilliance and gloom to show that Britain was facing an "economic Dunkirk". The fact that by March 1947 Britain had already spent 1.1 billion dollars out of the 3.75 billion granted in the American loan of December 1945 proves that Dalton was justified in his constant complaints to his colleagues that, in spending so much in Germany and Greece, we were simply spending at interest the money which the Americans should have been spending themselves.

The circumstances in which the American loan went through proved that a high price would have to be paid for it. The complexities and frustrations of the loan negotiations nearly drove Dalton to despair, and can be said to have killed Keynes. At the end of 1945, America was in no mood for interfering in Europe. Opinion polls showed that, in December 1939, forty-seven per cent of the American public placed foreign affairs above internal affairs in relative importance. The figure for November 1941 was eighty-one per cent. In October 1945 it was a mere seven per cent, and even by December 1946 it had not risen to more than twenty-two per cent. Only in March 1947, after the Truman Doctrine, did it rise to a level higher than December 1939. Bernard Baruch, Churchill's old crony, wrote to Congress, "no aid for Britain or anyone else till the national balance sheet has been drawn up to see what we have left over after taking care of domestic needs," and his letter received wide approval. Representative Buffet said: "Here is British imperialism in friction today with Russia. We walk over to Britain and say: 'Here we are on your team. Here is a new shot-gun.' " While his colleague Rep. Short declared: "Not one dollar for Britain as long as they have got the Crown Jewels in London."

It was all very much touch and go, and it is perfectly possible that the deal would not have gone through at all had it not been for the fortunate intervention of the Russians in Persia, in support of the Tudeh rebellion in Azerbaijan in November 1945, and of ex-Ambassador Joseph P. Kennedy in Washington, who declared on behalf of the Catholic hierarchy that Britain was the only bulwark in Europe against Communist atheism. Even so, the terms of the loan were almost impossibly onerous.

Thus, at a very early stage in its life, the Labour Government had been given a searing demonstration of the need for American support and the difficulty they would have in securing it.

But, even if the most optimistic forecasts of the Left had been fulfilled, and Europe had either found its own economic feet or been able to get American aid without the slightest political strings attached, it is equally doubtful whether at that stage a political basis for a European federation existed. It was only after Marshall Aid had sown the seed of a little stability in Western Europe that Churchill was able to start the movement which led to the Congress of Europe and eventually to the European Communities. But in 1946 all was still confusion and political strife.

Bevin did not need the advice of un-Socialist public school officials to see that some things were impossible, any more than he would have needed the advice of Socialist public school critics (such as most of the "Keep Left" people) to convince him of the opposite. What could be done with the situation he did by signing the Dunkirk Treaty with France in March 1947, and by trying to get a little economic freedom of movement through a quite abortive attempt to negotiate a trade agreement with Russia.

As for the renunciation of nuclear weapons, this was certainly a policy with some diplomatic possibilities in which Bevin was apparently uninterested. "I won't," he declared in his usual emphatic tones, " 'ave the Bomb in the Foreign Office." This was no doubt a failure of imagination. But in any case the policy suggested by "Keep Left" could only make sense on the assumption that the two Great Powers would never come into open nuclear competition – for in that case Europe's so-called independence would in practice deteriorate into military dependence on one side or the other – the very thing the Left wanted to avoid.

Left wing criticisms of Bevin, in short, were based on a totally unrealistic picture of Britain's capacity. The Left believed that Britain had the economic resources to finance her own and Europe's recovery without having to go to the Americans. They were wrong.

But then so was Bevin. For at heart he made the opposite mistake of believing that Britain could go to the Americans for cash and still retain her freedom of action as the third Great Power. He would occasionally bemoan the fact that if he had a few million more tons of coal to export he could save Europe from ruin. But in October 1947 he was still telling his colleagues with one breath that we must get more dollars out of the Americans for financing the British zone in Germany and declaring indignantly in the next that we must not get out of Germany because that would reduce us to the status of a third-rate power.

Poor Bevin. If hard work and the consummate bluff born of a lifetime in the trade union movement had been enough to retain Britain's place in the world he would have done it. And it was largely by the force of his extraordinary personality that he did manage for a time to conceal what was happening.

It was in the Greek crisis that the bluff first really failed to work. It failed first of all to provide a substitute for hard cash as a means of reducing the Greek economic situation to manageable proportions; it failed to convince either the Russians or the Greek Communists that their pressures would be too costly to be worth while; and it failed to convince the Americans that they were doing anything but bailing out a miserably enfeebled Britain.

This is not an indictment of Bevin, for the whole history of the affair shows that there was very little else he could have done. He held on as long as he could because he believed that Greece would go Communist if he did not, and that in the long run the standard of living of the British working-man would suffer in consequence. But he finally quit because he had to, and the ignominy of the retreat was rubbed home by the hullabaloo about world leadership which Truman had to make in order to get the Bill past Congress, and by the thoroughly unexpected belligerence of the Truman Doctrine, which Britain was given no chance to modify.

The transformation of British power signalled by the Truman Doctrine was not so great as the Americans made out: Britain still had the Commonwealth and a million and a half men under arms, but the change was real nonetheless. Until 1947 British relations with America were only theoretically an alliance—the cold dregs of war-time. In practice Britain was trying to keep going with a modification of the old balance of power policy. Bevin's original belief was that the Americans could be brought into Europe and the Middle East to offset the Russians and still leave Britain's hands free.

The remnants of this doctrine hung about until after 1956 and the Suez crisis. But by and large the withdrawal from Greece marked the British Government's realisation that there was no real way of inducing the Americans to do what was necessary except on the basis that they had full control. From the moment that this became established, Britain's only chance of retaining her influence was by developing a special relationship with America. Balance of power diplomacy had to give way to alliance diplomacy.

What is most striking is the inevitability of all this once Britain's economic situation was faced in a realistic way. Someone had said of Bevin in 1946: "He's a big bumble bee caught in a web, and he thinks he's the spider." At the time Bevin was at the height of his powers, and it may have seemed false. Greece proved how true it was.

6

THE NEW LOOK

PEARSON PHILLIPS

Pearson Phillips was born in 1927. He was educated at Sedbergh and Brasenose College, Oxford, where he read Modern Languages. From 1953–8 he worked for the *Daily Express*. Since 1958 he has been a feature and leader writer on the *Daily Mail*.

THE NEW LOOK

Pearson Phillips

A FEW minutes after ten-thirty on the morning of February 12th, 1947, a young English woman heard for the first time in her life what she afterwards described as "the sound of a petticoat." At last, at long last, she felt that the Second World War was really over.

She was one of a crowd of privileged people who had been squeezed into a grey and gilt *salon* at No. 30 Avenue Montaigne, Paris. The atmosphere was hot and heavy with scent, some of it from flowers, most of it from bottles. The windows were tight shut, and, in spite of protests, those in charge at this memorable occasion would not allow them to be opened. The crowd, most of them women, were expectant, impatient, slightly rebellious. They had gathered for the launching of a new fashion house, the House of Christian Dior.

Within a year that sound of rustling petticoats could be heard right round Europe and America, supporting the long, full skirts of the fashion that was launched that February morning, the fashion which later became known as "The New Look," which made the name of Dior and saved the name of Paris. A fashion which gathered some secret momentum of its own, and swept off to be very much more than a style of dress — a state of mind, an attitude to the times, and, eventually, a burnt-out cliché.

It also, in Britain at any rate, became a subject of controversy. It was what is called "an issue," and the way the British people reacted to it tells us something about the thoughts, feelings and desires of those times.

There was no sign of controversy, however, in that now celebrated gathering on February 12th. The other Paris collections of that year had not been of any great interest. Was Paris losing its grip? Would it ever regain its former position in the fashion world? Many people, particularly Americans, were ready to believe that it wouldn't. The materials were there, and so was the workmanship. But where was the style? Something that the fashion writers called *Bizarrerie* — an obsession with jazzy effects — had been allowed to swamp elegance. Could this man, Dior, an ex-designer with Lucien Lelong who had started on his own with the backing of Boussac's textile group, find the way back? Just before the first model walked in a sharp, imperious lady in the front row leant over to the

9

woman sitting beside her and made one small comment in a deep, chesty, Irish-American rumble. "Darling, it had better be good . . ." It was Carmel Snow of *Harper's Bazaar*. The Queen of fashion writers. It *was* good. Paris was saved.

What was it that Dior produced on that February morning? What was it that made some of the more emotional spirits present break down in tears (not an unusual occurrence at a Paris Collection, let it be admitted), and which brought him a smother of kisses and lasting shouts of "*bravo*", "*magnifique*" and "*ravissant*"? We can, perhaps, best get the idea from the way the British edition of *Harper's Bazaar* — a journal which normally prides itself on its suave matter-of-factness — breathlessly brought the good news to the fashion-starved drawing-rooms of Mayfair.

PARIS IS MARVELLOUSLY ELEGANT . . .
PARIS IS MORE FEMININE THAN EVER . . .
PARIS ROUNDS EVERY LINE.

"Paris swells with feminity. The big story is a curving, opulent day silhouette that is the most elegant fashion for decades. Its best blossoming is at the new house of Christian Dior, whose 'Corolle' line is the first major post-war fashion; a tight, slender bodice narrowing into a tiny wasp waist, below which the skirt bursts into fullness like a flower. Every line is rounded. There are no angles in this silhouette. Shoulders are gently curved. Bosoms are rounded out with padding, often fitted into the dress itself. Hips are very full, stiffened with padding or swelling with pleats stitched from waist to hips and then released. The longer day skirt is confirmed. Every house in Paris shows day skirts twelve inches from the ground, with even longer skirts for afternoon . . ."

Swelling, opulent, curving, full, rounded; those were the key words. It was a striking contrast to the way women were dressing at the time, in square, angular clothes that resembled uniforms, with wide, straight, padded shoulders that seemed to have been created to support badges of rank or rifles at the slope. The people whose job it was to advertise these grim, box-like garments, searching for a smart word, told the world that their suits and dresses were "man-tailored." But here was Dior encouraging women to be women again.

Encouraging them not only to be women, but "girls," and some of them needed little encouragement. Janey Ironside, who became Professor of Fashion Design at the Royal College of Art, describes being struck by the impact of Dior in these terms: "It was like a new love affair, the first sight of Venice, a new chance, in fact a new look at life . . ." He held, she says, "a mirror up to women, in which they saw themselves as they wished to be; no longer Amazons, but Nymphs; no longer Cinders, but Cinderella."

The British edition of *Vogue* had never really been happy in the role of Amazon, although it had tried. Its efforts to adjust itself to the gravity of the times had resulted in some richly comical absurdities, such as when it posed its models in front of an artistic panorama of bomb damage. (A question in Parliament wondered whether this was any help to the war effort.) With the coming of Dior it saw that perhaps its privations were nearly over. Adopting its dowager tone it permitted itself the following little lecture to the upper middle-class:

"There are moments when fashion changes fundamentally. This is one of those moments. Granted, we in England will not partake of it very fast, at present . . . it is still something which has happened, of which we should be aware, and of which we should reflect our awareness in every purchase and every renovation.

"Let us in small things as well as great hold to the idea of one world civilisation, from which we cannot be cut off by anything but the closing of our own minds . . .

"It all began when the word 'femininity' crept back . . ."

No one was more surprised at the effect of this "fundamental change" than the man who was responsible for it, Christian Dior himself. The term "New Look" was not his invention. It was a label tacked on by the American press. Dior himself would never have dreamt of calling his style "new," for in fact it wasn't. Paris had already started to accentuate "the feminine" in 1938 and 1939, but the war interrupted the process. Dior had taken the development up again when he worked for Lucien Lelong, and the traces of it could already be seen in the Paris Autumn collections of 1946. As he said himself in his autobiography, "It was time for fashion to return to base," base for him being the rudimentary female form, preferably wearing a corset.

Apart from this he was a man who liked dwelling in the past. His fellow-couturiers accused him of having a "grandmother complex." He didn't deny it. He confirmed it, saying that he had "fairy-tale memories" of his annual visits to his grandparents in Paris before the First World War.

"I thank heaven I lived in Paris in the last years of the *Belle Epoque*," he wrote in his autobiography. "They marked me for life. My mind retains a picture of a time full of happiness, exuberance and peace, in which everything was directed towards the art of living. The general, carefree atmosphere derived from the illusion that the existence and capital of the rich as well as the thrifty lives of the poor were immune from any sudden reverse . . ."

These were the thoughts behind the so-called "New" look of Dior's first collection, and behind the even longer skirts and more padded hips of his second collection in August, when hemlines came right down to the ankles. Some people have suggested that this was to please the mercantile interests of Marcel Boussac, his textile-making millionaire backer. But it wasn't. It was just Christian Dior, whose heavily draped Paris apartment looked like an Oscar Wilde stage set, having a shot at recreating the *Belle Epoque* of his childhood. And the women of Paris, old and young, were eager to join him in the fun.

In Britain, 1946 had been a vintage year for the word "new". The V.E. Day spirit was still carrying people through. Anything which pointed to the fact that a great new world had arrived was pleasurably received. In July 1946, before Dior's fashion was heard of, a woman's magazine even presented a "New Look" of its own.

"There's a new look about, a look of smoothness, serenity, and poise. It's the look of the new beauty; a young, burnished beauty, natural and free; a young beauty rooted in health and vitality, firmly planted on straight legs, fine sprung feet; soaring like an arrow out of the self-controlled, muscular girdle of a taut midriff and held-in stomach.

"It's a classic, truthful beauty, uncluttered by the flummery and chi-chi of the brittle pre-war phase; unimpaired by the drabness of the past years when, with husbands far away and war work never done, slovenliness was too often carried with an air of virtuous complacency.

"You can have this new look, too . . ."

During the course of the year the women of Britain were also invited to consider the "New American Look," the "new shiny look," and the "new stance."

". . . there are not only new clothes, but a new way of wearing them; a new way of walking, of standing. The new stance is a hippy one. Your hips become the most prominent part of your body. Your diaphragm above them is taut, so held-in it's practically concave. Your shoulders are held well back. Your seat is tucked away to vanishing point . . . it's a posture that's very much in tune with the hour . . ."

A new stance for a new era. And yet, where was this new era? As 1946 shivered into 1947, and the new women had got their seats almost away to vanishing point, the mood of freshness, hope and optimism began to fade, and give way to concern and despair. The word "new" lost some of its glamour. The magazines modified their message, promising that "there's a good time coming . . . one day you will be able to buy all the foundation garments you require."

It was a bad time for everyone, but the women seemed to get the worst of it.

It is worth looking closely at the situation in Britain at the time when the "New Look" seed was being planted in Paris. On the very day of Dior's success the Bishop of Fulham made a much publicised statement. "We are just drifting," he said. "We cannot see the end of it all." Possibly the one strand of hope running through those miserable winter days was provided by the Heinz advertisements: "They're coming back, those fifty-seven varieties, one by one . . ." They were about the only things that were. An advertisement for a tonic wine asked: "How does she get that pre-war feeling?" The answer: "By drinking the wine that does you good." A few months earlier the question would have been: "How does she get that post-war feeling . . .?" But the V.E. Day draught had been drained.

The problems of "an average housewife" were projected in the spring of 1947 by the magazine *Picture Post*, which set itself the task of finding out "What's wrong with Britain?" (Something was wrong, obviously, because during March many weekly magazines had been forced to miss out two whole issues because of the fuel shortage.)

"We won the war," she says. "Why is it so much worse?" In many ways it *was* worse. It had been calculated that every woman in Britain was still spending at least one hour of every day standing in a queue. She also believed that there were fewer things to spend money on in the shops. She wasn't quite right, here. She had the war-surplus sales, cheerless as they were.

For three days she was without any coal at all, and froze inside the house as well as out. She was fed up with queueing, hated the rudeness which had become general, and hated the drabness of life. But most of all she hated the ironic phrase "Don't you know there's a war on?" which people were beginning to use once more. It was war without *camaraderie* or cause.

It was a time of frequent fuel cuts, which meant that the ironing piled up, and the radio, beloved distraction, would cut out just at the time of a cherished programme. It was a time of incredible soap shortage. The rations were actually smaller than during the war, and *Picture Post*'s "Average Housewife" complained that it was impossible to keep the house clean, the clothes clean, and the family clean with what she was given.

Apart from that, the laundry service was now worse than it ever was, even during the height of the Blitz.

It was also a time of rising prices. The first tangible pangs of inflation were being felt. Two shillings for a frost-bitten cauliflower, and you had to queue for ten potatoes. Two shillings for a scrubbing brush in 1947, one shilling in 1939. 4s. 5d. for a bucket in 1947, 1s. 11d. in 1939. 1s. 9d. for a threepenny duster. The sinking feeling induced by inflation was something new in 1947. It aroused indignation. "During the war we were encouraged to save because things would be cheaper—now we are just cottoning on to the fact that things are going to be dearer . . ." Just when things were at their blackest, the sweet ration was halved.

It was young mothers who had some of the deepest grievances in these early days of the Welfare State. Normal necessities like nappies, prams, or baby clothes just could not be found. Baby cereals, such as Farex, were invariably "under the counter." Mothers had to make up their own baby foods. But, although there were luxuries like grapes and pineapples in the shops, at a price, it was difficult to get hold of simple things like carrots and onions. They complained about "shoddy goods in the shops," and did not like being told that "all the best goes for export." The women, too, felt something of a special grievance. There was still beer and tobacco about. The men were happy . . .

As far as the average woman was concerned, this sense of grievance did not crystallise in any political terms. It was not at that time "All the fault of the Labour Government." It would have been "just the same if the other lot had been in . . ." "They" were the enemies. The "officials," the people who pushed her around, the Food Office clerks, the great amorphous body of civil servants. The only really unpopular Government member at that time was Mr. Shinwell.

A great deal of this feminine indignation was directed towards "the men." This antagonism between the sexes may have been activated by deep-running psychological currents, but the rash of industrial disputes aggravated it. "The women" had stayed at home and had a dreary, uncomfortable war. "The men" had enjoyed themselves overseas. And now "the men" were slacking. That was the word for it, slacking. They don't want to work. They fight and strike over every little half-hour. The women can't strike. They haven't let up since 1940 . . .

What, then, did the women want? *Picture Post*'s "Mrs. Average" gave her answer. "She wants more leisure, more colour, more food and clothing, less weary work. But most of all she wants hope. That is why she is sadder now than during the war . . ."

But hope was not forthcoming. Slowly it began to sink into the national consciousness that "things for Britain would never be the same again." The meaning of the loss of our foreign investments was hammered home. In simple language the posters explained that "Britain must earn her keep . . . we cannot buy anything we cannot afford to pay for." One remarkable feature of this phase was the odd lack of partisan political activity. Conservative politicians sensed that it was shallow to make party points of the crisis. The onslaught was to come later.

"Monty," the hero, even suggested that perhaps the nation should close ranks "behind a man of leadership," someone who would "pull the country together." Some people took the cue and asked "Why not Monty?" General Slim asked the Press to refrain from gloomy sniping and rally behind the national cause, in the old, war-time spirit. The Bristol branch of the Electrical Trades Union even went as far as pronouncing that "what this country needs is another Churchill."

Then came the Control of Engagement Order, by which labour exchanges were empowered to steer workers away from "non-essential" jobs and put them into work that mattered. Entertainment, sport, hairdressing, window-cleaning and other "personal services" were all inessential. The women's lot became just a little drabber and harder. The illusive "normality" was pushed still further out of sight.

Indeed, for women there was little escape from the atmosphere of strain and concern. The Government took particular pains to explain to them exactly what it was all about. Poster and newspaper advertisements appeared, showing a woman at a shop counter who had ordered more goods than she could afford to pay for. That was Britain's plight. It was a metaphor which every housewife could understand in stark and dismaying terms. Another poster showed John Bull with his sleeves rolled up. "We're up against it," ran the caption. "We will work or want." The women felt that they had never had their sleeves rolled down.

Perhaps the whole feeling of the day can be extracted from a Government announcement which was made on September 25th, 1947, one of dozens of similar ones which appeared each week and which women had to take notice of.

"Take care of your 1947–48 clothing book.
To save paper it will have to last you two years.
The 20 yellow coupons on page iii of the General, Child's and Junior Clothing Books become valid on October 1st for the five months ending February 29th next.

This is how they are made up:

16 coupons "E" – value 1	=	16
1 set of ¼ coupons – value 1	=	1
2 token "F" – value 1½	=	3
		——
		20

Do not cut any of the invalid coupons from the 1947–48 books. They will be needed later."

During the war, dealing with this kind of thing had given women a feeling of importance. They had acquired prestige and self-esteem. They prided themselves on being able to "get round" difficulties, by "being in the know." But now they were tired of it. "Take care" of this. "Don't do" that. This is valid, that is not valid. They had had enough.

The British housewife was told that she belonged to the best-fed nation in Europe, but the desperate plight of others did not seem to make her lot any better. She was told that she was being better fed than before the war. She didn't believe it.

There was, however, at least one woman's publication, of admittedly limited readership, which, as usual, took a positive and optimistic line in the midst of these difficulties. Like a Colonel's lady in a crisis, *Vogue* mounted the ramparts and rallied the morale of "the girls."

"Our country's predicament presents a challenge. Here is our profession of faith and pledge of service.

"This isn't the place to discuss how best the crisis can be met. But it is the place to say how *we* mean to meet it. . . . We think the first need is to recognise this as a national emergency, calling for effort and understanding and unselfishness of the kind that we gave so unstintingly in the war . . . we shall help you make the most of your resources, in terms of practicality, good looks and good living. If there is less food, all the more reason to cook it superlatively."

There followed advice on what to do with windfall apples, patterns for renovating old clothes ("renovation" was a key fashion word in the forties), and ideas for a holiday in France on £20.

There were also some illuminating suggestions for "Party Food," supplied by a certain Phoebe Williams. The four items were cauliflower soup, creamed haddock, baked beans, and stuffed marrow. The spirit of 1947 seems to permeate the recipe for the cauliflower soup, nourishing as it undoubtedly was. Anyone wishing to recreate the era might care to try it:

Cauliflower Soup (8 *people*)

One large cauliflower
One teaspoon margarine
One medium onion
Two tablespoons semolina
Two quarts reconstituted milk
One heaped teaspoon nutmeg
Evaporated milk (if you can spare it)
Salt, pepper

Vogue suspected, however, that gracious living on cauliflower soup and baked beans was not enough to keep the spirits up. Every now and then this intrepid magazine would seek out indications that all was going to be all right with the world before very long. Things were "getting back to normal." "They are," said one report, "putting the plate-glass windows back in Dickins and Jones." There is plenty of fruit about, said another report. "It began with tangerines glowing on the barrows through the snow . . . now the stalls are piled with colour." There certainly was fruit to be had, for a price. Air Vice-Marshal "Pathfinder" Bennett had won himself a certain notoriety by flying peaches specially from France. But the feeling of the times was against expensive luxuries when so many necessities could not be had for any money. Some branches of the British Housewives League, a militant body, Amazonian in character, even went as far as swearing an oath to each other that they would not buy pine-apples at 7s. 6d., grapes at 6s. a pound, plums at 4s. 6d. and tangerines at 2s. Eventually the importation of what was called "luxury fruit" was stopped by Government decree. So that put an end to that particular sign of hope.

But *Vogue*, and other optimists, found more. The Dorchester Hotel had commissioned a carpet design from Graham Sutherland. That was one sign of civilised progress. Eros was back on his site in Piccadilly Circus. "Dolls with eyes that open and close are back once more . . ."

"The Royal Garden Parties are once more in flower." The "London Squares are getting a welcoming paint and shovel." The first Antique Dealers' Fair since 1938. For a jaded palate "why not try a change of bread?"

"They are beginning to dress for dinner again in London," said another report. Dressing for dinner became almost an act of social and political defiance. But while it was easy enough to get all dressed up (Moss Bros. opened a special "female hire department" under a Miss Laurie Giles, "a lady of tact and discretion") it was not so easy to find anywhere to go. London's night life was centred on a very small number of clubs and restaurants. "Getting a table" was an operation requiring skill and fore-sight. At some places you needed to book almost a fortnight ahead. For the younger generation the dance halls were doing a good trade. The rule, almost without exception, was "No Jiving." The term "teen-ager" was just being used. It came across from America during the war. But the British "teen-ager" had not yet emerged from the cocoon as a recognised, individualistic stratum of society. He was still relatively under-privileged. He had no idols. The older generations were still getting things their own way. No one needed to bother much about the "jitterbug fiends." After all, what had they done in the war? "National service will lick it out of them."

In its own inimitable way, *Vogue* portrayed also the frustrations of youth. It presented a picture of a girl in a flowing white dress leaning mournfully against the wall of a building which appeared to have been the victim of some past incendiary attack. What was the girl dreaming of? Perhaps "the graces and extravagances and charming absurdities that should be the natural inheritance of the young and that were snatched away with so much else from those who were still at school in 1939 . . ." Never mind. "You have a good time coming . . ." Meanwhile, "this season's strongest colour note is grey. There is always a shade of grey to suit you—no one can say 'I can't wear grey.' "

Grey. It was a perfect colour for the period. "What is missing?" asked an American correspondent. His answer—"cheerfulness and willing hard work."

Cheerfulness . . . but how was it possible to be cheerful without appear-ing to undermine what the irrepressible editorialists of *Vogue* called "the mood for these our sterner days"? In November 1947, there was a royal wedding. Princess Elizabeth was married to Lieut. Philip Mount-batten, R.N. A happy occasion, but . . . "It is officially announced that Princess Elizabeth will be given 100 coupons for her wedding. Brides-maids will get twenty-three coupons each. Pages ten coupons each." "It is the general impression among the workers," said Mrs. Mabel Ridealgh in the House, "that it would not be proper to spend large sums of money on this wedding when we are asking the workers themselves to economise even in the necessities of life." The wedding (formal dress was optional) played its part in what Sir Stafford Cripps called "an economic battle for democracy. If Western Europe fails, democracy will lose." The American loan was coming to an end. The Marshall Plan had not begun. Every man and woman was made to feel that they had a part to play in "saving Britain."

How was it possible to escape from the eternally grim severity of life? The cinema offered one release. It was a vintage period for escapist films and costume dramas. Michael Wilding and Anna Neagle were sweeping the crowds in with what one critic called their "sugar and saccharine comedies." (Cecil B. de Mille "has the courage of his own corn," wrote another critic, "Miss Neagle and Mr. Wilding have the courage of their own sweet corn.") Why, asked some discontented critics, can't we have films about today? What is wrong with tackling the problems of an ordinary family in the post-war era? Rightly or wrongly, the film-makers believed that their customers paid money at the box-office to be taken away from the drabness of their lives, not to be plunged further into it.

Escape, escape, escape . . . that was the national urge. There was an over-all spirit of claustrophobia. For eight years the women of Britain had been locked up and isolated in their island of hardship. For a brief period some of the luckier ones had been able to get away, and then the meagre foreign travel allowance was taken away again. It was as though the cell door had clanged shut once more.

It is difficult, at a distance, to appreciate just how much the inability to travel abroad, coming on top of all the other clamps and fetters, contributed to a feeling of imprisonment. "Don't Fence Me In," sang the Housewives League before Sir Stafford Cripps. Another popular tune of the moment was "Open the door, Richard." In fact, "Open the door, Richard" became a catch-phrase, a battering-ram applied to all kinds of restriction. Mr. Attlee was even told to "Open the door, Richard" and let some new blood into his Cabinet.

And then, there were the clothes. The experts in *haute couture* warn us against using words like "ugly" or "beautiful" to describe a particular fashion. These words are too grand, they say. Fashion is a fleeting, temporary thing. There are no permanent values on which we can create an aesthetic of the rag trade. This is all true. But, at the same time, there are clothes which flatter women, and clothes which don't. The style of the nineteen-forties manifestly and obviously didn't. And deep down inside them the women knew it.

Shoes were heavy and masculine. It was the era of "The Wedgie", of thick, platform soles and ungainly straps wrapped round ankles like a footballer's bootlaces. Skirts were short and jackets were long, with the result that legs were made to look short and squat. The figure was solid and square from the knees up to the wide, horizontally padded shoulders.

There were two main types of hat, both large and heavy. One was a variation of a Tam o'Shanter, the other looked like a civilian version of an A.T.S. officer's cap, and may well have been conjured out of war surplus supplies. Mr. James Laver, the costume expert from the Victoria and Albert Museum, did his best to cheer up the wearers of these garments by producing the theory that "it is always acknowledged that after a war, women, contrary to expectations, adopt a boyish, neat outline. Men will feel oppressed and frightened by excessive femininity when they return from war . . ." If this is so, the men of 1946 and 1947 should have been delighted. The colours matched the design, heavy and sombre. It was a time of purples and puces, midnight blues and bottle greens. They could either be bought as Utility garments, which were the Board of Trade's standard for the minimum any woman needed, or they could be purchased in what were called "non-utility" styles, which were a little more lavish but no more flattering.

This was the grey state of British womanhood. Weary, dispirited, cramped and cross. A celebrated cosmetics advertisement which blossomed out in 1947 provides an ironic sidelight on their plight. It was, runs the copy:

> "a day for looking young and gay, but
> '. . . darling, you look tired,' he said;
> (a tired look is no different from an old look)".

The women of Britain had a tired look, and it was no different from an old look. They were not quite sure what they wanted, but it must be something that would give them a little hope and gaiety, something that would take them out of the immediate past and the present and give them a taste of the better things which were eternally promised. Something that would take away that old look. What better than a New Look?

Dior's Messianic impact took a little while to make itself felt. The extraordinary scenes in the Avenue Montaigne on February 12th did not make headlines in the British daily press. The Paris fashion shows were not "news" to any great extent in the winter of 1947. They were too remote from ordinary life. The time when a whim from Paris could be seen rippling through the department stores and the typing pools like the wind through a field of corn had never yet been known in Britain. The great revolution in good, cheap, smart female clothing was yet to come. So that all the event rated in the non-specialist popular press was a small paragraph in Londoner's Diary in the *Evening Standard* for March 3rd, 1947:

"There is a new name in Paris fashions, I hear. It is Christian Dior."

On March 24th, *Life* magazine reported the show and the man. This article introduces an interesting thought. "Christian Dior's designs," it says, "are all founded on the premise that 'no fashion is ever successful unless it can be used as an instrument of seduction.' " During the war and in the late nineteen-forties, the adjective "seductive" acquired positive force. It became a "good" word, a term of flattery. "You are looking very seductive" was a fashionable expression of praise, commonly in use in "Young Conservative" circles. This, of course, was a time when hardly any woman *was* looking seductive. (Later when, thanks largely to Dior, practically all of them were, the term went out of fashion.)

Finally, with ecstatic proselytising from the fashion magazines and the added impact of Dior's second collection in the summer of 1947 (which was a more startling and definite version of his first) the message got through. But, as with most things, the New Look issue was radically simplified as soon as it became a subject of popular discussion. It developed simply into a matter of long skirts versus short ones. In mathematical terms the Paris hem-line was deemed to be from eight to twelve inches from the ground. This compared with sixteen, or even more, for the standard British short skirt.

To Miss Janey Ironside and the editorialists of *Vogue*, a swirling, feminine eight-inch-from-the-ground skirt seemed like "a new love affair". But to women of a different stamp it looked like a reckless betrayal of all they had worked for. A plunge back to non-emancipated womanhood. A disgraceful waste of material at a time when everyone was supposed to be "doing their bit" to save it, in the national interest, for the sake of democracy . . .

Sir Stafford Cripps, President of the Board of Trade, could hardly have been expected to feel the same way as M. Christian Dior and the fashionable women of London and Paris. He suggested to the British Guild of Creative Designers that they would be helping the national effort considerably if they would co-operate in keeping the short skirt popular in Britain. And the British Guild of Creative Designers, who should surely have known more about the hopelessness of trying to order the desires of women, agreed that they would boycott the Paris line "to save material." Said a Mr. Henry Scott of the Guild on September 24th, 1947: "We just have not got the materials. We cannot give way to Paris's irresponsible introduction of the longer skirt . . . there will be few long skirts in Britain next season." An unfortunate prediction.

While Sir Stafford was whispering into the ears of the clothing trade, some of the female members of the Labour Party took up the task of campaigning among the women. In the forefront of this battle were Dame Annie Loughlin (a former chairman of the T.U.C.), Mrs. Jean Mann, and Mrs. Bessie Braddock. All of them, perhaps, with their sympathies on the side of the Amazons rather than the Nymphs.

The Labour Party Conference at Southport that September was flavoured with a mood of sombre defiance. "What were legs given to us for?" cried out Dame Annie Loughlin. "To cover up? We are not going to lengthen the skirt at the whim of anyone . . ." Mrs. Bessie Braddock threw her weight behind the struggle with characteristic vigour. She scorned the longer skirt. It was "the ridiculous whim of idle people." Why? Because "the problem today as it affects British women is to get hold of clothes. They have not agitated for the longer skirt. Their strong feeling is that things should be left as they are. Most women today are glad to get any clothes they can get hold of, and people who worry about longer skirts might do something more useful with their time."

This could perhaps be cited as one example of the Labour Party's failure to catch on to the public's desire for some of the materialistic graces and frivolities of life. But it wasn't only Labour Party ladies who were against it. At the start, most women recoiled. Miss Prunella Stack, of Women's League of Health and Beauty fame, thought that "it is ridiculous in view of the shortages to use extra material for this purpose." Someone calculated that the extra few inches on the hem would mean that Britain's annual clothing production would have to be cut by 800,000 garments. A number of polls of public opinion were taken on the subject, and those against always seemed to outnumber those in favour. Plain-speaking women like Mrs. W. Hoyle-Smith, chairman of the Lancashire Executive of the British Housewives League, thought that "the idea of the longer skirt is preposterous."

There was one very simple explanation for this. Most women had never seen a New Look dress. They didn't even know what the New Look was. All the remarks quoted above refer not to the New Look, but to the "longer skirt." (It was not until the beginning of 1948 that the term became general.) There was almost total ignorance among most women about what the sheer femininity of the New Look could do for them. But then the new models started appearing here and there in the smarter stores. They began to be advertised in the daily press. Slowly the full impact sank in and the tide began to turn against Sir Stafford, Bessie Braddock, and those clothing manufacturers who were happy to turn out the old styles without having to bother about design.

The event which finally set the New Look irrevocably on its way was the arrival in autumn in London of M. Dior himself, with his models and his dresses. There was a sumptuous show at the Savoy Hotel which caused a sensation. The following day the dresses were shown privately, and indeed secretly, to the Queen, Princess Margaret, and the Duchess of Kent at the French Embassy. This was a ceremony which the public and the press were not informed about. Not even the Queen's dressmaker, Norman Hartnell, knew about it. Perhaps it was thought dangerous to involve royalty in something that had become almost a politico-patriotic issue. It had its effect, at any rate, Bessie Braddock notwithstanding. Princess Margaret was converted to the New Look, which sealed its success in due course.

In the face of these manœuvres the Amazonian opposition redoubled its efforts. A new Labour Party lady took up the struggle: Mrs. Mabel Ridealgh, M.P., a robust grandmother with a North Country background, at that time the parliamentary representative for Ilford. During the war she had held the post of Regional Controller for the Board of Trade's "Make-do-and-mend" campaign. She was a stern guardian of women's rights, and she tore into the New Look more fiercely than anyone yet. She told the *Daily Herald* on February 22nd, 1948, that it was "utterly ridiculous, stupidly exaggerated waste of material and manpower, foisted on the average woman to the detriment of other, more normal clothing." She said she was going to ask the Board of Trade to control its manufacture. She wouldn't stand for fashion experts decreeing longer this and padded that and proceeding to push women around to wear them. "The average housewife won't buy it. She can't afford the coupons, let alone the price. Yet this does not stop the manufacturers rushing it to the shops everywhere. When you think that normal dresses, skirts and blouses, which everybody wants, are not made because of the fashion experts' fad it is exasperating. I am all for a moderate bright change in fashion—every woman is—but this business is just completely silly." In a broadcast to America at the beginning of March she even went as far as stating that "The New Look is dead. British women deplore it." She quoted one store as saying that it was having to alter seventy-five per cent of the garments it sold, because its customers felt foolish in long skirts.

Some very deeply-felt motivation was obviously driving Mrs. Mabel Ridealgh, and a closer examination of some of the things she wrote and said reveals quite plainly what it was. "Padding and artificial figure aids, she thinks, are extremely bad, because they make for over-sexiness," wrote a reporter who interviewed her. "She does not mind a girl showing a good figure if it is her own. She is worried because she thinks the new padding craze is aimed at young girls." An even more revealing glimpse of her feelings (which represented those of a number of sympathisers at the time) can be found in an article that she wrote herself in *Reynolds's News*:

"Our fashion designers have shown a complete lack of touch with what is happening in the world. Our modern world has become used to the freedom of short, sensible clothing and prefers simplicity to over-dressiness, false padding, and exaggerated design. I am not suggesting that she does not like a change, but it must have some relation to the need of the times. I believe she is ready for a slightly longer skirt, one designed with a nice swing, but certainly not what the fashion experts would like to impose on her.

"Can anyone imagine the average housewife and businesswoman dressed in bustles and long skirts carrying on their varied jobs, running for buses and crowding into tubes and trains? The idea is ludicrous. Women today are taking a larger part in the happenings of the world and the New Look is too reminiscent of a caged bird's attitude. I hope our fashion dictators will realise the new *outlook* of women and will give the death blow to any attempt at curtailing women's freedom."

Women's freedom. That was what she felt was at stake. Were M. Dior and the league of dressmaking tyrants trying to drive women back into the drawing-room? Were they attempting to undo the work of emancipation, won through active participation in two wars? As far as M. Dior was concerned, there was probably nothing he would have liked more. He was confessedly in love with *La Belle Epoque*, and his fashion was a reflection of that. It was not so much a New Look as an Old Look, a Romantic last glimpse of a vanished era. This was part of its charm for the hard-pressed women of the forties.

In view of that it is not surprising that Mrs. Ridealgh and others like her should have been trying to stamp the evil movement out. Her enthusiasm, however, got the better of her facts. The announcement of the New Look's death was premature. And, on being closely questioned, it was discovered that the store she had had in mind when she spoke of seventy-five per cent of the garments sold having to be altered was not D. H. Evans or Dickins and Jones, but the Mansfield Co-operative Society. Mansfield was not setting the trend.

As the spring of 1948 progressed (it was the hottest March for a hundred years) the public demand for the New Look accelerated. Consider, for example, the effect on a square, shapelessly dressed regiment of women of the following advertisement, offered by Fenwick's of Bond Street:

"A ballerina suit, with softly-rounded shoulders, page-boy nipped-in jacket, gaily swinging skirt to give the new fashion look. Exciting colours and gay mixtures. 18 coupons. £5 12s. 6d."

Or this one, by Richard Shops:

"Exciting newcomer for pocket Venuses. Ballerina coat. Our Ballerina skirted coat with a Victorian bodice that accentuates your waist and your feminine curves. Soft velour in lovely pastel shades. 15 coupons. £6 2s. 7d."

"Far from losing its popularity," said a spokesman from the Fashion Trades Association on March 4th, "the New Look is definitely in to stay. Manufacturers are left with their old-length stocks, and the problem in the shops is how to dispose of existing stocks." There was some hesitation in the provinces, but in the West End of London "whenever women buy a new dress or coat it is the new length." "We are selling nothing but New Look clothes," said Marshall and Snelgrove, "with nipped-in waists and rounded shoulder lines . . ."

The fashion business was far from happy or unanimous about it. The top designers of the London Model House group were jubilant, but on March 17th a worried and indignant delegation called to see Mr. Harold Wilson, who had taken over from Sir Stafford Cripps at the Board of Trade. A Mr. Bert Alston, speaking, it was claimed, for three hundred dress firms, asked for a ban on the length of hemlines. "The London fashion houses may want the New Look," he said, "but the woman in the street, the utility clothes wearers whom we represent, do not want it. It is a shameful waste of material." It was a slightly pathetic plea. If the women in the street didn't want it what was he worrying about? Why ask for a ban? The truth was that the women in the street did want it. It was the small dress firms that didn't. Where you could get ten old-look dresses out of a length of material, only nine could be cut in the new style. The Board of Trade did not feel strong enough to maintain their original anti-New Look position. Said a Mr. Carruthers of the Board of Trade, making what must stand as the most curious abdication of responsibility ever uttered by a senior civil servant: "We cannot dictate to women the length of their skirts."

The struggle was almost over. A Miss Norah Alexander in the *Daily Mail* for March 13th, 1948, wrote that:

"I don't know how it is in your part of the world but you can't move in the Home Counties without hearing arguments about the New Look. I must say I'm getting pretty sick of them. The longer skirt is here, let's face it. The same is true of the nipped-in waist and the rounded shoulder line. In America they've dropped the 'New'. They rightly call it 'The Look'. You'd think that after all these austere years no one would grudge us this small token of pleasanter things to come. It's possible to wear skirts down to your ankles and still be one of the world's workers, as many a char and older countrywoman will testify. It is equally possible to make up Utility garments in line with current Paris fashions and sell them at practically pre-war prices and normal coupon rates. Don't let anyone persuade you it's wanton to covet the sort of clothes they're wearing in the other cities of the world."

"It's impossible to stop the New Look," said Mr. Frederick Starke of the London Model Group, a few days later. "It's like a tidal wave." Even frocks which could not by any stretch of the imagination be described as New Look were hopefully billed as such to catch the trend. One fashion writer offered some interesting advice about what to do if you hadn't got the coupons for a new-length coat. You could either let a band of fur into the midriff, or cut off the hem and turn it into a "boxy jacket".

By Easter, at the end of March, it was all over. The Easter parade in London was almost a New Look fashion show. At the Easter meeting at Kempton Park the New Look won—as one commentator put it—"by a length." The final signal came from Buckingham Palace, from Princess Margaret, at that time a young girl of seventeen, a representative of the new, post-war generation. On March 3rd she appeared publicly in a pink nutria coat with three velvet rings at the hem. On March 17th she appeared in the same coat, but it now had four rings at the hem, an alteration which did not escape notice. By April 26th, the celebration of the Silver Wedding of King George VI and Queen Elizabeth, she had progressed to a complete conversion, appearing in a Norman Hartnell suit described by an expert as having "a little jacket tightly waisted and buttoned with a short flared basque over an ankle-length skirt bouffant." The ridiculous whim of idle people? By the end of the year ten million women either possessed or coveted the same thing.

The "classic tailor-made" went into retirement. The British fashion industry sorted out its confusion and went "New Look" by popular demand. There was a boom in frilled petticoats. Every girl acquired a pencil-thin umbrella, part of the Dior "uniform." Often enough twopence worth of that year's weekly meat ration had to be taken in corned beef.

Punch, 30.3.49

"By 'New Look' I take it you mean what we now consider 'Old Look', but
not the 'Old Look' which preceded the 'New Look'."

We were, before Marshall Aid came to the rescue, down to the last drops of the American loan. We were forced to devalue the pound to avoid bankruptcy. And yet a little bit of hope and optimism arrived from Paris which was not there before. The phrase "New Look" began to be applied to other things.

A motoring correspondent discovered the British cars at the International Motor Show at Geneva, when compared with continental models, were "either unblushingly Old Look or a not very bold compromise towards post-war styling." We needed to wake up. There was a New Look in daffodils, a New Look in housing, a New Look in furniture, and a New Look Labour Party, with young men like Gaitskell and Harold Wilson moving up. The phrase was disastrously over-worked, but it did serve to swing people's gaze away from the past and the present and make them feel that at last they were moving forward. The old selling phrase "pre-war value" lost some of its attraction. Some articles even began to appear which were solely post-war in character. A ball-point pen came on the market "invaluable to businessmen, indispensable for writing out of doors." The price of this wonder, later selling at a shilling each, was 34s. 10d. in 1948.

It is very easy to look ridiculous when injecting philosophy and reflections about society into a discussion on silks and satins. Dior himself said that. But the New Look was a curious phenomenon, very typical of the late nineteen-forties. It was aspiring towards the future, but at the same time it was gazing nostalgically back towards the past. It was interpreting hopes for the unknown in terms of memories of the known. Looked at in retrospect, it seems an oddly pathetic episode. The phrase wore out quite quickly and was replaced by a much more brash and confident concept, characterised by the word "contemporary". Skirts rose again to the knee, and it was Dior, the sartorial Duke of York, who, having brought them down, let them up again. Photographs of those first bold bearers of the New Look make them seem strangely lost and bewildered, as though they had mistaken their cue and come on stage fifty years late. There was a revolution going on all around them which they didn't seem to be part of.

This, of course, was what it was. In musical terms it was a ghostly restatement at the end of the first movement of the Twentieth Century of the theme which had been heard at the beginning of it. It was Orpheus turning round to have a last look at an unemancipated Eurydice. And, having looked, we knew that we should never see her again.

7

BRITAIN AGAINST THE REST
The decline of British sporting prestige
BRIAN GLANVILLE

Brian Glanville was born in 1931 and educated at Charterhouse. He lived in Italy from 1952–5, and is the author of seven novels, including *Along the Arno*, *The Bankrupts*, *Diamond* and, most recently, *The Rise of Gerry Logan*. He is sports columnist for the *Sunday Times*, and left back for the Chelsea Casuals. He is married, with two sons and one daughter.

BRITAIN AGAINST THE REST

Brian Glanville

GREAT BRITAIN 6, The Rest of Europe 1: a delusion triumphantly confirmed. Not for another six and a half years, when the Hungarians came to Wembley on a November afternoon, scored six goals and might have scored ten, was the island myth of British superiority at football scattered to the winds. It was then, and only then, that the final, symptomatic breach in the wall was made: that British football fans not only acknowledged the names of foreign stars, not only remembered them – but managed to pronounce them correctly.

But 1947 – to be precise, May 10th, 1947 – was near enough to 1939 and pre-war times for players of the old, robust vintage to be still about. Frank Swift, the huge, dry-humoured goalkeeper who had fainted in 1934 during a Wembley Final, and roused the concern of the King; Stanley Matthews, ageless and inexplicable; Tommy Lawton, who could climb like a funicular and shoot like a cannon; the blond and impeccable Wilf Mannion. "Come the three corners of the world in arms . . ." They had come, after all, before, in 1938, the Rest of Europe against England, at Highbury when a Uruguayan centre-half, Italian for the occasion, had spat at the referee, and been firmly corrected by an English half-back. 3–0 to England was the score that day; Europe had seemed utterly disjointed.

This myth of supremacy rested on the fact that neither England nor Scotland had ever been beaten on home ground by a foreign team. True, they had failed time and again away, in that great, amorphous never-never land known vaguely as Abroad, where defeats, obscurely, somehow didn't count, because once-get-them-in-our-British-mud and we would kill them. (We often did.)

There had been the Spaniards, for example; cheeky fellows. They had beaten England 4–3 in Madrid in 1929, the first foreign side to do so, taking mean advantage of a heat wave. In 1931, the chips were down, the Highbury mud as thick as glue. The crowd, eager for the butchery, stormed the gates, and were fully rewarded. Ricardo Zamora, Spain's goalkeeper, a legend on the Continent, a nobody here, was overcome by the occasion, let through two goals a schoolboy might have stopped, and England ploughed inexorably on, to win 7–1. "If Zamora," wrote a complacent critic, "earns £50 a week, then Hibbs (the England goalkeeper) is worth a benefit once a fortnight."

There had, it is true, been the Austrians, perfectionists to a man, who came to Chelsea in 1932, astonished everybody with their technique, and just went down, 4–3. But that was a freak; on another day, said the captain of England, his team would have scored ten against them. Austria – in Vienna – beat England 2–1 in 1936. Hungary beat England; so did Belgium, Czechoslovakia, Switzerland, France and Yugoslavia. Scotland were beaten by Austria and Italy, Wales by France: but it was all, all of it, *Abroad*.

The war years saw the last, fine flourishing of British football; a swansong of which this match at Hampden Park was somehow an echo. There were still enough individualists, survivors of that old school of battle-toughened, quirky, intractable professionals, to survive the depredations of League football, the manic struggle for points; results, at the cost of style and virtuosity. Coaching might have supplied the growing dearth, but coaching was for foreigners. The unconscious fantasy, if put into words, would have stated that every British boy was somehow born with a golden football at his toe. Thus, the best British coaches were forced abroad; to Hungary, Germany, Italy, Scandinavia. Football could *not* be taught – except to foreign footballers who, by some process of uncertain chemistry, were Made, whilst British footballers were Born.

And yet, when the match against the Rest of Europe was first arranged, there were qualms. Would this celebration of Britain's return to F.I.F.A. (the International Football Association) be a celebration at our own expense? Could we, rationed and underfed, compete with the might of a whole Continent, with Swedes who had grown plump in the war, Italians who were already restored to the comforts of *vino* and spaghetti? If the England team seemed good, then our League soccer was indisputably bad: the Gap was showing – no youngsters, too many bald pates, familiar faces.

By the time May arrived, however, it was the Continent which quaked; Britain were indisputably the favourites. Meanwhile, there was the question of selection. On the face of it – at least until the annual match between England and Scotland, played at Wembley that year – England looked by far the strongest of the four home teams. Scotland, once proud and predominant, had gone horribly to pieces in the war; doubtless they would be thrashed, as they'd so often been in recent years.

But Scotland, disobligingly, were not thrashed; indeed, they should have won. A late, deflected goal gave England a shaky draw, to which they were certainly not entitled on the play, dictated as it was by two red-haired Scottish wing-half-backs, and a tiny, blond, dynamic inside-forward. The half-backs were Archie Macaulay and Alex Forbes; the inside-forward, Billy Steel. Of the three, Macaulay alone had a reputation, made in the war, when he was converted – playing as a "guest" for Doncaster Rovers – from a goodish, clever inside-forward into a right-half who combined classic style with a usually controlled ferocity. By now, he had left his war-time club, West Ham, to join another London team, in Brentford. Forbes, twenty-two years old, a former ice hockey star, had recently got into the Sheffield United team, and represented an inspired Scottish gamble. Steel, who was little older, and played then for Greenock Morton, the Glasgow club, had begun to make a name in the war, when service took him overseas. He and Macaulay surprisingly were picked for Britain.

There was also a third Scot, Billy Liddell, of Liverpool: a former R.A.F. pilot who had risen gamely from a raw, hard childhood, the son of a miner in the depression years. Now he was qualifying as an accountant and working in youth clubs; a tough, fast, functional player, who tore through defences with the impassive detachment of a runaway locomotive.

It was, inevitably, a "political" team, and, equally inevitably, great names were missing. It was really absurd that any British team should lack Carter and Doherty, those matchless inside-forwards, one English, one Irish – one of the silver hair, one of the red; those two who, a year ago at Wembley, had won the first post-war Cup Final for Derby County. But Carter, as the match with Scotland seemed to show, was inching over the hill, while Doherty gave way to the new *wunderkind*, Steel, that marvellous box of tricks.

Who else was there? Ron Burgess, the Tottenham and Wales left-half, a tireless greyhound of a man who had learned his football on the cinder-tips of a Welsh mining village; he had already played for the Football League (which traditionally called on English players alone) against the Scottish League, so that he could integrate himself with his English colleagues. Wales also provided the left-back, Billy Hughes, of Birmingham City, a pre-war hero, a teetotaller, a man who signed himself, to autograph hunters, "Yours in sport." George Hardwick, right-back and captain of the team, was a Middlesbrough player, who'd served in the R.A.F., handsome, elegant, with a moustache, he looked a little like a movie hero. He was frequently criticised after international matches for poor performances, but held his place for all that.

Ireland had but one representative, Jack Vernon, of West Bromwich

Albion, a hefty, solid man, the son of a Belfast butcher. Another slightly political choice, perhaps; Vernon was admired, but Neil Franklin of Stoke City and England – unhappy in the game against Scotland – was the great technician of his day.

And what of Europe? How was the mosaic to be made up: there was no question of the abundant talent. Sweden had its best team in history; Italy was recovering with customary resilience. Germany was still out of favour, the Russians (whose Moscow Dynamos had alarmed Britain two years before) weren't playing – but France still had a crop of pre-war stars, Switzerland was lively, Denmark full of promise.

In the event, the team was made up of two Swedes, two Danes, a Frenchman, a Czech, a Belgian, an Italian, a Dutchman, a Swiss and . . . an Irishman. The Irishman was Johnny Carey, chosen as right-half and captain, a bald, versatile player who had been with Manchester United since boyhood, turned out indiscriminately at full-back, half-back, and forward and played football in Italy, where he found himself with the Army at the end of the war. Technically, he would qualify, through his Dublin birth, as a "foreigner", although he played regularly for the (then) all-Ireland team which competed in the British Championship. Carey was a complete and studious footballer, admirable alike in his positioning and distribution.

The Swedes were a formidable pair, whose names were to resound through European football for a decade to come. Gunnar Nordahl, the dark and burly Norkopping centre-forward, was as mobile a player as Lawton; something of his power had been seen when Norkopping toured England, unbeaten, earlier that season. Gunnar Gren, from Goteborg, was a fair-haired, rangy, olive-skinned man of subtlety and clairvoyance; when he and Nordahl joined Milan, the following year, he quickly gained the nickname of *il professore*. The left-wing pair soon found their way to Italy, too: Faas Wilkes, a pale and lanky Dutchman with a mania for dribbling, Carl Praest, a cheerful, fair-haired Dane, who was one of the most talented and calm left-wingers of his day. Wilkes played for Internazionale, Praest for Juventus, where he teamed with the Rest of Europe centre-half, the swarthy Parola.

Parola, a strong but elegant player whose *rovesciata* – or aerial bicycle kick – always earned a cheer from the Italian crowd, was rather a surprising choice, for at this stage he was by no means unchallenged as his country's first choice. Moreover, Italy had a match to play the following day, against Hungary, from which Parola would inevitably be missing – press comment in Italy was a little wry.

Julie Da Rui, the French goalkeeper, was a brave, bouncing little man who had already been a stumbling block to England. Willi Steffen, a blond, perambulating alp, had been massively assisting Chelsea, as an amateur, while learning English; he had only just gone home. The team was completed by Ludl, a left-half from Czechoslovakia, Petersen, a large Danish right-back, and Lembrechts, a Belgian outside-right to whom might be applied that most solid of journalese encomia, "workmanlike". In charge of them was the smiling, enigmatic Jesse Carver, a Liverpudlian who was then coach of the Dutch national team; later he was to begin a ten-year love-hate relationship with Italian clubs.

The players gathered first in Amsterdam, then at the Scottish village of Troon. Communication was difficult, even impossible; "alas," Parola has written, "there was indeed an atmosphere of coldness among us." Parola, hungry for the Italian kitchen, suffered more than anyone, gaining the nickname of "*Parola pastasciutta*". There wasn't a strand of spaghetti to be found between Amsterdam and Troon. He whiled time away by trying to persuade Praest and Nordahl to join Juventus: Praest ultimately did, Nordahl did not.

The first training game went reasonably well; 70,000 spectators, in the Rotterdam stadium, watched the Europeans beat Holland 2–0; both the goals, ironically, were scored by Wilkes. "Yet we all had the feeling," wrote Parola (or his ghost), "that ours was essentially a fine mosaic, a rich complex of individualities, struggling to find a common language."

The sunny afternoon arrived: the great, terraced bowl of Hampden Park was almost full. Yet although the British team was to play in Scotland's dark blue, there was none of that tension and passion in the air which accompanies a match against England. Europe played in light blue. The teams lined up: Great Britain – Swift (Manchester City and England); Hardwick (capt.) (Middlesbrough and England); Hughes (Birmingham City and Wales); Macaulay (Brentford and Scotland); Vernon (West Bromwich Albion and Ireland); Burgess (Tottenham Hotspur and Wales); Matthews (Stoke City and England); Mannion (Middlesbrough and England); Lawton (Chelsea and England); Steel (Morton and Scotland); Liddell (Liverpool and Scotland).

The referee was a Southampton headmaster, Mr. George Reader.

For just over twenty minutes, Europe held out, showed signs of integration, and the game was open. Matthews, shuffling and accelerating his inimitable way past Steffen, fired the first real shot, an event as rare as a total eclipse; the joys of goal-making had long since outweighed those of scoring. But Da Rui saved that, and soon it was Europe's turn, Carey mounting the attack with a searching, typical cross-field pass.

Matthews, indeed, was responding to the occasion, inspired, as always, by the size of the huge crowd. What could honest, heavy Steffen hope to do with him, as he swerved and feinted, changed pace, swayed his body to the left and took the ball to the right, in that unique manner of his? Better backs had tried and failed miserably; and Steffen, in any case, was by nature and disposition a *Swiss* back, used to playing in the middle of the field, not out on the cold expanse of the wing. Once, he pushed Matthews in the penalty area, and the guillotine hung suspended; but Reader shook his head, and the game went on.

Europe found new heart; Lembrechts sped his functional way down the wing, and his cross flashed across the goal. But Swift, responsive to the occasion as Matthews, was untroubled. Little Steel, bouncing about the field, like a schoolboy among these famous veterans, ran on to Mannion's cross and shot past Da Rui; into the net, it seemed. But no, Petersen was there, on the line, to head the ball away.

It was Mannion, indeed, who was the surprise, his fair head everywhere, now moving neatly past his man, now darting for goal, now setting Matthews in motion, with an exquisite series of passes. In the twenty-first minute, Steel returned his compliment by gliding a pass through the defence to him. Mannion was on to it, Parola raced in, Ludl sprawled in an attempted tackle, Da Rui plunged for the point-blank shot; but the ball was home.

And yet – curiously indeed, in retrospect – this goal spurred Europe to equalise. Praest, who complained to me years later that he never had a pass from Wilkes, dribbled his casual, clever way past Hardwick on the goal line, beat him again – and again – for good measure, then gave Nordahl an easy goal. For the next ten minutes, an illusion was in the air; the illusion of a European rally. Parola, all power and elegance, was holding up Lawton, while Gren and Wilkes were tormenting the British defence.

Perhaps it might have been a different story had not Ludl panicked, handled a ball he had no need to handle, and given away a penalty, from which Mannion scored. Within a minute, Steel had run on, with Europe's defence retreating before him, waiting for the pass – only for the little Scot to unleash a thundering, dipping shot from twenty yards, which was past Da Rui before he could sense danger.

That was the end of Europe. Another two minutes, and Mannion sent the ball past Da Rui; Lawton ran in to kick it into the net, just before it crossed the line. Thus, at half-time, Britain led 4-1, an achievement which the crowd met with tepid indifference; blue jerseys they might be, but they were not Scotland's.

In the second half, there were two more goals – and both for Britain. Now it was the turn of Macaulay to show his paces, breaking up attacks with his fierce, firm tackling, blending perfectly with Mannion and Matthews.

Mannion was still unstoppable; once, he was pushed in the back – no penalty – once, he shot against a post. Swift jumped briskly to a shot by Nordahl, and flung himself at Wilkes' feet; but the die was cast, and everybody knew it.

Sixteen minutes from time, the unhappy Parola put through his own goal; he has described it in a plainly ghosted article (Great Britain are throughout referred to as "the whites" – the England colours): "Da Rui, alas, tired and demoralised, didn't anticipate my intentions, and allowed my very simple pass back to escape him: an 'own goal.' I could have wept and yelled with rage."

All one awaited now was a characteristic goal by Lawton; the one he had poached was grossly inadequate to his stature. And at last, after a flurry of close things, he got it, going up, up to soar above Da Rui, and head in Matthews' centre. 6–1; a famous victory, which had beyond doubt been Mannion's match.

In retrospect, the victory has grown in stature. At the time, it was too easily dismissed: first, on the mythical grounds of our natural superiority; second, on those of Europe's heterogeneity. But other European teams were to visit these islands and prove that great footballers can find a common language, whatever their provenance.

Moreover, one was also to learn, in retrospect, how many great players were included in the 1947 European team. Da Rui, Parola, Gren, Wilkes, Nordahl, Praest – not to mention Carey – were all to establish themselves as classic footballers. But, by the same token, so were Swift, Macaulay, Matthews, Mannion, Lawton, all of whom developed in the pre-war game, and none of whom found an adequate successor. Indeed, a match which seemed, when it was played, to confirm the power of British football in fact marked its brilliant sunset. It was certainly a landmark; one which has grown bulkier and more suggestive with the years.

*   *   *

If the supremacy of British football had by then become a legend, it was at least a legend which once had factual basis. By contrast, the pursuit of the British White Hope seems that of an *ignis fatuus*, a very folk myth, with its roots in the unconscious desires of the people, and the highly conscious desires of newspaper circulation departments. The development of the myth is significantly uniform. First, inevitably, the arrival of the new, young heavyweight, crushing all British opposition in his path. Local celebrity, qualified adulation. Next, a bout or two against Americans, always in Britain, each successfully overcome. Third, the Initial Disappointment: once more, against an American, often encountered in America. This gives way to the Period of Hope, in which it is conclusively, if variously, proved that the British Hope was not beaten fair and square. The referee was biased, he (the Hope) was butted above the eye, he wasn't fully fit, the American rules are different, he was thrust into the fight too early. There follows the Period of Rehabilitation, in which the Hope defeats one or two other moderate Americans, and is again pronounced to be "ready for a crack at the title." He is given his crack at the title – or, perhaps, at a favoured challenger – and is annihilated. From this point, the sequence may differ: the Hope may now be written off, or there can ensue a Period of Qualified Optimism, brought to an end by another American, or by an emergent New British White Hope.

The intriguing aspect of Bruce Woodcock's story is that, years after the fists of Baksi and Savold ground him to powder, one is tantalised. One can't be sure that, *had* things gone a little differently, he might not have fulfilled all that was predicted for him; might even, *mirabile dictu*, have won the world title. *If* his head had not clashed with Mauriello's; *if* he had not walked into that jaw-breaking "sucker punch" from Baksi; *if* he hadn't driven that truck into a tree . . . I suppose his fate would still have been the same, but there remains that troubling grain of uncertainty.

He was from the first a solidly appealing figure, his humble Yorkshire origins catering to all those Northern-superiority fantasies which George Orwell has laid bare. His father, Sam, was a miner, in and out of the pit during the depression years, afflicted by "miner's eye," for which he drew a disability pension. Young Bruce was a Boy Scout, an inveterate boy scrapper, a sturdy support to the family from his earliest years. Not only did he work for three and sixpence a day, lugging potatoes in the market; he toured the workingmen's clubs when he was seven years old with another seven-year-old called Micky Glennon – boxing exhibitions for money. For this, he wore an old blue pair of bathing trunks and two pairs of stockings – the family was too poor to buy him proper boots.

By 1939, he was working as a fitter for the London and North-Eastern Railway, and was one of the best amateur cruiserweights in the country;

indeed, he came near to winning a European Championship. When the war came, his work kept him out of the Army, and he was directed to an arms factory in Manchester, where he was recommended to a well-known manager, Tom Hurst. Woodcock twice lost his way, arrived at Hurst's house in darkness, and was sourly greeted by an unshaven man in a dressing-gown: Hurst, recovering from influenza. Their partnership for all that was to prove an apparently warm and harmonious one. Hurst persuaded him – with little difficulty – to turn professional, after Woodcock, according to the legend, had flattened Hurst's prize Irish pugilist in the gymnasium. His father was delighted, his mother anxious. "Tom," wrote Woodcock later, "has been like a second father to me." There was even, he claimed, a certain telepathy between them; thoughts would flash across the ring.

Woodcock made his professional debut at the Albert Hall in January 1942, by which time he was twenty-two, a relatively late age for a debutant. He knocked out a fighter called ex-Stoker Clarke in the third round, collected £25 for the performance, and went joyfully home with his father. He was still no more than a cruiserweight – 12 stone 4 – although he was fighting heavies. When, at Belle Vue, Manchester, he met a 19-stone colossus called George Davis, a woman stood up on her ringside seat and cried, "Take that baby out!" But the baby jumped two feet in the air in the second round, landed his punch on that elevated chin, and won by a knock-out.

By the end of 1942, he was Northern Area cruiserweight champion. In July 1945 he became heavyweight champion of Britain and the British Empire, knocking out poor old Jack London in the sixth round, on the Tottenham Hotspur football ground.

Briefly though he held the title, London's story was touched with a certain romantic pathos. He was a struggling, second-rate fighter, hard put to it at times to make a living for his family, whose career at the end was suddenly touched with glory. No one, after all, could take away from him the fact that he had once been Champion. It was a life and a situation which his namesake would have appreciated.

There were 38,000 at White Hart Lane where Woodcock, David again to London's Goliath, was giving away three stone: twelve stone seven, to the huge, bald London's fifteen stone eight. London, as Woodcock knew from having observed him, was a dangerous man to underrate. There was nothing graceful about the ponderous, crouching, almost Neanderthal style, but his defence was good, his jaw tucked in behind his shoulder, and he could move faster than one was entitled to expect.

For this occasion, he had decided to make Woodcock bring the fight to him. As the bell went for each round, he merely took a step or two from his corner, and calmly awaited the offensive. His left shoulder was cocked higher up than ever; a tribute to the fame of Woodcock's right hand. Thus, it was Woodcock's left hand which dictated the fight at first – as London allowed him to dictate it – till the Champion at last unleashed a massive right swing, which Woodcock hurriedly ducked inside.

After five unhappy rounds, the giant was goaded, and came thundering out of his corner, eyes hard, biting at his gumshield. A tremendous punch caught Woodcock in the stomach, but he tightened his abdominal muscles, took the blow, and didn't sway. Another mighty punch tore through Woodcock's guard and broke his nose. Woodcock bled, but endured. In his corner, Hurst whispered to him that his chance would come, that London would "want a breather."

In the next round – the sixth – provoked by a left to the nose, London at last dropped his mighty shoulder, Woodcock's right flashed in – and London was down. He was up again at two, but the fight was over: a feint, another fulminating right, and Hurst was shouting from the ringside, "That's done it! Step right back!"

Now followed the period of Hope. There was no one in Britain to extend Woodcock. Opponents went down quickly and regularly, in a handful of rounds. "It was a nice fight while it lasted," he said, after beating the Irish champion, Thornton, in three rounds. "How good is Bruce Woodcock?" asked the *Star*, that November. "We know Woodcock is easily the best of the British heavyweights and a worthy champion, but he has not yet been really tested."

The moment of truth arrived in May 1946. Woodcock, at last, was off to America, to fight the first opponent of standing he had met so far: a reflection less on himself than on the war years, and on the post-war state of British boxing. This opponent was a plump Italo-American called Tami Mauriello, 22 years old to Woodcock's 24, but infinitely, immeasurably more experienced, in the brutally hard school of American fighting. He stood 5 ft. 11 in. to Woodcock's 6 ft. 0½ in., but outweighed Woodcock by 14 stone to 13 stone 6½ lbs.

The railwaymen of Doncaster sped Woodcock on his way with a radiogram: just the thing, said the newspapers, for a homebody like Bruce. Equally true to the projected image Woodcock announced that he would buy a hat in America for his fiancée. He took up his training quarters at Bear Mountain outside New York. A posse of American boxing writers, those weather-beaten cynics, hardened by the battles of a thousand other men, descended on his camp, and found him wanting. "Woodcock," said Mr. Jim Jennings of the *New York Mirror*, "is a slugger, pure and simple – mostly simple. He's as easy to hit as an elephant at two paces. His defence is poor, he carries his hands too low, and is wide open when he leads." His first sparring partner, a merchant sailor called Barrett, tapped him on the nose and drew blood. Hurst, half tearfully, assured the boxing writers that "Bruce is fifty per cent better than what you have just seen."

And so to the fight. "If Mauriello's cornered or cracked," an American boxing manager had warned Woodcock, "he'll start his block-busting stuff. If that happens, the best thing to do is to get on your bicycle and keep out of the way."

Woodcock, alas, heeded him only too well. The aggressive Mauriello was sent hurtling back against the ropes in the second round. Woodcock, so he later said, remembered the advice and stood back – and Mauriello was left to fight on. Again, in the fourth round, Mauriello was in direst straits. Cary Grant, at the ringside, leaped on his seat to cry, "Woodcock, Woodcock, you've got him! I'm from England, too!" Woodcock heard, but did not act. The next round, his head clashed with Mauriello's. He reeled back, dazed, four left swings put him down, and his left leg crumpled beneath him. It was over. Bad luck, but above all, inexperience, had cost him the fight. The Americans dismissed him as still another British "horizontal heavyweight."

The rest of 1946, however, was propitious, showing that judgement to be harsh and unfair. Woodcock outpointed Freddie Mills, the British cruiserweight champion, on June 4th – though he finished the more badly marked – knocked out Renet of France at Belle Vue, Manchester, for the European title, and then, in September, knocked out Gus Lesnevich, the cruiser champion of the world, at Harringay. A powerful right on an already damaged eye put Lesnevich down and out in the eighth round. Illusions stirred again.

Alas, they were not to last long. On April 15th, 1947, came Joe Baksi, a title eliminator, and the affair of the "sucker punch." Once more, Woodcock was giving weight away to an American: 13–10 to Baksi's 15–2. He had already seen Baksi defeat Freddie Mills and – like every other boxer in history – felt sure that he would win. The first round had scarcely begun when Woodcock, deciding Baksi wasn't placed to deliver a good left swing, decided to try a right, and feinted with his left, to prepare the ground. At that moment, Baksi's own left came over like the judgement of God, smashed Woodcock's jaw, and landed him on his back.

It was a pity that the fight did not stop then, instead of dragging brutally on for another six rounds. But only after it was over was the injury diagnosed. Where and how did Baksi get the power? It remains a mystery still. A doctor who examined Woodcock told him he had seen only two men with their temporal bones thus damaged. One had been hit by a sledgehammer, the other by a truck.

The blow—it was clear at the time—must have been traumatic. It was all very well for Woodcock and his fans to say that it would not, could not, happen again; lucky punch or not, freak or not, it had landed, and a champion with pretensions to the world title had no right to let it land.

There followed months of despair. Working in a quarry, to refresh himself, Woodcock knocked a chip of stone into his eye. He had an operation, and another, the consequence of Baksi's punch, as much as the chip of stone. His weight went up to 19 stone, his impetus had gone.

He was back, though, the following year, sweating off the weight in a Turkish bath home-made by his father, knocking out an American called Lee Oma in four rounds, an anti-climactic return. Next, in December 1948, the month in which he was quietly married, it was Lee Savold, yet another American, yet another anticlimax. Woodcock boxed carefully to plan, he said, on the retreat, went down to a low blow in the fourth, and won on a disqualification. Hope had almost gone now.

"Why has Bruce failed?" asked the *Daily Mirror*. "Because he has learnt nothing. He has the same style, the same training set-up, the same outlook on life as when he was an amateur."

Ominous and significant indeed that even the popular Press should now turn its back upon him. But 1949 began well enough, with a third round knock-out of Johnny Ralph, South Africa's champion, in Johannesburg, a knock-out of Freddie Mills, and the renewed mirage of a title fight. Now it was more than an eliminator; for Joe Louis had retired, nominating two other negroes, Ezzard Charles and Joe Walcott, to fight for his title. Jack Solomons, the London promoter, leaped into the breach, to announce a rival fight between Woodcock and Lee Savold. It was an ersatz, unconvincing one, perhaps, but it got the recognition of the British Boxing Board of Control.

The fight was arranged for White City, on September 6th. On August 3rd Woodcock, driving a lorry full of training equipment, skidded on a bend in the road a few miles from Doncaster, ran into a tree, and damaged a right eye which was never to be sound again.

What in the name of logic, asked the hard Americans, was he doing driving a truck, a few weeks from a title fight? John Lardner, in *Newsweek*, devoted his pungent column to an account of how Woodcock had taken on, and been routed by, a British oak. It was June 6th, 1950, before the two fighters at last climbed into the White City ring, and by then, though Europe, New York, and Boston joined with Britain in recognising the fight, its validity was a pale and fragile thing. "I'll flay him alive," said Woodcock, in a newspaper headline, but he lasted a mere four rounds.

At first, he flattered to deceive. For a couple of rounds the embers of hope seemed faintly to glow again. But, though Woodcock forced the fight, Savold was shrugging off his hardest punches. By the third, the tide was turning. In the fourth, a short, vicious right split Woodcock's eyebrow, drew a well of blood – and that was the end. The towel was thrown in by Woodcock's brother, Billy, at the end of the round.

On November 14th, at Earls Court, the last illusion toppled. Jack Gardner, a ponderous, moustached heavyweight from Market Harborough, closed Woodcock's left eye, and took his title, in the eleventh round.

If, if, if. *If* – above all – Woodcock had had the experience, had spent those easy war-time years fighting in the clubs and halls of America, losing as well as winning, taking hidings as well as giving them. *If* he had arrived in boxing five years later, at a period when British boxers could start younger, and take on American opponents earlier. As it was, he returned to Yorkshire to run a public house. The British Board, thank goodness, turned down his pleas to make a come-back.

* * *

The London Olympic Games of 1948, the first for twelve years, have in retrospect something fetchingly placid about them. The absence of Russians and Germans deprived them at once of both colour and controversy. No Russo-American duel, no roaring, drilled, and disciplined phalanx of Germans, with their mechanical "hoi-hoi-hois" and "rah-rah-rahs", responding to their leader's straw hat.

Britain had not held an Olympiad since 1908. Wembley, that great glorified paradise for greyhounds, took the Olympiad in its stride, twenty-five years' experience of sports events behind it. A new track was laid down within weeks of the Games. Much play was made with the Opening Ceremony, when a lithe, inevitably blond, young Englishman – clearly chosen for his resemblance to Apollo – carried the sacred flame on its last lap, round the Stadium, firing (splendid anachronism!) the gas "fountain" which would keep it burning throughout the Games.

Though the Olympics have acquired over the years a plethora of other sports they are still essentially an athletics festival. Thus, they take on a curiously ambiguous position in Britain, where athletics – until Olympic year – is no more than a minor sport, watched and supported by the few. In later years, with the sudden rise of gilded milers, matters briefly changed. But in 1948 the war was too near for the New Wave of athletes to have arrived, and Britain's prospects were poor. Indeed the most substantial hopes lay in a coloured West Indian, Macdonald Bailey, a popular figure, allegedly the victim of prejudice from time to time. But Bailey was beset by muscle trouble, came sixth in the 100 metres, nowhere in the 200.

Athletically, it was America's Olympiad: 12 gold medals, to Sweden's 5, Holland's 4. But no American captured the imagination as did Mrs. Fanny Blankers-Koen, the flying Dutchwoman, with her gold medals in the 100 and 200 metres, 80 metres hurdles, and 4 × 100 metres. The consolations for Britain were marginal: 4 silver medals on the track. There was little here for the sporting public to savour.

Besides the anticlimactic finale to Bruce Woodcock's career, 1950 was a traumatic year for British sport in two other fields.

It was the year of the West Indian cricket tour, of calypso, Lord Beginner, Ramadhin and Valentine, of West Indians streaming in joyful triumph across the hallowed turf of Lord's after the Second Test had been won.

"The bowling was super fine . . . Ramadhin and Valentine!" Both were spin bowlers, Sonny Ramadhin a tiny tricksy fellow of just twenty, whose cunning leg-breaks were often unplayable that summer, Alf Valentine taller and graver, a few days older, who did almost as much damage at the other end. Then the batsmen: the graceful Worrell, the calm Stoll-meyer, the colossally powerful Everton Weekes, Clyde Walcott the wicket-keeper and run-maker. They won the rubber 3–1, investing a tired old game with new colour and excitement.

This was a stimulus. But the third disaster of 1950, England's World Cup defeat at Belo Horizonte in Brazil by the United States, was an unmitigated humiliation. It was the "impossible" result, a win for a scratch side, captained by a rejected English Third Division player, Eddie McIlvenny, who had been given a free transfer by Wrexham. So sure were the Americans of impending catastrophe that they revelled into the small hours of the morning of the game. But, on the bumpy little ground, an England team which included Tom Finney, Stanley Morten-sen – electric hero of a marvellous 4–0 victory over Italy in Turin in 1948 – and Billy Wright made nothing of endless chances. In the second half a cross by the American left-half was headed in by Gaetjens, a

Haitian centre-forward, for the only goal of the match. On the terraces, the amazed and ecstatic Brazilians burned newspapers, England's funeral pyre. It was the freak to end all freaks, that "couldn't" have happened again if the game had been replayed a hundred times. But England lost 1–0 to Spain also, fell out of the first World Cup for which they'd ever entered, and left Uruguay to beat their old rivals Brazil in the final.

Thus, in mid-century, British sport stood bare of prestige. The nation that had given cricket, football, and the Queensberry Rules to the world had at last to face the fact that in these and other sports the world had much to teach it. Yet everywhere delusions of grandeur persisted, to obscure this fact. The Fifties were to bring a new crop of delusions to replace the tattered old ones of the Forties, and to delay still further in Britain recognition of the need for a realistic and modern approach to the internationalism of sport.

Perhaps, if there are analogies to be drawn, they should be drawn above all from the football match, Great Britain v The Rest of Europe. Football, in microcosm, is a remarkable mirror of national characteristics and aptitudes, while in the second place, unlike cricket, it is a game which involves Britain with almost the whole of the rest of the world. By contrast, cricket remains for ever a family affair; even the defeat by West Indies was mitigated by that fact.

Our football supremacy—or rather, our belief in it, motivated by a splendid isolation from World Cups—seemed to be confirmed at Hampden Park. The three corners of Europe had come in arms against us, and had been pulverised. Indeed, looking back on that European team, with the knowledge of a more sophisticated hindsight, a later acquaintance with its stars, it does look very strong indeed.

Thus, the win gave birth to a further six years of illusions, for if Scotland's unbeaten record at home went late in 1950, to the Austrians, England's survived till 1953, when Hungary played them into the ground at Wembley. You couldn't laugh *that* one off, but you could—fortified by that win against Europe, fortified by England's 4–0 victory over Italy in Turin the following year—laugh off most defeats abroad, even dismiss the 1950 World Cup, and its disappointments. Brazil, after all, was thousands of miles away, and were we not playing out of season? Besides, the defeat by America was so obviously a freak and a fiasco, never to be repeated, that perhaps it tended to obscure the real lessons of the tournament.

We had thrashed Europe, ergo we were supreme. It was a dangerous, costly complacency.

8

SIR STAFFORD CRIPPS
The dollar crises and devaluation

DAVID MARQUAND

David Marquand was born in 1934. He went to Emmanuel School, London, thence into the R.A.F., where he learnt Russian. He won a Demyship to Magdalen College, Oxford, and took a First in History. After research at Oxford and teaching at Berkeley, California, he was a leader-writer on *The Guardian* from 1959–62. He is now a research Fellow of St. Antony's College, Oxford, and is working on a biography of Ramsay Macdonald. He writes regularly for *Encounter*, *New Statesman*, and *New Leader*. Married, one child.

SIR STAFFORD CRIPPS

David Marquand

"ANNUS HORRENDUS." For the Labour Government as a whole, and for the Chancellor of the Exchequer as an individual, Dalton's description of the year 1947 could hardly be bettered. The year began with a fuel crisis, which momentarily crippled the industrial recovery programme and put nearly two million people out of work. Four months after the fuel crisis had ended, the country staggered into the so-called convertibility crisis, in which 700 million precious dollars were lost in a month.

The crises themselves were painful enough, and to those alert enough to discern it the logic behind them was more painful still. In 1945 Britain had emerged from the war as one of the "Big Three", bankrupt but unbowed, and she had elected a Government pledged to carry through a social revolution. By 1947 it was becoming clear that Britain's status as a Great Power was no more than a polite fiction, that her loss of strength had created a power vacuum which others would fill, and that the country faced a desperate struggle for solvency, in which either the Government's social aims, or its inhibitions against pursuing them wholeheartedly, might have to be sacrificed. It was in 1947 that British troops left Greece, that India became independent, and that the Marshall Plan was launched. It was also in 1947 that the easy-going era of Daltonian finance came to an end, and that Sir Stafford Cripps was appointed Chancellor of the Exchequer.

His appointment was, of course, the result of an accident. No one could have foreseen Dalton's fall, for it was due to a momentary indiscretion rather than to any difference of principle with his colleagues. On the afternoon of November 12th, 1947, Dalton was on his way to the chamber of the House of Commons to deliver his fourth Budget, when he stopped for a few minutes' conversation with the lobby correspondent of *The Star*. The two men discussed the speech which Dalton was about to make. Later that afternoon, *The Star* published an accurate forecast of some Budget proposals, in an edition that reached the streets a short time before the proposals themselves were officially announced in the House. Next day,

Dalton resigned; and that evening it was announced that Cripps was to succeed him.

The episode was accidental, yet there was a kind of logic about it. The fact is that Dalton's blunder came at an opportune time for the Government. The two great crises of 1947 had so far produced disappointingly little in the way of scapegoats; and Dalton's indiscretion made him the ideal candidate for that edifying role. The fuel crisis of January and February, it is true, was due in the main to acts of God. But it created a general impression of Governmental uncertainty, which was reinforced during the summer.

Yet even the summer crisis cannot fairly be laid at Dalton's door. The true authors of the 1947 balance of payments crisis were the convertibility clauses of the American Loan agreement of 1945. In order to obtain a loan at all, the British Government had been made to promise that, a year after the agreement came into force, sterling would be made freely convertible for all current transactions. No one on the British side liked this commitment. But after six years of war, in which over £1,000 millions of assets had been sold and over £13,000 millions of external liabilities had been incurred, Britain was in no position to bargain. No matter that her losses had been incurred in the common cause, nor that her efforts had been proportionately far greater than those of the United States. Now that peace had come, the Americans were in no mood for sentiment. It was made plain to the British negotiators that no convertibility clause would mean no loan – and they already knew that no loan would mean national disaster.

President Truman ratified the loan agreement on July 15th, 1946. On July 15th, 1947, the convertibility clause came into effect. The result was what might have been expected. Already the British gold and dollar reserve had been ebbing away at an alarming rate, partly because of the effect of the fuel crisis on British exports and partly because of the rise of American wholesale prices. Convertibility turned the drain into a flood. During the second quarter of 1947, the average weekly drawing rate had been $75 millions. In July it was $115 millions. In the four weeks before August 23rd it was $150 millions. On August 6th, the Government announced a programme of cuts and austerities. The miners were to work an extra half-hour a day; food imports from hard currency areas were to be cut by £12 millions a month; the basic petrol ration was to be reduced by one-third. On August 20th, full convertibility was suspended, having lasted for little more than a single disastrous month. On August 23rd, the meat ration was cut, public dinners were restricted, foreign travel was suspended, and the basic petrol ration was abolished. Dalton's emergency budget in November was designed to cut down internal spending still further.

The Opposition pounced on these disasters with the ferocity traditionally shown by the Gentlemen of England when they believe that the country is in the hands of their social inferiors. On August 16th, Winston Churchill made a speech on the radio in which he forecast a still lower standard of living, and the death or dispersal of a large proportion of the population. These prophecies could be discounted; but at the same time the Government was widely criticised in the Press for lack of drive, even by papers like the *Manchester Guardian* which had generally shown it at least a benevolent neutrality. Even before Dalton's fall, the growing sense of *malaise* in the country had been reflected in a minor political crisis and a major Government reshuffle. Towards the end of July, Dalton and Cripps had tried to persuade Bevin to depose Attlee and become Prime Minister himself. Their blandishments were rebuffed. The end result of a tortuous series of negotiations between leading members of the Cabinet, in which Attlee showed once again that he was easily the cleverest politician in the Government, was that on September 29th Cripps became Minister of Economic Affairs, taking over some of the co-ordinating and planning functions previously discharged by Herbert Morrison.

Cripps's appointment was popular. But it was not popular enough to prevent the Government from losing 652 seats in the municipal elections on November 1st, or to remove a widespread impression that tougher measures and stronger men were needed at the Treasury. Even before his resignation, Dalton's stock had fallen in relation to Cripps's. In September, the *Economist* praised Cripps as "one of the few Ministers who has always seen clearly what was coming on the road the country is travelling"; and the sentiment was general.

In part this was because of Dalton's monetary policy. "Cheap money" was widely attacked as inflationary; and although the criticisms made of it were probably too sweeping, the best that can be said for it in retrospect is that it did no real harm. But the main reason for the growing reputation of Cripps and the sinking reputation of Dalton was the temperamental contrast between them. As Mr. Charles Curran once remarked, the British people like their leaders to resemble either bishops or bookies. Dalton was a bookie. Cripps, on the other hand, was pre-eminently a bishop; and in November 1947 a bishop was just what was required. His appointment as Chancellor of the Exchequer was greeted with enthusiasm.

Even Mr. Osbert Peake, speaking for the Opposition, congratulated the Government on having sent for the plumber who was needed.

In 1947, these sentiments seemed natural, almost conventional. Ten years earlier, coming from either front bench, they would have seemed proof of mental disorder. British politics are generally conducted on the principle of Buggins's turn; and the most striking feature of Cripps's political career is that he was not Buggins. Out of the twenty years he spent in the House of Commons, eight were spent in violent conflict with the leaders of his own party – and six more were spent as a member of no party at all. Cripps the rebel had, in fact, a longer innings than Cripps the Chancellor; and Cripps the Chancellor is incomprehensible without first examining his stormy political past.

The first fact to notice is that he came into politics late. He was born in 1889 of an old and wealthy family. His father and grandfather were both distinguished lawyers; and he himself was called to the Bar in 1913 after a scientific education. Until the late twenties most of his energies went on his successful and lucrative legal practice. The remainder was spent, not on politics, but on the Anglican Church. It is true that his father, Lord Parmoor, was Lord President of the Council in the Labour Government of 1924. But although Cripps himself was attracted during the twenties by the moderate socialism of Ramsay MacDonald and the Labour Party leadership, he delayed some time before taking the plunge into active politics. At thirty-nine he was not even a member of the Labour Party; at forty he was Solicitor-General in the second Labour Government. The election of 1931, in which he was one of the few Labour ex-Ministers who held their seats, thrust him still further into a precocious prominence. From then on, he was one of the leading members of the Labour Party, and one of the idols of the rank-and-file.

Like most reforming parties, the Labour Party has always been torn by divisions over doctrine and personality. In the 1930s these divisions were particularly acute. MacDonald's alleged treachery in 1931 had created a bitter suspicion of leadership as such. What MacDonald had done, other leaders could do. Better, then, to have no leaders at all – or, if there must be leaders, at least subject them to searching and incessant scrutiny. It is doubtful whether Cripps was ever completely carried away by this reasoning, though he certainly profited from it in his conflicts with the party leadership. He undoubtedly did accept, however, another and equally embarrassing ideological legacy of the 1931 crisis. This was the widespread belief that the fall of the second Labour Government had been engineered, in some mysterious way, by the "capitalists"; that any future Labour Government would face equally nefarious "capitalist" plots; and that in order to defeat them it would be necessary to by-pass, or at least to overhaul, the entire Parliamentary and constitutional machine.

In the early thirties, most of Cripps's conflicts with the leaders of his party were fought on this issue. The lesson of 1931, he wrote in the Socialist League pamphlet *Can Socialism come by Constitutional Methods?*, was that "the ruling classes will go to almost any length to defeat parliamentary action"; and he concluded that the first decision of a newly-elected Labour Government must be to arm itself with an Emergency Powers Act. But the objects and nature of Emergency Powers remained obscure. At times, Cripps talked of the need to prevent a "capitalist dictatorship", speculated on the possibility that a Socialist Government might have to stay in power illegally, and even warned of armed conflict. At other times, he stressed the moderation of his proposals. "Emergency Powers," he told the 1933 conference of the Labour Party, "have no relation to dictatorship whatsoever," and he claimed that they were needed only to scotch the machinations of "financial strikers." His purpose, he insisted, was to combat the "temptations of Fascism and Communism" and to satisfy the electorate that "using its constitutional and democratic methods we are capable of bringing about the transformation which it is our desire to bring about."

His stand on foreign and defence policy was marked by a similar lack of clarity. In the great debates on sanctions and rearmament which divided the Labour movement in the mid-thirties, there were two logical positions: Lansbury's and Bevin's. According to Lansbury, war was wrong and therefore sanctions and rearmament must be wrong. According to Bevin, sanctions and rearmament were necessary as the only way to stop Fascism before it was too late.

Cripps hovered between these two arguments in a state of dialectical schizophrenia. He was not a pacifist; he did not underestimate the Fascist threat; he was prepared in principle to resist Fascism by force. But although he wanted Fascism to be resisted, he was not prepared to give the British Government the wherewithal to do so. Cripps objected to sanctions against Mussolini if the price was to strengthen Baldwin. "There is no man in this Conference who more cordially detests Mussolini and all his acts than I do," he told the Labour Party conference in 1935. "If I could feel that British imperialism had turned over a new leaf . . . then my difficulties and doubts would largely disappear, but . . . the driving force behind our Government, overpowering all humanitarian and liberal sentiments, is, and must be, the urgent necessities of the capitalistic economic system itself."

It followed that rearmament, far from helping to defeat Fascism, would merely strengthen imperialism. In 1937 he referred to the support given to rearmament by the leaders of the Labour Party in the following terms: "Let us, if we seek praise from the capitalist press for our statesmanship, become organisers of the rearmament campaign for our rulers and recruiting sergeants for our militarists. Then we shall be able to ape the antics of the Labour Front in Germany, safely ensconced as lackeys of the capitalist system." But if the leaders of the Labour Party were capitalist lackeys, the party must be given new leaders and invigorated with new blood. As Cripps put it: "We must concentrate within it every available element of working-class political activity."

These passages are taken from a speech defending the campaign for a "united front" of the Labour Party, the Communist Party, and the I.L.P. It was on this issue that Cripps's most savage battles with the leadership were fought, and on the superficially related issue of the Popular Front that he was actually expelled from the Labour Party. Yet his arguments on these issues were more convincing than they had been on emergency powers, or on rearmament as such. Nothing has been easier since 1945 than to point out the dangers of a united front with the Communists. In 1937 it was less easy. The intellectual and moral climate of the 1930s cannot be understood unless one remembers the pitiful record of contemporary liberalism and democratic socialism. The great Social Democratic Party of Germany had scarcely lifted a finger to stop the rise of Hitler. The Socialist Prime Minister of France seemed powerless to help his brother Socialists in Spain. In the late thirties the Communists could present themselves as the only determined anti-Fascist force in Europe. The intellectuals who joined them, or who worked for close association with them, were duped. But there are times when it is as honourable to be duped as it is to keep one's head.

The real weakness of Cripps's united front campaign was not that he made common cause with the Communist Party, but that he did so in pursuit of the wrong aims. The united front, he declared, would "reverse the definite and well-defined drift towards a complaisant reformism" which had crippled the Labour Party. It would "galvanise" the workers, whereas the party leaders had been content to accept the capitalist framework. It would act on the logic of the 1931 crisis, which showed that capitalism could no longer concede the piecemeal demands of a gradualist party. It would resist the imperialist designs of the National Government, and the rearmament plans which those designs had entailed. Couched in these terms, the united front campaign was, of course, a monstrous irrelevance; and the party leaders could rightly argue that it would make a Socialist victory less likely rather than more.

The same did not apply to the Popular Front. On the Popular Front, Cripps was for once in the right—yet it was on the Popular Front that his relations with his party reached breaking point. In his early united front days, Cripps denounced rearmament as imperialist. By the summer of 1938 he was denouncing the Government for failing to rearm fast enough. The united front campaign was based upon the assumption that no "capitalist" could be trusted to resist Fascism. The Popular Front was to be an alliance of Socialists and "capitalists", formed to resist Fascism more effectively. To supporters of the united front, the victory of Socialism at home seemed an indispensable prelude to the defeat of Fascism abroad. The Popular Fronters were prepared to postpone Socialism inside Britain for the sake of a change in British foreign policy.

These inconsistencies put Cripps in a vulnerable position. The party leaders were now able to attack him on his own ground, as someone who was cravenly prepared to dilute his Socialist faith for the sake of power. Their argument was politically effective, for there is nothing the average member of any party hates more than the sight of a clever man changing his mind. Moreover, the case for a Popular Front rested on one of two assumptions: either that Labour had little hope of winning power on its own, or that the times were too grave to wait for the next election. Neither argument could be expected to appeal to a party machine whose *raison d'être* was the independent winning of power at parliamentary elections. In January 1939 the Labour Party executive rejected Cripps's memorandum on the Popular Front by seventeen votes to three. Cripps proceeded to circulate it to Labour M.P.s, constituency parties, and affiliated bodies. The executive ordered him to withdraw the memorandum and reaffirm his loyalty to the party, on pain of expulsion. He refused, and was duly expelled. In May the party conference upheld his expulsion by a majority of more than 1,500,000. He was out of the party for almost six years.

Cripps's character can be understood only in the light of his activities in the thirties. Yet the light they shed is singularly ambiguous. To his trade union colleagues on the Labour Party executive he was the quintessential intellectual; to the general public, he was the sea-green incorruptible of British Labour, a semi-revolutionary with leanings towards totalitarianism. It is clear that, except in the most superficial sense, the first of these descriptions is almost wholly misleading. Cripps had little of the true intellectual's restless passion for ideas, or his ability to penetrate beneath the surface of an argument to the assumptions beneath. The most obvious feature of his ideas was the zeal with which he applied them, not that with which he examined them.

Three characteristics marked his speeches and writings in the thirties: a rigid absolutism of doctrine, a notable lack of political imagination, and a lonely obstinacy which was, according to taste, either heroic or pig-headed. It might seem, therefore, that the picture of him as a revolutionary is the appropriate one. Yet even this is misleading. The first requirement of a successful revolutionary, as of any other political leader, is a grasp of political forces: an ability to smell the way the wind is blowing, to sense shifts in public opinion, and to gauge the weight of the different groups with which he has to deal. In these qualities, Cripps was remarkably deficient. The outstanding fact of European politics in the 1930s was the rise of Fascism, and the failure of the democracies to deal with it. Cripps, as a Left-wing Socialist, might have been expected to recognise this danger sooner than others did. In practice, the stand he took did little to resist it.

The explanation lies less in his quasi-Marxist ideology than in the way in which he interpreted it. Interpreted flexibly, Marxism might have furnished a more accurate guide to European politics in the thirties than that provided by any other political creed. But Cripps's Marxism was not interpreted flexibly. For much of the time he was more Royalist than the King: more doctrinaire than the Communist Party. His central assumptions in the thirties were that the logic of capitalism was bound to drive the National Government into imperialism, and that therefore Britain must not rearm until she had "a Workers' Government, as they have in Russia." It was the kind of reasoning which had led the German Communists in the Weimar Republic to regard the Social Democrats as a greater menace than the Nazis. The strange thing is that in the 1930s the Comintern showed a greater willingness to abandon it than Cripps did.

The truth is that Cripps was in no real sense a Marxist intellectual, and still less a revolutionary. The clue to his behaviour, in the thirties and later, lies in his education, his profession, and his religion. He was above all a distinguished lawyer and a devoted Churchman, with a scientific training. It has often been noticed that scientists, trained in the exact measurement of quantifiable data, are apt to make heavy weather of the nuances of human behaviour. The same applies, in a different way, to lawyers. The skills of a trial lawyer, adept at manipulating a jury, are not far removed from the skills of a politician. But Cripps was not that kind of lawyer. He shone at the precise and lucid presentation of legal arguments, and the handling of expert witnesses. He was, in fact, a lawyer's lawyer: more at home with a judge than with a jury. At that level, legal skills consist chiefly in the application of general principles to particular cases. It is a skill akin, in some ways, to that of the theologian. The framework is taken for granted; and great ingenuity is devoted to fitting the facts into it.

Here is the most important clue of all. To Cripps himself, the most significant and valuable part of his life was not politics or the law but the Christian Church. He went into politics in the first place primarily because he was convinced that it was through politics that God's work could best be done. Christians, he believed, must fight the forces of Evil and complacency in this world, and not wait passively for the next. "The truth is that we are living God's life here and now," he wrote in *Towards Christian Democracy* in 1945. "Whether good or bad, it is the life ordained by Him; it is His creation, and through it His purpose is constantly being served." Socialism, for him, was the practical expression of Christianity; and he attacked the Churches for compromising with society as it existed. It is in the light of this belief that the complexities of his politics can best be understood.

There is nothing new in a British politician, and especially a British politician of the Left, trying to do what he believes to be God's work. For generation after generation, British Radicalism has been enriched by the Nonconformist conscience. But Cripps did not belong to that tradition. He came of a different and more esoteric line: that of the Anglican conscience. The distinction is difficult to describe, but important to grasp. Nonconformity, in Britain, is on the whole democratic and plebeian: the Anglican Church is patrician, and in an important sense authoritarian. In recent years, at least, the Nonconformist conscience has stressed Works and adopted a rather robust and unsubtle attitude to the intricacies of Faith. For the Anglican conscience (though doubtless not for the average member of the Church of England), doctrine seems to have had a greater emotional significance. The difference is the difference between John Bright and Gladstone – or between Arthur Henderson and Cripps.

Cripps's religious beliefs showed themselves in two ways. In the first place, they help to explain the sweeping extremism with which each successive change of heart was expressed. It is a commonplace that a doctrinaire in one faith can become a doctrinaire in another. Cripps was no exception, only in his case there were two changes of doctrine, not one. In the early twenties, he was first and foremost a Churchman, with little interest in conventional politics. Hugh Gaitskell, then a schoolboy at Winchester, remembers Cripps telling him, the first time they met, that the "only hope" for the world was the union of Churches. By the thirties, the prescription had changed; but the single-mindedness of the dispenser remained. Now the "only hope" was the destruction of capitalism, and the purging of reformism from the Labour movement. After the war, the prescription changed again. Now it was national unity and class co-operation.

"Leadership and popularity often appear to be almost opposite," Cripps wrote in *Towards Christian Democracy*, "as can be seen in the life of Christ, and in those of the early Christians. Yet in the long run, moral leadership will justify itself with the people, not because it plays down to their momentary desires or emotions, but because it ultimately wins the support of all that is best in human nature." That passage is perhaps the most revealing Cripps ever wrote; and it illuminates both his greatest weakness and his greatest strength.

The cement of democracy is compromise. Aneurin Bevan once wrote that "democratic socialism is the child of relativist philosophy"; and the same is true of all democratic creeds. In all democratic institutions — whether nations or political parties — there is an implicit assumption that the method of settling disputes is more important than the content of the disputes, and that both sides in any controversy are prepared to admit the possibility that they may be mistaken. But if you believe that you are in politics to do God's work, and that your case is bound in the end to appeal to all that is best in human nature, such an admission is hard to make. For if your case appeals to the best, to what does your opponent's case appeal? And if you are doing God's work, whose is he doing? The answers are only too obvious; and they do not encourage a mood of philosophic doubt.

Yet in the end these attitudes were a source of strength. Cripps's confidence in the rightness of his own case made him an impossible subordinate and a difficult colleague. It also made him an inspiring leader who was in fact able to appeal, as he hoped, to the best in his listeners. Perhaps it was unfortunate that so many of the most idealistic people in the Labour movement followed him in the thirties rather than Bevin or Dalton. The fact remains that they followed him because he could appeal to their idealism in a way that Bevin and Dalton could not.

A party of the Left stands or falls on its ability to generate an intense moral commitment among its supporters. That can only be done by leaders who show intense moral convictions themselves – and the sad fact is that such leaders are unlikely to prove co-operative colleagues.

The same applies to a nation in an emergency. The Pitts, Lloyd Georges, and Churchills come to the fore in times of crisis, not because they make wiser decisions than their rivals, but because they are able to communicate to others their own intense belief in themselves. Such self-confidence usually comes from ambition. In Cripps's case it came from religion. Churchill's gibe is well-known: "There, but for the grace of God, goes God." Properly interpreted, however, the comment is a reluctant tribute to the only man in British politics who might conceivably have challenged Churchill as a national leader.

It is from this point of view that Cripps's record as Chancellor of the Exchequer must be judged. He became Chancellor at one of the most difficult moments of modern British economic history; and so far as the broad outlines of policy were concerned he was less an architect than a prisoner. In the schoolboy's vision of politics, statesmen are Great Men who take the Great Decisions that determine the course of history. In reality such decisions are taken by default more often than by design. No Minister is ever a free agent – and Cripps was less a free agent than most. The chief aims of his policy were determined for him by economic circumstance; for most of the time even the means were conditioned, within fairly narrow limits, by the political situation and the state of public opinion. Nevertheless, he was sometimes able to give public opinion a lead: and the direction in which he led it contrasted sharply with his own earlier career.

The Labour Government had four basic aims. It had to bring the country's balance of payments into equilibrium as quickly as possible, and to bridge the dollar gap. It had to maintain the standard of living of the British people at a tolerable level. It wished to play a leading part in world affairs, and had therefore to support armed forces of the appropriate size. Finally it had to remember that it was a *Labour* Government, pledged to carry through drastic social and economic reforms, and to defend the interests of the working-class. Of these four aims, only the last two allowed much room for manœuvre.

The export drive was not, as it was sometimes represented in the popular Press, an economist's whim: it was the condition of Britain's survival, and the necessary lodestar of Government policy. Any Government, of whatever political complexion, would have been forced to adopt a policy for exports substantially the same as the Labour Government's. Before the war, Britain had lived on her ancestors. She had exported less than she imported, but the balance had been made up by income from foreign investments made in the past. During the war that cushion had been removed. According to Dr. Balogh, Britain's net income from foreign investments fell from £175 million in 1938 to £73 million in 1946. In the meantime the prices of imports had multiplied fourfold. Thus the real purchasing power of Britain's income from foreign investments had fallen to about £30 million in terms of 1938 import prices – or less than a fifth of its pre-war level.

To fill this gap, it was calculated that Britain would have to surpass her pre-war level of exports by seventy-five per cent. To this there was no alternative. It is true that the export gap was, for many years, filled by American aid. But although it is clear in retrospect that no sane American administration would have allowed Britain to starve, it was not always clear at the time that sanity would prevail. The negotiations that preceded the American loan were a cruel warning. Until 1947 the United States appeared anxious to return as fully as possible to her traditional isolationism. The Marshall Plan was announced in 1947, but it did not come into force until a year later. Even then the volume and direction of American aid were subject to Congressional caprice. No responsible British Government could afford to count on American generosity indefinitely, or to give up the attempt to become self-supporting as soon as possible.

The claims of the export drive competed with the claims of Britain's existing standard of living. In theory, no doubt, it was possible to cut the level of consumption still further. The British people were far from starving, although a casual newspaper reader might have been forgiven for doubting the fact. The working-class was better off than it had ever been, and even the middle-class was better off than it felt. In strictly physical terms, more could have been squeezed out of the British people, and less given back. A Government ruthlessly determined to obtain maximum production at the minimum cost would have reduced still further the quantity of luxuries available, and met the problem of morale by giving higher and better rations to those engaged on work of national importance. Politically, however, that course was out of the question. After six years of war, the British people were in no mood for heroic sacrifices. Even as it was, "austerity" became the subject of a violent propaganda campaign by the Conservative Press, and the greatest single cause of the Government's failure to hold its position in the 1950 elections. A deliberate decision to reduce the standard of living would have been tantamount to political suicide—unless it had been accompanied by restrictions on the freedom of the Press, and perhaps on the freedom of the trade unions also.

No Government could have abandoned the export drive, and only a Government of masochists could willingly have cut the level of domestic consumption. The level of defence expenditure, however, was more controversial. Throughout Cripps's time in office, eager voices were raised on the Left, suggesting that cuts in defence expenditure might solve the country's economic problem. In September 1949 Mr. Ian Mikardo, in a typical passage, compared the Government to "people who do without

Giles, *Daily Express*, 12.2.48

"Once more unto the breach, dear friends, once more . . ."

their Sunday dinner or give up smoking cigarettes, but nevertheless buy a new set of plush curtains to impress their neighbours." The comparison was apt; but it remains doubtful whether the money saved on the plush curtains would in fact have made much difference to the Sunday dinner.

Two years earlier, military expenditure overseas had undoubtedly played a major part in damaging the country's balance of payments, but by 1949 this was no longer true. In 1947, when the country faced one of the worst foreign exchange crises in its history, and the balance of payments deficit was £600 millions, over £200 millions went on military expenditure overseas—by any standards an impressive example of conspicuous consumption. In 1948, however, the figure was down to £113 million; and by

1949 it was only £98 millions. The Government's critics were on stronger ground when they pointed to the number of men under arms. Manpower was one of the scarcest commodities of all – and yet as late as December 1946 there were still a million and a half men in the Services. In 1946 the Government could point, in its own defence, to the unhappy consequences of the breathless demobilisation after the First World War. By 1948 that argument had worn thin; yet in the spring of 1948 the armed forces swallowed up 940,000 men who might have been used on productive work. Even in 1949 the figure was close to 800,000; and it was not until 1950 that it fell much below 750,000. This was undoubtedly a drain on the country's meagre resources. Whether it was a serious drain is more doubtful. The phrase "a cut in commitments" was used as an incantation rather than as a tool of analysis. During Cripps's Chancellorship, even if the armed forces had been cut to half their actual level, the numbers released would have been less than 3 per cent of the total labour force.

The level of defence expenditure was a matter of controversy only within the Labour Party. To the Opposition, the most controversial feature of Cripps's policy was: "Socialism". Quite what Opposition speakers meant by this was not always clear. To Churchill, "Socialism" seems to have meant partly the Government's sacrilegious interference with the economic laws he had been taught to revere in his youth, and partly what he characteristically called "the morbid doctrine that nothing matters save an equal sharing of miseries." More sophisticated Conservatives, however, agreed with the *Economist* that "Britain's difficulties are not due, save in a minor degree, to anything that can properly be called 'socialism' "; and objected primarily to what was euphemistically known as "over-full" employment. The great bulk of the Conservative Party in the House of Commons, on the other hand, professed to accept the goal of full employment, and openly objected only to the way in which it was reached.

The Conservatives' technique of opposition was distinguished by vehemence rather than coherence, and it is therefore difficult to pick out the main points of their attack from the morass of minor objections within which they were embedded. Roughly speaking, however, three main criticisms emerge. The Conservatives imagined that in some mysterious, and largely unspecified, way the nationalisation programme was swallowing up resources which could have been devoted to the export drive or to the domestic standard of living. Less frivolously, they attacked the high rate of taxation, and called for cuts in Government expenditure in order to provide more "incentives". Finally, they objected to the network of controls by which the economy was sporadically regulated, and called on the Government to "set the people free." The paradox is that the first of these points was economically irrelevant; while on the second two Cripps's policy was almost as un-Socialist as it could safely have been.

Behind Conservative criticisms of the high rate of taxation there lay an unspoken assumption that, in some sense, the country could not "afford" an egalitarian fiscal policy, and the high rate of expenditure that went with it. As Churchill put it in 1949: "In these last four lavish years, the Socialist Government have exacted upwards of £16,000 million and spent them: over four times as much every year as was the cost of running the country in our richer days before the war." Conservative orators painted a Hogarthian picture of a profligate Government wasting the country's hard-earned foreign exchange. As David Eccles put it: "They themselves have set the pace in extravagant spending. How can they hope to have any influence on anyone else? What influence would they expect the father of a family to have, if every day he exhorted his children to produce more and to save more, and then every night he jammed on his hat and went off to the local to spend their earnings?"

In fact, as intelligent Conservatives knew well, the high rate of Government expenditure was not a drain on the country's income: it was simply a mechanism for redistributing part of that income from one class to another. The use of Budgetary policy to redistribute the national income from the rich to the poor has been an indispensable weapon of every Left-wing Government since the days of Lloyd George. As the *Economist* recognised (though most Conservative M.P.s were too coy to follow suit in public), the demand for a cut in Government expenditure was in fact a demand for a cut in social services – and that in turn was a demand for a less egalitarian fiscal policy. But this, contrary to the opinions of most Conservatives and even of some Socialists as well, would have made the Government's task harder, not easier. Significant cuts in the social services would have stimulated inflationary wage demands by the unions. They in turn would have crippled the export drive, unless the Government had deliberately broken the unions' bargaining power by the creation of unemployment. This, of course, is exactly what did happen in the 1920s – and, even by the narrowest criterion of economic efficiency, the precedent was not encouraging.

Short of launching such an assault on the social services, it is hard to see how Cripps's fiscal policies could have been significantly less egalitarian than they were. It is true that he appealed frequently for equality: but for equality of sacrifice rather than of reward. His great powers of eloquence and moral leadership were devoted not so much to persuading the rich to accept a greater degree of equality as to convincing the poor that their share of the national income could not be increased. In *Towards Christian Democracy* he had written disparagingly of a "democracy with purely materialistic standards"; and as Chancellor a recurrent theme of his speeches was that true, unmaterialistic Socialism now consisted in not asking for more wages. "There is only a certain sized cake," he told the Trades Union Congress in 1948, "and if a lot of people want a larger slice they can only get it by taking it from others." His listeners were evidently too bemused to point out that it was precisely to take larger slices of a "certain sized cake" that the Trade Unions, and indeed the Labour Party, had been created.

His budgets told the same story. One of his former junior Ministers remembers reminding Cripps of the hardships of the pensioners. "And I," Cripps replied, "am thinking of the hardships of the taxpayers." Considering the economic circumstances, his concern for them could hardly have been more solicitous. His first budget, it is true, contained the celebrated "special contribution" or "capital levy." But the special contribution was at most a faint echo of the kind of capital levy Socialists had advocated in the past; and it seems to have been imposed as a sop to Cripps's critics on the Left rather than as part of an onslaught against economic privilege.

Apart from the special contribution the chief feature of the 1948 budget was its shift from direct to indirect taxation. In 1949 the pattern was repeated. Redistribution of wealth, Cripps told the House of Commons, could go no further until new wealth had been created – and in the meantime there must be a ceiling on the social services. Mr. Oliver Stanley, the Opposition spokesman on finance, commented that the budget marked "the end of an era of Socialist policy and Socialist propaganda." In 1950, Cripps cut the food subsidies still more; and even Mr. Anthony Crosland remarked that he had condemned himself to a spectacular intervention later in the year to buttress the policy of wage restraint.

Much the same was true of the Conservative slogan: "Set the people free." The real objection to the Government's economic policy was not so much that there were too many controls, as that there were too few controls of the right kind, and those few too timidly administered. The "people," in the Conservative sense of the term, were too free already. The 1947 *Economic Survey* declared that, "There is an essential difference between totalitarian and democratic planning. The former subordinates all individual desires and preferences to the demands of the State. . . . But in normal times the people of a democratic country will not give their freedom of choice to their Government. A democratic Government must therefore conduct its economic planning in a manner which preserves the maximum possible freedom of choice to the individual citizen." Un-exceptionable sentiments – but Ministers interpreted them to mean that, in a number of vitally important sectors of the economy, the Government must rely on exhortation rather than on direction. Cripps's exhortations were, no doubt, loftily conceived and nobly phrased; but in the last resort they remained exhortations.

So far as economic planning and the redistribution of wealth were concerned, it might be argued that Cripps had no real alternative to the course he followed. On devaluation, however, he had more room to manœuvre; and here too he was remarkably orthodox. The devaluation crisis serves, in fact, as an ideal case study of his attitudes in operation.

To the economist, devaluation is nothing more dramatic than a device to be resorted to, coolly and without emotion, when prices in one country are out of line with prices in another. Money has no intrinsic "value". Its "value" is what men choose to place on it; and men are the masters, not the servants, of their currencies. To the general public, on the other hand, money is an arcane mystery to be approached with reverence and dread; and the price of a nation's currency is a magic index of its standing in the world. To the economist, the news that the price of the pound sterling has fallen in terms of the dollar means only that prices have risen in the sterling area faster than they have done in the dollar area. To the man in the street, it means that Great Britain and the sterling area have suffered a humiliation as terrible as it is inexplicable. The intellectual gap between these two attitudes was largely responsible for the severity of the balance of payments crisis and of the political storm that followed it.

The foreign exchange crisis of 1947 had been caused partly by an American boom. The crisis of 1949 was caused chiefly by an American recession. In the early months of 1949, Britain's balance of payments position seemed healthier than at any time since the war. By the summer, the slight down-turn in the United States had transformed the situation: Washington had caught cold, and Britain was on the point of dying from pneumonia. On July 6th, Cripps told the House of Commons that the dollar deficit in the four quarters of 1948 had been, respectively, £147 million, £107 million, £76 million, and £93 million. In the first quarter of 1949 it was only £82 million – £60 million less than in the corresponding period the year before. But in the second quarter of 1949 it was £157 million; and all the progress of the last eighteen months was wiped out.

Cripps's remedy was to cut dollar imports, and to hold out the prospect of long-term solutions after the talks to be held in Washington in September; he had not, he told the House, the slightest intention of devaluing the pound. In July and August, however, the situation failed to improve. On September 18th, following his return from the Washington talks, Cripps announced that the pound was to be devalued from $4.03 to $2.80.

The House of Commons debated the decision at the end of September; and Cripps was attacked with almost equal ferocity from two opposite sides. To the Opposition, devaluation was a shameful humiliation, a final proof that "Socialism" had failed, and a desperate expedient which might degrade solid, respectable Britain to the level of some flighty Latin Republic. Mr. David Eccles declared that it would work only if it were accompanied by a programme of "harder work" (whether he proposed to work harder himself he did not say), sweeping reductions in Government spending, and a decision to "unfreeze the factors of production." Should it fail, "and the degraded pound be again degraded then gone is the last chance to restore London as a financial centre. The Socialists will then have reduced the status of sterling to that of one of the untrustworthy currencies of Europe or South America." Churchill, floundering now in deeper waters than those of his youth, declared that so far as he was concerned, "the true exchange value between pound and dollar or between all other currencies and the dollar or the pound: the true one is the right one; and the one at which we ought to aim." Mr. Oliver Stanley warned that: "Whatever views we may have upon the present devaluation, all of us are agreed that it is a thing which cannot and must not be repeated. It is dangerous enough now and may be disastrous enough now; but if this were to be followed at some interval by a further devaluation, then indeed there would be nothing for this country to look forward to."

Such sentiments were perhaps to be expected from the Opposition, although they might fairly be considered somewhat harsh in view of Mr. Eccles's own speech in the House of Commons on July 14th, in which he said that: "The purpose of this debate is to discover whether there is a chance left, however small, to save sterling from a collapse" – a remark which must have played at least a subsidiary part in undermining confidence in sterling. The strangest feature of the debate, however, was that the Left clung to the canons of fiscal orthodoxy even more tenaciously than the Right. To the Labour Independents, devaluation was a "capitalist remedy," and as such bound to fail. "There is no element in it," complained Mr. D. N. Pritt, "of a Socialist attempt to remedy the situation"; and he hinted darkly that, if there had been, it would not have been acceptable to American Big Business. The orthodox Left-wing of the Parliamentary Labour Party was only slightly happier. Mr. Richard Crossman (whose pronouncements on economic matters occasionally betrayed the limitations of a classical education) wrote in the *Sunday Pictorial* on the very day that devaluation was announced: "Devaluation would . . . create unemployment and force up the cost of living. So Sir Stafford Cripps said no." In the House of Commons he was less emphatic, but even there he declared that: "This suggestion that we could and should seek to earn sufficient dollars to pay for all we are receiving in Marshall Aid seems to me an insanity," and he urged the Government to work for "a sane economic unit in which we can live and work, instead of becoming an appendage of the United States."

Both sets of critics took it for granted that, whether it was justified or not, devaluation was at any rate a momentous and highly controversial step. In fact, it was not momentous in the slightest degree; and the only controversial thing about it was that the Government delayed far too long in taking it. As the *Economist* pointed out on September 24th, "The majority of sober judges of affairs in this country have long felt that it was only a matter of time before the decision to devalue was taken, and to many of them it had become apparent months ago that the time had come — indeed was in danger of going by."

The inner story of the devaluation crisis has not yet been told. Cripps's official biographer says nothing about the way in which the decision was actually reached; and the other memoirs dealing with the period are equally reticent. Nevertheless, two facts seem reasonably clear. The first is that the decision to devalue was delayed until the last possible moment, presumably because the Cabinet shared the orthodox prejudices of the City and the Treasury, where devaluation has traditionally been regarded as a sign of extreme fiscal irresponsibility if not of downright moral turpitude. The second is that these prejudices cannot have been altogether foreign to Cripps. In 1931, the second Labour Government was brought down partly because the Chancellor of the Exchequer refused to abandon the Gold Standard. It is not certain who deserves the credit for avoiding a similar catastrophe in 1949. The greatest paradox of his career is that it was evidently not Cripps himself.

9

PARTITION IN INDIA

The Attlee Government and the independence of India and Pakistan

JOHN HIGGINS

John Higgins was born in 1934, went to school at K.C.S., Wimbledon, learnt Russian during National Service, and read French and Russian at Worcester College, Oxford, from 1954–7. After a year in advertising, he joined the *Financial Times* in 1958, and is now Features Editor and Arts Editor.

PARTITION IN INDIA

John Higgins

"THERE was no hesitation or complexity about this Bill," wrote Hugh Dalton of the 1947 Act granting independence to India and Pakistan "It was in our best stream-lined style. It passed without a division in either House of Parliament."

His words reflect what was probably the general mood in Britain over the transference of power in the sub-continent. There was a curious lack of general involvement in the creation of the two new countries, though clearly it was one of the most important acts of the post-war Labour Government; many would argue *the* most important.

Close observers of the complex negotiations heaved the deepest sigh of relief. For years agreement between Britain on the one hand, and the Hindus, the Muslims, the Sikhs and numerous minority groups on the other, seemed not merely distant but at times impossible. Those, however, who, like Dalton, were not principally concerned with colonial affairs, were delighted that another moral task to which Labour was pledged had been accomplished, particularly as the winding up of our commitments in India would help ease the economic pressure that was building up at home.

There was little sense of occasion when the Indian Independence Bill came before the Upper House for its final reading; for all that it concerned the fate of millions of people and broke a centuries-old link, it was treated as a fairly mundane piece of legislation. As the *Daily Herald* reported the following morning: "Only a few peers, members of the Commons, and the public saw the historic final ceremony in the House of Lords yesterday which marked the passing of British rule in India."

That, everyone said, was that.

It is true, of course, that bills by themselves are fairly unexciting, and there were plenty of domestic problems to engage the attentions of politicians and the public, and to compete for space in the austerity-size newspapers. India and Pakistan were a long way away, and, as Dalton remarked, "I don't believe that one person in a hundred thousand in this country cares tuppence about [India] so long as British people are not being mauled about out there."

The Bill had been raced through the Commons, and by July 16th it had

received the approval of the Lords. Independence Day had already been
fixed for the following month—August 15th. Only the usual formalities
remained: the tributes to Attlee, the instigator of independence, and to
Viscount Mountbatten, the negotiator; the despatching of fraternal
greetings to the two new nations. With few dissenting votes (among them
the Earl of Selborne) these formalities were carried through. And in their
routine execution there was little recollection of the sweat and tribulation
that had been so much a part of the journey towards Indian independence
over the previous five, if not fifty, years.

Indian demands for independence date from the mid-nineteenth
century, but it was not until the First World War that the possibility of
the British moving out of the country was considered seriously. It was at
this time, in 1917, that Mahatma Gandhi became leader of the Indian
National Congress Party, not long after his return to his native country.
Throughout the twenties and thirties various British committees considered moves towards self-government (not without a certain amount of
Conservative opposition) but they brought no results. Gandhi's answer
was his series of civil disobedience campaigns, using techniques which he
had developed in South Africa (from 1908 to 1914). His first major
campaign in India was staged in 1920-1.

The Second World War turned the seething discontent with British
inactivity into an absolute and grim determination to end British rule, and
end it soon. The Viceroy, Lord Linlithgow, announced on September 3rd,
1939, that India was at war with Germany. This statement, made without
consulting the Indian leaders, incensed Congress.

Although a number of Hindus, including Jawaharlal Nehru, expressed
sympathy for the British cause, it was pointed out that after the 1914-18
war (which India had supported unconditionally) no reward in terms of
independence had been offered; that India was now engaged in a war
which she had not provoked, and had been involved without being consulted; that, if this was indeed a war of freedom, then some post-war
guarantee of *Indian* freedom must be given.

Linlithgow tried very hard indeed to get Congress support, but, lacking
any firm promise, let alone a firm date, Congress refused. Linlithgow was
not prepared to consider independence until the war was over, and for
Congress this was simply not good enough. By 1942, when the war in the
East had brought the Japanese army almost to the Indian border, Sir
Stafford Cripps was sent out to negotiate a settlement. Superficially, he
had all the right qualifications: a deep interest in Indian affairs, a radical

desire to give the country the freedom it desired, and the personal friend-ship of Nehru. All Cripps lacked was a *carte blanche* from the Coalition Government. He offered what he could, but again it was not enough – Gandhi contemptuously described the Cripps proposals of peacetime independence as "a post-dated cheque." Cripps returned empty-handed.

From the Indian point of view by far the most important event in the years from 1937 to 1945 was the hardening and strengthening of the All India Muslim League, under its leader Mahomed Ali Jinnah. Jinnah was a tall, ascetic intellectual. Like most Indian politicians he had been trained as a lawyer, but by all accounts he was not a very successful one. In the early thirties he worked with Gandhi for a united India – indeed Jinnah's grandfather had been a Hindu – but the two men quarrelled, and Jinnah turned his attention to the Muslim League. (He had been president of the League in 1916 and 1920, and from 1934 was re-elected annually.) Before he assumed the leadership, the Muslims had been divided into a series of disputatious cabals; under him they united. The 1937 elections saw the League emerge as a serious opponent to Congress and with it Jinnah as the first important voice of Muslimism. Jinnah began to attack Gandhi publicly, something which had previously been unthinkable, and he also started to demand special treatment for Muslims in the event of an independent India.

The war in 1939 gave him the perfect opportunity to advance his plans. Linlithgow, the Viceroy, finding no support from Congress, was forced to turn to Jinnah, who offered help on the condition that the British make suitable provisions for the Muslims after the war. Before long the Muslim League formulated the so-called "Pakistan Resolution," which stated that where the Muslims were in a majority (i.e., in the north-east and north-west) independent and autonomous states should be set up. From here it was but a short step to the famous slogan of 1943 – "Divide and Quit" – and to the appearance of pressure groups working for a partitioned India.

Throughout the Second World War the Muslim League became increasingly strong, with Jinnah correspondingly more powerful. Mean-while the gulf between Muslims and Hindus grew ever wider. On October 20th, 1943, Lord Linlithgow ended his term of office as Viceroy, and, as V. P. Menon wrote in *The Transfer of Power in India*, he left the country more divided than he had found it in 1936. During his rule Pakistan had developed from an Islamic dream, an ideal discussed by students at midnight, into an inevitability. But very few people realised it, least of all Linlithgow's successor, Lord Wavell.

The end of the war brought with it an increased demand for freedom, and not surprisingly, high up on the list of priorities for Britain's new Labour Government, was the Independence of India. The whole party agreed that India should be free; the only problem was to devise the method of achieving this. Once again Cripps was despatched to India (with him went Lord Pethick-Lawrence, Secretary of State for India, and Mr. A. V. Alexander, Minister of Defence and First Lord of the Admiralty), but this time he was able to act from a position of strength. The principle of independence was agreed. There was no Government constriction operating on Cripps from Whitehall; Britain did not want anything from this action except perhaps a little of the reflected glory of magnanimity. Yet Cripps failed again, and again scarcely through any fault of his own.

In March 1946, when the Cripps Mission left Britain, the balance of Hindus to Muslims was roughly three to one – 250 million Hindus and 90 million Muslims – and the Muslims had received a guarantee that their interests would be protected. At the end of the normal prolonged debates and arguments the Mission came up with the so-called three-tier plan. At the top there was to be the Constituent Assembly, responsible for Defence and Foreign Affairs, in other words a kind of pontoon to span Hindus and Muslims. Next were to come a series of Provincial Groups, which would be roughly comparable to the sections of the country in which the two religions held sway – the body of India would be Hindu and the north-western area Muslim. Finally, Bengal and Assam, where there was only a small Muslim majority, would form two Independent Provinces.

The plan was provisionally accepted on both sides, which meant that Jinnah had made a major concession in not holding out for a separate state of Pakistan. Then came disappointment. Nehru, after consultation with Gandhi, began to press for a much stronger Constituent Assembly – which would of course have the effect of increasing the power of Congress. Jinnah, for his part, became suspicious and declared that Congress would not honour the letter of the Cripps Mission's law. Nehru, in trying to push his command too far, seriously underestimated the strength of Jinnah, just as everyone else had. Michael Brecher, Nehru's biographer, admits that a bad tactical error was made, for through Nehru's demands "Jinnah was given an incomparable wedge to press more openly for Pakistan on the grounds of Congress tyranny."

This has been seen as the last possible chance Britain had of leaving a united India. Yet was it a chance at all? Probably not. The Cripps Mission had devised a plan which on paper came very close to pleasing everyone (that in itself was no mean achievement), but would it have worked? In the emotional and political climate of India at the time it is most unlikely that the Muslims would have been content for long with their areas of control, and it is even less likely that Jinnah would have been prepared to co-operate with Nehru. For a short period there might have been the semblance of a single country, but the paper bridge of the Constituent Assembly would surely have caught fire sooner or later.

The Cabinet Mission's reaction to Nehru's words was one of bitter disappointment. Cripps might have tried to put a brave face on things, but this was the second time he had to return to England empty-handed. "The real situation," wrote Penderel Moon in *Divide And Quit*, "was truly mirrored not in Sir Stafford's cheerful smiles but in the woebegone face of Lord Pethick-Lawrence as he stood at the airport waiting for the plane. Three months in the heat of India seemed to have aged him ten years."

Jinnah's reaction was the declaration at the end of July of Direct Action Day. The Bengal Government announced that August 16th should be a public holiday in Calcutta, and a mass meeting of the Muslim League was staged. This rally led to the first major carnage in the partition of India. For four days the city was in turmoil, and by the evening of the fourth day 5,000 lives were lost—mainly Hindus. Few people in Bengal emerged from the event with any credit. The British officials showed that they were powerless to control such a disturbance, and the native police revealed little inclination to take action. In fact, Suhrawardy, the Muslim Premier of Bengal, has subsequently been accused of conniving at the riots, which reverberated outwards through the surrounding countryside. Yet no one drew the now obvious inference that they were a prelude of worse to come.

Jinnah's call for direct action was the final token of his supreme power. He had shown that he was well able to withstand Nehru and Congress, and he had proved that Nehru had underrated him. He had also demonstrated to the British that he had no more liking for the Hindu Raj than for the British Raj.

Of the Calcutta disaster Gandhi said: "We are not yet in the middle of civil war, but we are nearing it." Yet no firm action was taken in India. Lord Wavell still strove to arrive at some solution through the Constituent Assembly. He had almost no success, although he did persuade Jinnah and four other Muslims to join the Government. Jinnah agreed to this more to prevent a total Congress stranglehold on events than to open the door to a *rapprochement*. Realising that Wavell was making no progress, and probably warned by Gandhi and Nehru of the retrogressive turn of events, Attlee called the Indian leaders to London at the end of 1946.

Like all previous meetings the London conference had the external semblance of deadlock. Nehru and Jinnah continued to stand up for a united and divided India respectively. But out of the conference came a statement from the British Government clearly indicating that a separate state of Pakistan was a good deal nearer reality than had hitherto been supposed. The statement in part read:

> "There has never been any prospect of success for the Constituent Assembly except upon the basis of an agreed procedure. Should a constitution come to be framed by a Constituent Assembly in which a large section of the Indian population had not been represented (i.e. the Muslim League), His Majesty's Government could not of course contemplate . . . forcing such a Constitution upon any unwilling parts of the country."

This meant that the plan Wavell had just devised was quite unacceptable to the Government. It proposed the gradual withdrawal of British troops and officials from the remoter parts of India, until eventually they were gathered at Karachi and Bombay, ready to embark and quit altogether. This so-called "Operation Ebb-Tide" had already been severely criticised at home as being an undignified scuttle. Such criticism was unduly harsh, but the plan was clearly the desperate solution of a soldier trapped between warring factions, baffled by polemics, unable to assert his authority, and in general totally disheartened by his task.

Wavell was clearly not cut out for the job of Viceroy at such a time. He was a poor speaker, an indifferent debater, and an unsatisfactory conciliator. In many ways he represented the old-style British Raj, unable to adjust himself to the currents of thought which came in with the new men of 1945. Certainly he was no match for the casuistry of Jinnah, let alone the skilful manoeuvring of Nehru and Gandhi. His greatest mistake was to keep pushing forward on the road to a united India when all the signposts pointed towards partition.

On February 20th, 1947, the Prime Minister made a double announcement in the House of Commons. First, he declared that independence would be granted to India not later than June 1948; second, that Admiral Viscount Mountbatten would replace Wavell as Viceroy. Attlee's public reason for the change was that Lord Wavell had been placed in command of India during the war, and that the new and final phase before independence "was the appropriate time for the termination of his wartime appointment." But it was clear that Wavell had been fired, and that Mountbatten was being sent to clear up the mess. The Conservative Opposition fiercely demanded some explanation of Wavell's recall and indeed directly asked whether it was a dismissal. On this occasion, as on many others, Attlee was giving away nothing, and stuck to his original story of "terminating a war-time appointment."

Subsequently it was revealed that the proposition had been made to Lord Mountbatten in December 1946 – in all probability the London Conference had confirmed Attlee's dissatisfaction with Wavell's handling of affairs. At first Mountbatten refused the appointment, and only when Attlee stressed that it was the King's wish that he should become Viceroy of India did he accept.

So Viscount and Viscountess Mountbatten arrived in India on March 22nd, 1947, and were installed as Viceroy and Vicereine two days later. The handing over by Wavell was as brief as possible, which, in the circumstances, is not surprising. *The Times'* treatment of the event sums up the situation admirably. It devoted considerable space (at a time when newsprint was scarce) to the Mountbattens' arrival, and then near the bottom of the same page carried a small item with the by-line "From our own correspondent," and the date-line "Bombay, March 23":

"Lord Wavell and his party left Karachi this afternoon for Britain."

Wavell's only consolations were that civil war had been avoided during his Viceroyship, and that Nehru paid tribute to him on the eve of his departure. The latter fact speaks well for both men.

Short of insurrection, things could scarcely have been worse on Mountbatten's arrival. The gulf between Muslims and Hindus was as wide as it had ever been, a major food shortage was threatening, a series of minor riots had developed out of the Calcutta massacres, and in Britain those who considered the Indian problem viewed it with gloomy concern.

Mountbatten had few illusions about his task: he was there to do a deal and do it fast. He said as much at his inauguration ceremony – making his first break with tradition as the only Viceroy to deliver a speech on the occasion of swearing in:

"I believe that every political leader in India feels, as I do, the urgency of the task before us. I hope soon to be in consultation with them . . ."

Once again a down-column item in *The Times* is as revealing as the lead news story:

"Delhi, March 24" (the date of swearing-in).

"Lord Mountbatten today had a private meeting with Pandit Nehru and Mr. Liaquat Ali Khan." (Liaquat Ali Khan, who had gone with

Jinnah to the London Conference during the winter, was to be the first
Prime Minister of Pakistan.) The new Viceroy had arrived with a reputation for speed of action and decision, and made every attempt to live up
to it from the start.

Mountbatten's other great quality was his immense personal charm.
This, too, he utilised to the full. Nehru, always susceptible to flattery, was
overwhelmed by it in 1947, and not for the first time. He realised the fact,
too, according to his biographer.

"Mr. Nehru," said Mountbatten, "I want you to regard me not as the
last Viceroy winding up the British Raj, but as the first to lead the way to a
new India." Nehru turned, looked intensely moved, smiled, and then said:
"Now I know what they mean when they speak of your charm being so
dangerous."

After the partition of India had been accomplished Mountbatten stated
publicly that he arrived in India with the idea of a united country firmly
in his mind. This again shows that few people in the British Government
had fully appreciated either the hatred that existed between the Hindus
and the Muslims, or the very considerable power that Jinnah had built up
for himself over the preceding few years. Attlee had long taken a deep
personal interest in Indian affairs, Cripps had twice negotiated with the
Indian leaders, yet there is no evidence that either had suggested to the
new Viceroy that partition might be the solution. Certainly Wavell had
always fought against it, as had his predecessor, Lord Linlithgow. In
March 1947, nearly all those concerned with the problem were hoping,
and indeed expecting, that a sudden compromise would magically appear
(it could not in the circumstances have arrived any other way), and that
both sides would make concessions.

It did not, however, take Mountbatten very long to decide that a united
India was little more than the impractical dream of idealists or constitutional theorists. Jinnah was now demanding not only two separate states,
in north-west and north-east India, but also a corridor through the body
of the country to link them. Meanwhile the continuation of civil disturbances and the increasing bitterness between the two parties was putting
pressure on Mountbatten to come up with a solution in a quarter of the
time that he originally thought he had at his disposal.

In the middle of May the British Mission *did* produce a plan – a variant
of the Cripps solution of 1946 – which was thought sufficiently feasible
to be taken to London for Government approval. As with all its predecessors, the work done on it went for nothing. But with lizard-like
speed Mountbatten switched to an alternative set of proposals produced

by V. P. Menon, his reforms secretary. Menon had spent his life in the Civil Service, and had risen with remarkable speed. In his job he had contact with both Muslims and Hindus, and knew precisely what the leaders of both parties were likely to reject or accept. Earlier in the year he had discussed his personal solutions to India's problems with Sardar Patel, Chairman and Chief Whip of Congress, and had obtained a measure of agreement from him.

Menon's proposals (given in full in his book *The Transfer of Power in India*) were basically very simple. The country was to be divided into two states, India and Pakistan. A vote was to be taken in the Muslim areas to find out which side they wished to join; moreover, both the Punjab and Bengal were to be divided according to the vote and following the report of a boundary commission. No special provisions were to be made for the Sikh community.

So in the last resort Menon emerges as the originator of the plan, and Mountbatten as the salesman. Mountbatten succeeded in his role: Jinnah accepted, Nehru accepted – though, if Nehru had known that the plan had already been discussed with Patel, he might well have turned it down out of pique. The British Government also accepted. On June 3rd the Viceroy, Nehru, Jinnah, and Sardar Baldar Singh (representing the Sikhs) announced to the nation that henceforth there would be two countries. On this occasion Jinnah was probably the happiest of the four. He had got precisely what he wanted, although he was still on the look-out for further gains. Mountbatten had achieved agreement on all sides – far more than any of his predecessors had done. Nehru himself appeared philosophical: "It is with no joy in my heart that I commend these proposals, though I have no doubt in my mind that this is the right course." Gandhi's role in the negotiations had steadily decreased as partition became increasingly probable. He expressed horror at the prospect of a divided India, as he always had done, and fasted the whole day.

Having achieved agreement, Mountbatten wanted it implemented at once. On his visit to London, at the end of May, he impressed on the Prime Minister that the Indian Independence Bill must go through Parliament during the current session. He also urged that it should go through unopposed. Attlee's reply to this was that Mountbatten himself should talk to the Opposition leaders. Having completed one selling job in India, the Viceroy took on another at home. The Opposition, which had disapproved of his appointment and had advocated a fairly lengthy stewardship in India, were won over. The Bill was drawn up and passed in record time. Once again, as in the war, Mountbatten had demonstrated his almost frightening speed of decision, coupled with an impressive ability to win approval, or at worst acquiescence, from potential opponents.

In addition to assisting that the India Bill should not hang over until Parliament reassembled, Mountbatten also demanded that August 15th, 1947, be announced as the official date for the transfer of power in India. Thus the ending of the British Raj was cut back by exactly ten months from the date fixed by Attlee on the day of Mountbatten's appointment.

The timetable for the transference of power is remarkable. A month elapsed between the appointment of Mountbatten and his arrival in Delhi, and a further nine weeks from the swearing-in ceremony to the announcement of the terms of partition. Between Mountbatten's broadcast to the nation over All-India Radio, and the creation of two new countries, there were a further nine weeks.

Menon, with typical self-effacement, remarked that the evolution of the partition plan was simple compared with its implementation. Nevertheless, nine weeks is not a long time for dividing up a sub-continent of 400 million people, for settling the status of 600 princely states, for disbanding and reassembling a vast army and a complex civil service, for creating a new capital, for transferring the entire power previously wielded by the British Parliament and its Government in India, for appointing Governor-Generals of Pakistan and India, for delineating the boundaries in Bengal and Punjab.

The boundary problem was uppermost in Mountbatten's mind. It was agreed that an English barrister, Sir Cyril Radcliffe, should be responsible for this, aided by two High Court Judges, from the Congress Party, and two nominated by the Muslim League. Radcliffe was chosen on the grounds that he would be an impartial judge – in other words he had never set foot on Indian soil and had had no previous dealings with the country. His briefing at the Colonial Office is said to have lasted no more than thirty minutes, and he left England with no more than this information and a couple of maps. There is some disagreement about the day on which the Radcliffe Commission produced its recommendations (both August 9th and August 13th have been quoted), but the important thing is that they were not announced until after Independence Day: the surprising thing is that they were produced in time at all.

The other major decision reached before August 15th was the nomination of the Governor-Generals of India and Pakistan. Clearly, Mountbatten would have been happy to have accepted both posts, as a reward for his own negotiatory skill and in order to keep the balance between the two countries. It was Nehru's wish that the last Viceroy of

India should become its first Governor-General, so Mountbatten agreed. Jinnah's attitude was very different. After some debate, the Muslim League announced that Jinnah himself would be Governor-General of Pakistan. Behind this action can be seen the last public demonstration of Jinnah's lifelong distrust of British aims and motives.

Even so, Mountbatten agreed to attend the Birth of Pakistan ceremony at Karachi, the new capital, on August 13th. Before the procession there was a warning that an attempt would be made on Jinnah's life; Mountbatten's characteristic reaction was that he would share Jinnah's car. In fact nothing happened, and the Karachi ceremony proved a dull and ill-attended occasion – quite understandably, as Karachi was a predominantly Hindu city.

New Delhi presented an entirely different scene. On the eve of independence, a crowd, which was estimated by *The Times* correspondent to be between 100,000 and 200,000 strong, massed in the main streets. To them Nehru made the most moving speech of his life:

"Long years ago we made a tryst with destiny, and now the time comes when we shall redeem our pledge, not wholly or in full measure, but very substantially. At the stroke of the midnight hour, when the world sleeps, India will awake to life and freedom."

The speech reveals the same Nehru as the broadcast two months earlier – careful, contemplative, realising that he was not the leader of Gandhi's united India, yet convinced that compromise was the best solution. On Independence Day Nehru appealed for unity and tolerance in a speech which was marred only by a vehement reference to the Portuguese enclave of Goa.

The celebrations in New Delhi were peaceful, but elsewhere sporadic outbursts of violence indicated the shape of things to come. In Amritsar a number of Muslim women were raped and murdered by Sikhs. In Lahore Sikhs were attacked by Muslims. Then, on August 16th, the Radcliffe boundary awards were announced, and the holocaust began. Old scores from the Calcutta massacres of a year before were remembered and settled, and new ones were chalked up. As the stories of Muslim atrocities, of Sikh atrocities, of Hindu atrocities accumulated, the flames of hatred were fed.

No attempt had been made to move the Hindus into India or the Muslims into Pakistan before Partition, and now, as neither race felt safe in an alien country, a mass migration began. The divided Punjab was the scene of the bitterest strife, as caravans of Muslims trekked west to Pakistan and trains of Hindus moved east into India. In their paths were the now stateless Sikhs, who raped, looted, and murdered indiscriminately, and received similar treatment themselves. Mountbatten had created a boundary force of 50,000 in the Punjab, but against violence on this scale it was powerless. As in Calcutta in the previous year, the native police showed little inclination to take action against their compatriots, when rumours of slaughter of their own kind reached them daily across the frontier and from the lips of arriving refugees.

It will never be possible to assess the extent of the carnage which followed partition. At the time figures of over a million dead were bandied about. Even now calculations vary between 600,000 and under 200,000. It is known that some four and a half million Hindus moved out of Pakistan to India, and something like six million Muslims moved the other way. Once the migration had started it was quite clear that nothing could be done about it, short of having a Gandhi at one's disposal. Gandhi, in fact, had set up headquarters in Calcutta, where he preached his doctrine of mutual tolerance to such effect that the slaughter in Bengal was kept to a very low figure — "the one-man boundary force who kept the peace while a 50,000-strong force was swamped by riots," as Mountbatten described him in a broadcast later.

The question which has been asked ever since partition is whether this mass killing could have been prevented, or, put in a different way, was the total of 200,000 dead (to take the more conservative estimate) a reasonable price to pay for the creation of two new countries? Another aspect of this problem is the question: "Did Mountbatten act too fast?"

Mountbatten, though never short of admirers, has never been short of critics either. He was once described as a man "happy to make too many important decisions too swiftly," and his denigrators have found this tailor-made phrase very useful.

It is no secret that Mountbatten was sent to India against his will: he claimed to be a sailor, not a political negotiator. Attlee was anxious to obtain a settlement in India as quickly as possible, and Mountbatten for his part was not going to set foot in India unless there was a date clearly specified for his return to Britain and the Navy. Thus Parliament's original announcement of the termination of British rule in India by June 1948 was as much a declaration of Mountbatten's refusal to be away from the Navy for more than fifteen months as it was of the Government's approved timetable for withdrawal. Mountbatten's task was to secure action quickly in India, and it so happened that a speedy timetable accorded very closely with his own wishes.

But the suggestion that Mountbatten raced partition through, steam-rollering both British and Indian politicians in the process, does him considerably less than justice. Mountbatten undoubtedly wanted a quick solution to the Indian problem, just as he wanted the honour of being the Englishman who fathered two new countries. But he certainly was not prepared to jeopardise lives in order to get back to the Fleet.

Mountbatten's arrival in India came at a time of great difficulty for Britain both in Europe and Asia. Labour's crest of exhilaration of 1945 and 1946 was seen to be past in the early months of 1947. Dollar credit was becoming exhausted, and expenditure had to be cut back somewhere. British commitments overseas provided one obvious sector for reduction: one division was stationed in Greece trying to bolster up the depleted Greek army, more troops were engaged in Palestine, and, to the eyes of many people at home, the rewards for this sort of expenditure were slight. Moreover, Britain was desperately short of manpower – the so-called Manpower Budget of 1947 was to reveal a deficit of some 600,000 men in the country's labour force – which was only to be expected after the depredations of a six-year war.

Could Britain afford, either in terms of money or of men, to hold India any longer? The purely practical answer to this question was clearly "NO".

These considerations apart, both the Labour and Conservative parties were committed to eventual Indian independence, and the Government had affirmed all along that this should be done at the earliest possible moment. Both Russia and the United States had made it quite clear that they would view with disfavour any continuation of imperialism after the war – the words of the Atlantic Charter on the right of all people to choose the form of government under which they would live had been cited in the Indian context for six years. And in a general mood of freedom few countries would have supported a British attempt to maintain control in India.

The other main difficulty in 1947 was that there appeared to be no possibility of the internal Indian situation improving in the near future. A. V. Alexander said quite categorically that Britain either had to leave India at once, or be prepared to stay there for ten or fifteen years – for his own part, he was in favour of another decade of control. Cripps at the same time agreed that the Indian leaders must be brought together at once, or else steps would have to be taken to strengthen British garrisons in India with a view to continuing responsibility there "indefinitely." Cripps, as opposed to Alexander, believed and stated that a period of indefinite rule would have been both "undesirable and impracticable." In other words, most members of the Government were convinced that independence had to be now in 1947 or not in their term of office. And they were no doubt quite right.

Nevertheless, when the Independence Bill was presented to the Commons, little reference was made to these considerations, apart from an occasional comment about easing the manpower situation. The Bill was seen as a moral duty, and Cripps produced something of a *volte face* when he said that Britain was taking this action because it was just and right, "not because it was forced upon us by circumstances beyond our control."

If domestic and international pressures demanded that Britain withdraw, then the same applied to the pressure of events in India itself. As has been said earlier, during the last months of Wavell's viceroyship the rift between Congress and the League grew ever wider, and personal relations between the leaders of the two sides deteriorated correspondingly. In addition, sheer distrust of British motives, and suggestions of deliberate delay by Britain, meant that each successive British plan was likely to be greeted with more suspicion than its predecessor. When Mountbatten arrived in India the only unifying factor between Muslim and Hindu was a lack of confidence in the manœuvrings of the British Raj. After Calcutta the cauldron of physical violence was on the boil – indeed, a visit by Lady Mountbatten to one of the riot areas of the Punjab, and her subsequent report, played a considerable part in persuading the Viceroy that action must be immediate. It is indeed arguable that civil war would have followed if the British had kept their hold on the country.

So Mountbatten had to get agreement, and, when he had it, paper decisions and promises had to be put into effect at once. In the mood of India during the summer of 1947, a false move, or an unguarded statement, by any of the signatories to the Partition agreement, could have meant the negation of all their work and achievements. Having steered the Indian leaders into a position where they had come to terms with one another for the first time, it would obviously have been stupid on Mountbatten's part to offer an extended period for reconsideration of their action. That these thoughts were well to the fore in Mountbatten's mind emerges clearly in the first presentation of Menon's proposals. Jinnah wanted a week to think the matter over and present it to the League. Mountbatten countered by demanding his *personal* approval or rejection on the spot. Plainly agreement must be followed by action.

If the speed of Mountbatten's actions now appears justified, can it also be said that sufficient precautions were taken in the nine weeks before August 15th against communal rioting after Partition? It can not. But apportioning the blame is not easy.

On July 22nd Mountbatten had a meeting with the leaders of the League, Congress, and the Sikhs. It was decided to set up a boundary force in the Punjab. In addition, a statement was issued on behalf of all parties which said, among other things:

"Both the Governments further undertake that there shall be no discrimination against those who before August 15th may have been political opponents."

As in many instances, both before and after Partition, paper declarations, however admirable in intention, proved useless in practice.

The fact is that almost no one in authority, whether British, Hindu, Muslim or Sikh, envisaged outbreaks on anything like the scale on which they occurred. Mountbatten himself expected some upheavals, but nothing which could not be controlled by the measures already taken. Nehru anticipated some individual attacks of a sporadic nature, and little else. The British Government could only rely on the information from its advisers, and Attlee admitted some years later that he was not only appalled, but completely surprised, by the turn of events after August 15th. Just about the only warning voice was that of Sir Evan Jenkins, Governor of the Punjab. Jenkins was opposed to the division of the Punjab in any case – primarily on the grounds that outbreaks of violence were inevitable – but during the general pre-independence rejoicings few people were inclined to take any notice of either his public or his private warnings and prophecies. There was a second warning voice at home. During the final reading of the India Bill in the House of Lords, the Earl of Selborne, dissociating himself from the general sanguine mood of self-congratulation, announced sourly – and only too accurately – that the human misery which had occurred so far was only a foretaste of what was to follow.

There is no doubt that the jubilation of the weeks before independence distracted attention from, and blunted any understanding of, the growing ferment among the masses. Michael Brecher has put forward the additional theory that many of India's leaders, Nehru among them, were out of touch with the people. In preaching their own doctrine of tolerance and non-violence, they found it difficult to believe that others would not follow them. These highly educated men (graduates in many cases of English universities) had necessarily grown away from the mass of their followers – if they had ever been close to them in the first place. They had an idealised picture of their average supporter, and found it difficult to appreciate the purely animal in man. Thus the élite were just not equipped to forecast what would happen, and they found it difficult to understand when it finally did.

The lesson of the 200,000 dead is that paper safeguards by themselves are never enough.

August 15th came, and India was partitioned. A few months later the Congress Party was also divided. Nehru was Prime Minister, but the rift between him and his deputy, Sardar Patel, became wider. To some extent the division was a personal one. Patel was a much older man than Nehru, and he had hoped to be rewarded with the leadership, or at least the nominal leadership, of the party as reward for his services to it. When he found that this was not to be, and that his hopes had gone for ever, his bitterness increased. Fortunately, there in the background was Gandhi, whose anguish over the division of India never affected his love and respect for Nehru, and who acted as *bapu*, or father and confessor, to both Nehru and Patel.

The main disagreements between Patel and Nehru centred on the attitude to be taken towards Pakistan during the period of massacre. In particular, under the Partition agreement India was due to pay Pakistan 550 million rupees. Patel, arguing that India's economy was in a shaky state, and emphasising the mass murder of Hindus that was going on, stood out for postponing the payment of this sum. A further factor was the knowledge that the money could be used by Pakistan to purchase arms for the fighting which had broken out over Kashmir in autumn, 1947.

Gandhi, ever the moralist, declared that the sum should be handed over, and Nehru, ever the disciple, agreed. So in 1947 a statement was issued that India would pay its debt. From this moment Patel, realising that he was out of favour, completely renewed his agitation, and insisted on firmer treatment of the Muslims on Indian territory. Patel's words increased the hatred which was being incited by extremist Hindu groups. Gandhi went on preaching his doctrine of tolerance.

On January 30th, 1948, Gandhi called Patel and asked that the breach with Nehru be sealed. The indications are that Patel was unwilling to do this. Gandhi then left Patel, and went to his habitual five o'clock prayer meeting. On the way, a young man stepped out of the crowd and fired three bullets into Gandhi's body. The Mahatma was dead, assassinated by a Hindu right-wing extremist, Nathuram Vinayak Godse. (In the days that followed, one hundred leaders and members of the Mahasabha, Godse's group, died in communal rioting.)

Mountbatten at once hurried to the scene and found Nehru and Patel confronting one another over Gandhi's body. Immediately he insisted on the reconciliation between the two that Gandhi himself had asked for. Nehru and Patel embraced one another.

Four months later Mountbatten left for England. With Mountbatten gone and Gandhi dead, Nehru, Patel . . . and Jinnah . . . were on their own.

10

TOWARDS THE COCKTAIL PARTY
The conservatism of post-war writing
DAVID PRYCE-JONES

David Pryce-Jones was born in 1936. He was educated at Eton and at Magdalen College, Oxford, where he was an open scholar. In 1961 he was literary editor of *Time and Tide*. His first novel *Owls and Satyrs* was published by Longmans Green in 1961. He has also written a book about Israel, which will be published by Weidenfeld and Nicolson.

TOWARDS THE COCKTAIL PARTY

David Pryce-Jones

"THE great marquee of European civilisation, in whose yellow light we all grew up, and read or wrote or loved or travelled, has fallen down; the side-ropes are frayed, the centre-pole is broken, the chairs and tables are all in pieces, the tea-urns empty, the roses are withered on their stands, and the prize marrows; the grass is dead."

Cyril Connolly's introductory comments to the post-war numbers of *Horizon* are like the temperature charts of a patient beyond recovery, recording the persistent disease, with rare lapses into hopefulness. The garden fête was never to be as gracious as it had been: in place of the great marquee there were a great many small and dingy tents pitched at random. Efforts were certainly made to co-ordinate elsewhere. "What are *Penguin New Writing*'s post-war plans?" asked its editor, John Lehmann. "We can reveal that *Penguin New Writing* has planned bigger and better poets, short story writers, critics for you after the war. They will be made of a new kind of plastics evolved in our laboratories while you weren't looking." This regular anthology was to keep "a sharp lookout for the new authors coming back from the war."

The literary reactions to the mass society now set loose in the ruins of European civilisation were either, like John Lehmann's, unchanged since before the war – a vision of young writers stepping forward uninterruptedly – or far more hesitant and negative. "There is a feeling abroad – even among quite unobservant people – that life will never be quite the same again," wrote a *Spectator* critic in a review of H. G. Wells' *Mind at the End of its Tether*, in November 1945. The feelings of the quite unobservant people and of the quite observant have never held each other in much respect, and rarely tried to come to terms. The observant tend to adopt an attitude rather like that of the Walrus and the Carpenter, in Lewis Carroll's poem, towards the Oysters:

> But answer came there none –
> And this was scarcely odd because
> They'd eaten every one.

The Oyster masses, "thick and fast they came at last, And more and more and more," had proved too much for the bourgeois Walrus and Carpenter to digest. Cyril Connolly regarded this as the chief and most lamentable cause of the withering away of literary values. "There is a decay in communication owing to the collapse of that highly cultivated well-to-do world bourgeoisie who provided the *avant-garde* artists – writer, painter, musician, architect – with the perfect audience." And against that "The fact remains that a Socialist Government, besides doing practically nothing to help artists and writers (unless the closing down of magazines during the fuel crisis can be interpreted as an aid to incubation), has also quite failed to stir up either intellect or imagination; the English renaissance, whose false dawn we have so enthusiastically greeted, is further away than ever. Even Socialist magazines like *Tribune* and the *New Statesman* seem desperately short of new talent and the sole outstanding Socialist writer remains J. B. Priestley."

The war may have enlarged the reading habits of a great many people. Certainly a wider market for cheaper books was created. The success of Penguins established the habit of slipping a paperback into one's pocket. The strict allocation of paper prevented *avant-garde* magazines such as *Polemic* from getting off the ground, and it restricted the existing publications. But more serious than any material shortage was the intellectual failure to respond to those readers in whom the *Spectator* critic had observed the new feelings that things would never be the same again, and who were wondering in what way they would be different. Hence the *cri-de-cœur* of *Horizon* in 1947, echoing over the gap between supply and demand: "It is disheartening to think that twenty years ago saw the first novels of Hemingway, Faulkner, Elizabeth Bowen, Rosamund Lehmann, Evelyn Waugh, Henry Green, Graham Greene, to name but a few, for no new crop of novelists has arisen commensurate with them. Viewing the scene in 1947, moreover, one is conscious of the predominance of a certain set of names, the literary 'Best People', who somewhat resemble a galaxy of impotent prima donnas, while round them rotate tired businessmen, publishers, broadcasters, and civil servants who were once poets, novelists, and revolutionary thinkers." It was as if we had "enslumbered the arts, like a skilled anaesthetist, into final oblivion," with the gods deserting "their bitter little hairy experiment – western man." John Lehmann's conclusion in 1950 is not far removed in spirit: "Is it merely that an altered situation, a changed mixture of feeling is waiting, as so often before, for a new catalyst, a new formula, a new innovation of genius to lead the dance of our tomorrow?"

The immediate problem, then, was that the war did not alter the nature of the people who wrote the books, just as it singularly failed to provide material for British prose and poetry in the way that the First World War had done. An American novel, Norman Mailer's *The Naked and the Dead*, concerned with the most brutal and brutalising aspects of fighting, had a success in 1948 which found no English parallel. The first result, of course, was that many of the post-war books might well have been exactly the same if there had been no war: an amalgam of left-over sentiments from the Thirties and Twenties. And in so far as literature tried to come to terms with social and political change, to assess what sort of feeling was abroad among the unobservant, it assumed a peevishness. It was not so much a question of how the new world was to be fashioned, as how much of the old world had survived in order to be reincorporated. Rummaging around in the social attics might provide scraps to patch up the torn fabric and show the unobservant that as usual they were wrong.

"The people of England were long habituated to queues: some had joined the procession ignorant of its end – hoping perhaps for cigarettes or shoes – but most were in a mood of devotion. In the streets few words were exchanged; no laughter . . . women predominated . . . the civilians were shabby and grubby. Some, for it was their lunch-hour, munched 'Woolton Pies'; others sucked cigarettes made of the sweepings of canteen floors." So Evelyn Waugh has described the joyless, deluded crowd shuffling to see the Sword of Stalingrad in 1943, victims of the Locust Years, as he christened the period . . . or possibly the locusts themselves, with their unaccountable "Woolton Pies" as a makeshift for the finer fare which was now beyond the grasp of one and all.

"But a very large proportion of the (road) accidents were due to strain and fatigue borne over a number of years and accentuated since the outbreak of peace by deliberate under-nourishment of the people of England to make them too listless to resist petty tyranny. To the same cause may be attributed a number of very bad railway and mine accidents besides the increasing tendency to go out without one's shopping list, lose one's purse, put one's ration book down on the counter and forget to pick it up, go to a room to get something and stand in a daze completely unable to remember what one wanted and have to go back to the place where one was when the thought first came to one's head and wait for it to return, to be perpetually flurried or anxious about things which really did not matter, and in the case of the majority of housewives who were giving their weekly rasher of bacon and their one monthly egg to a husband or growing child not to speak of their ration of so-called meat, a growing wish to sit down and die except that one's death would mean a weekly rasher of bacon the less and a monthly egg the less!" In so displaying her opinions, in her novel *Love Among the Ruins* (1948), Angela Thirkell was less synthetic than Evelyn Waugh, more rumbustious, more generous with her emotions. But the substance gives off the same bitter, satirical fume: this is the duet of the cross Walrus and the frustrated Carpenter.

For both of them the war seemed a watershed: civilisation and all things nice on the far side, and anarchy, snails and puppy-dog tails on this side. The immediate post-war years in this view of things constituted an unprecedented bleakness. It was with surprise that anybody emerged into the springtime, like a tortoise after the winter hibernation. Angela Thirkell was emphatic about the miles of arid sand stretching in the post-war desert as far as the eye could compass. "We have seen the end of a civilisation," one of her characters explained. "It began to crash in 1789 and this is its last gasp. It's a sickening thought, but there it is. All our scrattlings and scutterings, our trying to save a bit here and a bit there, are useless. We are out of date." Such an admission counted for a good deal more than the firm Edwardian resolve of upper-class bankrupts to sell off the horses or the plate. It was Talleyrand who lamented that those who had not known life before 1789 had no conception of what *douceur de vivre* implied. *Brideshead Revisited*, published in 1945, said much the same. Lord Marchmain dies in his *chinoiserie* bed just before the holocaust; his eldest son has gone off with the vulgar Mrs. Muspratt; Ryder is left billeted in the shell of the big house, fouled by wrecker-occupiers. There was no question here of nostalgic scrattlings and scutterings to keep the concern going: Evelyn Waugh carried Angela Thirkell's desolation to the end of the road. Brideshead falls with a crash so savage that there is a joy in it: if we can't have it, so the mocking ghosts rejoice together, then we'll see you don't either. And still the last word was Evelyn Waugh's, referring to *Brideshead Revisited* in the preface to a later edition, published in 1960: "It was impossible to foresee, in the spring of 1944, the present cult of the English country house. It seemed then that the ancestral seats which were our chief national artistic achievement were doomed to decay and spoliation . . . And the English aristocracy has maintained its identity to a degree that then seemed impossible."

In many ways Angela Thirkell is more instructive than Evelyn Waugh because of her inferior style, literary quality, and intellect. She recorded her version of the truth unadorned, and, far from crying *après moi le déluge*, she showed an intense fear of being sprinkled by any precipitate drops of rain. Her books enjoyed an enormous post-war vogue in Britain and in the United States, selling in many tens of thousands. I can re-member a clever though reliably conventional school friend rebuking me for never having heard of Angela Thirkell. "At home we think she's the best living author. Everyone reads her." Home was in Camberley. Dutifully, I read.

These latter-day Barsetshire chronicles, in the setting and the assumed manner of Trollope, seemed to fill a contemporary need for continuity. There was no need to readjust to a new set of characters with each novel, no difficult wrestling with strange values or newfangled *mœurs*. Certainly, the rich man was only living in one wing of his castle which had been turned into a prep. school, and the poor man was only at the gate if it suited him to be there, but still the landmarks were familiar. And so, as if to dam the post-war flux, there were the boulders of Angela Thirkell, Mazo de la Roche, Warwick Deeping, Howard Spring, and the best-selling novel of Robert Henriques, *Through the Valley*, another massive and Thirkellian reconstruction of county life adapting itself to change.

If these years produced social change, the adjustment was certain to be felt more acutely in the countryside than in the towns where class barriers had already been dissolving for some time. The war had obviously made less impact on the countryside than on the factories and the bombed areas, on the men in the forces. And so a literary saga unfolding as if nothing had happened to shake the real deep roots of old England made compulsive and reassuring reading to those who wished this to be true. If Evelyn Waugh was at the bedside of the dying aristocracy, Angela Thirkell was taking the pulse of the county gentry, that hard core of conservative guerrillas. Some-times the apologetics were quite modest. " 'What worries me,' said Noel, 'is the deliberate extinction of the upper middle-class. We aren't running to seed yet, as some of our betters are. There are some very honourable families of old title who really need suppressing altogether, because all the brains and vigour have gone to the winds, and the men are spineless or fanatics. But I think we have still a few generations of good work to do.' " Sometimes the opinions were more extreme. When the old family of Marling finally crashes: "There was really nothing to say. The same thing was happening all over England and no one could stop it." And a conversa-tion on the subject is ended by Captain Belton, "I daresay there is a dictaphone behind the wainscot, and whoever is in charge of liquidating landowners taking it all down in shorthand." Or again, "When they have exterminated the middle-classes, England won't be any better."

The county families were seen as all that was best in Britain, although the definition of a county family was too subtle for crude words. It had something to do with continuity, for each generation seemed to make a point of modelling itself on its predecessor. Hence the survival of values which allot each person his place and take away the anguish of self-determination. But more importantly, it had to do with behaviour. There were some people, and only those, who could set a good example, just as there were others who could only labour, or be artists, or foreigners, or belong to an inferior culture. To muddle it all up, as was happening, was only to confuse the system that sorted out, as it were, which human letter should go into which social envelope.

Angela Thirkell's books were nothing if not topical. She responded immediately in her novels to shifts in the system, so that unreflectingly she wrote a fictionalised journalism, the kind of thing that was later superseded by Mrs. Dale's Diary, which was started in 1948 and was by no means unlike Angela Thirkell's books in intention and execution. Her first book after the war, *Peace Breaks Out*, was published in 1946. Its very significant title gives some indication of the views expressed, for in it war was seen as a chivalrous exercise of brave men fighting to defend un-questioned and therefore good values. Just as Waugh's Guy Crouchback could find a place in the battle against "the Modern Age in arms", so Angela Thirkell's naval officers and army captains and decent men were engaged in an issue of black and white, or perhaps red and white. But peace would be far more complicated for it would bring forward all the intermediary shadings. England was introduced like this: "Old people conscientiously doing their duty in a world they didn't understand, a world which did not want them; middle-aged people losing their charm under the endless strain of sons and daughters in danger, public duties, aged and failing parents, and growing discomfort and privation at home, or, if they did keep their charm, doing so with a plodding determination which ruined everything; young people mostly being so good and doing what they had to do, emerging for leaves in which there was so little fun to be got that they had almost stopped trying to get it . . . Everything in fact was beastly for everybody." Against this background of knowing exactly where you stood and whom you were fighting, even if it was unpleasant, the outbreak of peace could only be confusing and deleterious, while it would also give opportunity and impulse to the social change which had been menacing. In the next two books, *Private Enterprise* (1947) and *Love Among the Ruins* (1948), she was still concerned to show how the upper middle-classes kept their backs to the wall. As the tension yielded with the passing years, the books lost their vitality. If this battle was not won outright, at least it was disengaged with success. The complaint which threatened to turn into a lament could switch key to a hymn of conservation. Mrs. Thirkell's obituary in *The Times* in 1961 pointed this out, although it did not draw the full conclusion: "The wit shone rather less brightly in the later novels, the inventive high spirits drooped a little, the admixture of High Tory views grew more pronounced—increasingly the novels tended to become a satirical running commentary or lament on the times, particularly those of an England pinched after the Second World War." The further the war receded, the duller the High Tory views became.

Backs cannot be kept to the wall without some encouragement: the weaker fighters will be only too likely to jump over the wall and hide on the other side. Angela Thirkell provided the stiffening view of life, the call to resistance, which struggled for articulation and for a standard to rally around, in so many Georgian halls and manors, converted rectories, dower houses, and squires' residences. "We need a more eighteenth-century set to see us through this mess—if they were gentlemen in the proper spirit of the word, if they drank and gambled and whored . . . and put people in the pillory or cut their ears off and encouraged child-labour, I'd feel some hope for England." The same woman in *Private Enterprise* goes on: "What I really mind is their trying to burst up the *Empire* . . . I mean like leaving Egypt and trying to give Gibraltar to the natives. If they try to do anything to Gibraltar, I shall put on a striped petticoat and a muslin fichu and murder them all in their baths, because TRAITORS ought to be murdered." In a review of this book in the *Spectator*, Hester Chapman first acknowledged Angela Thirkell as a Recording Fury: "I am told by a friend who has read every single one of Mrs. Thirkell's novels that she has a special gift for recording the difficulties, disappointments and frustrations of the upper middle class housewife," and then she went on to point out that this amounted to a world picture, and an excusable one at that: "The Labour Government seems to worry her a bit and every now and then there is a nostalgic reference to Mr. Churchill and his days of power (Ah! those were the times when we were all killing one another) while foreigners, intellectuals and working-class folk are treated as figures of fun. But what of it? This is one of the traditions of English humour." Elizabeth Bowen put it rather more intelligently in the *Tatler*: "If the social historian of the future does not refer to this writer's novels, he will not know his business." Sentimentally the *Daily Telegraph* found that "She is the High Priestess of good cheer."

Obviously the best exhortation Angela Thirkell could give was to marriage, for the upper middle-classes traditionally maintain and perpetuate their way of life by carefully chosen alliances compounded out of a regard for money and position and an ideal of Romantic Love debased from an ancient literary tradition. All her plots turn on questions of marriage and the social suitability of the two people involved. " 'One good marriage and the county will be taking those Deans up' and though the Dowager Lady Norton was a snob and a quite dreadful bore, her social sense spoke truly." Marriage provided the sense of limited change within a context of continuity and a prolonged tradition. It could reassure the gossips and the Lady Nortons at all levels and yet be something static. The characters who distress their author were those eligible young men who were refusing to marry in spite of their desirability and qualifications, and the equally eligible young women who were more interested in finding out about the world than in adding to a family tree. They took jobs and left Barsetshire, and sometimes even married foreigners. This was described as "the descent of decent young people into real squalor, the terrible *nostalgie de la boue* to which so many of them fall a prey."

For if the square should once be broken and the resistance at the wall dissipated, the barbarians would have won the day. Two young people who have not fallen a prey take part in a conversation with their parents:

" 'The Dark Ages are upon us . . . And we shall have to spend our holidays in Mr. Butlin's camps and do everything communally with common Communists.'

'And learn Russian.'

'I always think that if people are wicked to their Royalty, there is a kind of curse on them.'

'I know what mother means. Look at the French guillotining the King and Queen and torturing the Dauphin. They've never had a decent Government since and serve them jolly well right.' "

Shortly afterwards a don adds the weight of his learning to the discussion: "What is interesting, though I must say even to a philosopher damnably galling and uncomfortable, is that we are living under a Government as bad as any in history in its combination of bullying and weakness, its bid for the mob's suffrages, its fawning upon unfriendly foreigners who despise it, its efforts to crush all personal freedom."

These two passages seem to unite every emotive response to the post-war years from the class most directly forced to retrench. Angela Thirkell was speaking for all those who felt that the new equality and socialism were a discrimination against themselves. The hazards of the future were weighed and found wanting against the comforts of the past, and Angela Thirkell was the most blatant, or perhaps the most honest, of the Preservationists At All Costs. There were others during these years,

Nancy Mitford, Sir Osbert Sitwell – who was recreating a past even before the First World War with the five volumes of his autobiography, which were nearly always at the top of the best-selling list. Imaginative literature was either at a standstill or cast in the mould of the Thirties. The high-brows had turned their attention across the channel to Sartre and Camus – as early as 1945 Raymond Mortimer was introducing the *"engagé"* arguments to *New Statesman* readers. This was countered by the trans-atlantic impact of Arthur Miller and Tennessee Williams, whose play *A Streetcar Named Desire* in 1949 led the *New Statesman* critic to suggest that he would "decline into the most successful playwright of our day." But it was generally considered that seven lean years were upon literature without the prospect of seven fat years anywhere. The fashionable questions took the form, "Can the novel survive?", "Where is the Redbrick Lawrence?". The periodicals died, *Horizon*, *Scrutiny*, *Penguin New Writing*. Angela Thirkell of course did not come into the highbrow terms of reference.

If Angela Thirkell represented the attitudes of upper middle-class resentment to permeation by what she called the Brave New Revolting World, Christopher Fry, who came to the public attention during these years, seems to epitomise the attitude of resignation. Angela Thirkell was the daughter of J. W. Mackail, a classical scholar and professor of poetry at Oxford, and the granddaughter of Sir Edward Burne-Jones. Christopher Fry was born in Bristol in a family with Quaker antecedents, although his father had been a Church of England lay preacher. He was a schoolmaster and a professional actor, and later a resident director at the Oxford Play-house. Much the same kind of people who read Angela Thirkell's novels went to see Christopher Fry's plays, although the professional critics at first responded with marked enthusiasm to the latter, an enthusiasm which veered round the contemporary compass to abuse. But similar sounding comments were made about both writers: "A voluptuary in gay malice," "a very witty woman," compared with "the verse may be 'sliced prose' but it is backed by an abundant vocabulary and a pretty wit," "Mr. Fry can let down his bucket into a sea of dazzling verbal invention where he wishes, and bring it up brimming."

At first sight Christopher Fry's plays appear to be just high jinks, rather like Angela Thirkell's books. But just as the Barsetshire reconstructions were directed by a sense of social outrage, so the plays were grounded in a pervasive melancholy. Perhaps the bitter-sweet quality – almost as if Noël Coward had tried to infuse a sad moral into his tinkly tunes – accounted for their instantaneous West End success. For the public reception of

Christopher Fry's plays was of the kind generally reserved for musicals. And like musicals, there cannot be enough of the same thing, so, between 1947 and 1952, eight different Fry plays and his one translation from Anouilh were staged, and all almost universally well received initially. That this was a mood on the part of the public is best seen in Raymond Williams' corrective that Fry's brilliant success was a very good thing for the theatre and had a definite place in modern English drama, "but it is important to emphasise that this place is neither innovating nor directive."

But the mood was innovatingly euphoric: it seemed as if the new original star could twinkle uninterruptedly. "The outstanding event in the British drama since the war is the arrival of Christopher Fry" was typical of contemporary judgement. Christopher Fry was retained at the Arts Theatre as a staff-dramatist by Alec Clunes, and *A Phoenix Too Frequent* was revived there shortly after its première at the Mercury Theatre. *The Lady's Not For Burning* was first presented there. Later, in 1949, he was commissioned to write a play for Sir Laurence Olivier, and the result was *Venus Observed* at the St. James' with Olivier in the lead part. This seemed only a natural progression at the time, for Sir John Gielgud had taken the part of Thomas Mendip in the production of *The Lady's Not For Burning* at the Globe in 1949. In January 1950 two Fry plays, *Venus Observed* and *The Boy with a Cart*, opened on successive nights, while his translation of Anouilh's *Ring Round the Moon* followed only a week later.

Until then the critics had been favourably impressed by the unforeseen commercial success of the new verse drama. There came to be much talk in fashionable circles of a revival of poetic drama; the "death of the novel" was temporarily relegated. But with *Venus Observed* the critics rounded. There had been a few warnings. Gerard Fay had written, "If he is not careful Fry will be labelled 'clever' and that will be the end of him." Reviewing *The Lady's Not For Burning*, the *New Statesman* critic, T. C. Worsley, had referred to "the almost continuous ripple of amusement, punctuated by frequent outbursts of laughter, which greeted it on the second night. It is enormously high-spirited." But he had closed with an admonition: "after being greatly entertained, we are left unsatisfied; that is something to do with the conception, not with the realisation." And of *Venus Observed*, only a year later, he was commenting, "Mr. Fry's second full-length comedy is, to be perfectly frank, a real mess." "Mr. Fry may well be rather puzzled at the coolness of the critical reception of his second play when it is really so little different from his first," was the fairly general judgement. "Mr. Fry spills a delicious bibful of witty phrases, but that does not make him the Messiah long awaited by the Arts Council," Philip Hope-Wallace decided, presenting perhaps a rather too private interpretation of the role of the Arts Council in English culture. Christopher Fry expressed his surprise by trying to think of the picture of himself which emerged from the Press cuttings. "His typewriter continues to chatter long after it has been put back in its case. Words will grow out of him, like fingernails, for some time after his death," he rue-fully concluded. The producer, Peter Brook, referred to Fry's work as "a dance of words" attempting to "free the theatre from realism and the novel," but a dance of words now appeared to provide only a chorus, as it were, in front of which no dramatic characters emerged.

"The fashion of the moment is for fantasy and fancy dress, nostalgia and pictorial wit," wrote Richard Findlater in a book about the con-temporary theatre, *The Unholy Trade*, written at the height of Fry's success. "The popularity of Jean Anouilh and Christopher Fry is a symptom of the change in taste. This is what sterner critics mean when they lament the coming of 'the era of Christopher Fry' and the death of honest-to-God naturalism or true-blue literary drama." In a world where communication was largely in the hands of the upper middle-classes, it was improbable that naturalism or realism would be the order of the day, for if it were it could only produce a gloomy eclipse. Nor does it seem surprising in retrospect that so obvious a symbol as an eclipse should be the framework for *Venus Observed*. It is only unexpected that Fry should have reached it by such a long and winding progress. His plays worked their way through to modern times, from Moses, from the Romans, then the Jutes, to medieval England "more or less or exactly" and so finally to *Venus Observed* set in the present.

Christopher Fry himself explained that the mood of *Venus Observed* was autumnal. The ageing Duke lives in a decaying mansion – Angela Thirkell would have known all about that – to which he invites three mistresses so that his son may, like Paris, judge them and choose one for his mother. The arrival of Perpetua, the agent Reedbeck's daughter, causes both the Duke and his son to fall in love with her. The chosen mistress fires the Duke's mansion while he is making love to Perpetua. The Duke, however understands Perpetua's motives, that she wants to marry him in order to protect her swindling father, forgives her and agrees to marry the chosen mistress once she is released from prison, where she will serve a sentence for arson. Christopher Fry elucidated the meaning of this situation. The Duke has remained unsatisfied since the death of his wife, and the absence of love and domesticity has driven him to a sexual lust which can never provide a reasonable alternative. At the beginning of the play "he is prepared to marry anybody: all are alike." The agent Reedbeck too is overpowered "by a passionate longing for the nobility and leisured civilisation that is passing away from the earth, and is quite conscienceless in the way he tries to attain it."

For the only things that human beings cannot put up with are rootlessness or loneliness. As the Duke says to his son:

"Loneliness. The note, my son, is loneliness.
Over all the world
Men move unhoming, and eternally
Concerned: a swarm of bees who have lost their queen.
Nothing else is so ill at ease."

Or, as Fry says elsewhere:

". . . this great orphanage
Where no one knows his origin and no one
Comes to claim him."

It was just this business of being very precise and nice about one's origins which so occupied Angela Thirkell. Christopher Fry was the pessimistic reflection of the same inquiry. Once again marriage was the essential key to survival: although the three mistresses do not know the Duke's intentions, they naturally come to his house together when he calls them. "One good marriage and . . ." But everything to do with the Duke is decaying, his house, his sexual appetite, his honour. And outside, the world is under eclipse. When his house and possessions go up in flames, the Duke is left to resign himself to a marriage that may salvage his need for domesticity. We understand the moral: the Duke and all he stands for are consigned to the ashes, although the survival of his actual person is immaterial. As a person, he may continue existence at a low level with a former mistress. Resignation is marginally better than destruction. The ship is sinking, but the captain has the wisdom to climb into the only lifeboat available.

It was quite natural for the critics to couple Fry with T. S. Eliot. *The Cocktail Party* was first performed at the Edinburgh Festival in September 1949, and was brought to London in May of the following year. *Venus Observed* was therefore produced midway between these two dates. The publication of these plays in book form was more or less simultaneous, generally giving the reviewers an opportunity to digress about verse drama. Raymond Williams, writing shortly after *The Cocktail*

Party had been produced, summed up this new trend: "In our own day, the phase of naturalism . . . has, so far as serious, original work is concerned, already ended." There were furthermore several playwrights who seemed to flourish under the Christian skirts of Eliot and Fry: Ronald Duncan, Anne Ridler, and Norman Nicholson, whose plays were taken to point towards a revival of poetic drama. Much of this centred upon the Mercury Theatre and the productions of Mr. E. Martin Browne, but both Eliot and Fry were fortunate in their actors. Alec Guinness took the part of Sir Henry Harcourt-Reilly, and was succeeded in it by Rex Harrison. Superficially *The Cocktail Party* was greeted as an enjoyable evening in the theatre – "entertainment of much distinction," it was called by Desmond Shawe-Taylor. I can remember being taken to see the play at Brighton. There was a large crowd at the theatre; it was the opening night. There was rapturous laughter and applause. I have an image of glasses raised upon the stage: it seemed to be the way grown-ups did behave at their solemn functions, but it was interesting that they should enjoy laughing at it so much.

I was not alone in responding to this as a play of mood. Peter Fleming, for instance, politely self-deprecating – "I am speaking for the more honest of the Philistines" – wrote: "It seems to be a distinguished, exciting and stimulating drama; but I find the greatest difficulty in explaining why it possesses these qualities . . . The plays of poets are more apt to be analysable in terms of their mood than in terms of their message."

The Cocktail Party was also staged on Broadway, where it had a successful run not far short of a year, or what *The Times* correspondent referred to in the vernacular as "a long innings". The *New York Times* ambiguously called it "a verbose and elusive drama that has to be respected", but James Thurber, in a *New Yorker* article, "*What* Cocktail Party?" may have touched nearer the truth: "Ever since the distinguished Mr. T. S. Eliot's widely discussed play came to town I have been cornered at parties by women, and men, who seem intent on making me say what I think *The Cocktail Party* means, so that they can cry 'Great God, how naïve'." Stephen Spender, too, noticed that the play formed the chief subject of conversation at New York cocktail parties, "thus providing the title with a wry, Eliotish, ironic overtone." And in his book *Drama from Ibsen to Eliot* (1952), Raymond Williams recorded that an American actress, after seeing the play, returned home to advise American playwrights to smash their typewriters.

Certainly some of the more exaggerated claims made on behalf of the play were due to the fashionable criteria, and to the debate among high-brows on the function of verse in the theatre. Thus Henry Reed in *The Listener* could make this tremendous claim: "I believe that in English only the use of verse on the stage can elevate the drama to a position where its achievements may be taken as seriously as those of the novel; and I also believe that this elevation has been achieved with illuminating certainty and success only once in the last two hundred years, in Mr. Eliot's *The Cocktail Party*." Eliot's success was largely that he had taken a well-established convention, that of the drawing-room comedy, with a long and prosperous history behind it, and presented it in terms which appeared more meaningful than audiences usually supposed from other plays of this genre. Mr. Eliot himself explained his view in a lecture in 1950. "It is the function of all art to give some perception of an order in life, by imposing an order on it," which he elaborated: "It is ultimately the function of art, in imposing a credible order upon reality, and thereby eliciting some perception of an order *in* reality, to bring us to a condition of serenity, stillness, and reconciliation." In order to do this he postulated that prose was an inadequate medium, too direct for the communication of ideas whose intangibility could only be captured in verse.

A few critics stood out against this, notably Ken Tynan, who sub-sequently expressed his view in the *Atlantic Monthly*: "I have been finding myself in a beleaguered minority. The post-war vogue of T. S. Eliot and Christopher Fry has brought back into the play that ancient battering-ram of criticism, the assumption that the upper reaches of dramatic experience are the exclusive provinces of the poet." About Fry he wrote, in his book *He that Plays the King*, in 1950: "Like Olivier, Gielgud recognised in Christopher Fry the only modern dramatist to whom he could adapt his own rhetorical style, and accordingly took him up and made a commercial success of him. Fry is a producer's nightmare: he bears, I have sometimes felt, the same relationship to a first-class playwright as the man who engraves the Lord's Prayer on pinheads bears to a sculptor. But Gielgud, incomparably alert to Fry's poetry, demonstrated in *The Lady's Not For Burning* that here at last was a dramatic verse which could be spoken at the speed of dramatic prose." And, in the *Atlantic Monthly* article, Tynan extended this: "In poetry, Fry gilds where Eliot anoints; in neither procedure are there seeds of real dramatic vitality. If they, the foremost heretics, can be persuaded off their crosses away from their martyrdom in a lost cause, the theatre would immediately benefit."

The nature of Eliot's martyrdom stems from certain of the upper middle-class attitudes brought out earlier in the work of Thirkell and Fry.

Although immensely articulate and not comparable as a work of art or literature, *The Cocktail Party* completed the contrasting moods of upper middle-class outrage and resignation by furnishing its own mood or spirit of defiance, that is to say, of the need to carry on at all costs. "IF you can keep the bloody audience's attention engaged, then you can perform any monkey tricks you like when they ain't looking, and it's what you do behind the audience's back so to speak that makes your play IMMORTAL for a while." This was one of Eliot's "Five Points on Dramatic Writing," written to Ezra Pound. It is worth looking at the monkey tricks in order to understand the influence this play had, the immortality for a while, and so to learn what it was trying to impart, for it was nothing if not didactic.

Essentially this is a play about the unhappy marriage of two upper middle-class people, Edward and Lavinia, whose love for each other has died and who have found lovers, a fact they try to conceal from each other. This is a stock situation of its kind, of many a hundred such drawing-room plays. Eliot's originality lay in his attempt to show that, although the pressures of personality drive people apart once the initial impulse of love has worn down, yet the higher response to this will be an acceptance of the inevitable and a return to a life wholly orientated by conventions. Human feelings are too dangerous for ordinary people, and they must accept all the support that society has devised to prop them up. Hence the play ends with the reconciled Lavinia and Edward giving a cocktail party, that most artificial form of human contact, depending entirely on conventional manners, and paying each other stilted compliments. There is an alternative, which is taken by Celia, who was in love with Edward. It is not clear to most of us that this second possibility exists, for to realise it requires faith—"the kind of faith that issues from despair." But Celia chooses it when she learns that neither way is better in itself. "Neither way is better. Both ways are necessary. It is also necessary to make a choice between them." Celia's choice leads to a horrible death in a distant and savage place.

Both ways of life are manipulated by Sir Henry Harcourt-Reilly, a psychologist who features as a kind of Orwellian Big Brother, half god, half guardian, ordaining, teaching, supervising, occasionally having a private joke at his own expense—"What's the matter with One-Eyed Reilly?" He is interested in helping people find solutions in much the same way as the Church is, and it is a sign of the times that he is a psychologist, not a priest. The problem which afflicts these characters, and which they excuse as loss or nonfulfilment of love, is loss of origin and purpose, of impermanence, having no sense of belonging. These are particularly the problems of a disorientated upper middle-class. Loss of origin is not so terrible, if the origins were abandoned with relief because they were extremely poor, or else if they are always there to return to. Rootlessness may be a liberation, unless the roots provided sustenance, and the best way of finding out may be to pull them up and have a look. The preoccupation with security is something naturally pertaining to those whose possessions are the most important thing in their lives, and who therefore toil and spin and take every precaution for the morrow. Since this is essentially a selfish action, they are reassured by the sort of authority provided by Sir Henry Harcourt-Reilly.

It is interesting that the most important outcome should be the reconciliation of Edward and Lavinia. They offer each other security in spite of the awareness that they do not love each other, and they have no illusions about it. They live in a world which is threatened on all sides. The alternative has led to Celia's revolting death. Outside the framework of their marriage lies disintegration and the end of all they stood for. Yet again, it is a case of "One good marriage and . . ." Angela Thirkell's characters married in order to perpetuate the old way of life. Christopher Fry's Duke married because, once the human plight becomes manifest, any woman to share it is better than none, given the general insufficiency of all. Edward and Lavinia stay married just so that they can perpetuate what they represent, and not fall into the self-aware unhappiness of the Duke, knowing that what they represent is worthless because the life has gone out of them. What linked these tight-lipped viewpoints together – different as the expression so plainly is – was the sense of patching up, of the choice between letting the dry rot eat up the whole social fabric, or else preserving just those parts which were selected as indispensable for what had always been recognised as a proper way of life. Everybody here was observant: all had understood that life would not be quite the same again: together they formed three points of a defensive post-war bastion.

T. S. Eliot had long made his position clear. But by 1950 he was speaking with greater authority than before. "One seems to become a myth, a fabulous creature that doesn't exist," Eliot told an interviewer at the time. The myth grew from the distant island of his poetry, which seemed to rise above the surface of the waters and to be accessible to those few who were prepared to make the effort of rowing across, while underneath were the increasingly disparate refractions of Eliot's prose which were knocking a hole in the bottom of the boat. Hugh Kenner has described Eliot's fundamental critical strategy, until fame overtook him, as "a close and knowing mimicry of the respectable." Certainly there was much of the don in Eliot's critical writing. After all, as a graduate research student of Harvard, he had written a thesis on F. H. Bradley, and from Harvard had gone first to the Sorbonne and then to Merton College, Oxford. On the whole it was the work of dons which elucidated much of his poetry, and in particular Helen Gardner's *The Art of T. S. Eliot*, which appeared in 1949. But the obscurity of his writing, it is fair to say, restricted Eliot's audience to a small number of people. It was not until his social criticism and his plays were more widely known that he became a public figure, that the myth appeared – fully-armed, for Eliot had been in his adopted country since 1915.

His social criticism was expounded in two books before the war, *After Strange Gods* in 1934, and *The Idea of a Christian Society* in 1939. Eliot saw perfectly well where social change was leading. "A society has not ceased to be Christian until it has become positively something else. It is my contention that we have today a culture which is mainly negative, but which, so far as it is positive, is still Christian. I do not think that it can remain negative, because a negative culture has ceased to be efficient in a world where economic as well as spiritual forces are proving the efficiency of cultures which, even when pagan, are positive; and I believe that the choice before us is between the formation of a new Christian culture and the acceptance of a pagan one." It was not with culture as a concept that Mr. Eliot was interested: he saw culture as a kind of mechanism which allowed us to regulate society and make judgements about it. This came out most clearly in his *Notes Towards a Definition of Culture*, published in 1948, and the book which gave Eliot a reputation as an upholder of traditional values, although he was only elaborating what he had said already. The myth was carrying him along.

The argument was rather opaque. E. M. Forster objected to this: "When he is writing for people who may answer him back, he becomes wary. By its caution and astuteness the title forestalls many possible objections. But what cumbersome English!" Basically Eliot argued that we had developed within a Western religious tradition, and that our culture was essentially an aspect of this, a complement to it. "We have to face the strange idea that what is part of our culture is also a part of our *lived* religion." Eliot tried to forestall the obvious objections to this in an introduction, when he stated that he had political convictions and prejudices, although he did not want to impose them, and, if his beliefs conflicted with any passionate faith of the reader, "if he finds it shocking that culture and equalitarianism should conflict, if it seems monstrous to him that anyone should have 'advantages of birth' " Eliot asks him to stop "paying lip-service to culture." Really Eliot was here expressing the general dismay of the observant post-war bourgeois that their culture had declined into nullity, and could only be resurrected by observing the old social forms. Angela Thirkell had also reached this conclusion, although she was perhaps interested in the rather crude characteristics of "advantages of birth." Eliot presented it more elaborately: culture was the highest expression of man; if you accepted culture, you must also accept the things that fashioned it, religion, the rich, and so on: plainly the people who were most fortunately placed to enjoy and improve this culture should have every opportunity, because it was self-evident that man ought to express himself as well as he could; anybody who did not believe this should not dabble in culture. As the *New Statesman* reviewer, R. D. Smith, said: "There are higher and lower degrees of culture and we must not pretend that the higher kind of culture ought to be accessible to everybody." Mr. Eliot also dropped some asides: "It is essential for the preservation of the culture of the minority, that it should continue to be a 'minority' culture." He pointed out how the lower culture was "destroying our ancient edifices to make ready the ground on which the barbarian nomads of the future will encamp in their mechanised caravans." Even the language was for once intriguingly like Angela Thirkell's: certainly the same conclusions emerge. Mr. Eliot too wanted the family to propagate the traditional culture, and, the better placed the family, the higher the culture, so that an élite was formed. A carefully regulated attitude to marriage must be at the centre of such an existence. He too wanted the regional culture—not dissimilar to Barsetshire, if I understand it correctly. In many less important social attitudes—towards foreigners, or the Royal Family—similar parallels could be drawn between the two writers.

This gives a better perspective on *The Cocktail Party*, or rather on the monkey tricks while we aren't looking, and while our attention is held by the brilliance of the verse and the theatre. For surely here was a play defending a minority culture at a time when the barbarian nomads appeared to have got the upper hand, even to have elected a government of their own choice. The characters accept the authority of Reilly to arbitrate over their destinies. Celia dies, which does not surprise Reilly, and Lavinia and Edward return to each other in a reaffirmation of his values which do not take their feelings into consideration. They accept Reilly's definitions of the world against their judgements. But, if it were a case of resisting the barbarian nomads, it was important to do precisely this, or else they might find that they were at one with the nomads. If Angela Thirkell urged her readers to keep their backs to the wall, Mr. Eliot told them, if they could understand him, which wall it was, and how they should recognise it.

Mr. Eliot appeared after the war like one of the thinkers of the nineteenth-century reaction, gathering together the strands of conservative emotion and placing the garland before the public far more intelligently than the other more direct partisans on his side. Besides publishing *Notes Towards a Definition of Culture*, 1948 was the year in which he emerged into the limelight, into the gossip-columns where before he was an object of ill-informed and Philistine fun. Partly he was treated as the Celebrated Poet and Playwright, and partly as the Thinker, the social critic behind the Establishment. The culmination of his worldly triumph was the award in November 1948 of the Nobel Prize for Literature. *The Times* devoted a leader to the subject, incidentally pointing out that "In the course of a single year Mr. Eliot has received degrees from the universities of Oxford, Aix-en-Provence and Munich." The world press carried a photograph of Mr. Eliot in evening dress receiving his award from the Crown Prince of Sweden. The same leader talked about "a happy irony, for it is not so many years since Mr. Eliot was the object of general criticism as an opaque and wilful poet with an ancillary talent, not always well employed for prose criticism." However, the leader writer tried to justify the honour: "It must be supposed that the Nobel award has been bestowed upon a quality which he exemplifies better, perhaps, than any of his eminent contemporaries — a coherence of outlook reflected by an exceptional sense of responsibility." In the 1948 New Year's Honours List, Mr. Eliot had also been awarded the Order of Merit. About this distinction Raymond Mortimer commented in the *Sunday Times*: "The Order conferred on Mr. Eliot honours two men, the dramatist who has moved a large public in churches as well as in theatres, and a recondite poet who has further widened the gulf between literature and the general reader . . . He has evolved a style exactly fitted to render his imaginative vision, a style that expresses with equal intensity the heart-rending vulgarities of the modern world and the life-enhancing mysticism of historic Christianity." The Nobel Prize was the top of the crescendo. The myth was being taken out of Mr. Eliot's control, if it had ever been within it: the apotheosis was under way.

At the Edinburgh Festival in 1949 Eliot was confronted by a journalist with a set of written questions about *The Cocktail Party*. He defended himself: "I should like to suggest to you a useful exercise. Imagine that you have just seen the first performance of *Hamlet*, and try to set down fourteen questions for Shakespeare to answer, parallel to these fourteen.

Then consider whether it is not all for the best that Shakespeare never answered these questions, or, if he did, that the answers have not been preserved." Certainly publicity and fame are more damaging to the creative writer than to other people. Christopher Fry had pleaded: "The difficulty of the poet-dramatist is to create himself in the glare of the public eye, to be given the opportunity to fail, and then half-fail and to avoid being stamped on before he can achieve." But Eliot, although so blandly discouraging to journalists, was wholly in command of his published or performed work, and it was essentially as a controlled and didactic writer that he emerged in the post-war years, perhaps the most influential high-brow on either side of the Atlantic, the focus of intelligent reaction against the new mass society, revealing in his attitudes what other writers could only express with less dignity. What he was saying was in itself not in harmony with the reconstruction necessary during these years, and contains little compassion for his fellow-men, perhaps not even a disinterested curiosity in the future. He did not like the times, and in the social forms evolving after the war he found little to rejoice over and much to regret. The apotheosis of Mr. Eliot might be embodied in a marble statue of a Roman senator crowned with the appropriate laurels, and surveying the thronged forum below with a stony, sculptured stare.

Many others were holding the same kind of opinion, although not so provokingly because not so skilfully. A few, like George Orwell, who published his two best-known books, *Animal Farm* and *1984*, during these years, were as dissatisfied with the state of society, but for opposite reasons. Although perhaps more interesting, such writers were in the intellectual minority, and seem to be shipwrecked or marooned from the Thirties. One new writer, Angus Wilson, was beginning to probe the uncomfortable middle classes in his short stories. His first collection, *The Wrong Set*, immediately received as the work of a new talent, was a breakaway from the post-war strait-jacket: his stories of the late forties probably reflect the nature of the times more faithfully than the work of any other writer: and as for the Oysters, whom everyone was getting at, they hardly put a sound down on paper. It was as if their day had never come, as if the "bloodless revolution" had not happened – or, rather, was not to become effective for many more years. It was still the day of the Walrus and the Carpenter, wondering if the sand could ever be swept from the shore, spoiling the treat for the young Oysters, as if the new feelings abroad could be painlessly stifled.

11

BEVAN'S FIGHT WITH THE B.M.A.

Labour and nationalisation

PETER JENKINS

Peter Jenkins was born in 1934. He was educated at Culford School, and was a scholar of Trinity Hall, Cambridge, where he took a First in History. He was the Emma Perry Ogg fellow at the University of Wisconsin from 1957–8. He worked for the *Financial Times* before joining the London staff of *The Guardian*.

BEVAN'S FIGHT WITH THE B.M.A.

Peter Jenkins

WINSTON CHURCHILL did not miss the opportunity in 1948 to suggest that Aneurin Bevan should be among the first to receive free psychiatric treatment under the National Health Service. Others, more sympathetic towards Bevan, wondered if he was in his right mind in choosing the eve of the Appointed Day for nationalisation to tell a Manchester audience that he regarded the Tories as "lower than vermin." Even Harold Laski, himself no mean exponent of putting his political foot in it, estimated that the remark would cost two million votes at the next election. Certainly, long after the hubbub had died down, and the painted words "Vermin Villa – home of a loud-mouthed rat" had been removed from the Minister of Health's front door at Cliveden Place, Chelsea, the insult had not been erased from the political memory.

What rankled so about this particular piece of Welsh invective was its timing. Bevan had said many offensive things before about his political opponents, and he was to say many more. But he had chosen to speak of his "deep, burning hatred of the Tory Party," which, as the architect of mass unemployment between the wars, had obliged him as a young man in Tredegar to depend on the earnings of a working sister, on the eve of July 5th, 1948. On this day Britain committed finally to history more than four centuries of Poor Law legislation. The means tests, "Robin Hood medicine," and all the anomalies and abuses which had grown out of a hundred years of piecemeal reform were swept away. Under the National Health Insurance Acts "workmen's insurance" became National Insurance. Citizens, not merely paupers, were covered by the National Assistance Act. Medical treatment, including dental and ophthalmic services, for the first time became free to all. The bad old days were supposed to be over and done with: the Welfare State had arrived.

"The main outlines of a social service state approaching maturity are now plainly discernible in a logical array," said *The Times* leader writer cautiously. An "important reform," Churchill called it down at Woodford. The Prime Minister, in a broadcast to the nation, recognised the non-party roots of the plant which had flowered under Socialism. Bevan

himself, in his final message to the medical profession, had commented
gently "there is nothing of social groups or class in this."

Why, then, did he speak of class hatred on July 4th, 1948? It was
typical of the man and the moment. The achievement of a Welfare State
built around a free National Health Service marked for Bevan, and for the
many who had waited through the years for power, the realisation of a
personal goal. Bevan's father, a founder member of the Tredegar
Working Men's Medical Aid Society, had died in his son's arms of the
dreaded pit disease—pneumoconiosis. Aneurin Bevan had seen poverty,
ill-health and squalor in abundance. In 1945, with Labour's massive
victory at the polls, came the opportunity to sweep it away. For Bevan,
it was the "revolutionary moment." When Attlee made him Minister of
Health, with responsibility for housing, local government, and the setting
up of a National Health Service, there were plenty of voices to urge upon
him caution and delay. A National Health Service was a gigantic project –
should it not be brought into being gradually? Bevan resisted a phased
programme; the revolutionary moment waited for no man. "We are going
to make the right people squeal for a change," he said in 1945, catching
the mood of the day. Three years later, in July 1948, the revolutionary
moment had almost vanished. Crisis had followed crisis, sapping the
strength of the Government which had set out to build a new Britain.
The horizon had been darkened with the threat of bankruptcy. There was
not the money to build the new hospitals and health centres. The timber
for Bevan's housing programme could not be afforded. The people and
the Government were divided on the next step forward—the public
ownership of steel. The discipline of the nation was cracking: strikes in
the coalfields were holding back recovery; the black market was undermining the policy of fair shares; the squatters preferred a roof over their
heads now to high-standard permanent houses later; the miners found it
difficult to understand that nationalisation could mean harder work;
householders who wanted a pot of paint obtained one as best they could,
not worrying that it threw the planners' arithmetic out. But, for all the
disappointments of three years of Labour power, and for all the doubts
which hedged around the future, Bevan's health service, despite the
seductive voices of delay, and despite its near-sabotage by an organised
group of doctors, was there to see, safely and soundly established. It was
with a sense of achievement that Bevan voiced his hatred of the past.

The National Health Service was the most ambitious and one of the
most successful pieces of Labour legislation. Within a year of its inception

41,200,000 people – ninety-five per cent of the eligible population – were covered by it. In the first year 8,500,000 dental patients were treated and 5,250,000 pairs of spectacles dispensed, illustrating the pent-up demand for the dental and ophthalmic services, which had never been a part of the old insurance system. Working people no longer had to test their own eyes at Woolworths. In the first year 187,000,000 prescriptions were written out by more than 18,000 general practitioners. "I shudder to think," said Bevan as the statistics soared, "of the ceaseless cascade of medicine which is pouring down British throats at the present time." The National Health Service employed 34,000 people, and cost nearly £400,000,000 a year. In terms of money and manpower it became the second largest undertaking in the country – second to the armed forces. It was the largest single item in the civilian budget, and accounted for about 3½ per cent of the national product.

That some form of National Health Service should be set up after the war was not a matter of controversy among the parties. In 1943 Sir John Anderson, for the Coalition, provisionally accepted the Beveridge Report, including its "Assumption B" that after the war there would be "a national service for the prevention and cure of disease and disability." The next year Henry Willink, Coalition Health Minister, presented Parliament with a White Paper entitled *A National Health Service*, which envisaged a service hardly less ambitious than that which Bevan later introduced. The war had produced a broad consensus of opinion on medical planning. It had quickly exposed the inefficiency and inadequacy of the hospital system, the grave lack of equipment, and the shortcomings of a non-unified health administration. It had led to an experiment in central medical planning in the Emergency Medical Service and when many, especially middle-class people, found themselves publicly hospitalised for the first time, their not very pleasant experience helped to arouse public opinion in favour of reform. "Disease must be attacked in the same way that a fire brigade will give its full assistance to the humble cottage as readily as it will give it to the most important mansion." "The essence of the satisfactory health service is that the rich and the poor are treated alike, that poverty is not a disability and wealth is not an advantage." The first words are Churchill's, the second Bevan's.

There was no guarantee, however, that a Conservative Government would have introduced a thorough-going health service after the war. The medical profession, though committed to reform, and in theory in favour of a wholly free, comprehensive service, was already alarmed as the prospect of something actually being done grew more imminent. After publication of the 1944 White Paper the doctors turned the pressure on Willink, and in backstairs discussions persuaded him to press in Cabinet for a number of important concessions. These included remuneration of general practitioners by capitation fees, not by salary as envisaged in the White Paper for doctors in group practice. Suspicious of what was taking place, Labour announced that it would not be bound by anything that had passed between the Ministry of Health and the British Medical Association. Thus there were the makings of a grand row before the war ended, and before the Labour Party was swept dramatically to power.

When Bevan arrived at the Ministry of Health he inherited the broad outlines of a health scheme inspired by a Liberal and drawn up by a Conservative. He added Socialism. The entire hospital system was now to be brought under public ownership; the principle of nationalisation was to be applied to medicine no less than to fuel or transport. The size of such an invasion of the private sector by the State did not escape Bevan, and he recorded with evident satisfaction "it takes away a whole segment of private enterprise and transfers it to the field of public administration." Looking back, he commented, "A free health service is a triumphant example of the superiority of collective action and public initiative applied to a segment of society where commercial principles are seen at their worst."

An entirely free, comprehensive health service, equally available to all, had been a principle of official Socialist policy since 1934. Bevan intended not to depart from it; he rejected suggestions that an incomes ceiling should limit entitlement to free treatment – "The really objectionable feature" of this would have been the creation of a two-standard health service, "one below and one above the salt." He determined that the principles of his scheme, approved by the electorate, were not to be a matter for discussion nor its execution a subject of delay. The service was to be financed according to Socialist principles; Bevan rejected a flat-rate contributory method in favour of direct finance from the Exchequer out of progressively applied taxation. Less thought was given to the overall cost of the scheme or of the social services generally. The mood of 1945 was "push on and hang the expense" – the end was taken to justify the financial means. With the enthusiasm of a fervent Socialist, and the obstinate determination of a Welshman to have his way, Aneurin Bevan set out to carry through the most far-reaching piece of social legislation in British history.

If Bevan's attitude towards the National Health Service helped to surround it with an unfortunate and unnecessary air of controversy in its formative days, it was not without the assistance of two obstinate doctors. One was Dr. Guy Dain, a veteran medical politician of seventy-five who had sat on the B.M.A. Council since 1921, and been its chairman since 1942. The other was Dr. Charles Hill, secretary of the B.M.A., but more famous as the B.B.C.'s Radio Doctor, who, during the long period of food rationing, with its unpalatable whale-meat and snoek, maintained a continuing paternal concern for the normalcy of the nation's bowels. The electorate had clearly expressed at the polls its desire for a National Health Service, all political parties had welcomed the Beveridge Report and the Coalition White Paper, and the doctors themselves, in reply to a B.M.A. questionnaire in 1944, had substantially approved the major proposals of the White Paper, including the abolition of the sale of practices and remuneration by salary of general practitioners in group practice – later two of the most explosive issues. Yet Dain, Hill, and the medico-politicians at Tavistock Square succeeded in whipping up such an opposition within the profession that by 1948 it was feared that the whole scheme might be sabotaged.

The B.M.A.'s annual representative meeting happened to be in session at Tavistock Square when the results of the 1945 General Election were coming through. Despite Labour's sweeping gains, delegates found reason to cheer the news of Sir William Beveridge's defeat as Liberal member for Berwick. Relations between the doctors and the new Minister of Health began promisingly. Bevan's blunt and good-humoured informality went down well with medical audiences and, ever jealous of the mysteries of their scientific art, the doctors approved of his frank admissions that he was very much the layman who knew no more about the subjects on which he was required to speak than his officials at the Ministry had set down in his brief – which for this reason he frequently refused to read. During the months in which Bevan's Bill was in preparation, Dr. Dain's negotiating committee of sixteen B.M.A. representatives, three representatives of each of the three Royal Colleges, and seven representatives of other medical organisations, stood by, waiting to negotiate. But there was no negotiating to be done. Bevan considered the views of the medical profession to be already well known and the last thing he intended was to engage in horse-trading with a pressure group on the principles of the Bill that he would present to Parliament. Anxiety mounted at B.M.A. House as some of Bevan's proposals leaked out to the Press. Shortly after Labour's first Christmas he presented the negotiating committee and other interested parties with a confidential statement of his draft proposals – but still he refused to discuss them. Effectively gagged from publicly discussing the proposals, the *British Medical Journal* struck a gloomy note in the February of 1946. "Doctors share the general weariness of the spirit that descends on everyone in the immediate post-war phase, made less easy to resist in the present gloom of austere living on short commons in front of fires that burn very low. As a people we have missed the elation of victory . . . As a profession which has had to negotiate with two war-time ministers, we are faced with a peace-time Minister who consults but does not negotiate, or, in the ordinary sense of the term, discuss."

Bevan's Bill was published on March 26th, 1946. It received, on the whole, a good press. However, Bevan's refusal to discuss his proposals in advance with the medical profession made it inevitable that the White Paper would find little favour with the B.M.A. Regional control of the hospital system was welcomed, but nationalisation was opposed. Local *ownership*, it was argued, was compatible with public control. "It will no longer be more blessed to give than to receive," said Hill piously, but Bevan shed no tears for the passing of the voluntary system—it was repugnant to him, he said, to see nurses selling flags in the streets when they should be tending the sick. The proposal to prohibit the purchase and sale of the good-will of practices ("A reform," said *The Times*, "now probably supported by at least half the medical profession") was completely unacceptable to the B.M.A. The Minister's powers provided by the Bill were held to be too great—"dictatorial" became a favourite epithet for Bevan. The Local Authority Health Centre programme was too radical for the B.M.A., which considered that the centres should be introduced on an experimental basis only in the first instance (in the end the building materials shortage saw to it that none could be built). Most obnoxious of all to the B.M.A. was the proposal that the remuneration of the general practitioner should contain a basic salary component. It was on this that B.M.A. propaganda concentrated. Hill's tactic was to stir up ill-feeling towards Bevan for his refusal to negotiate with the profession, and to play on the doctors' fears that his Bill was the thin end of the wedge that would turn them into full-time salaried civil servants. B.M.A. members were encouraged by their leaders to consider the proposals in the Bill not from the point of view of an efficient health service, but from the standpoint of principle, the principle of professional freedom.

A few days after the publication of the Bill an audience of more than a thousand doctors, gathered at Wimbledon Town Hall, was told by Hill: "We are on trial now. This is the most essential phase in the history of the profession. Let us not consider it as a matter of compensation (for sale of good-will) or remuneration. Let us look at the principles and determine where in fact the principles lie, and let us, at last, learn to stick together." This meeting—typical of many which Hill and Dain were to address up and down the country—ended with an elderly doctor observing, "If the Bill comes into operation in anything like its present form it will represent something very much like that régime which is now coming to its sorry end at Nuremberg."

The Bill was read a second time on April 30th, spent two months upstairs in committee, received a third reading on July 26th, and the

Zec, *Daily Mirror*, 2.5.46

Hill meets mountain!

Royal Assent on November 6th. The committee stage was hard fought. In the first week alone one hundred and thirty-two columns of *Hansard* were filled—twenty-nine by Bevan, twenty-seven by Willink—in disposing of three clauses out of the Bill's seventy-four. In the end Bevan had to have the committee meet both morning and afternoon in order to get the Bill through before the recess. Nevertheless the B.M.A. failed to get the Bill amended in any important detail. By midsummer the conflict had sharpened. Bevan accused the B.M.A. leaders of allying themselves in a spirit of partisanship with the Conservative Party. Dain told the B.M.A. annual meeting "A conflict is inevitable." It came in December 1946.

Acting on the mandate of a referendum which showed fifty-six per cent of the doctors to be opposed to co-operation with the Government in the introduction of the scheme, the B.M.A. informed Bevan that it would refuse to negotiate with him on the terms of service. The medico-politicians had succeeded in swinging a majority of the organised medical profession into declared hostility towards an Act of Parliament.

The deadlock did not persist for long. On January 2nd, 1947, the social and professional gulf which separated the local general practitioner, the backbone of the B.M.A., from the grand consultants and specialists of the ancient Royal Colleges, became apparent for the first time. To the great disgust of Hill and Dain, the three presidents of the Royal Colleges, Lord Moran, Sir William Gilliat, and Sir Alfred Webb-Johnson, wrote to Bevan in a spirit of compromise, defining the area of difference between the Government and the profession, and requesting certain clarifications and assurances. It was a move that heralded the final ignominious collapse of the B.M.A.'s campaign nearly eighteen months later.

From the beginning, the specialists were more favourably disposed towards a National Health Service. They stood to gain from State employment in the hospitals, in which they had hitherto served in an honorary capacity in order to acquire the prestige essential to a lucrative business as a private consultant. A unified, more efficient, and more adequately financed hospital system was to their professional advantage. Many of the general practitioners' problems, such as the buying and selling of good-will, or payment by capitation, did not directly touch them. The B.M.A., on the other hand, was dominated by the general practitioner, and in its composition tended to reflect the views of the well-to-do, older, and often suburban practitioner. The young doctors, the medical officers of health, the doctors who had found in the services that their clinical freedom had not been impaired one bit by salaried service under a discipline far more rigorous than anything envisaged in a civilian health service, were less fearful of lay interference than the vocal group in the B.M.A. which had the time and money to engage in medical politics. It was this group which egged on Hill and Dain in their immoderate opposition to Bevan's scheme.

Bevan was quick to seize upon the opportunity given by the letter from the three presidents. He disarmed the B.M.A. by a conciliatory gesture which effectively invalidated their mandate to refuse negotiations with him. He assured Lord Moran and his colleagues, in a published correspondence, that no doctor need fear that discussions on the terms of service would compromise his freedom to make up his mind when the time came whether or not to join the service. The method of remuneration, he said, was "open to discussion" and he would "gladly discuss" the question of appeals against expulsion from the service. He gave the assurance that he had "no powers to direct a doctor to go anywhere or do anything." Significantly, he agreed with all the points raised of special concern to specialists and consultants – satisfactory arrangements would be made to encourage them to work within the precincts of hospitals; he also attached the "utmost importance" to this.

The B.M.A. Council decided, with a not very good grace, to talk with Bevan, on the understanding that amending legislation would not be excluded from the discussions, and that a second plebiscite would be held at the end of the negotiations. From February to December 1947 the negotiations proceeded between B.M.A. leaders and Ministry of Health officials in a series of specialised sub-committees. The surface was undisturbed by whatever currents were running beneath it until, on December 2nd and 3rd, 1947, Bevan met personally with the full negotiating committee. A second crisis exploded. According to Bevan, Dain presented him with a duplicated statement of the B.M.A.'s position, which had been decided before the meeting ever began. According to the B.M.A., Bevan was as obdurate as before, refusing to make a single concession to the B.M.A. while, by his concessions to the specialists, making finally clear his intention of splitting the profession. By all accounts this meeting marked the low point in the history of the Minister's relations with B.M.A. House. *Tribune*, which may be presumed to have enjoyed some access to its former editor and director, reported that Bevan warned the doctors not to push him too far on the issue of compensation for loss of good-will, as they had no right to any at all. "Don't be impudent," he told one B.M.A. representative during the meeting.

But, if Bevan had done nothing to allay the doctors' fears that the salary element in their remuneration would lead before long to the dreaded full-time salaried service, which technically he had the power to introduce at any time by administrative order, he had gone very nearly the whole way towards meeting the remaining reservations of the specialists and consultants. He had agreed in negotiation to set aside a limited number of pay beds in the State hospitals for the use of specialists attending private patients, he had waived the limit imposed on the fees they could charge, and he had agreed to exclude the nursing homes from nationalisation. Two further carrots were held out to the specialists: the teaching hospitals, the most famous and distinguished of the British hospitals, were not to fall under the jurisdiction of the Regional Boards, but would be independently administered by Boards of Governors; and specialists were to be remunerated on a generous scale. In this way Bevan made powerful allies within the profession, who were to help him yet again, and this time decisively, within a few months.

Barely six months remained before the Appointed Day when the B.M.A. ordered the second referendum. To the public, through a Press by now exasperated with the B.M.A.'s stubborn behaviour, it appeared as a delaying tactic. Doubts were cast on the genuineness of the plebiscite as an attempt to find out what the doctors really thought about Bevan's scheme. *The Times*, which had little more patience with Bevan than with the B.M.A. leaders, commented irritably, "The dispute has been allowed to drag on as though it were a private wrangle between the Minister of Health and a score of elderly doctors."

The doctors voted by nine to one against accepting service under the Act. It was a declaration of war which seemed to threaten the implementation of Labour's legislative showpiece in the social field. But it is unlikely that Bevan was greatly disturbed: he had more cards to play yet. He had done nothing to conciliate the doctors when, on February 9th, 1948, while the referendum was in progress, the Government had staged a full-dress Commons debate with no apparent purpose other than to influence public and medical opinion. In fact he had used this occasion to mount his most bitter attack on the B.M.A. He described its leaders as "a small body of politically poisoned people," who had misrepresented his Act to the profession, and were currently engaged in the "organised sabotage" of an Act of Parliament. "It looks like a squalid political conspiracy," he had said. But Bevan knew by then that nothing he could do or say was likely to win round the B.M.A. leadership, and detach their rank-and-file support. It was Lord Moran who helped him do this by acting, for the second time, to undermine the popular mandate obtained by Hill and Dain.

Moran, President of the Royal College of Physicians, the oldest and grandest of the Royal Colleges, had come to be on friendly personal terms with Bevan. Moreover, they seem to have indulged in some successful horse-trading, which resulted in the important concessions and attractive terms offered to the specialists. It certainly looked like a put-up job when, on March 22nd, the comitia of the Royal College of Physicians adopted a resolution, published on April 4th, which called on the Minister to amend his Act in such a way as to make it impossible to introduce a full-time salaried service except by further Act of Parliament. Bevan swiftly took his cue: on April 7th he announced in the Commons that full-time salaried service would not be introduced by statutory instrument, and added that he would consider making the £300 a year basic salary for general practitioners optional after a doctor had been in practice for three years. He called for new talks with the B.M.A. In the Lords that afternoon Moran was dutifully up to welcome Bevan's statement. The Minister, he said, had boldly met the main fears of the doctors, and it was now to be hoped that he would be rewarded by the loyal support of all reasonable members of the profession.

Dain saw what was coming immediately the R.C.P. resolution was published, and wrote at once to *The Times*. He pointed out that not only did the Act make it ultimately possible to introduce a full-time salaried service by statutory regulation, but that it made "here and now" a number of harmful changes, among which he instanced the universal basic salary. This, he warned, the profession would not accept, whatever the amount. The B.M.A. leaders were in for another shock, however, for, when Bevan met with them a week later, he informed them that four thousand doctors – about twenty per cent of the total – had already signed on for service under the scheme. The National Health Insurance doctors were faced with the expiry of the Lloyd George scheme on July 5th. Bevan had the B.M.A. in a cleft stick, and he knew it.

Still they fought to the last ditch. The B.M.A. council issued a statement which said, "Bearing in mind what we have secured falls short of what we sought, the council's view is that, while progress has been made to that end, the freedoms of the profession are not sufficiently safeguarded." Dain made an intemperate speech at Shrewsbury, which went beyond the B.M.A.'s more cautious official policy. The famous physician, Lord Horder, who led the opposition in the Royal College to Moran, announced in a letter to the *Daily Telegraph* that the situation was "unchanged" by Bevan's conciliatory move. Nevertheless, when the B.M.A. ordered yet another plebiscite, it wisely provided itself with an avenue of retreat by announcing that a vote of at least 13,000 against service would be required before the B.M.A. would feel justified in recommending a boycott. The wily Hill by this time could see the end of the affair; the Conservatives had become frightened by the virulence of the doctors' opposition and, wishing to escape from the pressure of the militantly reactionary section of the B.M.A., Hill attached to the plebiscite a condition that he knew could not be met. In February 1948, 17,000 general practitioners had been prepared to refuse service. When the results of the third plebiscite were declared early in May the number had dwindled to 9,588. In February, nine doctors were prepared to refuse service for every one prepared to take part. Two out of three doctors were now willing to co-operate. More than 7,000 general practitioners had changed their minds, and another 2,000 had not troubled to vote. A special representative meeting of the B.M.A. was called to consider the situation. When it met on May 28th it was known that 26 per cent of the doctors in England, 36 per cent in Wales and 37 per cent in Scotland had already signed on. Yet there were still those who wished to continue the fight—Horder was one, but not Dain this time. He told the meeting that he had never been so disappointed in all his life as at the result of the plebiscite. He admitted regretfully that, on the good-will question, the B.M.A. had received no support from Parliament, nor from any political party. He referred to the differences which had become apparent in the B.M.A. council, between the majority and the sizeable minority, who, it turned out, really did not want a health service at all. Trying to put a brave face on the B.M.A.'s defeat—for so it was—he said, "We have not given up anything. It is the Minister who has given up all the time." And with these heartening words the B.M.A. at last decided to recommend its members to serve Aneurin Bevan under the National Health Service Act—barely a month before the service was due to begin.

Bevan was able to out-manœuvre the B.M.A.'s negotiators because they never knew what they really wanted. They spent too much of their time and energy defending principles which were not at stake. While the eminent surgeons were busy persuading Bevan to allow pay beds in State hospitals in order to avoid a mushroom growth of private nursing-homes – a concession he was later to regret—the ordinary G.P. was being encouraged by his leaders to worry about whether he would be free, under the National Health Service, to write a letter to his local newspaper. Dain's and Hill's only major achievement in their dealings with Bevan was to negotiate the salary component of the general practitioner's remuneration virtually out of existence. In all the other matters of principle they sought to defend they were charging either at securely bolted or wide open doors. Their opposition to the nationalisation of the hospitals, or the prohibition of the sale of good-will, was useless, because these measures in the eyes of the Government were fundamental to a National Health Service. Their efforts to protect the doctor from becoming a civil servant were unnecessary, because Bevan never intended it. Throughout, the B.M.A. insisted that it was in principle in favour of a National Health Service. But it became clear that many of its leaders were fundamentally opposed to what the Government in power meant in practice by a National Health Service.

By concentrating on the method of remuneration, the B.M.A. neglected attending to the amount. The specialists and the dentists fared better under the service than the general practitioner, especially the general practitioner with the medium list. The basic salary, which was unobjectionable in its proposed form, would have been welcome to many doctors had not the B.M.A. set against it, not so much in its present form but in its hypothetical future form. In the end it was limited only to those doctors who desired it and were able to persuade their local executive council that they would suffer hardship without it.

Bevan regarded the fear of lay interference as the most legitimate cause of the opposition he encountered from the medical profession. "Any health service which hopes to win the consent of the doctors must allay these fears," he wrote later. He could have done more to allay them at the time had he understood them better. The medical profession had always been extremely sensitive to any change that might in some way intrude upon the doctor-patient relationship, an emotive concept which no doctor could quite define but which was held to be in jeopardy the minute the State appeared upon the threshold of the surgery. A Labour Government, particularly a Labour Government which included Bevan in its Cabinet, not surprisingly exacerbated the traditional fears of a predominantly middle-class professional group. There were a number of incidents which contributed to the doctors' alarm. At Willesden municipal hospital there was the case of the doctor, matron, deputy-matron and thirty-six nurses who were given notice for refusing to join a trade union. There were the cases where doctors' prescriptions for extra rations were overruled by Ministry of Food doctors who had not seen the patients in question. There were the letters in the newspapers complaining of red tape, bureaucratic high-handedness, and inter-departmental muddles. There were the epic tales of form-filling feats. Bevan had every reason to lose patience with the B.M.A. leaders, but more tact on his part and a greater willingness to listen sympathetically to the doctors' fears might have prevented some of the bitterness which surrounded the introduction of the National Health Service.

The doctors' opposition to the National Health Service was the most serious that the Labour Government encountered during the three years in which the major part of its programme was carried into effect. Because of the peculiar phobias of the medical profession, this was not a true reflection of the mounting hostility to nationalisation, hardly a foretaste of the campaigns which were to centre on steel, sugar and cement. But it contained, nevertheless, an element of general political disaffection, and the doctors were, after all, the first middle-class and predominantly Conservative interest group to offer concerted resistance to the Government.

By 1948 Britain had consumed a large and rather stodgy helping of Socialist legislation in a very short period of time. She was suffering from indigestion. The nationalisation of the Bank of England, the coal and fuel industries, the railways, and the wireless and cable services all aroused little opposition. The case for taking each of these industries into public ownership for the sake of national efficiency had been well made, not least in the reports of the various independent committees which the Conservative Governments had set up to look into their shortcomings. But by 1948 industry was beginning to organise against further invasions by the State into more profitable sectors of the private economy. To the public, more nationalisation began to seem irrelevant to the pattern of recurring crisis. The consumer had begun to discover that public ownership of coal made it no more abundant, nor prevented its price going up. British Railways took their place in the repertoire of music-hall jokes. The worker discovered that the State was an employer much like any other employer, and just as interested in maximising productive effort. The social services, although undoubtedly popular, seemed to their critics unwarrantably expensive and grandiose at a time when the nation tottered almost daily on the brink of bankruptcy. Until Cripps reminded the nation that it could not have its cake and eat it, the people had not seemed to realise that free teeth and spectacles were just another form of consumption and unrationed, at that. It had not been appreciated that social services, subsidised housing and controlled food prices were just as much a part of the standard of living as another pound note in the pay packet. Ultimately the whole range of social services made freely available cost the equivalent of an all-round wage increase of about £2 15s. 0d. a week. Few realised that they were not paid for by the weekly insurance stamps.

When the war ended, nobody was in the mood to reckon what the peace would cost. A cartoon by Zec used in the 1945 election campaign showed a returning soldier and his young wife banging on the counter of the Tory peace stores. Under the counter are hidden "jobs", "proper medical attention", "good homes", "decent schools" – "the fruits of victory" marked "reserved for the rich and privileged." The returning soldier says to the storekeeper, "What do you mean, you're out of stock? I've paid twice for those goods, once in 1914 and again in 1939." Post-war Britons wanted all these things, and Labour had promised them, but few quite realised how seriously the country had been weakened by the war. More than half the national wealth had been lost, two-thirds of the export trade was gone. Britain was the largest debtor nation in the world. Almost everything was in short supply – raw materials, dollars, labour, food, equipment, accommodation, and, as Herbert Morrison observed in the crisis days of August, 1947, above all, time. "An impoverished, second-rate power, morally magnificent but economically bankrupt," was how the *New York Times* correspondent found post-war Britain. More than half a million houses were needed to replace just the worst slums, coal production was 50,000,000 tons down on pre-war, demand for electricity had increased by twice the amount of generating capacity, millions of pounds' worth of damage had been done to the railways. During six years of war the people had consumed less than four years' normal supply of clothing, and less than three of household goods. It was under these conditions that Labour set out to build the new Britain – to maintain larger peace-time armed forces than ever before, to build more houses, to provide more leisure, to nationalise and modernise the basic industries, to maintain full employment, and to erect the most comprehensive welfare state in the world. It was hardly an austerity programme.

So much depended on coal. Ernest Bevin even said that he could give the country a new foreign policy if it could only give him more coal. On January 1st, 1947, Emanuel Shinwell and Lord Hyndley stood with hats raised at the gates of Murton Colliery, County Durham, before a notice board which announced jubilantly, "This colliery is now managed by the National Coal Board on behalf of the people." Within two months of this historic day there were 2,300,000 unemployed, and £200,000,000 worth of exports down the drain, all because of a shortage of just 6,000,000 tons of coal. It was nothing of course to do with nationalisation, and Shinwell could not be blamed for the coldest winter since 1881. He could be blamed, and was, for the one per cent error in his forecasting which helped to bring about the first, and perhaps the worst, of the three major economic crises which afflicted the Labour Government. His offence was aggravated by his jocular pooh-poohing of the dire predictions which had been made in the previous autumn, by such well-informed persons as Arthur Horner, the general secretary of the mineworkers' union. The fuel crisis set the national recovery back for a whole year, and made almost inevitable the dollar crisis of the summer. It illustrated Britain's utter dependence on sufficient supplies of coal.

Nationalisation of the industry had long held pride of place in the

Labour Party programme. The miners had been demanding it for more than fifty years, the Sankey Commission had recommended it as long ago as 1921. Partly because of its emotive significance for Labour it was made number one priority among the Government's post-war tasks. Winding up the second reading of the Coal Nationalisation Bill, Hugh Dalton said, "In this Parliament we are going to nationalise many industries and services, but the Government has decided that the miners shall have pride of place; that theirs shall be the first industry to be transformed from private inefficiency into public service, that in the great forward march of Socialist accomplishment the miners shall lead the way." But the transformation of the coal industry was easier said than done. Psychologically and physically, it was in a dreadful state. The legacy of the pre-war period was not only an old-fashioned, ill-equipped, and inefficient industry, but a store of bitterness and suspicion in the heart of the miner against the treatment he had received at the hands of the colliery owners. The "coal industry" also turned out to be a gigantic undertaking, the largest single business in the Western world. On Vesting Day the nation found itself the proud possessor of not only 1,634 pits, but also 55 coke ovens, 85 brickworks, 30 briquette plants, 250,000 acres of farmland, 141,000 houses and a mixed bag of hotels, swimming-baths, holiday camps, shops, a bicycle track and a slaughter house. Shinwell had gone to the Ministry of Fuel and Power innocently believing that somewhere in the Party archives a blueprint was ready. A few weeks later he was telling a luncheon gathering at the Dorchester Hotel, "We are about to take over the mining industry. That is not as easy as it looks. I have been talking of nationalisation for forty years, but the complications of the transfer of property had never occurred to me."

Lord Hyndley, the National Coal Board's first chairman, had spent his life in the industry, and had long been in favour of its nationalisation. He was liked and trusted by the miners. No man could have better bridged the old days and the new, but his task was an impossible one. On the one hand he was expected to produce more coal, on the other to modernise the industry. Modernisation involved closing or reconstructing old pits, and sinking new ones, but meanwhile the country needed every lump of coal, every shovelful of nutty slack that could be extracted from below ground or above. Mechanisation helped to increase output (although the machines came from abroad and cost dollars) but ultimately the coal supply depended on the miners. As Shinwell said, "We do not produce coal at the Ministry of Power. People seem to think we do. Coal is not produced by statistics, or by Government departments, or even by speeches, however eloquent they may be. Coal is produced by miners working underground." There were not enough miners, and those that there were were not producing enough. In May 1947 a five-day week was introduced in the pits, not because the country could afford to do without the Saturday output (Saturday working had later to be reintroduced at overtime rates) but because the miners expected something from nationalisation, and had waited a long while for it. The Government could hardly deny them the main point in their Charter. All it could do was to hope that the shorter hours would boost pit recruitment. Output per man-shift had fallen well below the pre-war rate, absenteeism was more than twice as high. In the year before nationalisation there were 1,329 unofficial strikes, in the year after, 1,635.

In the late summer of 1947, when the dollar crisis obliged Attlee to trim his programmes all round, and to give the country its first dose of post-war austerity, the *Manchester Guardian* summed up Britain's needs: "We must at once make a new effort to get more coal. Without that nothing else will help us very much. Only the Government can lay down the programme for that effort. The National Coal Board has neither the authority nor the ability to do it. *It has turned out to be little more than another Government Department.*" So, at any rate, it seemed to the miners of the little Yorkshire village of Grimethorpe. It had long been the custom in the Yorkshire coalfield for men to knock off before the end of their shift if they had fulfilled their output target. One of the conditions of the five-day week, however, was that coal-face stints were to be reassessed, and the miners were henceforth to work a full shift. The reassessment went smoothly enough, until the one hundred and thirty-two men who worked the Melton Field seam at Grimethorpe were ordered to work an extra two-foot "stint". On August 11th they struck.

At the height of the strike, which raged erratically through the Yorkshire coalfield during the next five weeks, 50,000 men were out in sympathy, thirty-three pits were idle, and steelworks in Sheffield were reduced to below half their working capacity. As a result of the strike 600,000 tons of precious coal were lost. Workers went on to short time at engineering and textile factories hit by power cuts. Wakefield bakeries had to import loaves from Lincolnshire. Coal had to be carried to Yorkshire from Newcastle.

Shinwell broke his holiday at Eastbourne and rushed north. Horner and the other miners' leaders left the annual Trades Union Congress at Southport, where the need for more coal was high on the agenda, to try to end the strike in Yorkshire. But the Grimethorpe men obstinately refused to go back, and a Labour Government and the Board of the newly nationalised coal industry looked helplessly on at a dispute which, in bitterness, exceeded many of those in the bad old days. Partly the fault may have been the handling of the situation by the chairman of the North-Eastern area board, General "Mickie" Holmes, whose action in threatening the Grimethorpe strikers with the sack sharpened the dispute. But the real culprit was the past. The mental scars of the inter-war years could be no more repaired overnight than the physical damage to the mines. The traditional hostility to the boss remained, and the National Coal Board was turning out to be just another boss. The miners had expected more of nationalisation than it could possibly give. Newspaper reports during the Grimethorpe strike quoted miners as blaming it on the "obstinacy" of the top-heavy Board in London. Some said it would all have been settled in a day under the old coal owners. One spokesman for the strikers said, "If we lose now, officialdom will make us their door-mats. We are sticking out for a principle against a new kind of officialdom." A Coal Board spokesman, later repudiated, said "This is a test case of our authority. We cannot afford to have our prestige shaken by withdraw-ing the extra stint order." The official union appeared to the men to be ranged on the side of authority. They ignored the warnings from Horner, a Communist, that they were risking another fuel crisis that winter, which might bring the Government down and ruin the country. When Will Lawther, the miners' president, accused the strikers of damaging nationalisation, they put up a caricature of him at Grimethorpe with a noose round his neck. But, to the public, it seemed that the miners were obstinate and irresponsible, especially when it read in its newspapers of coaches being organised to take the strikers to Doncaster races. On Saturday, September 13th, Sayajirao won the St. Leger. On the Monday 35,000 men went back to work.

"Planning" was a key word in the Labour vocabulary, almost a magic word. *Let Us Face the Future*, the 1945 manifesto, promised, "Labour will plan from the ground up, giving an appropriate place to constructive enterprise and private endeavour in the national plan." But where was the plan, how was it to be carried out? Herbert Morrison, responsible in the early years for the co-ordinating of home policy, was understandably vague when pressed on this point. In 1946 he told the House of Commons, "I am happy to say that the machinery of economic co-ordination and administration has undoubtedly improved enormously during recent years. We have learnt a lot about this in the war, and those lessons are now being applied to peace." Attlee was a little more frank when he said,

"Although we may have to plan without having all the data, it is better than having no plan at all. We must make some kind of economic forecast."

Shinwell made "some kind of economic forecast" in the autumn of 1946, and, by getting it slightly wrong, failed to take the precautionary measures which might have averted or at least softened the blow of the February 1947 crisis. According to Dalton, usually malicious when Shinwell was concerned, the Fuel Minister, challenged by Attlee on his estimates, advised the Prime Minister not to be blinded by statistics, and to take account of the "imponderables". The affair alerted Labour to the grave weaknesses of the planning machinery. The re-thinking which ensued led in the end to the supremacy of Cripps, whose task it was from November 1947 to devise means of paying for what had gone before, trimming the nation's coat to the size of its cloth.

Labour came to power prepared and equipped to fight the traditional enemies – unemployment and over-production. It encountered unforeseen foes – under-production and over-consumption. When Morrison told the 1946 Party conference, "We have turned our backs on the economics of scarcity," it sounded like a foolish boast. But he meant – and it was true – that no longer would goods go unproduced for want of paying customers. The situation was the reverse: there was more money than goods, more jobs than labour, more needs than a dislocated, war-damaged industry could answer. And Morrison's words were true. It was not what he meant, but Labour *did* turn its back on the economics of scarcity. During the first two years, Bevan's "revolutionary moment", it pushed its programme through without too much regard for the cost. In November 1945, for example, George Tomlinson, Minister of Works, asking the Commons for £100,000,000 as a revolving fund for the purchase and supply of building materials, said that, as he had never heard it suggested during the war that a military operation should be held back for financial reasons, he hoped that his Bill would be treated in the same spirit. It was the spirit in which the Government treated the whole of its programme until the day of reckoning came.

Even then, in August 1947, when the convertibility crisis forced Attlee to reverse the trend away from war-time austerity, no clear system of priorities had been evolved. There was still no "national plan", and the hatchet fell where it would hurt least politically. The left wing succeeded in shielding the housing programme from a direct blow, although it was to suffer from the £10,000,000 cut in timber imports. It was capital investment which suffered the largest proportionate cut when the programme was trimmed. The Working Parties set up by Cripps, as President of the

Board of Trade, were all finding that much of the equipment in their industries was out-dated and inadequate. If the economy was to be planned from the ground up, as Labour had said, it was here, above all, that the money needed to be spent. It was estimated, for example, that the country required £30,000,000 worth of machine tools annually to maintain a moderate rate of industrial recovery. But £12,000,000 worth was all that was provided in 1947–8. It was in areas like this that austerity really pinched.

Without foreign aid, it would all have been quite impossible. In 1948 the Board of Trade estimated that, had Marshall Aid not come to the rescue, rations of butter, sugar, cheese and bacon would have had to be cut by one-third, cotton goods would have disappeared virtually from the home market, timber shortages would have reduced the housing programme from about 200,000 new buildings a year to about 50,000, and shortages of other raw materials would have led to 1,500,000 unemployed, with the situation worsening. It was not until 1947 that the Government began to square up publicly to these realities. The Economic Survey for 1947, and those for the following years, were the nearest the Government came to producing the "national plan". The first Survey recognised many of the factors which limited Labour's power and ability to plan the economy. There was "democracy", which made it impossible in time of peace to compel too many people to do too many things. There was the external situation, which committed the country to a day-to-day, hand-to-mouth struggle for survival. And there was the complexity of British industry, which made central direction through the existing machinery virtually impossible. Other limitations were not mentioned. There was the lack of information on which rational planning decisions could be based (the economic section of the Treasury had no more than fifteen graded economists, and the Central Statistical Office the same number of professional statisticians). There was the vacuum at the top where the plan, such as it was, gave way to naked competition between departmental Ministers. The first economic Survey itself was a watered-down compromise between the conflicting demands of the service Ministers and those engaged on drawing up a civilian manpower budget. Thus, at the centre of the first "plan" was the "manpower gap" which it was *hoped* could be closed by increased productivity. Failure to recruit enough men to the pits was one of the great planning failures of the period, which inhibited all other efforts towards economic recovery. The 1947 Survey warned that the central fact for the year was that "we have not got enough resources to do all that we want to do. We have barely enough to do all that we must do." Everything was priority; it was a question of priority priorities. In such circumstances, without the machinery, the personnel, the materials or the time, there could be little in the way of planning "from the ground up." By necessity the Government was limited to attempting to direct the economy from the top down – simply by allocating scarce resources. Using the war-time machinery of materials controls, the planners were able, in crude fashion, to organise the limited resources where they were most required to give flesh to the bare bones of the Government's political decisions – wood for pit props, bricks for the housing programme. Planning was rationing, scarcity the only effective weapon in the whole of Whitehall.

"A good plotter but a bad planner," Derek Walker-Smith called Bevan in a housing debate. But Bevan, within the physical limitations which beset his ambitious programme, got most of his houses built. Against a target of about 200,000 new permanent dwellings a year, Bevan built 558,261 by the end of 1949. In addition, about 125,000 temporary houses were erected, and more than 140,000 damaged homes repaired. Bevan's policy was to build houses for the workers. Private building for sale, and the repair or redecoration of owner-occupied premises, were ruthlessly restricted. A private house, built under licence, was limited to a cost of £1,200, repairs and decorations to £10. Bevan's council houses, he insisted, were to be good houses, worthy of a natural life of eighty years. Despite their expense – including fittings and fixtures they came to £1,500–£1,600 – he resolutely refused to reduce standards, and he was never more than half-hearted about the prefab programme which he had inherited from the Coalition. His idea of houses fit for workers to live in was "spacious homes fitted with all the labour-saving appliances invented by domestic science." They could be made available to all, and at low rents, only, Bevan told the electors of Ebbw Vale in 1945, if the task of house-building was organised on a national plan.

Control over the building programme was from the first hopelessly divided. As Minister of Health, Bevan was ultimately responsible, but the Ministry of Works was responsible for the bulk purchase of basic building materials (bricks, glass, cement, etc.) the Ministry of Supply for fittings (from bathtubs to nuts and bolts) and a multitude of local authorities for actually putting the houses up. Completions were continually delayed by bottlenecks of supplies. There were bricks with nobody to lay them, or bricklayers with no bricks to lay. Houses were finished except for the electrical fittings. Houses were even occupied without their kitchen units. Partially built houses became a familiar part of the early post-war landscape. "We are having to close down brickyards because they cannot get orders," Bevan told the House in 1947, "and the reason they cannot get orders is because the rate of bricklaying is not what we are entitled to expect it to be . . . There will be found, on sites all round London, wherever one likes to look, stacks of bricks."

The planners added up the numbers of bricks, tiles, doorknobs, and windowpanes which were required to meet the housing programme, and eventually satisfied themselves that the output of materials squared with the planned output of houses. But this did not mean that a bathtub was where it was wanted, when it was wanted. And the planners, who as a race hold human nature in high esteem, took no account of the materials siphoned off into the black market for illicit repairs and decorations. The problem of distributing building materials efficiently was never solved. At Bristol, in 1946, Bevan was urged by an angry member of his audience to "deal with" the black-marketeers. "They are myriad," he replied. "How can I get at them if I cannot find them? I should want an army of policemen. That is why I say that in these difficulties what we want from the British people is self-discipline and self-restraint."

"Self-discipline and self-restraint." Under the menace of Hitler there had been enough of this to support an elaborate system of controls, rationing, and regimentation. It lasted over into the period of Labour Government, in the first flush of peace and enthusiasm for building the new Britain. But gradually it broke down: among the doctors, the miners, the householders, the frustrated people on the housing lists who became squatters, and among everybody who had more money to spend than before the war and less to spend it on. "Planning in itself is no substitute for the increased effort and efficiency which are essential to our national prosperity," said Attlee. Planning, Labour was discovering, was people.

12

THE LYNSKEY TRIBUNAL

JOHN GROSS

John Gross was born in 1935, educated at City of London School and Wadham College, Oxford, where he read English Literature. Coming down in 1956 he joined the publishing house of Victor Gollancz, which he left in 1958 for a year at Princeton University. He taught from 1959–62 at London University, and in 1962 was appointed to a teaching fellowship at King's College, Cambridge. He contributes regularly to the *New Statesman* and other journals.

THE LYNSKEY TRIBUNAL

John Gross

THREE years after the war had ended most war-time economic controls were still in force, and Britain was still a country of licences, permits, coupons, and allocations. Inevitably a great deal of business was done under the counter, and even official statements spoke rather primly of "the so-called Black Market"; at the same time the Opposition kept up a steady campaign against "snooping", "meddling", "Whitehall busybodies", and so forth. There were also malicious whispers about "jobs for the boys." But the harshest critics of the Government stopped short of hinting at corruption; French tax-evasion or American graft might be regarded as a bit of a joke, but even those who detested Socialism took it for granted that English Ministers and English civil servants were beyond the reach of a bribe.

Then, in October 1948, came the first whiff of a scandal. It was announced that for the past month the head of the Metropolitan Police fraud squad had been leading an investigation into the Board of Trade, at the request of the Lord Chancellor. A few days later there was a brief statement from 10 Downing Street: as soon as Parliament reassembled, the Government were proposing to set up a tribunal of enquiry into alleged irregularities at the Board of Trade. The allegations concerned a football-pool promoter and a firm importing fun-fair machinery; the name of the Parliamentary Secretary to the Board, John Belcher, had been mentioned, and it was with his agreement that the President, Harold Wilson, had asked the Lord Chancellor to organise an enquiry.

For a few delirious days the wildest rumours had been circulating: was this to be a scandal of Panama or Teapot Dome proportions, were senior members of the Cabinet implicated, would the Government fall? The Downing Street statement, with its suggestion of a much more limited, altogether homelier affair, went some way towards quelling the rumours, but, throughout the remaining three weeks of the parliamentary recess, there was still a good deal of extravagant gossip and speculation. The Press had to confine itself to reports of "foot-high" stacks of documents being sent to the Lord Chancellor; there were only two fresh developments to make public. Belcher, thrust uncomfortably into the limelight, asked for leave from his official duties until the enquiry was over. And on the same day that Attlee and Harold Wilson agreed to his request, a man who, even more than Belcher, was to be the central figure at the tribunal made his first appearance on the front page: "an alien" was detained by the police and taken from his flat in Park Lane to Brixton. Three days later he was released.

At the end of October Parliament reassembled, and decided, on the Prime Minister's own motion, to set up a tribunal of enquiry. Attlee explained to the Commons that, during the summer, officials of the Board of Trade had told the President of allegations being made that the Parliamentary Secretary and other Ministers or officials had been offered or received bribes. When the police were called in, it was revealed that they had been pursuing independent enquiries along the same lines, and further allegations were subsequently brought to light. As all the allegations centred on the activities of one man, it was right for them to be considered by the same tribunal; and the terms of reference of that tribunal should be wide enough for it to undertake "a general roving enquiry." For the Opposition, Churchill offered Attlee his full support, and advised M.P.s to set an example by not spreading scandal. Almost immediately it was announced that the tribunal would have three members: the chairman was to be Mr. Justice Lynskey, assisted by two K.C.s, Gerald Upjohn and Godfrey Russell Vick.

The tribunal was set up under an Act of 1921, which gave it certain judicial powers: it was able to take evidence under oath, and to compel witnesses to attend or documents to be produced. But it was again and again pointed out that it was not a court of law, and that its purpose was to establish facts, not to allot guilt. One important question of procedure was in doubt: the role of the Attorney-General. When the House of Lords agreed to the setting up of the tribunal, Lord Simonds expressed the hope that the law officers would not be left with the conduct of the proceedings, as they might be faced with a conflict between duty and loyalty to colleagues. But, at the first session of the tribunal, the Attorney-General, Sir Hartley Shawcross, speaking as a law officer and not as a member of the Government, offered his full services, and it was agreed that under the instruction of the Treasury Solicitor, and with the assistance of other counsel, he should present the case and examine witnesses. Lord Simonds' doubts must have been set at rest; certainly no more was heard of them, and it has never been suggested that in the course of the tribunal Sir Hartley Shawcross pulled his punches.

The first session of the tribunal dealt only with procedure; so many statements and letters had been received, many of them anonymous, that a fortnight was needed to sort them out. Consequently it was not until the middle of November that the tribunal began its proceedings proper. The hearings, which lasted for five weeks, were held in the antiseptic atmosphere of a hall on the first floor of Church House, Westminster. At one end was a dais, where Lynskey and his colleagues sat at three tables draped with blue cloth; facing them were rows of chairs for witnesses, officials and lawyers (most of the key witnesses were represented by counsel). There were no wigs or gowns, and at the end of each session participants, journalists, and onlookers streamed away to tea together. Public interest was immense, even after it had become clear that any revelations at the tribunal would be less shocking than had been at one time supposed (or perhaps hoped). There were long queues at Church House, while the newspapers were full of little else. Osbert Lancaster had a series of cartoons commenting on the national preoccupation; one showed two clergymen bumping into each other at Church House, and one asking the other sheepishly: "What sudden diocesan crisis brings *you* up to London in the middle of Advent?"

In his opening speech the Attorney-General explained how the whole tangled web which the tribunal had to unweave centred on the activities of one man, Sidney Stanley. Stanley earned part of his "not inconsiderable" income by representing to businessmen who had dealings with Government departments that by bribery and other means he had great influence with those departments. He lent plausibility to his claims by forming an intimate acquaintance with Belcher, and much lesser friendships with George Gibson, a director of the Bank of England, and Charles Key, the Minister of Works. He also claimed to be a close friend of other Ministers, and, in fact, of the leaders of all the main political parties. One witness alleged that Stanley had boasted of paying Belcher £50 a week and making gifts to Mrs. Belcher, whom he knew as "Lulu", of £100 a time. This was hotly denied by the Belchers, and there was not a shred of evidence to support it.

With one exception (which concerned a man called Liversidge), all the major cases which the Attorney-General outlined bore the imprint of Stanley's methods. Three of them involved Sherman's Pools Ltd. of Cardiff. Owing to the paper shortage (those were still the days of salvage drives), the amount of paper allocated by the Board of Trade to the football pool promoters was strictly limited, and the promoters decided among themselves how this allocation should be divided up. Sherman's Pools was a firm which had expanded rapidly, and the Sherman brothers laboured under a grievance that their quota of paper was inadequate. In January 1948 the firm was prosecuted by the Board of Trade for a breach of the paper regulations; the magistrate reserved his decision, but died before he could deliver judgement. The Shermans were anxious that the case should be dropped, and twice wrote to Belcher. Then, at the end of March, Stanley introduced himself to one of the Shermans in the lounge of the Grosvenor House Hotel, allegedly armed with details of the case, and offering to help. Subsequently he met the head of the firm, Harry Sherman, whom he immediately tried to interest in buying various shares, including a controlling interest in Aldford House, the block of flats where he himself was living. He also said (so Harry Sherman reported) that other pools promoters had offered Belcher between £50,000 and £100,000 to put Sherman's out of business. Later he introduced Harry Sherman to Belcher, although both he and Sherman claimed that there was no discussion of the prosecution (which was withdrawn late in April). The Shermans were still eager to get an increased paper allocation. In June Stanley received two cheques from Harry Sherman, for £5,000 and £7,000. According to Sherman these were loans secured by three cheques which Stanley deposited with him, all of them subsequently dishonoured. Stanley, however, claimed that they were on account of a sum of £50,000 which he said Sherman had promised him for work in connection with the flotation of Sherman's as a public company. Stanley had also told Sherman that he could arrange for the Capital Issues Committee to give their consent, and introduced him to George Gibson, who warned him that such consent was in fact unlikely. In the event, the flotation wasn't proceeded with, and the paper allocation wasn't revised.

Apart from Stanley's dealings with Sherman's, a number of other cases were sketched in. There was the importer of amusement machinery who was told that he could obtain an import licence for £150,000 if he paid £10,000 through a solicitor to an unnamed recipient, who turned out, not very surprisingly, to be Stanley. Then there was the managing director of a paint firm, whom Stanley approached with an offer to obtain building permits for a site in Berkeley Square. When a fee of £500, or even £1,000, was mentioned, Stanley waved his arms and exclaimed "Chickenfeed!" and demanded £10,000 in notes. The affair went no further. Other building permits and import licences were also mentioned. Finally, there was the general question of gifts and favours; it seemed that, among other things, Stanley had paid for the Belcher family's hotel bill at Margate, given Belcher a gold cigarette-case, and had suits made for Belcher and

Gibson. At the beginning of August, when the storm was already starting to break, Stanley's munificence had culminated in what must have been an extraordinary gathering: a so-called birthday party which Stanley gave for Belcher, footing the bill (it came to almost £90 for six or seven people) and providing a cake with one candle and the odd inscription, "For Dear John on the first birthday" (the actual wording was later disputed).

The facts were tangled and obscure, and the written statements which the tribunal had received were often sharply at variance. It was therefore necessary to hear a great deal of evidence, and, after Hartley Shawcross's opening speech, there began a long and extremely well-assorted parade of witnesses. In quick succession the tribunal heard from detectives, bookies, senior civil servants, showmen, the President of the Board of Trade, and a lady from the Garter Club. A good deal was made of alleged talk of Stanley needing money "to grease palms." There was the witness with the faintly Proustian-sounding name of Sir Maurice Bloch, who was in fact a whisky distiller from Glasgow, greatly concerned with getting permission to import sherry casks, butts, and hogsheads for storing his produce. Sir Maurice admitted that he made gifts of wines and spirits to Belcher to secure "an easier approach," but explained that this was in order to persuade Belcher, when the time came, to speak at a Refugee Appeal meeting – an explanation which the tribunal declined to accept. Some of the evidence came straight from a cheap thriller; there were stories of anonymous threatening messages, bogus phone calls, and meetings with "Mr. X". Cheques bounced like tennis-balls. The tribunal heard about fruit-machines, dog-racing, gifts of sausages and cosmetics, rabbit-skins from Russia, exhibitions at Earls Court, an imported Packard which disappeared, and, of course, about football pools. If the world which was revealed was often seedy, it was seedy in the style of 1948; much of the evidence would have been unintelligible to a time-traveller from an earlier period. A writer in the *Spectator* pointed out that this was a drama which had unfolded at Harringay and Grosvenor House, although casual references to Ascot and the Savoy "introduced a welcome touch of tradition."

Many of the witnesses were businessmen, some of them displaying a nonchalance which must have startled the public in those pinched years of crisis and austerity. An amusement-arcade proprietor, asked if he wasn't surprised by a solicitor's letter embodying an agreement to pay £10,000 to an unspecified person, replied stolidly that it was not for a layman to be surprised at any document a solicitor presented to him.

Much of the evidence given by the businessmen had a quality of impenetrability. In particular Harry Sherman raised the circular argument to a fine art. One exchange ran:

Q: You thought the whole thing was extraordinary?
A: Yes, I did.
Q: Why was it that you thought it was extraordinary?
A: Well, the fact that this man knew so many people in high places.
Q: Well, why did that strike you as being extraordinary?
A: For the reason I have said.
Q: What was the reason, Mr. Sherman?
A: Well, it just struck me as extraordinary that he would know so many people.

Yet despite the doggedness of witnesses and the seriousness of the issues involved, there were frequent bursts of laughter from spectators, sometimes rather heartlessly, as when a witness called Colonel George described his first meeting with Belcher. The Parliamentary Secretary had said, "You probably know who I am?" and George recalled that he had answered, "Yes, I know all about you, Mr. Belcher," adding that it was a reply which he hadn't intended to have a sinister meaning. If the proceedings remained good-humoured, it was largely due to Lynskey's benign chairmanship. Lynskey came from Liverpool, and, although he had been a High Court judge for four years, he had not been previously well-known to the London public. But now, with his genial face and bulbous nose, he made a distinctive impression, while his dry observations to witnesses always went home. When Hirsch Teper, the tailor from South Audley Street whom Stanley had been employing, said in his evidence that he'd been using his imagination and putting two and two together, Lynskey remarked: "One of your twos was missing, Mr. Teper."

One episode in the tribunal stood by itself. A businessman called Green wanted to export twenty million paper cement bags to Belgium and France, but, when he went to the Board of Trade, he was told that it was unlikely that he would be granted a licence. In Brighton he ran into a man called Robert Liversidge, to whom he confided his problem. Liversidge had once been the central figure in a case of constitutional significance involving his temporary internment in the early days of the war. He was now a businessman interested in various companies with names of a fairly abstract nature: Transatlantic Service Representatives Ltd., the Allied General Investment Trust Ltd., the Allied General Trading Co., General Planning and Development (Holdings) Ltd., RWI. Productions

Ltd., and Plastilities Ltd. He also knew Belcher, and offered to help Green get his licence. According to Green, he later said that "they" wouldn't grant a licence, and it would have to go through him (Liversidge) at a cost of 1d. a bag. As this amounted to a fee of over £80,000, said Green, there were angry words, and he put down the receiver. Liversidge, on the other hand, told the tribunal that all he expected if he put Green in touch with the right department was "a nice box of cigars." He was questioned closely by the Attorney-General, and produced at least one neat distinction in reply. When asked whether a phrase which had been used was a lie, he retorted: "It's not exactly a lie, it's a commercial term." In the end the tribunal decided that there was no case at all for either Liversidge or Belcher to answer. But the most curious feature of the whole episode was that Green had initially gone to the wrong department of the Board of Trade, and that in fact no licence at all was needed to export the paper bags.

All this was something of a digression; the chief object of attention at the trial was increasingly Sidney Stanley. He sat brooding, or occasionally shrugging as one of his gaudier pronouncements was recalled. (Belcher, a few feet away, spent most of his time taking notes). Gradually a picture of what one witness termed "the Stanley approach" was pieced together. The tribunal heard about his gambling, his attempts to sell property to acquaintances, and, above all, about his boasts of friendship with the great ones of this world. He was "a man who would claim to know His Majesty, if he were pressed," according to one statement. Certainly he had told one witness that he was a close friend of the Prime Minister, and warned another to "hold himself in readiness" for a call from Dalton and Cripps. Yet he had been taken fairly seriously by tight-fisted and supposedly shrewd financiers. No doubt his activities on the fringe of politics lent a certain colour to his claims, although they can't always have inspired much confidence. There was the period when he busied himself in the affairs of a highly respectable organisation called the Freedom and Democracy Trust, for instance. He turned up uninvited at a dinner being given by the Trust, professed great interest in its work, borrowed a cheque from another guest, and made it out for £50 payable to the Treasurer; "the cheque, however, was irregular in its drawing and was never paid." Such stories might have been merely unsavoury if they hadn't also been so preposterous, and if Stanley himself hadn't obviously taken such pleasure in his bare-faced performances. An M.P. who was a friend of Belcher described how Stanley had pulled a scrap of paper from his pocket, and, in the midst of laughter, insisted on reading aloud what he purported to be its contents: "Dear Stanley, We are very pleased with the way you are helping us in the Government and the work you have done for the Party. Yours sincerely, Stafford Cripps." Undoubtedly the figure of Stanley in his big overcoat, taking huge baskets of fruit round to his friends, sounded rather jollier than some of the grey-faced tycoons who had been taking the stand. Belcher's former private secretary described how Stanley had told him that he had to hurry off to an appointment with some senior Ministers; later that afternoon he passed the Houses of Parliament and noticed "Mr. Stanley waiting in a queue with the public outside." The spectators in Church House burst into laughter at this, but it wasn't clear whether they were amused by the deception, or by the thought of this quasi-mythical figure standing amid the mere public.

The real facts about Stanley were less sensational, though perhaps only because they were so obscure. He had been born in Poland, but had come to England as a boy, shortly before the First World War. At various times he had been known as Solomon Kohsyzcky, Schlomo Rechtand, and Sid Wulkan. He had had to fend for himself from an early age; he claimed that he had been managing a workshop when he was only sixteen. He had been declared bankrupt in 1927 ("but I was only a kid then") and possibly again in 1936, under the name of Blotts. He was still an undischarged bankrupt. Before the war he had lived in the East End and Stoke Newington, and worked in the clothing trade. In 1933 a deportation order had been made against him, but the police had lost track of him, and little was known of his whereabouts until 1945, when he emerged as the tenant of a flat in Park Lane, describing himself as a "business agent". He was now in his late forties, a stocky figure with a pale face and heavy-lidded eyes (like a Victorian heroine's, according to Rebecca West, who was covering the tribunal in a series of articles. One of these drew a protest from Stanley's counsel which was followed by a general warning from Lynskey against prejudicial reporting). This was the man who came before the tribunal as the forty-fifth witness.

Stanley was examined and cross-examined for fifteen hours. He explained how at the end of the war, unable to go back to his old job of selling dresses, he had tried to start buying and selling department stores instead. (When the Attorney-General expressed surprise at so drastic a change in the scale of operations, he was told: "I was never interested in selling ten or twenty dresses – I sold thousands.") In 1946, Stanley said, he first met Gibson, when he was asked to take the fourth hand in a game of solo whist on the train to Manchester. It turned out that Gibson had met his brother, Marcus Wulkan, in America. Wulkan was visiting London, and a dinner party was arranged at which Belcher, who had not previously met Stanley, was also a guest. At first Gibson and Belcher were interested in Stanley because they thought he might be able to secure overseas trade through his New York connections (in his statement to the police Stanley said that his wife had gone to America to buy steel for the British Government, though this was later emended to "for the British country"). Later a friendship between Stanley and Belcher developed. Stanley vehemently denied that he was a contact man, or that his technique had been to scrape an acquaintance with leading politicians by inviting them through nominees to dinners (like the one to launch an anti-Communist magazine) for which he footed the bill. When he was asked whether he had ever offered, or talked of offering, sums of money to Belcher and Gibson, he was indignant: "Oh my God, never. How dare you suggest that?" He admitted that he had forced the gold cigarette-case on Belcher "against his wish and against his will," but it had been lying around in his flat since 1940. In any case, businessmen often handed out small gifts without any question of influence being involved; he had given Ernest Bevin twenty or so cigars, but "I didn't ask him to declare war on anybody." (Stanley had in fact met Bevin, but the Attorney-General said that the story about the cigars had been investigated and was completely untrue.) Sometimes a note of pathos was sounded. Stanley had introduced businessmen to each other because he felt sorry for them, and he had taken Belcher round to his tailor because he "couldn't bear it" when Belcher pointed out that he had patches in his trousers. But, if he wasn't a contact man, how had so much money passed through his bank account? Stanley explained that, until the previous April, he had been able to draw cash by cheques at the Greyhound Racing Association's banks. The cheques were not presented to his own bank for several days, and this gave him "three days' grace to play about with the money." Stanley had been described by an earlier witness as "not very conversant with the more elaborate procedures of business," but this was quite elaborate enough for most people. (It is a dizzying thought, too, that he had been pursuing almost all his various schemes simultaneously.) When Lynskey intervened to give a clear account of how the G.R.A. manœuvre had worked, Stanley was the first to congratulate him: "I'm very thankful to your Lordship for explaining what I could not explain myself."

Something of Stanley's winning ways came across as he gave evidence, although naturally he was largely on the defensive: he drank glass after glass of water, and continually wiped his palms with a handkerchief.

Sometimes he was rebuked after exclaiming "My God!", but in general he was unruffled. When Lynskey pointed out to him that an operation which he was describing was illegal, he immediately said, "In that case, my lord, I will have nothing to do with it." When he thought that a question might be better put, he offered to rephrase it for opposing counsel. What was most remarkable was his inability to say "yes" or "no". His evidence abounded with such phrases as, "put it on the other foot," "I disagree entirely," "it was mutually both ways," "nothing of the sort," "If I am right or wrong I don't know, but . . ." and, when he was hard pressed, "I defy you to prove it," or "it's news to me." At the time an observer wrote that "he was always level with Sir Hartley, and sometimes a little bit ahead." In retrospect this seems exaggerated, since prevarications never look at their best in cold print, and, in any case, Stanley was often at a disadvantage (as when it turned out that he didn't know the meaning of the word "bogus"). But to be questioned for fifteen hours by Hartley Shawcross was an ordeal which few would readily undertake, and Stanley certainly showed astonishing resilience, and an unusually good memory (even if it was for fabrications as often as it was for facts).

Interest now switched to Gibson and Belcher. Gibson was in his sixties, a burly Scotsman who had once been chairman of the T.U.C., and was now a director of the Bank of England, chairman of the North-Western Electricity Board, and a Companion of Honour. In 1941 he had been in America collecting funds for this country, and Marcus Wulkan claimed that he had met him at a lunch at the Commodore Hotel in New York, and handed him a cheque for $30,000. Gibson could recall the lunch (though not meeting Wulkan) and he accepted this claim, which is why he first let Stanley befriend him. (The Attorney-General later quoted a report on Marcus Wulkan, which had been undertaken on behalf of the British Iron and Steel Corporation, describing him in decidedly unflattering terms. In New York Wulkan called a Press conference, defending his reputation and offering to fly over to London and give evidence.) There was no question of Gibson having received anything more than a suit of clothes from Stanley. What was at issue was whether Stanley had dangled a well-paid directorship in front of him, and what he had meant when he spoke in a letter to Stanley of exercising "a greater degree of influence in the future than perhaps I have in the past." At any rate Gibson admitted that he had been "a little extravagant" when he wrote a letter of introduction to various American labour leaders on Mrs. Stanley's behalf, describing her as the wife of "an eminent businessman with large interests who is greatly concerned with assisting in the re-establishment of world trade and world prosperity."

Next came the Belchers, and the most painful part of the proceedings. John Belcher was forty-three. He had started life as clerk for the Great Western Railway, taken a diploma in Economics at London University, and entered Parliament in 1945. He had the air of a bank manager; he and his wife were obviously a hard-working couple, with three children and a small house in Enfield that must have seemed a very long way from Park Lane. In particular Mrs. Belcher, with her forthright manner and Old Look clothes, won a lot of sympathy when she broke down after being questioned about her fairly modest housekeeping budget. Belcher himself, before he gave evidence, announced through his counsel that he was resigning from the Board of Trade, as he realised that he had been wrong to accept small gifts (though there was no question of corruption) from Stanley, Sir Maurice Bloch, and a cosmetics manufacturer. He told a reporter afterwards, however, that he wouldn't be applying for the Chiltern Hundreds (" – or the Chiltern Thousands. It's all right. I know all the stories"). On the stand, he described how he had found Stanley a good companion: "interesting, amusing, generous." If he had told a businessman that, when the Labour Government went out of office, "some of you might be inclined to offer me a directorship," it had been a pure joke. Although, he added wanly, "during this tribunal I have had many causes to regret my sense of humour." It was generally agreed that Belcher was a good witness, whose candour and efficiency contrasted favourably with the evasions of some of the previous witnesses. But one point weighed heavily against him: the letter which he had written to the Lord Chancellor in September, when asked for a statement about the Sherman case and his associations with Stanley. He now admitted that his account of his dealings with Stanley had been inadequate, and that he had been wrong to say that the decision to drop the Sherman prosecution had been taken in his absence (the phrase was interlined as an afterthought), when he had in fact made the decision himself.

Several other Ministers appeared as witnesses, though far more briefly. The Solicitor-General, Sir Frank Soskice, flew five hundred miles from The Hague and back in order to say "no" seven times when asked about allegations connecting him with Stanley and the Shermans, none of whom he had ever met. Charles Key, the Minister of Works, said that Stanley had taken him to be measured for a suit by Teper, but he had been under the impression that Stanley owned Teper's firm, and there had been no question of not paying for the suit. As it was, he had only had one fitting, and the suit had never been collected. A better-known witness was Hugh Dalton, who appeared at his own request to scotch Stanley's allegation that he (Dalton) had sought a directorship from Isaac Wolfson, the chairman of Great Universal Stores. Stanley had in fact introduced Dalton to Wolfson, but no one believed the allegation about the directorship for a minute. Nor had the acquaintanceship between Dalton and Stanley been more than very slight. Dalton had brushed aside Stanley's overtures; the only odd detail was a letter which he had written to Stanley (in fact declining flatly the invitation to any further meetings), which had begun "Dear Stan". Dalton explained that this was a mistake by his secretary, and that he must have dropped his voice during dictation. The tribunal didn't think it worth pursuing the matter further, though Stanley's counsel couldn't resist a harmless little joke at the expense of Dalton as a man not exactly notable for lowering his voice.

After all the evidence had been taken, witnesses' counsel were allowed to address the tribunal. A bevy of K.C.s appeared in succession. In several cases counsel representing the pot devoted much of his energy to blackening the kettle represented by his learned friend. Stanley's counsel, on the other hand, stressed his client's kindness, though he conceded that he could be wilful and impetuous and had what Gibson had called "a tendency to oriental exaggeration." Finally, the Attorney-General summed up. He hoped that tendentious reporting of the tribunal in some papers would not undermine public confidence in the parliamentary form of government itself. There was plainly not a shred of truth in the allegations against any of the civil servants in the case; nor was it necessarily wrong for Ministers to associate with businessmen. But he couldn't help thinking that Belcher had been unfortunate in his friendships, particularly with Stanley, whom he labelled "the spider of Park Lane." It had been a grief to cross-examine Gibson so severely. If he hadn't always been an impressive witness, it should be remembered that he had recently been very ill. (Gibson had in fact never completely recovered from being gassed in the First World War.) Finally, and this was the heart of the matter, the standards of integrity and propriety in English public life were very high ones, which had to be jealously protected if the whole country was not to suffer, and sometimes individuals had to be sacrificed for errors which might seem comparatively trivial in another context. He hoped that the report of the tribunal would put an end to the "mean innuendoes and reckless gossip" which had been circulating freely.

There was now a lull of a month, with nothing for the Press to fasten on to apart from a few of Stanley's antics: he threw a party for journalists

Osbert Lancaster, *Daily Express*, 11.12.48

"*Well* IF *Santa Claus has not come out on strike in sympathy with the Euston porters, and* IF *he isn't subpoenaed to give evidence at the Tribunal, and* IF *you've been a very good boy, it* MIGHT *be worth while to hang out your stocking as usual.*"

and cracked jokes with the photographers who followed him when he went
out shopping. Then, at the end of January 1949, the report was published,
a document of some 50,000 words in length and, at 1s. 6d., a best-seller.
Despite the tremendous complexity of the evidence, the findings of the
tribunal were brief and straightforward. Belcher had received small gifts
or favours from Stanley, Sir Maurice Bloch, and a cosmetics manufacturer,
as he had already admitted. On account of these obligations he had intervened to secure an import-licence for Bloch, assisted two businessmen
(in connection with a lease and a licence) introduced to him by Stanley,
and decided to withdraw the prosecution against Sherman's. There was
no evidence whatsoever to support any other allegations against him. As
for Gibson, the tribunal was satisfied that Stanley had offered him the
chairmanship of a proposed new company, to induce him to help in getting
permission for the flotation of that company. Gibson had refused the
offer, but had continued to assist Stanley in his efforts, "in the hope of
some material advantage to himself," although all he had actually received
were some trivial gifts and a suit of clothes. All the other Ministers and
public servants involved were completely exonerated. Of Sydney Stanley
(the report gave his first name a new spelling), the tribunal contented
itself with saying that he was a man who would make any statement, true
or untrue, if he thought that it was to his own advantage.

Gibson was shattered by the report, Belcher "surprised and grieved."
Stanley told reporters that it was too long to read in bed, and went out to
have dinner in Soho instead. A week later, the report was debated by the
Commons, and its findings accepted. Before the debate, the Attorney-
General said that he thought justice could best be met without criminal
proceedings, since "in general great discretion should be exercised in the
use of statements obtained in the exercise of compulsory powers of
interrogation as evidence against the person who under that interrogation
actually made those statements." That needn't rule out proceedings under
the bankruptcy laws or the laws affecting aliens.

Belcher then made a personal statement. He apologised for his mistakes,
and recalled the day in August 1945 when he had been sworn in as an
M.P. – his fortieth birthday, and "the happiest and proudest day in my
life." Now he touched the depths of wretchedness, since he was proposing
to apply for the stewardship of the Chiltern Hundreds. There was
sympathetic cheering as he strode to the Bar, turned and bowed, and
hurried out. His wife was in the gallery watching.

The debate which followed was quite short. Attlee sounded the
dominant note when he said there were no party differences when it came

to being determined to maintain the highest standard of integrity in public life. In agreeing, Churchill added a word of sympathy for Gibson, whom he had known personally. The only difference between the two leaders was over Stanley; Attlee thought the best thing would be for him to be deported, Churchill hoped that he might be prosecuted. From the Conservative back benches, Earl Winterton suggested that Stanley should be parachuted over Warsaw, and wondered why Belcher had not been expelled from the House, as had happened in the case of Garry Allighan, former Labour Member for Gravesend, who was expelled in October 1947 for "offences against Parliamentary privilege and decorum."

For several weeks there was falling debris, and witnesses at the tribunal were still in the news. The name of Sir Maurice Bloch was removed from the list of Glasgow's Justices of the Peace, while Mr. Teper of South Audley Street, tired of being pointed out as "Teper the Tribunal Tailor," decided to emigrate to Florida. He ran into difficulties, however, which delayed him on Ellis Island, while the papers tried to build him up as a somewhat Chaplinesque figure. For Belcher and Gibson there was less publicity. Belcher retired into private life, while Gibson, who had already quit the Bank of England, now resigned from the Electricity Board, though not without reluctance. He announced that he had no intention of relinquishing the Companionship of Honour. He died in 1953.

Stanley's farewell bow was altogether more spectacular. Guarded by detectives, and claiming to receive seven hundred letters a day, he was now playing to the gallery for all he was worth. He announced that he was writing a book, from which the royalties would be used to set up a Sydney Stanley Children's Trust. In the meantime, he had sold his memoirs to *The People* for an estimated £10,000. *The People* announced that Stanley "would be the poorer for disclosing his secrets, and the public would be the richer for hearing them." It is to be doubted whether the public got the better of the bargain. There were no startling disclosures, apart from a cock-and-bull story about Stanley stoutly resisting the blandishments of Russian agents, and what one can only call some ghostly memories ("As I look back down the years, memories come flooding back. Gordon Selfridge smiling and shaking his head as he said: 'I must hand it to you, Stanley, you were too smart for me . . .'") Other papers kept up a campaign urging that Stanley be deported as quickly as possible, but it was not clear where he should be sent to. The Polish authorities declined to accept any responsibility for him, while the Israelis announced that he would be unwelcome (although there was some difference of opinion, since Israel was pledged to grant admission to all Jews). Meanwhile, Stanley was reporting every day to the West End Central police station. Then, early in April 1949, he disappeared. For a few days nothing was heard of him. Then he turned up in Paris, and a few days after that in Israel, where the authorities accepted his presence as a *fait accompli*. One of his first actions on landing was to send a greetings telegram to Sir Hartley Shawcross signed "Stan". For some while his name still made news. He bobbed up in France again, with schemes to buy up department stores, and, during meat negotiations with the Argentine, he sent a telegram to the Board of Trade, assuring them that he had no intention of putting in a rival bid. Then he, too, faded out of the headlines. When a British reporter interviewed him in Tel Aviv, early in 1962, he didn't appear very well-to-do, though he spoke a great deal about his contacts with leading political figures and his backstairs role during the Suez campaign. What had started as a confidence trick sounded as though it were turning into an obsession.

Although there was naturally resentment that he should get off scot-free, most people were glad to see the last of Stanley, and certainly, in the light of the damage which he had done, the Stanley joke had long since worn thin. But his choice of Israel as a refuge brought out very sharply one of the ugliest aspects of the affair. Deploring his activities, and urging that he should be refused admission (this was before his arrival), the Israeli paper *Ha-aretz* had coupled his name with the Stavisky scandals in pre-war France and predicted that the case would contribute to an upsurge of anti-Semitism in Britain. In 1948 such a warning was not altogether fanciful. Relations between Britain and the new state of Israel were very bad (on the day after the Lynskey report was published there was a bitter debate in the Commons over Bevin's Palestine policy), while at home and abroad minor but widely-reported instances of friction piled up: riots over the Alec Guinness film of *Oliver Twist* in Berlin, Mosleyite demonstrations in North London, pronouncements from Ben Hecht in Hollywood. Against such a background, it was a particularly unhappy thought that Stanley and many of the businessmen whom he had known were Jews. Newspaper readers became accustomed to being told that witnesses at the tribunal had taken the oath with head covered "in the Jewish fashion." In his summing-up, Hartley Shawcross stressed that the behaviour of a small group was no reflection on the Jewish community as a whole, and gave a warning against gossip which stirred up racial animosities. Belcher echoed these points in his resignation speech, and deplored the reactions "with a racial basis" which one overheard listening to conversations on bus or train. But such reactions could be heard, in private if not in the Press, for a long time afterwards, together with any number of canards and exaggerations. It was even widely assumed, on account of his unusual name, that Lynskey was a Jew, and that this was somehow reprehensible (he was in fact a Catholic of Irish descent). Most Jews wished Stanley good riddance, with some relief. But gradually he was forgotten, as fresh sensations filled the newspapers. Within a few years, relations with Israel had improved considerably, and the anti-Semitic campaign which *Ha-aretz* had feared mercifully failed to come about.

It is ultimately rather depressing to turn over the tattered and yellowing pages of an old scandal, and one which didn't turn out to be that much of a scandal after all. What is the moral of the whole affair, and did it have any lasting significance? The only immediate official consequence was a decision by Attlee to set up an enquiry into the role of contact men, under the chairmanship of Sir Edwin Herbert. After consulting twenty-seven Government departments and ten major public organisations, the Herbert Committee published its report in March 1950. It had discovered twenty-nine individuals acting as intermediaries between the general public and Government departments, thirteen of them specialising in the affairs of aliens. In a society where many people were baffled by proliferating and often highly technical Government control, there might be a place for such men, just as there was for tax consultants, and the committee did not propose any restrictions. Obviously the system was open to abuses, but none of the twenty-nine seemed to be operating on Stanleyesque lines.

Everyone agreed that the tribunal itself had carried out its job thoroughly, and, equally, that there had been no widespread corruption to reveal. Instead of Augean Stables, editorials now invoked Caesar's Wife. Perhaps £500 worth of small gifts had changed hands. Gibson and Belcher had been fools, but nothing worse, and they had paid a heavy penalty. Still, the principle of complete integrity on the part of public servants came first. By the end of the affair, there was a distinct note of self-congratulation in many newspaper comments, which amused or occasionally irritated foreign observers. Harold Nicolson reported that the French papers were either tickled by the spectacle of Englishmen self-righteously making a fuss about next to nothing, or inclined to believe that the real corruption hadn't been brought to light.

The Civil Service was completely vindicated, and journalists who had been hoping to snipe at bureaucrats were disappointed. But inevitably

Conservative opinion argued, with the *Daily Express*, that "a speedy return to the free economy should be the aim of every Government bent on maintaining the moral fibre of Britain." On the other side, it was repeatedly said that capitalism had emerged as the villain, and that a devastating light had been thrown on the big-business mentality. There was only a limited truth in this. For a start, Stanley was, to put it mildly, an exotic. For another thing, the businessmen involved had almost all been self-made men engaged in inessential or highly specialised types of trade. To many observers at the time, the Lynskey Tribunal underlined in a melodramatic way the inconsistencies which are bound to arise when a Socialist Government presides over a largely capitalist economy. The whole question facing the tribunal, Lynskey remarked at one point, was to decide what was "legitimate business". In a free economy, whether its moral fibre comes up to the standards of the *Daily Express* or not, this can never be an altogether simple question. Most businessmen in 1948 would have argued that the same Government which was exhorting them to export more, and increase their turnover, was merely hampering them with its restrictions.

The question remains as to whether or not the outcome of the tribunal seriously damaged the reputation of the Labour Government. In the most direct sense, plainly not. The prospect of a major scandal quickly melted away, and there was little out of which opponents of the Government could make capital. For a few days hecklers made garbled references to "tribunal sherry" and so forth, but only for a few days. Rebecca West wrote, in the last of her *Evening Standard* articles, that the affair would be used to discredit Socialism in America and capitalism in Russia, while at home the names of Belcher and Gibson would be used by enemies of democracy "to convince the impatient that Parliamentary government is the rotten ally of a corrupt business system." This was getting the episode wildly out of proportion, and few would have agreed. On the contrary, the promptness and severity of the Government's reaction were, in the eyes of many Conservatives, the strongest proof that ultimately, in spite of everything, the Socialists were at least respectable. But to suggest that the tribunal did the Labour Party positive good would be too much of a paradox. For every reader who pondered on the true significance – and triviality – of the affair, there must have been ten who snatched from the headlines a hazy impression of politicians living it up in Mayfair orgies. Long after the details of the tribunal, and even the names of the other protagonists, had been forgotten, Sydney Stanley held a place in the mythology of primitive Socialist-baiting. Perhaps, too, the period flavour of the whole affair, with its ersatz luxuries and down-at-heel restrictions, contributed to the associations of shabbiness which dog the Labour Party, but this is more difficult to decide. At any rate, justice had been done; and business – legitimate business – went on as usual.

13

J. ARTHUR RANK AND THE SHRINKING SCREEN

The struggles of the film industry and the rise of television

PETER FORSTER

Peter Forster was born in 1926, educated at Wycliffe School and New College, Oxford. He went through Sandhurst, and held a commission in the Wiltshire Regiment. Since leaving the Army, he has lived between journalism (book, drama, film critic) and authorship (three novels published — *The Primrose Path*, *The Right People*, *The Self-Made Man*). In 1962 he retired to write novels in a farmhouse in Provence.

J. ARTHUR RANK AND THE SHRINKING SCREEN

Peter Forster

IF you had decided to go to the cinema in January 1945 – and more than twenty million people did each week – you could have seen a film biography of Goebbels called *Enemy of Women*, or Ronald Colman and Marlene Dietrich, ageless as the East, in *Kismet*. There was a Selznick weepie, *Since You Went Away*, featuring the combined tears of Jennifer Jones and Claudette Colbert – though the latter could also be found in more characteristic mood in a Norman Krasna comedy, *Practically Yours*. Scarcely less comic was *A Song to Remember*, now remembered only for the performance in which Merle Oberon put on trousers, puffed daintily at a cigar, and pretended she was George Sand.

The great majority of the films you might have seen were American, but offerings from other nations reflected no less well the tastes of the times. The French put out a stern documentary, *Journal of the Resistance*, and *L'Homme Qui Cherche la Verité*, one of the last comedies of the great, still-lamented Raimu.

Great Britain entered four films in the competition for the twenty-million-a-week patrons: an inheritance melodrama starring William Hartnell, *The Agitator*; an animal documentary, *Animal Wonderland*; a reissue of the ancient Aldwych farce, *Rookery Nook*; and another reissue, *Goodnight Vienna*, featuring Jack Buchanan and the young Anna Neagle. The monthly bulletin of the British Film Institute summarised the plot of this last as follows: "Captain Maximilian Schletoff is in love with Viki, who works in a florist's shop in Vienna, but is forced into a betrothal with a countess. He goes off to war, and on the return of peace takes a job as a shoe salesman. Viki, in the meantime, has become a famous singer and will have nothing to do with her former admirer when she meets him one day in the shoe shop. Eventually, however, all misunderstandings are cleared away and the course of true love runs smooth."

Twenty million people, I suppose, could not be wrong . . .

If you were still doing your duty by the box office in December 1950 – and the gallant twenty million still were – there would have been a chance to see Gertrude Lawrence in *The Glass Menagerie*, and Judy Garland in *If You Feel Like Singing*; *Treason* dealt with the sufferings of Cardinal

279

Mindszenty of Hungary, and possibly added to them with a portrayal of the Cardinal by Charles Bickford; Joan Crawford sank her teeth into the strong meat of George Kelly's old drama, *Craig's Wife*, renamed *Harriet Craig*; and James Cagney played yet another of his jerky little killer roles in *Kiss Tomorrow Goodbye*.

The majority of new films were still American, but there was a rape-and-inheritance saga from Italy, *Lupo della Sila* (The Wolf of the Sila), and from France came one of the most charming musical biographies ever made on film, *La Valse de Paris*, with Pierre Fresnay as Offenbach and Yvonne Printemps as Hortense Schneider.

Great Britain produced *The Mudlark*, with Alec Guinness as Disraeli and Irene Dunne imported to play Queen Victoria in a way that might well have amused the Queen, though many thought the performance not a bad effort, and, by a certain gentle irony, the film was selected for the Royal Command Performance. For the rest we remained true to form with *The Clouded Yellow*, a comedy-thriller with Kenneth More and Trevor Howard, and *The Elusive Pimpernel*, in which David Niven found the Orczy hero rather too elusive for him. There was also a reissue of *City Lights*, made by Chaplin in the days before he talked and became Charles.

From all of which it might seem that, during the six years under review, little had changed in the world of films. There was the same mixture of varied qualities, of "A" and "U" certificates with the occasional "H" for "Horrific" ("X" arrived on January 1st, 1951), and the members of the general public, who buttoned up their overcoats and made their way through the winter weather to the local Odeon or Gaumont or Granada, were probably not aware of any specially deep-seated change in the industry which produced their weekly ration of entertainment.

But, in fact, during these years a cataclysm took place from which British films did not recover—indeed, there was one vital period in the drama when the weather was so unseasonably fine that the public did not button up and go out to the cinema, but sat shirt-sleeved in the garden while men in Wardour Street prayed for rain. But of this more in due course.

There is something peculiarly compelling about the spectacle of a commercial empire coming a cropper—*La Grandeur et Décadence de César Birotteau* is not one of Balzac's best novels, but it remains one of his most popular, though it is simply the story of a man who makes hair-oil, then loses his head: and recently American novelists have discovered that the boardroom drama is an almost infallible formula. Perhaps it is that even those who most worship Mammon do so without respect, and can feel a kind of temporary virtue when they witness one of his occasional failures.

So here: with a graph as clear-cut as any dramatist could wish, British films rose to an apogee, then fell to an apology. At the same time, the details of the story are anything but clear-cut – in comparison with the politics of films, the politics of independent German states in the eighteenth century were simple, sincere and unsubtle. And it must be emphasised at this early stage that there was a great deal of admirable, honourable, even brilliant work going on during the period, affected by, but not involved with, the political crises. Mary Field was still making films for children, John Grierson was still in documentaries – and the Marshall Plan for aid to Europe benefited from the services of many clever youngish men who duly combined excellent propagandist film-making with expensive free travel.

But the complex must be simplified to be understood at all, and inevitably the drama centres upon what happened to the empire associated with one man, Joseph Arthur Rank. Subsequently the public saw the name of J. Arthur Rank on divers enterprises – as the Welsh might put it, he became Rank the Dance-hall, Rank the Gymnasium, as well as Rank the Odeon.

But, as often when dealing with the past, the context is all. The J. Arthur Rank story (which will probably be made as a television film one day) cannot be understood without recalling the atmosphere of the times. In the 1930s, films were still something of a novelty. In a way, they fully came into their own during the war, when the film industry found itself in the rare and delightful position of being able to have something both ways, because Entertainment served a Purpose. Whether it involved Rita Hayworth and Betty Grable cheering up the boys with displays of leg, or Noël Coward and John Mills inspiring them with displays of stiff lip, films were generally agreed to have made a contribution to the war effort.

Here is where Rank came in. He started as a miller, became a million-aire, entered the film world and remained a Yorkshireman: also, and perhaps above all, a religious man – a devout follower of Methodism, the Free Church in which the Almighty probably gives the maximum latitude of free thought to his worshippers, and vice versa. In his time Rank has been much mocked for his do-good, religious approach, as exemplified by his famous remark, "I am in films because of the Holy Spirit." But his career does not make sense unless it can be accepted that he has always been concerned, not simply to make good films, but to make films a force for good.

Thus, although he was established in films before the war, it was during the war that his mentality came into its own. He offered Idealism and Patriotism, and he was assumed to have that other ingredient without which the first two are seldom successful, Commercial Flair. Unfortunately, what stood him in good stead as a financier and miller was often easily misled among the absurd, fairyland mazes of the film world. There must have been an inner groan of sheer bewilderment in Rank's breast when he found himself underwriting a film which involved the export of sand and a dummy Sphinx to Egypt, as happened while Gabriel Pascal, a flamboyant genius of a kind Rank can seldom have met in the City or the milling worlds, was making *Caesar and Cleopatra*. And when the film proved a flop *d'estime*, one half of Mr. Rank may well have said "I told you so!" to the regretful other half. But Rank's viewpoint explains how that immensely expensive failure came to be made: in the climate of 1944–5, it was held to be worth doing.

However, there was never any pretence that British films were a philanthropic activity bestowed upon the public with the aim of educational uplift. Here the commercial necessities obtruded, and here, of course, those who relish the discomfiture of Mammon reserve a special sneer for Rank, because he tried to do the right thing and make it pay. But, in all that has been written against Rank, no serious charge of personal hypocrisy on the Chadband model can be brought: that is the true tribute to the man. There is, surely, something very touching about the picture painted by his brilliant biographer, Alan Wood, of Rank muttering a prayer on his way from his suite in the Dorchester to a board meeting in South Street. The fact that his prayers seldom seem to have been answered is neither here nor there.

The contrast between Rank and Alexander Korda, the best known other figure in British films at this time, is charmingly striking. Korda had been in charge of M.G.M.'s British production since 1943, the sophisticated, worldly Hungarian who understood studios and actors and temperaments. ("My artists cannot start making love at nine o'clock in the morning," he told a union delegate who wanted an earlier start.) It is also not without irony that Korda was knighted, though Rank never was.

But Rank stood massively, almost monolithically, for British films. Hence his promotion of the "prestige" films, like Olivier's *Hamlet*, and in passing let it be noted that, while Olivier was later among the most commercially-employed as well as the greatest of actors, at that time the emphasis was upon his status as ambassador of culture, in which role he served most nobly.

And here it is necessary to come to a closer examination of the subtle, perpetually shifting balance between principle and prudent calculation of which the film industry offers such a complex, special example.

Again, context obtrudes. In the early days of the Labour Government there was social idealism in the air, likewise cynicism and bitterness. Some proposed that the State should nationalise cinemas and take over production, thus supposedly ensuring that we would get the best films. As against this, distributors and exhibitors clung to Wardour Street's traditional conception of what was "box office", and many films continued to be made which took a lowest-common-denominator view of what the public wanted. There were demands, spurred by films like *Brief Encounter* and *The Way to the Stars*, for a truly British school of film-making, to be encouraged by some kind of preferential treatment. Others worked on the assumption that the best way to rival Hollywood was to copy it. In the press and trade, discussion raged as to who should be got into films, and who should be got out. Many saw the export market as both challenge and answer. Others were more concerned to appeal to audiences at home. The lavish, all-star "prestige" picture had its advocates (especially among the export school). Others thought this wasteful, and said that, for the money spent on one such epic, several modest and more worthwhile films could be made, true to national life and realities. (The influence of Rossellini and de Sica, with their small-budget masterpieces made on location, was strong.) The British are not, on the whole, a polemical people when they came to consider the arts, yet in those years films inspired an unwonted amount of lively disputation.

But, for all this ideological and practical turmoil, the British film industry appeared to thrive. In the year ending March 31st, 1946, eighty-three feature films were made: the following year, 107; the year after, 170. On November 3rd, 1947, Rank announced a programme for making forty-seven first-feature films at a cost of £9,250,000. He was by far the biggest man in British films, controlling most of the production and two of the three big distributing organisations. He was a firm believer in prestige products and exports in the national interest. He was at the height of his power.

Now, however, there must be taken into account the omnipresent fact that the film industry is an integral part of the country's economy, not a cul-de-sac for the pursuit of private enterprise and arguments. No Government could ignore the cinema as it does the theatre. The overwhelming national need was to prevent the drain on our dollar resources – this was the time when the dollar gap affected all lives so closely that many came to feel they had passed through it personally. Since the majority of films shown in England were American, the outgoing payments in dollars were obviously enormous – by 1947 Hollywood was earning about 70 million dollars a year in this country.

Thus, on August 6th, 1947, Dr. Hugh Dalton, Chancellor of the Exchequer, made one of the most momentous moves in the history of British films by sanctioning a Treasury order, under the Import Duties Act, 1932, imposing a Customs duty of 75 per cent on the value of all imported films, the sum to be prepaid. Rank was not forewarned, and barely consulted – he had actually been in America for two months previously, persuading the big circuits to show his films, with some success. Now, angrily, he found all his good-will work negatived, for there was no mistaking the vehemence of the American response: the day after the 75 per cent duty was imposed, the Motion Picture Association of America announced that all further shipments of films to this country would be suspended indefinitely.

Rank rang up Herbert Morrison to protest about what was being done. Morrison merely remarked: "I can't pretend to be expert in international finance. The dollar business is mainly in the hands of Dalton and Cripps." To which Rank is said to have replied: "Well, I don't know about international finance, but I *do* know something about Americans. I know they'll be —— mad with you. Perhaps you'll save sixteen million dollars, but you'll have to spend sixty million getting back the good-will you'll lose."

Even so, when Cripps made a special, private appeal to him to increase his group's production in the national interest (again, note the approach, typical of the times), Rank responded with enthusiasm: hence the stepped-up programme to make forty-seven films. And now the big film battle was on in earnest.

The Americans won, though some may argue that it was a Pyrrhic victory. Against this, it must be allowed that the British generalship was of a quite startling ineptitude. Dr. Dalton seems completely to have miscalculated the American reaction to his tax, never expecting that the Americans would simply not send any more films. Worse still, he appears not to have realised that there were a great many American films already in this country, enough to keep the cinemas busy for quite a long time, and that the dollars on these must still go out of the country.

But, of course, eventually the supply of old films would be exhausted, and there must be something to put in their place, unless the cinemas were to shut down, and it can hardly have been the Government's aim in the matter to put people out of work. Here Rank's expanded programme was expected to fill the bill, but the Government was in effect forcing Rank to run before he could walk. That is the simplest summary of the complex, often chaotic sequence of events that followed.

For the British film industry found itself hoist with an American petard. One of the long-accepted axioms about American films was that they covered their production costs at home, then went abroad to make profits. Dalton had virtually presented the British industry with the British home market—but where abroad were they likely to get enough of a showing to make a killing? Our home market was in any case smaller than America's, and the Americans were naturally not in a mood to welcome British films. And was the British industry capable of the sudden, mighty spurt required to meet the shortage of American films? It was not.

Inevitably, then, the Government, having marched right up to the top of the hill, had to march back down again. When Dalton resigned as Chancellor, after his Budget gaffe, and was replaced by Cripps, Mr. Harold Wilson became President of the Board of Trade. It was Wilson who opened negotiations with Mr. Eric Johnston, spokesman for the American interests. The 75 per cent duty was lifted, and so in return was the American embargo. It was agreed that 17 million dollars yearly could be taken out of the country, which was the amount that would have been left over had the tax been deducted. The balance, instead of being taken by the tax, was left for the Americans to use in this country—a device of far-reaching importance, since it may be that from this time stemmed the trend of making major American films outside America.

The other effect of this dispute and deal was to strike the Rank Organisation a blow from which it never fully recovered. Rank had been losing money on production even before the dispute, and gambled on American distribution to recoup. Whether he would have succeeded can never be known for sure, because the winter of 1946-7 deprived him even of the chance of testing his luck. He was again not consulted by the Government in their parleying with Mr. Johnston, and, to cap all for him, the weather in the spring was so exceptionally fine that people stayed away from the cinema when he most needed to pack them in.

The new agreement with America was signed on March 11th, 1948: in October of that year, Rank had to inform his shareholders that bank loans and overdrafts with the National Provincial Bank stood at £13,589,858. In four years he was to lose over six million pounds. At one point he announced that he might have to give up film production altogether, and throughout he was fortunate in commanding the support and personal friendship of the National Provincial's chairman, Captain Eric Smith. The City was known to be chary of investing in films.

And no sooner had the film agreement been settled, than the Government sprang another surprise: Harold Wilson announced that the quota of British-made films to be shown in this country was to be raised from 20 per cent to 45 per cent. Not the least of the results was to increase ill-feeling among the Americans, many of whom took this to be a piece of decidedly sharp practice.

But the brunt of Wilson's bright idea had to be borne by Rank. The quota was an old protective device – as long ago as 1925, Stanley Baldwin had laid down in Parliament that it was "desirable on natural grounds to see that the larger proportion of films exhibited in this country is British." In fact, the larger proportion had always been foreign, but the quota was a typical mixture of patriotic desire to encourage the home product, and plain economic advantage in the idea that a proportion of films should be produced here.

But 1948 was hardly the best time to increase the proportion to nearly one-half. The Rank Organisation was already seen to be over-extended, independent smaller producers could not quickly fill the gaps, with the result that poor quality films were turned out in a hurry – then flung into the line against the best of the American films that had been stockpiling during the embargo. Inevitably, the public preferred the latter, and one of the cruellest aspects of Rank's situation was that, as major exhibitor, he was bound to show his own bad films in his own cinemas, to try to cut his losses, knowing that he was bound to lose patrons and so lose his profits as exhibitor. He lost on both swings and roundabouts.

This classic example of how a theory may go wrong in practice was bluntly summed up in July 1950 by Lord Archibald in the House of Lords: "The quota is supposed to protect the producer in the home market, and an increase in quota should therefore lead to an increase in production. The size of the quota is determined by the volume of production, and not the other way round, although it is supposed to be that way round in theory."

Another major factor – some would say the most crippling of all – in Mr. Rank's catalogue of problems must be mentioned: Entertainment Tax. In 1948, total box-office receipts were £109 million – of this the Government took £39 million in Entertainment Tax, and, whilst the heavy tax had been supportable during the war-time boom, its effect was bound to be devastating on an industry suffering from smaller audiences and a rise in production costs.

So, by this time, making British films had ceased to be a paying proposition. Looking back, the marvel is that many notable films were made – during 1948, this harassed and groggy industry produced *An Ideal Husband*, *It Always Rains on Sundays*, *Mine Own Executioner*, *Brighton Rock*, *Anna Karenina* and *Vice Versa*.

But by 1949 the full, frantic hullabaloo was under way. Philip Guedalla once said that cold blood was what one murdered one's relatives in: likewise, crisis might almost be defined as the perpetual condition of the British film industry. Every pundit in the land seemed eager to perform a post-mortem on the still-breathing body.

The producers blamed the exhibitors and distributors, pointing out that they took the lion's share of a picture's profits. They, in turn, pointed to high production costs, then explained that they themselves had high costs. Producers pleaded that they needed more money to turn out the number of films required under the new quota. Sir Laurence Olivier remarked: "It is wrong to say that British films don't pay – they pay very well, but they pay the wrong people." He was rebuked by people who said that stars took over-large salaries, and they were duly rebuked by those who explained that total salaries seldom amount to more than about fifteen per cent of a picture's budget.

Some actually mentioned that, quite apart from the economics, the creative artists, who have more to do with making a good film than anyone else, were being asked to work under increasingly intolerable conditions. But the artists would have been the first to agree that, more than any other art, the cinema is a group-creative effort, conditioned by economics.

At all events, by the spring of 1949 the remarkable state of affairs had been achieved whereby more British films were needed than ever before, yet seventeen out of twenty-six British studios were idle, and three thousand out of ten thousand studio operatives had been dismissed. Good directors, too, were simply not working. In despair, men look to the Government for help, and at this time (again the context: there was still a strong Socialist Government) many looked with hope and idealism. Moreover, Mr. Harold Wilson, having got into films, was in no sense eager to get out. In his ideology, it was natural and desirable that the State should be in films as in most other industries. In 1947 he set up a National Film Production Council, under his own chairmanship, with representatives of all sectors of the industry. In Alan Wood's words: "Mr. Wilson beheld the whole crazy, much-criticised edifice of the British film industry toppling down in ruins. He gazed, appalled. And then – he did his best to prop it up again." Against this implicit criticism it may be argued that

Mr. Wilson's job was not to see the industry in ruins, and there was a
certain amount to be said for his next move: the founding of a National
Film Finance Corporation, as a kind of State-owned bank with five
million pounds capital to subsidise independent producers. Clearly it was
a move to counterbalance Rank: new-style Socialism was in collision with
old-fashioned capitalism.

The result nearly ruined both. The one big thing on which almost
everybody in films agreed was that the distributors had too much power:
the Government therefore prescribed that N.F.F.C. loans should be made
through distributors. And, since Rank was in official disfavour, the bulk
of the available money was given to Korda's British Lion, whereupon
Korda proceeded to perpetuate many of Rank's mistakes by making costly
prestige flops like *Bonnie Prince Charlie*. Indeed, there is a strong case to
be made that Wilson's biggest blunder was to interfere in the production
sector of films, and that, if the State was to be in films at all, it should
have reorganised and rationalised the unwieldy system of distributing
and exhibiting. Also, relief was urgently needed from Entertainment Tax.
In all, Rank calculated that a producer was left with only thirteen per cent
of his film's takings at the box office: the margin made trade almost
impossible.

Not that the N.F.F.C. was unhelpful – it helped to finance such notable
films as *The Third Man*, *State Secret* and *Seven Days to Noon*. But it was
not help enough, and inevitably it quickly lost most of its money. The
press continued to offer all sorts of solutions, and, of course, throughout
the period there was a sizeable section of the public which understood
nothing of the nature of the crisis which they read about, and merely
continued to regard British films with varying degrees of indulgence as if
they amounted to nothing more than sixty glorious years of Anna Neagle.

Meantime, Rank was doing his best to set his organisation in order by
the most obvious, if least imaginative, device – economy. His chosen
instrument was Mr. John Davis, a tough, hard-working administrator
with a talent for saying "No". There was much sacking, trimming,
reducing and recrimination. Davis probably saved the Rank Organisation
from financial ruin, but the inability of artists to create according to a
balance sheet (a crucial factor in filming, to be solved by neither politics
nor good-will) was underlined when Carol Reed departed from the Rank
Organisation because he overshot by a third his budget on what proved
to be one of the finest British films ever made, *Odd Man Out*.

The happier, more positive side of Rank's activities was an agreement
with Michael Balcon, formerly a Socialist opponent of Rank, whereby

Rank distributed, and to some extent underwrote, the financing of Balcon's Ealing Studios, thus helping on their way a series of the brightest, wittiest, most original comedies ever made in England: the summer of 1949 saw the premieres of *Passport to Pimlico*, *Whisky Galore* and *Kind Hearts and Coronets*.

At the end of 1948, in mid-crisis, Mr. Wilson acted as Governments do at such times, and set up a committee. The crisis being exceptionally severe, he set up two committees, the Gater Committee on Film Production Costs and the Plant Committee on Distribution and Exhibition. The former drew up a mass of data, but failed to elicit those vital, confidential figures that were the hub of the investigation, which is not entirely surprising since representatives of many of the big producers sat on the committee. But at least nobody could disagree with their grave conclusion that, "At no time since the substitution of sound for silent films has the British film industry been on a satisfactory financial basis."

The Plant Committee for a time had difficulty in getting any statistics at all – apparently no official figures existed for the aggregate seating capacity of British cinemas, of weekly attendances, of amounts paid in film hire, and so on. However, the committee happened upon a gentleman named Mr. Williams, whose hobby was compiling statistics about films, and with his help they were able to come up with a number of proposals for increasing the producers' share of the box-office profit and cutting the distributors'.

Harold Wilson was thought to have endorsed this, but in the event he did nothing. Then, having failed to arbitrate decisively as to who should have what share of the cake, he rather surprisingly agreed that at least the Government's share, Entertainment Tax, was a little excessive. Steered by Sir Wilfred Eady – with the result that it became known as the Eady Plan – a scheme emerged from the deliberations of all concerned, whereby the price of cinema seats was increased. It was calculated that this would give the industry three million pounds more each year, of which half must be paid direct to the producers: contrariwise, the exhibitors must pay one farthing per ticket sold into the British Film Production Fund, a non-profit-making company set up to administer the levy. The fund was to dole out money quarterly according to applications, properly attested, from individual companies, though a percentage was set aside to finance a Rank-owned company for producing children's films. Children are sacred, even in the film world.

And there, in 1951, the matter rested. Socialism had tried to come to grips with the Cinema. The result? It is hard to disagree with Alan Wood:

"The verdict of history will be that the slaughter of the British film industry was one of the most tragic blunders of the years after the Second World War. Lenin said in 1918: 'For us, the most important of all the arts is the cinema.' President Wilson declared in 1917: 'Trade follows the film.' Ever since, both the Russian and American film industries had enjoyed the wholehearted support of their Governments, but the British Government, thirty years later, had still failed to see the point."

It can hardly be said that any Government since 1951 has seen the point any more clearly, but there has been a kind of excuse, in that the most obtrusive medium of entertainment in the lives of the masses is no longer the cinema. On June 7th, 1946, a cloud appeared on the horizon of the world of films, no bigger in most homes than a seven-inch screen: B.B.C. Television reopened, and Lenin would very likely have been the first to revise his estimate about which is the most important of the arts.

It is commonly believed that the first performer to appear on British television was Mr. Leslie Mitchell; in fact that distinction belongs to "Bill", a ventriloquist's dummy televised by John Logie Baird on October 2nd, 1925. Baird suffered a pioneer's fate, and died poor and neglected, although, in case it should be thought that England has been entirely forgetful of his memory, it is only fair to add that in 1959 a public house in Muswell Hill was christened "The John Baird", by Leslie Mitchell.

Meantime, of course, the B.B.C. had acquired a monopoly of television broadcasting with the service which was opened on November 2nd, 1936, by Leslie Mitchell. There was a seven-year closure from 1939–46, due to the war, and then Mr. Mitchell again performed his usual office. The first great occasion was the televising of the grand Victory Parade from London that summer – a freak of transmission made the picture visible at a village in Somerset, 169 miles from London – but there were more far-reaching consequences from the presence in London of T.V. people from many nations, all suitably impressed by the B.B.C.'s achievement.

In fact, although the whole continuing history of television is primarily beset with political factors, whether of principles or personalities, the background to development turns on technical achievement, and during these years B.B.C. engineers and the radio industry progressed strikingly, often under severe handicaps of Government control and financial restriction. Early in 1949 a new outside broadcast unit came into being, shortly afterwards the "zoom" lens was introduced, and the following year the first broadcasts were made with the Eurovision Link. Give a B.B.C. technician a problem, and he will seldom fail to overcome it somehow: it is the planner or administrator who will tell you that something is impossible.

And inevitably the general trend in 1946 was to take up what had been put down seven years before. Miss Jasmine Bligh returned as an announcer. Miss Joan Gilbert had been with Cecil Madden's magazine programme "Picture Page" before the war, so now she resumed, and in passing one may note that, in many memories, some of the early magazine programmes were as good as any since. Then there were fashion demonstrations, Philip Harben teaching cookery, and plays which cautiously started to evolve something specifically televisual, instead of being simply photographed stage dramas – though one producer resolutely refused to employ more than a single, uncomplicated camera, and became known as "One-Eye" in consequence. Actors liked to work with him because he was thought to understand their problems. The Controller of Television at this time was Maurice Gorham, a genial Irishman who had been with B.B.C. sound services for many years.

And in this early period B.B.C. T.V. was very much the Cinderella of the B.B.C.'s services. Certainly few in the Corporation seemed to consider the possibility that, once properly shod, Cinderella might start to kick her older sisters. The actuality of T.V.'s news coverage was an obvious asset – underlined on such occasions as the wedding, late in 1947, of Princess Elizabeth to Lieutenant Mountbatten, and the Olympic Games in 1948. But hours of transmission were short, and so was money.

The B.B.C.'s Director-General from 1944 was Sir William Haley, and the story is told of a senior television executive who, in order to show his chief the poor quality entertainment which shoe-string budgets forced upon the service, lured Sir William to Lime Grove and forced him to sit through an excerpt from a fourth-rate provincial music-hall show. Not a word was said, but afterwards, going downstairs to the D.G.'s car, Sir William, not known as the gayest of men, started to whistle, then hum, then gaily bellow "Lily of Laguna", which had been featured in the show. He had not, he said, departing, enjoyed an evening so much for a long time: it quite took him back to old times.

Sir William, an extremely able man (how charming that a ship's wireless operator should have become head of the B.B.C.), soon showed that a principal feature of his administration was to be decisiveness – subordinates knew where they stood with him; direct questions received clear answers. But in the climate of 1946-7, even afterwards, television was a beguiling toy. Not many realised its fantastic potentialities, and few of those who did wanted to face up there and then to the issues involved.

It was neither a hot political problem nor even a nation-wide enthusiasm. The film industry noticed its ragged little rival, but without alarm. During the fuel crisis, early in 1947, television actually closed down for a month.

But late that year Cinderella acquired a new kicking power. Gorham was succeeded by a formidable, forty-year-old author-administrator, Norman Collins. At the age of twenty-two, Collins had been Assistant Literary Editor of the *News Chronicle*, progressing to become Deputy Chairman of Victor Gollancz Ltd., thence to the B.B.C., where he became Controller of the Light Programme, then of the General Overseas Service. Along the way he wrote novels, which inevitably became best-sellers. Success seemed to sit upon Mr. Collins like a comfortable tweed suit: he was to the manna born.

His personality counts enormously when it comes to disentangling accurately the pattern of events from the obscuring mass of rumours and hearsay. When precisely did Mr. Collins become disaffected with the B.B.C. ? It would be fascinating and convenient to have a distinct answer – there is for instance a version, much put about in the B.B.C., that he wanted promotion to the post of Director of Television in 1950, when it was created, and resigned when it was given to George Barnes, an old hand from sound radio. But, even if this is true, it came as the culmination of a long process, not as a blinding conversion. The B.B.C. is a bureaucracy, cumbersome, pompous, overweight and over-righteous as any other – especially so when it held the television concession for England by what (Sir John Reith being then of even more vivid memory than he was later) must have seemed divine right.

So quite when and how Mr. Collins started off on that road which led him to found a counter-bureaucracy of his own, is almost irrelevant. Suffice to say that he found himself short of money and encouragement, and to guess that, as an organisation man who had hitherto thrived on manipulating the machine, he must have found it galling, if not humiliating, to find even his hardest punches sinking ineffectually into a midriff of cotton-wool.

But this is rather to anticipate, for undoubtedly Collins tried to do his duty by the B.B.C. Indeed, in November 1948 he went to the United States on a mission to gather facts with which to fight the B.B.C.'s case before a Parliamentary Commission set up to investigate the subject of sponsored television. Four years later he was to go over again with a very different objective.

And all this time, be it remembered, the general public was gradually getting addicted obsessively to the small screen, talking about Sylvia Peters and Dimbleby and Terry-Thomas, little aware that it was shifting the whole national ballast of interest from films to television.

Then in flooded politics. In 1946 the B.B.C.'s Charter, due for renewal, was extended to the end of 1951 without over-much concern or debate, since there were other more pressing problems just after the war. But towards that date, in 1949, a committee was appointed under Lord Beveridge to consider the future of broadcasting, sound and television. With the significant exception of a little-known Tory back-bencher named Selwyn Lloyd, the committee recommended an extension of the B.B.C.'s Charter and monopoly.

What happened next is truth of the order which is disbelieved in novels. In 1950 Ernest Bevin, the Foreign Secretary, was persuaded by his wife to go to Brighton for some fresh air; he caught a chill, and so began that last, sad illness which forced him into resignation on his seventieth birthday, March 9th, 1951. Herbert Morrison, Lord President of the Council, was appointed Foreign Secretary; Patrick Gordon-Walker was made Lord President. The significance to the B.B.C.? Simply that Morrison had been responsible for Government policy in that field, and was a fervent B.B.C. supporter, eager to renew the Charter. Under Gordon-Walker, less interested and less powerful, the issue was treated as less urgent, and had not been decided when the Tories were returned at the general election on October 25th, 1951.

All was now in the melting-pot, and there was one hand eager to start stirring: on October 13th, 1950 Norman Collins had resigned from the B.B.C., and set about campaigning to break the B.B.C.'s monopoly, the campaign which was to lead to the establishment of commercial television. Nothing indicates more sharply the nature of the opposing mentalities than the account of the actual break in the memoirs of Lord Simon of Wythenshawe, then Chairman of the Board of Governors. In Lord Simon's presence, Haley sprung it upon Collins that Barnes was to be appointed Director of Television over his, Collins', head, hoping that Collins would stay on. Lord Simon's recollection is that Collins asked for two hours to think over his decision. "Like damned fools, we agreed, with the result that Collins filled the afternoon papers with the story of his resignation because the B.B.C. wasn't interested in television." It would take a long book to explain why each side felt its attitude and behaviour right and permissible, and the other's wrong.

To sum up, in 1945 entertainment had been under the domination of the cinema: by 1951 the rival shortly to supersede it as money-maker and public draw had emerged. One might have thought the trend was plainly there for those who cared to notice it—in 1946 figures were not even collected to show how many people bought television licences; the estimate for 1947 is something under fourteen thousand; in 1951, there were 763,941 licence-holders.

Did the cinema people foresee the future? Norman Collins likes to tell how, in the early stages of commercial T.V., he offered some project to Mr. John Davis, only to receive the cheery reply: "We'll wait till you're all bankrupt, then buy you out!" The Rank Organisation later became a shareholder in one of the lesser commercial companies, Southern Television.

Not that the old rivalries have led to total cleavage: television still provides a fine graveyard for old films.

14

THE STEEL DEBATES
The Tory Recovery
GODFREY HODGSON

Godfrey Hodgson was born in 1934. He was a scholar of Winchester and of Magdalen College, Oxford, where he took a First in History. In 1956 he joined *The Times*, which he left in 1960 to write the "Mammon" column on *The Observer*. In 1962 he became the *Observer* correspondent in Washington. He is a member of the Bow Group, and is married, with two children.

THE STEEL DEBATES

Godfrey Hodgson

"A s the election results came tumbling in, it became clear that six years of increasing danger and discomfort . . . had left the peculiar English so desirous for change of any kind, so blindly making themselves believe in promises of everything for nothing (except even higher taxes and discomfort), that Mr. Churchill's friends were swept away by huge majorities, and the Brave and Revolting New World came into its own."

In her 1946 novel, *Peace Breaks Out*, Angela Thirkell sounded the mood of the Tory classes in the hour of the country's victory, and their defeat, as accurately as usual. The defeat of Mr. Churchill's friends might be ungrateful, foolish, catastrophic – so it seemed to the squires and butlers, tradesmen, clergy, and ladies of Barsetshire – but it was all too inevitable in a world where so much that had been taken for granted could be taken for granted no longer.

As the tenderly-nurtured Emmy put it, looking up gruffly from a pig she happened to be grooming: "I know. Sir Robert and Mr. Adams (the two candidates for Barchester) say the same things, but Sir Robert says them in a gentleman's voice, and Mr. Adams doesn't, so Mr. Adams will get in."

If, for many people, the morrow of the General Election in 1945 was a blissful dawn, the morale of the Conservatives was at its nadir and that of the Left at its height. An Oxford don remembers setting out in those first weeks to give Workers' Educational Association lectures with an old Labour stalwart. As their car went round the roundabout on the Oxford by-pass, the old man turned to him with moist eyes and said, "We're in for ever." Most rank-and-file Conservatives, like those who rushed to Wimbledon Post Office on the morning after the poll to withdraw their savings, would probably have agreed with him. When Sir Hartley Shaw-cross was reported as crowing in the House of Commons that "We are the masters now," Conservatives hated him for the taunt, but suspected it was no more than the truth. What Sir Hartley actually said was, "We are the masters at the moment", but he was always quoted as having said "now", and in that form the saying entered the language.

This demoralisation operated differently in the case of the Conservative leaders and their rank-and-file. In Barsetshire, so to speak, the fall of "Mr. Churchill's friends" came with the numbing effect of shock, for all its inevitability. For the leaders, the fact that defeat was not altogether a surprise did nothing to encourage optimism. They knew that their parliamentary majority was largely an illusion, the rump of support gathered in the special circumstances of November 1935. They knew that, if there had been a General Election in 1938 (as there would have been, but for the imminence of war), Labour would almost certainly have won it. And they knew that, in the last two years of the war, the swing had been to the Left.

So the Tory leaders were not surprised; but they had all the more reason to despair for the future. And they were mortally tired. Not that they had spent themselves in the war effort any more than had the Labour Ministers; but some of them had been in power for as long as fourteen years. One Minister in the Caretaker Government told me with feeling how he longed to get back to his house and his businesses, his family and his private affairs. Most Labour leaders had less private affairs to get back to. And they had all to go for. In 1945, their finest hour was in the future.

Nothing in the story of the years of Labour rule is more striking, and more puzzling, than the contrast between the Tories of 1945, without hopes, without ideas, and numb with traumatic defeat, and the revitalised party which came back off the canvas to win power in 1951.

It is always hard to try to catch the moment when the political tide turns. Many forces, some of them deep strong currents, some of them mere swirling eddies on the surface of politics, contributed to the total reversal of political fortune between 1945 and 1951.

Perhaps the most important single cause of this reversal was the fuel crisis of 1947. Certainly the Gallup Poll shows clearly enough that in 1947 the Conservatives, who had been supported by barely thirty per cent of the electorate when Labour enjoyed an actual majority of popular support in 1945, came back with a rush to be within striking distance of the Government. Indeed, after 1947 the two parties never swayed out of the same bracket, with forty per cent to fifty per cent each of the sample's vote, except when one party or the other momentarily topped fifty per cent on some burning issue.

The economic crisis generally, and the fuel crisis in particular, meant that the Government was condemned to a policy of austerity, whether it liked it or not. At the same time crisis provided an excuse and an opportunity for that strain in the Labour movement's thinking, strongest among the powerful perhaps in Cripps, which actually welcomed austerity – the "let 'em eat dog-biscuits" school. And again, the economic crises weakened the faith of those floating voters who had come to associate Toryism with hard times.

One factor which helped the moderate Right all over Europe in the post-war years was the fact that America, the citadel of anti-Socialism, was also the land of plenty and food-parcels, whereas in the Thirties it had been hardest hit by the crisis of capitalism. Those who were young in these years remember the effect of ads. saying things like "America believes in competition," and lusciously displaying ham, steaks and eight-cylinder cars in full colour across a couple of hundred pages of the *Saturday Evening Post*, at a time when competition, newsprint, food, cars, and colour were all conspicuously absent on this side of the Atlantic.

The memoirs in which most leading members of the Labour Cabinet looked back in anger on each other lay a good deal of stress on natural exhaustion among the causes of Labour's fall from popularity. It is true that the premature deaths of Bevin and Cripps, the serious illness of the Prime Minister at a critical moment in 1951 – he went into hospital at Easter with a duodenal ulcer – and Dalton's unlucky departure after the Budget leak, would have been heavy blows for any Government. But not all the memoirs also mention something that was not mere bad luck – the resignation of Nye Bevan, Harold Wilson, and John Freeman on the "glasses and false teeth" issue – significantly enough an issue where Attlee had to choose between this Left-wing Cave of Abdullam and young Mr. Gaitskell.

There were many other reasons for the turning of the tide between the two parties: the natural swing away from the party in power, the fact that the special circumstances of the slump and the war had drawn to Labour many reformers who were no Socialists, and who tended to ebb away in the more humdrum battles of peace-time.

But Labour has perhaps been too apt to blame its fall on these negative factors. There were two mighty reasons for the turn of the tide which had nothing to do with the natural mortality of governments. One was quite simply the Tory revival. Recovering in bulldog style from the traumatic defeat of 1945, the Conservatives put their house in order administratively to such effect that, whereas in 1945 they had been frankly ineffective as an electoral machine, after 1951 Labour tended to accept as part of the natural order of things that the rich and businesslike Tories should show an un-British and undemocratic professionalism in elections.

But the Conservatives also literally changed their ideas. They spring-cleaned themselves ideologically under the impetus of Rab Butler and his bright young men just as thoroughly as they revamped the machine under Lord Woolton. This double rejuvenation had as much to do with the Conservative victory of 1951 as anything else; and it must count as one of the most important things that was happening in Britain. Secondly – and intimately connected with the Tory revival – was the question of nationalisation.

The Conservatives got back into power in 1951 under the banner of Free Enterprise. But it is often forgotten that the Conservatives of 1945 were in two minds about whether to attack nationalisation in principle at all.

In the debate on the King's Speech, in the very hour of defeat in 1945, there was a curious little passage of arms in the House between David Eccles and Sydney Silverman. "I think today," said Eccles, "no sensible man would oppose the principle of nationalisation or public enterprise in all its forms." It was just a question of timing, he argued, only the present, with its menacing economic conditions, was not the time. Up jumped Mr. Silverman. This was very interesting, he implied: just when would Mr. Eccles nationalise, and what? Mr. Eccles hummed and hawed, of course. The incident was trivial. But it does suggest how far an ambitious young Member at the time seems to have sensed that the country wanted nationalisation – however dangerous it might be with Conservative stalwarts actually to approve the nationalisation of anything in particular.

It is easy to forget how boldly and how truculently Labour called for nationalisation in 1945. The election manifesto, *Let Us Face the Future*, was written in what seems today an impossibly fustian, almost Stalinist style. Businessmen, big and small, were called "hard-faced men." They and their "political friends have only learned to act in the interest of their own bureaucratically-run private monopolies which may be likened to totalitarian oligarchies within our democratic State." "No more dole queues in order to let the Czars of Big Business remain kings in their own castles," cried the pamphlet. Finally, and flatly, it proclaimed that "The Labour Party is a Socialist Party, and proud of it. Its ultimate aim is the establishment of the Socialist Commonwealth of Great Britain." The electorate voted for this aim.

Let Us Face the Future presented the electors with a shopping list of industries and institutions to be nationalised. The Bank of England, fuel and power (the coal mines, both the generation and supply of electricity, gas), transport (the railways, road haulage, civil aviation). And next on that list came the iron and steel industry.

Essentially, steel was as far as Labour got with its programme. This was the high-water mark of Socialism in Britain, and there are good reasons for regarding the struggle over the Iron and Steel Nationalisation Bill as the moment when the political tide turned.

Curiously enough, the nationalisation of steel scarcely figures in the memoirs of Lords Attlee, Dalton and Morrison of Lambeth. But there is nevertheless plenty of evidence that, at the time, Labour took a different view of its importance.

To take one example: in 1948, the year that the Bill was presented to Parliament, Wilfred Fienburgh and Richard Evely, both of them then in the Labour Party's research department at Transport House, wrote an eloquent little book which was published between the proud yellow covers of Gollancz, or what Oliver Lyttelton called "the yellow-backed romances of the Socialist Grub Street." It was called *Steel is Power: the Case for Nationalisation*. And, in the foreword, to give the case the stamp of authority, Morgan Phillips, secretary of the Party, wrote: "The battle for steel (is) the supreme test of political democracy — a test which the whole world will be watching."

That was it: the case for nationalising the steel industry was in the last analysis a political case. It was first and foremost a question of power. That is why both Labour and Conservatives treated it quite differently from earlier nationalisation measures.

Other Conservatives, besides David Eccles, had been somewhat half-hearted in their opposition to the earlier nationalisations. After all, in the beginning, it was not the Tories but the Liberals who were the arch-opponents of interference with business. As early as 1889 a Conservative Government had passed a sort of delayed-action public ownership measure, binding the private electricity companies to hand over to local authorities forty-two years later. More than one-third of the country's gas supply was in public hands. The railways, though still owned and operated by private companies, of which by hallowed tradition most of the middle-class were shareholders and many leading Conservatives were directors, had long been subject to public control, had been especially so during the war, and in any case had not been really profitable since the First World War. Coal was an industry which Conservative Governments had passed Mines Acts to control in 1930, 1932, 1936, and 1938. More-over, those Conservatives who were not personally ashamed of the sufferings of the miners were well aware by 1945 how strongly others felt on the subject. Coal, decidedly, was not worth fighting over.

The Tories (who had themselves created the Central Electricity Board and the B.B.C. in 1926) had only the vaguest of ideological objections to its nationalisation. So long as Labour contented itself with taking over public utilities, and especially unprofitable ones, Conservative opposition took the form of sensible enough attacks on the proposed structure of the industries, and unimpressive sniping at the rather generous terms of compensation offered to shareholders.

But steel was another matter. It had been a profitable industry within living memory, and would obviously be so again. Huge sums had recently been invested in it. It was therefore defensible in theory on the record of private enterprise – and well worth defending on its prospects.

Although some Labour champions tried to make out that the industry's record in war-time had been poor, in fact their case was not strong, and they made little of it.

Steel, unlike all the other industries slated for nationalisation, was a manufacturing industry. What is more it was – indeed it always must be – intimately connected with the engineering industries as a whole. He who controlled the citadel of steel, it was felt, would control shipbuilding, the motor industry – in effect, British industry as a whole. This aspect of the issue was rather exaggerated at the time, since the Government already had a good deal of control over the industry. But the feeling that the battle had moved beyond the outworks, to the citadel of private industry in Britain, undoubtedly hardened the hearts and nerved the arms both of the attackers and of the garrison.

Finally, and not least important, there was a difference in the attitude of the workers in the industry itself. Much of the impetus for nationalisation as a whole had come from the Trades Union Congress. In particular industries, notably the mines and the railways, there was a strong syndicalist tradition: the union claimed the right to have its industry nationalised on behalf of the workers. But in steel not only had labour relations been exceptionally good, the steelworkers' leaders were known to be lukewarm about nationalisation, and, in the two important cases of Lincoln Evans and Harry Douglass, they were on record as opposing it.

During the struggle, the Tories made a great deal of alleged divisions in the Labour ranks on the question of nationalising steel. It is true that over the years the Labour Party seems to have hesitated. Steel had been explicitly mentioned as an industry to be taken over in a 1934 Transport House document, *Socialism and the Condition of the People*. Yet, six years before, *Labour and the Nation* spoke only of nationalising the Bank, coal and transport: and, six years later, *Labour's Home Policy*, published just before Labour joined the war-time coalition, again did not specifically mention steel, though it was a strong document, with many fierce professions of Socialist faith. It also seems certain that some Right-wing Labour leaders, notably Herbert Morrison, had their private doubts about either the wisdom or the feasibility of taking over steel.

It is said that the question of shelving the nationalisation of steel was discussed among Labour leaders at the highest level after the Election in

Illingworth, *Punch*, 3.11.48

Design at Work

1945. Herbert Morrison is recorded as saying, during 1946, that steel nationalisation was "a matter of business," and "not really a party political matter at all." He is thought to have approached Sir Andrew Duncan, of the Iron and Steel Federation, with a compromise plan, whereby the Government would take greater powers to control the industry, and keep ownership in reserve for particular companies that seemed to need taking over.

But these doubts and divisions never reached a formal Cabinet, and those who felt them most strongly were discreet about expressing them. For the mainstream of thought in the Labour Party reckoned that it had the mandate of the electorate to nationalise steel, and the only question was when to get on with the job.

One of the workers who so skilfully passed up the ammunition to the Tory front bench during the steel debates has confessed: "We managed to dig in a bit of a crossbar and work it around a bit, suggesting that the Bevanites and the Left were demanding steel as a sop. I think now that may have been a bit of a debating point. They had so much trouble about it, maybe they really did want it."

As far as the Government and the parliamentary party were concerned, they certainly did want it. The lot of preparing a measure to carry out the alleged mandate fell on a new Minister of Supply – George Russell Strauss.

Strauss, a handsome, slightly shock-headed man, with the air of a successful musician, was forty-six at the time, and the kind of Socialist whom elderly Tories used to call "traitors to their class." In other words, he was a relatively rich man and an Old Rugbeian, whose father, after making his pile as a metal broker, had sat first as a Conservative Member of Parliament, and then crossed the floor to join Labour. Strauss had both the will and the experience for the task. He was – or at least he had been – a man of the Left within the Labour Party. He had been an ardent pacifist, he had made a trip to Russia in the days when that was something of a pilgrimage, and in the enthusiastic company of Nye Bevan and John Strachey. He had even got himself temporarily expelled from the Labour Party, along with Cripps, over the Popular Front to-do in 1939.

But he was also a metal broker, who knew the steel industry to some extent at first hand. And he had been involved in drafting and carrying through nationalisation Bills before, as Parliamentary Secretary to the Minister of Transport.

Almost as soon as he took office, in the summer of 1947, he was asked by the Cabinet if he could be ready with a steel nationalisation measure for the autumn session. He said "No": there was far too much detailed work to be done in the time. In this, as in all their nationalisation plans, Labour did not take office with a plan of campaign waiting only to be applied. There was nothing but a firm intention of pressing on, a vague notion of how this should be done – and a brimming confidence in the good things which would follow. Strauss had to settle down with his officials – not all of whom were privately in favour of nationalising steel, but all of whom, in the best Whitehall tradition, gave of their best none the less – and work out his scheme from a clean sheet of paper. He put up a paper to the Cabinet, a mere thousand-word sketch of what he proposed to do. It was accepted, and he and his men went to work.

So it was not until October 9th, 1948, that the Government published the Iron and Steel Nationalisation Bill. And this delay was important. It made practically inevitable one of the most controversial features of the Bill – its provision of a vesting date, May 1st, 1950, which was almost certain to be very close to, and perhaps actually after, the date of the next General Election.

The Bill was given its second reading in the House of Commons on November 15th. This was the Tories' opportunity for full-dress debate, and they had three days allotted to make the most of it.

The House met as usual on the first day at two in the afternoon. But it was four minutes past four before George Strauss rose and begged to move his Bill. In the meantime, it had been the Ministry of Supply's turn to answer questions: and the questions Strauss had to answer bring back the impossible burden of detailed administration which the Government took on, and the almost sadistic relish with which the Opposition ridiculed it. Behind any question time in those years one can catch a glimpse of an over-stretched bureaucracy, an echo of those other clerks at whom the hidalgos used to jeer: "If death came from the King of Spain, we should all be immortal."

The first hidalgo was Captain John Crowder. He had picked up a story from the *Graphic*: OUR WAR TOOLS FOR IRON CURTAIN: and he wanted to know the reason why. So did Sir Waldron Smithers.

Next Mr. Hugh Fraser. He had done some deeper digging, and found 36,000 pieces of radio equipment which, he alleged, had been first dumped down a mine-shaft at Cheadle, Staffs., under two hundred tons of muck, and then heroically (and profitably) rescued by Private Enterprise. What about that?

An honourable and gallant Member complained of the delays of a body called the Co-ordinating Committee on Hand Tools.

A lady Member pleaded the cause of 250 monkeys, recently arrived by air from Calcutta. She suspected they were to be used for some "nefarious purpose". Here poor Mr. Strauss got it both ways. Sir Waldron was on his feet in a flash, and witty too: "in view of the shortage of Labour candidates," he wondered, "would safe seats be found for the animals?" While Emrys Hughes, in deadly earnest, sniffed bacteriological warfare.

So it went on. A Government department had put advertisements in a Labour paper in Cornwall. Potash supplies. Parsonage houses. Sewage. Fowl pest. Almost lost beneath this rain of trivia were two topics of more than passing interest. The birth of a royal prince who was to become heir to the throne of England was duly noted. And Emrys Hughes, again, asked the Prime Minister whether he was aware that he was missing a splendid opportunity to give moral leadership to the world by declaring that Britain would neither manufacture nor use atomic weapons. The Prime Minister was of the opinion that unilateral disarmament had not proved effective in the past.

There was still one more tangle to be sorted out before the House could debate the Steel Bill itself. Major Sir David Maxwell Fyfe asked the Speaker for a ruling: was the Steel Bill, or was it not, a Hybrid Bill? In other words, was it a Bill that affected the interests of individuals rather than those of all individuals in a category? With much learning, the Speaker foiled this ingenious piece of sapping and mining. At last Mr. Strauss could introduce his "profoundly important, and vehemently controversial" Bill, as he called it.

There were three possibilities for steel, he began by arguing. Both ownership and control could be left with the steelmasters. Or the ownership could be left, subject to State supervision. Or ownership and control could both be in the hands of the State.

The briefest of historical excursions, into which he managed to work the magic name of Jarrow, convinced Mr. Strauss that number one was unthinkable. Under number two, the Government would still not have all it needed. It would be unsure of having enough positive control over capital investment, and it risked the non-co-operation of the steelmasters. Indeed, the Minister said, their divided loyalties had already brought them to a state of schizophrenia, which must be cured before it became chronic.

Mr. Strauss droned capably on with the details of his scheme. There was hardly a sound from the Opposition until he came to the question of compensation. The Tories, and even the non-Tory press, had argued that the basis proposed – Stock Exchange prices on certain days – was unfair, because market prices had been artificially depressed by dividend limitation.

Now a Tory back-bencher ruffled Mr. Strauss by putting this same argument less delicately. He was like "one barrow boy throwing dirty water over the fruit of another barrow boy, so that he may buy it more cheaply." This set off a gentle drip of interjections. But on the whole Strauss was able to plough steadily on to his low-toned peroration after an hour and twenty minutes on his feet. He came to it at last: the Bill was designed to make the steel monopoly the servant, not the master, of the people.

Oliver Lyttelton led for the Opposition. To many on the Labour benches he was a symbol of the privilege, the arrogance, and the formidable determination, of Toryism. There was always something in his manner – the elegant correctness of the clothes, the uncompromising edge of instinctive authority in the voice – which rankled with the working-class rank-and-file in the Labour Party, and provoked its intellectuals to paroxysms of fascinated hatred, such as Michael Foot's vitriolic pen-portraits.

But Lyttelton was more than an aristocrat, a Guards officer, and an archetypal capitalist. He was also highly intelligent, and he was brought up in the Whig tradition. Beneath the haughty tone of his speech there were subtle touches. He knew how to take for granted some hotly disputed generalisation, slipping it between two cheerfully brutal imputations of motive, and leaving it to sink in.

He began with a nice debating trick. The Bill had caused him anxiety, he said. He waited until the Labour benches began to jeer. No, he said quickly, to the unspoken suggestion that the anxiety was financial. The trouble was that the Bill had said nothing about how the industry was to be run. No plan, in fact, from the planners.

He dragged up a little string of quotations from Labour speakers – what he called "flashes of candour," to suggest that it was power Labour was after in taking over steel. "This was the real stuff. Let us agree that, if the nationalisation of steel is carried out, a revolution, not evolution, will have been carried out, and that revolution at the end of a Parliament."

He, too, turned to history, to prove his contention that there was no case for nationalisation, either on grounds of inadequate capacity, or of bad labour relations. He quoted the pamphlet, *Steel is Power*, by Mr. *Fienberg*. (The *Hansard* spelling seems to indicate his xenophobic pronunciation of Mr. Fienburgh's name!) "They give the whole thing away . . . they believe in the doctrine of centralisation of power in the hands of the State . . . it has long been our doctrine that, in a democracy, power should be dispersed." So, softly imputing the worst motives between the lines of his credo, he came on to his confident, menacing ending: "One day, and not far off, the people will decide."

For the rest of the night, until the adjournment at ten o'clock, the debate continued rather coolly. There was only one significant little skirmish, though it was hardly even that. The Honourable Hugh Fraser was a very superior young person, thirty years old, son of a sixteenth baron, and a member of all the right clubs. He turned some aggressive phrases in his speech, talking about Marxists, and jobs for the boys, and calling the Government "sterile and ignorant."

He was neatly deflated by a Member with a very different experience of life, and twice his age. "If he had anything to do with the practical side of the industry, I do not think the furnaces would ever lack heat," said David Llewellyn Mort.

Mort went on to make, in his South Wales voice, more eloquently than most, two points that were to recur in speech after speech from the back benches, that emotional Spion Kop where the old men sat and watched their champions. He spoke of the bad old days, when he as a steelworker had known unemployment, and as a trade unionist had been obliged to stand up in the presence of the manager.

"Those conditions have gone," he went on. "These blessings which we have gained were not conferred upon us. We fought for them." And he spoke for the deepest instincts of the rank-and-file in his conclusion: "It may be old-fashioned, but we on this side of the House still believe that the earth is the Lord's and the iron ore thereof. This nation wants above all things security, stability, and protection against the cold winds of uncontrolled economic force."

The second day was stormier than the first, and more partisan. But ironically it began with one of those little ceremonies of party truce that so delight the foreign observer of Parliament. The occasion was an address of congratulation to the Sovereign on the birth of a son (later christened Charles) to Her Royal Highness Elizabeth, Duchess of Edinburgh.

Mr. Attlee was at his most benign. In his habitual short, colourless sentences, he said a few nice things about promise, and responsibility, and happiness. Mr. Churchill, a few minutes before sweeping the debate on to a new plane of partisan sharpness, rolled out with obvious pleasure a few inimitable sentences, about our ancient monarchy, and how refreshing it was to break off from the ebb and flow of party strife. Only Willie Gallacher, the Communist Member for West Fife, obstinately chose the moment to remember "far too many babies being born in sub-lets and in appalling slum conditions."

Then the Member for Woodford was up again. Was the Steel Bill, he began by asking, going to help the country or was it a partisan manœuvre? With an elevation of language that no one else would have dared to adopt, he set out to show that it was the second. Suddenly, in mid-period, he was interrupted, and by Sir Richard Acland, the Member for Gravesend.

Churchill switched immediately to almost childish vehemence. "Go back to Gravesend!"

Acland rose, to press his point. But the old man was off on a noble period: "It is indeed a base and a most melancholy sequel . . ." Acland refused to be over-awed. Churchill told him rudely that he had no intention of interrupting the thread of his argument to help the Honourable Gentleman to make himself a footing in the Socialist Party, and ploughed imperturbably on with the story of the base and melancholy sequel. The conclusion, reached only after a serene series of lofty and polysyllabic insults, was the outrageous charge that the Government was pressing the Steel Bill only to increase its powers of patronage.

Mr. Churchill, in fact, was in his best vein. Among a mint of striking phrases, he hit upon one which perfectly expressed the basic Tory contention that Labour wanted to nationalise steel for political, and not for economic, ends. "This is not a Bill, it is a plot; not a plan to increase production, but rather, in effect, at any rate, an operation in restraint of trade. It is not a plan to help our patient struggling people, but a burglar's jemmy to crack the capitalist crib."

Finally, with a characteristically powerful archaism, he reiterated his basic indictment against the Labour Government: that they were factious — a feeling which was no doubt fed subconsciously by his own understandable resentment at the electorate's ingratitude: ". . . the one thing that fills their minds, the one thing which they fear and shrink from, is the General Election which is coming upon them, and which will end in obloquy and censure their dismal and evil reign."

To that cadenced condemnation, Jack Jones, one of Strauss's aides, had the temerity to oppose a less dignified charge. Mr. Churchill was jumping about a bit, said Mr. Jones in his broad Rotherham.

"What?" said Churchill, as if his honour had been tarnished. Mr. Jones repeated the phrase, and explained it. "Today the Right Hon. Gentleman takes off his hat to the steelworkers. Not many weeks ago the Right Hon. Gentleman referred to the workers of this country as being members of a democracy of Tired Tims and Weary Willies."

"Really!" said Mr. Churchill, and for some time these two grown men argued about whether or not the one of them had used this nursery insult, and, if he had, what he had meant by it. At last Jack Jones went on, defending the workers, "these ordinary fellows, men such as myself, who, generally speaking – there are exceptions – sweat and slave, swear and drink," from the monstrous imputation of not wanting their industry to be nationalised.

Clement Davies, the Liberal leader, was caught out as having signed a pamphlet in favour of steel nationalisation, which the Liberals now opposed, eight years before. His answer had charm: the relevant part of the pamphlet had, he bizarrely revealed, been written by that well-known Liberal, Dr. Thomas Balogh.

Sir John Anderson, lawyer, ex-Chancellor of the Exchequer, and Scot, drily expounded the Tory case against compensation. But he was out-lawyered, out-argued, and out-gunned, in the closing speech of the night, by the Chancellor.

Cripps's speech exemplified the strengths and the weaknesses of a man, intellectually as able as ever spoke in the House of Commons, yet who never understood the House, and usually irritated it. He began by taking Sir John's case apart at a galloping pace, and finally sank it with a devastating quotation from the *Financial Times*: "Yesterday's near-boom conditions in Iron and Steel shares reflected a gamble, pure and simple. Buyers are gambling on the contents of the coming Nationalisation Bill."

But, when he turned to his general argument for the Bill, he blundered, under a constant fire of heckling interruptions from Churchill, into indiscretion and an immoderate over-statement of his case. Dropping the grandiloquent dignity of his earlier manner, Churchill harassed the Chancellor with street-corner interruptions: "Nonsense!" or "Have a General Election!"

Eventually Cripps went too far. He said that some of the opposition to the Bill came from those who bitterly resented an attack on their property. This was a challenge to democracy. Democracy must assert its rights. "The ugly alternative would then be that any such change that is to occur must be brought about by other and more violent means."

Somebody shouted "By gunpowder?"

Cripps glossed hastily: "It is because we are preventing that, that Socialist democracy is the true barrier against Communism."

This was too much for Churchill. Again and again he rose, in real or simulated rage, amid cries of order and counter-cries, until the day's debate adjourned in near-pandemonium.

After this, and with one notable exception, the speeches on the last day of the debate were anti-climax.

They had their moments, of course. That bantam-weight Cheshire champion, Mr. Ernest Marples, told the House the old commercial travellers' tale about the American railroad which had a standard form of letter for passengers bitten by bed-bugs. Alas, he spoiled the point by his evident belief that American railroads were State-owned, and only recovered his aplomb by quoting Aristotle. Mrs. Jean Mann also achieved a felicitous quotation: she delighted Tory members with her assertion, in the course of a diatribe against "unearned increment," that "even Solomon in all his glory was not arrayed" like one of their grandmothers or their aunts.

The two speeches to wind up the debate came from Mr. Eden and Mr. Morrison. Both made some solid points; Eden returning effectively to Oliver Lyttelton's charge that neither the Bill, nor the speeches in support of it, had disclosed a clear plan for the future of the steel industry. Eden was urbane, Morrison rumbustious. But the one was never at his best on home affairs; and the other was suspected, rightly or wrongly, of not having his heart in this debate.

Both were overshadowed by the first speaker of the day, Sir Andrew Duncan. Then sixty-three years old, an ex-Minister and Member for the City of London, Duncan was the undisputed chieftain of the steel industry, wielding his power through the Iron and Steel Federation. He had also been one of the captains, if not the epitome, of British heavy industry as a whole in the inter-war years. A deep, cautious man, who smoked huge cigars, Duncan, so they said, "was what Socialism was about."

Yet oddly enough Duncan, though the acknowledged champion of the steel industry, was in a sense neither a steelmaster nor a capitalist. A Scots family lawyer, he had risen by his talents as an industrial diplomat, and by being what Michael Foot called "the great co-ordinator, the brilliant amalgamator." He was an exponent, not of ruthless competition and productive vigour, but of defensive combination.

He put the case for the Federation in typical fashion, at once factual and partisan. He denied, with a mass of figures, that the industry had been to blame for the lean years. How for example, he asked, could it be said that the industry had deliberately kept capacity below demand? The trouble had been the surplus of capacity. Duncan went through the Labour charges one by one – monopoly, cartelisation, stagnation, and excessive profits – and sought to disprove them. The British industry had grown faster than the German or the American in the bad years, it had invested £50 million in new plant – and its alleged monopoly profits had amounted to a return of no more than two per cent on the money invested.

It was a masterly performance. Indeed, the Conservative performance in the debate as a whole was masterly. No dispassionate observer could have failed to judge them the winners – if Parliament were a debating society, and there were any such thing as dispassionate observers.

But of course the Bill was passed, by 373 votes to 211. There were few on the Labour benches who would have allowed themselves to be persuaded by a member for the City of London, though he spake with the tongues of men and of angels. Indeed, one can go as far as George Strauss himself, who has said, "Nobody is ever convinced by a debate."

Certainly one should not exaggerate the effect even of this debate. A week before, the Conservatives had won a famous victory in a by-election at Edmonton. Their vote was up by fifty per cent. Yet steel was hardly mentioned. And that perceptive political journalist, Hugh Massingham, could write in the *Observer* that this was a "curiously stagnant hour."

There is a moment at the turn of a tide when the water is slack, as if stagnant. Perhaps this was that moment in the life of the Labour Government: the retreat had not yet begun, but the impetus of the great series of measures of reform had become feeble.

The after-history of steel nationalisation charts the slow stages of the retreat. All winter the Bill was argued over in committee. But hard as Oliver Lyttelton, and Harold Macmillan, and a young provincial lawyer called Selwyn Lloyd, and their friends argued their amendments, they could have no hope even of delaying its passage. Herbert Morrison, as Leader of the House, had set a guillotine, which fell, after thirty-six sittings, on St. Patrick's Day, 1949, with two hundred amendments still undiscussed. The Bill went up to the Lords, substantially as George Strauss had brought it in.

In their lordships' house, the Marquess of Salisbury had to tread delicately. He had a huge but largely backwoods majority. He could not afford to risk the reputation – and even the future existence – of the House of Lords by using it to obstruct the passage of a Bill which carried out, as Labour claimed, a clear mandate of the democratic electorate. He could not obstruct. But he made plain his view of the Bill: he called it "a definite step towards Communism." The strategy must be Fabian: he would delay. He urged his peers to amend the vesting date, so that it would fall after a General Election, and give the electorate a second chance to express their will.

The Lords' debates, the constitutional issue of the mandate, the short, unhappy life of the Iron and Steel Corporation of Great Britain, and the eventual denationalisation – these are all important chapters in the political history of the time, and the slow ebbing of the Labour tide. But they are not part of the story of the Tory revival. For other threads we must return to 1945.

On August 1st, 1945, Mr. Churchill's friends had to sit, angry and miserable, in the Commons through the Red Flag, or such of its words as their conquerors could remember.

Less than three years later, those two hundred demoralised Conservatives had become the most effective Parliamentary Opposition of the century. This change was not only due to the exhaustion and to the mistakes of the Government, nor even to the groaning of the people under austerity. Great things were happening within the ancient body of the Conservative Party.

There were two sides to this rejuvenation. First, the party organisation was rebuilt from the ground up. This was essentially the work of Lord Woolton.

There is an ancient piece of Lancashire wisdom which distinguishes between Liverpool gentlemen, Manchester men, and Salford lads. Fred Marquis, first Earl of Woolton, was a Manchester man. His whole career and personality exemplified that downright city. A scholar of Manchester Grammar School, then a student at Manchester University, he taught maths. at a grammar school, and did social work in Liverpool. He was Controller of Civilian Boots in the First World War, and he rose to the top of a great group of department stores before accepting the vast administrative responsibilities of the wartime Minister of Food.

This was not a characteristic background for a Tory leader of that generation (Woolton was born in 1880), and in fact, on the day of the election in 1945, Woolton was still not a Tory. He had a lively social conscience, and a streak of Lancashire radicalism; but he was no Socialist. He had come to believe that "the British way of life . . . was in danger of losing its old sense of the importance of the freedom of the individual." And he was passionately loyal to his war-time chief, Winston Churchill. On the morrow of the defeat, he wrote and asked to join the Conservative Party. On July 1st, 1946, he was appointed chairman of the Party Organisation.

He arrived at Abbey House to find little more than a couple of chairs and a typist – or so it seemed to people a few months later. Certainly demoralisation was so complete that many wanted to change even the name of the party. The organisation was, as Woolton himself said, "the most Topsy-like arrangement I had ever come across." There was devotion there, and even some talent. But there was no direction, and no co-ordination. The constituency associations were not controlled in any way by the Central Office. Functions such as research were divided between rival bodies. The appointment of candidates was a matter of bizarre and complex protocol. There was not even enough money.

Woolton began by spending five times more than he had. By 1948, he was spending the party's annual income ten times over. Remembering that, as a social worker, he had once failed to get £400 that he had appealed for, but had succeeded when he asked for £10,000 for the same object, he asked Conservatives to raise the apparently impossible sum of a million pounds. He got it; and much of it came in small sums from thousands of contributors (though much, too, came from industrialists who felt the hot breath of nationalisation on their necks).

Before the election of 1950, this million had been spent. Woolton set about remodelling the party organisation with the long-sighted thoroughness of big business – and with some of its techniques. He trained 278 new agents, and he paid them salaries that would attract capable men. He advertised. He appointed, and personally trained, a publicity officer (Mark Chapman-Walker, who became an enthusiast for commercial television and commercial radio, and a director of the *News of the World*). Woolton himself was no mean propagandist: it was he who insisted on calling the Labour Party "the Socialist Party."

He rationalised the proliferating wings of the organisation. He re-organised the party conference, and left a big place in it for his newly created Young Conservatives. And he did not stop at organising. He put the party on the stump. Operation Knocker – the name alone would have been inconceivable before Woolton! – was a massive national campaign of person-to-person persuasion, to supplement the countless hours which Woolton himself and front-bench speakers put in on platforms all over the kingdom. Most important of all, a commission was set up under the lawyer David Maxwell Fyfe, to modernise the appointment of candidates. No doubt for long to come Tory candidates would speak in "a gentleman's voice": at least henceforward they would not owe their nomination to their subventions to the party funds.

Of course, the Tory New Look did not come from Woolton alone, even on the purely organisational side. That alone could not have made a Tory revival: but it made a Tory victory at the polls possible. However, this work would have gone for nothing without new ideas to attract the electorate. And ideas were above all the department of Rab Butler and his young men.

Far younger than Woolton, Butler (only forty-two at this time) was also a more orthodox Tory in background and thinking, wealthy, an Etonian, a scion of Cambridge and the Indian Civil Service. But he was, if in the slightly strangled Tory manner, an intellectual, and one who cared deeply about social issues. Moreover, as the Minister responsible for the Education Act of 1944, the one great measure of domestic reform of the war years, he was identified with progressive social thinking.

In 1946, he was chairman of the Conservative research department, whose functions were solely those of research into possible long-term policy. This was a baby of Neville Chamberlain, founded by Lord Davidson after the defeat of 1929. The day-to-day briefing of the Opposition in Parliament was the responsibility of the Parliamentary Secretariat.

By 1948 these two bodies were merged, and housed in a Queen Anne house in Old Queen Street, backing on to St. James's Park. What was more, both department and secretariat dipped their nets into the shoals of bright young men who were just coming out of the forces – men who in peace-time would have been deeply committed to their careers. They came up, for example, with Brigadier Enoch Powell, a pre-war Greek teacher, back from the Far East; with Major Iain Macleod, of 50 Div. H.Q.; with Michael Frazer, who had been an intelligence officer in Germany, and with Reginald Maudling. Altogether ten of the research department's recruits over the next few years were to find their way into the House.

It was not a group of the Left particularly – though still less of the Right. It was not even a group of new men, sociologically speaking. But, as one of its members said: "It was not a group of boneheads," and these clever young men threw themselves both into the day-to-day briefing of the Opposition in Parliament, and into the preparation of new, long-term policies.

"In 1946," Michael Frazer remembers, "we dropped a lot of catches." But in 1947, as the Opposition warmed up against a stream of major legislation, the department produced 397 briefs for Tory speakers. The party ceased to be in the House of Commons "the stupid party": the technique of the Fabian Society was turned against its inventors.

The long-term thinking was even more important. One must beware of exaggerating the influence of Butler's bright young men. Most sections of the party were involved, more or less willingly. A group of by-no-means-radical young Members of Parliament, for example, Quintin Hogg, Hinchingbrooke, Peter Thorneycroft, were pamphleteering as the Tory Reform group. And, on an initiative of the Blackpool conference of 1946, official party committees were set to work to produce charters, one for agriculture, and one for industry. The membership of the committee which produced the Industrial Charter of May 1947 is significant: it included Oliver Stanley, Lyttelton, Macmillan, Derrick Heathcoat-Amory, Maxwell Fyfe, Eccles, with Butler in the chair, and Maudling and Frazer as its two secretaries. This was the party as a whole taking policy seriously, acted upon by the leaven of the research department. The Charters in turn served as a basis for the domestic sections of the first general statement of Conservative policy produced since before the war, *The Right Road for Britain*, which came out in June 1949.

A few weeks before, by coincidence, Labour had also produced a policy document. It was called, with the terrible banality which neither party seems able to avoid on these occasions, *Labour Believes in Britain*. And it contained, on the essential point of public ownership, a notable retreat from the principles of 1945 and the dream of the Socialist Commonwealth: "Unless there is economic necessity, there is no reason for always socialising whole industries."

So the great debate on nationalisation, which reached its climax and its turning-point in the fight over steel, worked its effect upon the philosophy, as well as the morale, of each of the parties. For Labour, steel was a Pyrrhic victory. Its cost was too high, both in future divisions within the Party and in stiffening opposition in the country. Never again did Labour advocate nationalisation with the same unquestioning fervour. But the Tories, who fought the early measures of nationalisation with their well-tailored backs to the wall, did not only pick up new confidence in the course of the struggle: they also forged new weapons of party organisation. Equally, they evolved almost without noticing it an ideological opposition to nationalisation that had been no more than a vague jumble of interests and prejudices in 1945. And lastly the sinners had again learned from the reign of the Saints. Just as Charles II learned his politics in the hard school of exile, so when the merry Tories brought in the Restoration of Affluence to dispel austerity, they brought one firm intention with them: they were in no hurry to go on their travels again.

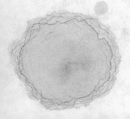

15

FESTIVAL

MICHAEL FRAYN

Michael Frayn was born in 1933, educated at Kingston Grammar School and Emmanuel College, Cambridge. In 1957 he joined *The Guardian*, first as a reporter and then with his own column, "Miscellany". In 1962 he moved to *The Observer*, where he writes a weekly satirical column. He appears on Granada Television. Married, with one daughter. A selection of his *Guardian* articles was published by Collins in 1962, under the title *The Day of the Dog*.

FESTIVAL

Michael Frayn

"IN 1951," wrote Evelyn Waugh, in the epilogue to his novel *Unconditional Surrender*, "to celebrate the opening of a happier decade, the Government decreed a Festival. Monstrous constructions appeared on the south bank of the Thames, the foundation stone was solemnly laid for a National Theatre, but there was little popular exuberance among the straitened people, and dollar-bearing tourists curtailed their visits and sped to the countries of the Continent where, however precarious their condition, they ordered things better."

Poor Evelyn Waugh. It was certainly not the Festival of his Britain. For those sections of the upper- and middle-classes of whose subconscious anxieties he is the curator the Festival marked the climax of a decade in which almost every single act of government had been inimical to their immediate interests. For a decade they had lived in unprecedented austerity — austerity which could have been ended for *them* years before if it had not been artificially prolonged by egalitarian theorising. For a decade they had been watching — or thought they had been watching — the gestation of a monstrous new state, in which their privileges would be forfeit, their influence dissolved, and their standards irrelevant. When they said — as they frequently did in the years that led up to the Festival — that there was pathetically little for Britain to celebrate in 1951, it was their own private Britain that they had in mind. Perhaps if they had realised that 1951 was to mark the end of this era, and the entry into a decade of stable, moderate Conservative government, when it soon became plain that the balance of power and privilege had hardly changed after all, they might have enjoyed it more.

On the other hand, it was scarcely the Britain of the working-classes that was being fêted. With the exception of Herbert Morrison, who was responsible to the Cabinet for the Festival and who had very little to do with the actual form it took, there was almost no one of working-class background concerned in planning the Festival, and nothing about the result to suggest that the working-classes were anything more than the lovably human but essentially inert objects of benevolent administration.

In fact, Festival Britain was the Britain of the radical middle-classes –

the do-gooders; the readers of the *News Chronicle*, the *Guardian*, and the *Observer*; the signers of petitions; the backbone of the B.B.C. In short, the Herbivores, or gentle ruminants, who look out from the lush pastures which are their natural station in life with eyes full of sorrow for less fortunate creatures, guiltily conscious of their advantages, though not usually ceasing to eat the grass. And in making the Festival they earned the contempt of the Carnivores – the readers of the *Daily Express*; the Evelyn Waughs; the cast of the Directory of Directors – the members of the upper- and middle-classes who believe that if God had not wished them to prey on all smaller and weaker creatures without scruple he would not have made them as they are.

Perhaps this domestic split in the privileged classes, rather than any struggle between classes, is the basis of all democratic politics. Anyway, for a decade, sanctioned by the exigencies of war and its aftermath, the Herbivores had dominated the scene. By 1951 the régime which supported them was exhausted, and the Carnivores were ready to take over. The Festival was the last, and virtually the posthumous, work of the Herbivore Britain of the B.B.C. News, the Crown Film Unit, the sweet ration, the Ealing comedies, Uncle Mac, Sylvia Peters . . . all the great fixed stars by which my childhood was navigated.

The idea of celebrating the mid-point of the twentieth century, and the centenary of the Great Exhibition, was one which had naturally been in the air for a long time. The Royal Society of Arts, which had been closely concerned with the 1851 Exhibition, put it to the Government privately as early as 1943. In September 1945 Gerald Barry, the editor of the *News Chronicle*, urged the project in an open letter to Sir Stafford Cripps, the President of the Board of Trade, and followed it with a campaign to whip up support among industrialists. Cripps scribbled a reply to Barry in his characteristic red ink, saying he thought it might be quite a good idea. Presumably the Board of Trade had been thinking about it already, for, eleven days after Barry's letter appeared, the Government set up the Ramsden Committee to consider the question.

The idea had now been fed into the official Government processing machinery, from which ideas habitually emerge squeezed to the pips by the intermeshing teeth of incompatible political expediencies. But it did the Festival project nothing but good, reducing the grandiose pretensions that mar most undertakings of this sort to the modest and practical functionalism which was in the end its greatest virtue. Again and again pure expediency deflected the plans from the dismal disaster towards which they seemed naturally disposed to gravitate. The Ramsden Committee, for example, reported in favour of a "Universal International Exhibition, to demonstrate to the world the recovery of the United Kingdom from the effects of the war in the moral, cultural, spiritual, and material fields," in Hyde Park. Unwilling to deprive Londoners of their main open space, the Government set up an interdepartmental committee to find another site. It recommended using 300 acres of Osterley Park, in the outer western suburbs, and the scheme was only abandoned when the Government discovered that it would cost the taxpayer £70 millions, and absorb a third of London's building labour for three years. So, by the spring of 1947, the universal international exhibition had been ground down to a national one, and Cripps, now that the Board of Trade was no longer concerned, handed over responsibility to Herbert Morrison, the Lord President of the Council.

By this time the project had a name, and was sufficiently mature to begin breeding a profuse genealogy of organisational units. The Cabinet begat the Great Exhibition Centenary Official Committee. The Great Exhibition Centenary Official Committee begat the Festival of Britain Office. The Festival of Britain Office begat the Festival Council and the Festival Executive Committee. The Festival Executive Committee begat the Presentation Panel. And the Presentation Panel begat the Design Group, which was to bring honour upon the entire family.

Expediency still ruled. The Government had failed to find a site big enough to hold an international exhibition; the Festival Council and the Executive Committee, respectively the Lords and Commons of the new organisation, were almost defeated in their search for a site big enough for a national one. The main exhibition halls at Earls Court and Olympia, they discovered, were already booked for the British Industries Fair. They proposed putting it in Battersea Park, under "recoverable standard shedding." The Government rejected this awful idea for fear of upsetting the people of Battersea, but, having saved the Festival from a living death in recoverable standard shedding, went on to propose a fate worse than death – housing it in the museum buildings at South Kensington. It was only the inexpediency of turning the regular museum-goers out for two or three years that persuaded the Festival Council to refuse.

By the summer of 1948 complete deadlock had been reached. If the L.C.C.'s plan to build a concert hall in time for 1951 on the South Bank had not come up for endorsement by the Festival Council at this point, the deadlock might never have been broken. Afterwards it was widely supposed that it had been Morrison who swung the South Bank on the

Festival as a way of getting the area redeveloped – a project in which as an old L.C.C. man he had long been interested. In fact it had been first suggested by the Ramsden Committee, and overlooked in the excitements of recoverable standard shedding and remote, mysterious Osterley. It was now revived, not by Morrison, but by the Festival Council.

It had taken three years to find a home for the Festival. There were only another three left in which to find a Festival for the home. It is difficult to know whether it made the task easier or harder that no one had ever clearly explained what the whole undertaking was *for*. But then, apparently, no one thought it necessary to ask. There seems to have been a mixture of motives taken for granted. It was intended partly to fulfil the abstract but curiously compelling task of marking the mid-century and the 1851 centenary; partly to be a sort of national prestige advertisement; partly as an attraction for tourists. Under attack, Gerald Barry, who in March 1948 had been appointed Director-General, sometimes tried to justify it on the purely materialistic grounds, which, he must have hoped, even a Carnivore would understand, that it would make people work harder; there was, he insisted, an appreciable increase in national production after the pageantry at the wedding of Prince Philip and Princess Elizabeth. Still, a certain vagueness about its purpose lingered to the end; as Noël Coward wrote, in his song "Don't Make Fun of the Fair", in the Lyric Revue in 1951:

> Take a nip from your brandy flask,
> Scream and caper and shout,
> Don't give anyone time to ask
> What the Hell it's about.

Coward was for a time a member of the Festival Council, and if he didn't know what the hell it was about one can only wonder if anyone else did. Morrison probably made the closest guess afterwards when he described it as "the people giving themselves a pat on the back." After five years of war, and a disillusioning peace which had brought nothing but continued austerity, continued restrictions, and the threat of war again, the nation craved a brilliant holiday as some sort of tangible reward for its labours and sufferings.

What sort of holiday, though? The strange thing is, looking back on it from a Carnivorous age, that at no point was it ever suggested that the people should be given what Carnivores usually allege they want – a gigantic national booze-up, perhaps, with hostesses giving away free washing-machines, and gigantic, gas-filled facsimiles of chorus-girls' legs floating over all the major cities, picked out at night by searchlights.

But then the whole tone of public life was curiously different in those days; and besides, the Festival was securely in Herbivorous hands. The Press identified it with Morrison, particularly after he was given a convenient handle by a member who put down a question on the Festival for the Lord President, and by a spoonerism addressed him as the Lord Festival. It was the Lord Festival's energy that pushed the project through, and his surprising tact and statesmanship that brought it through the criticism in the House still looking something like an all-party undertaking. The actual making of the Festival, however, he left entirely to the Executive Committee. They were a purely Herbivorous herd – two civil servants, a scientist, an industrial designer, the former general manager of the Stratford Memorial Theatre, a representative from the British Film Institute, Huw Wheldon from the Arts Council, a public relations officer from the Coal Board, Hugh Casson the architect, and Barry himself. These were the men who were to administer the national pat on the back – with not a Val Parnell, not a Billy Butlin, not a Herbert Gunn, not a shadow of a giver-of-the-people-what-they-want among them. In this Carnivorous age, the mind boggles at the idea.

More than anyone else, it was Barry who set the tone of the Festival. Appropriately enough, his appointment had been suggested by Max Nicholson, the Secretary to the Office of the Lord President, who was well known for his interest in the profoundly Herbivorous pastime of bird-watching. Barry himself was the son of a clergyman, and was educated at Marlborough and Cambridge. An anxious, sensitive, conscientious, rather dry man, he had spent his life as a radical journalist. The tone of the Festival was not unlike the tone of the *News Chronicle*, which he had edited for eleven years – philanthropic, kindly, whimsical, cosy, optimistic, middlebrow, deeply instinct with the Herbivorous philosophy so shortly doomed to eclipse.

The Committee met for the first time in May 1948, for a week-end session at Barry's house in Sussex. It must have been something like a Fabian house-party; they sat on the terrace in the sunshine, or paced the lawn in pairs, discussing the First Principles of Festivity, before a background of rolling English parkland brilliant with the first translucent green sheen of summer. It was the pastoral prologue to three furious years, in which waking hours were working hours. Barry recalls them as a period of almost continuous elation – even when, in the later stages, he would be still reading official papers in bed at three in the morning. The

Festival, he wrote afterwards, was made not only in committee rooms. "It was made on hill-tops, in gardens, round a log-fire, wherever half a dozen people could foregather and talk. It was made clambering among rubble and cement mixers, amid the uproar of cranes and pile drivers, in over-heated railway carriages and under-heated motor-cars, tearing through the English landscape. It was made in mayoral parlours, on fog-bound airfields, in dingy studios, on visits to experimental building stations, in lecture halls, youth centres, and standing on street corners waiting for a bus. I sometimes think that those who jostled us in a queue might have detected a special smell, for all that time we breathed, thought, imagined, willed, inhaled, and exuded – Festival."

There is something about this exuberant toil that makes one think of putting on a school play – a super-colossal school play, perhaps, to mark the end of a super-colossally long and trying term. But the daily contact with bus queues and youth centres kept the reality of Britain's reduced circumstances perpetually before their eyes. "One mistake we should *not* make," wrote Barry: "we should not fall into the error of supposing we were going to produce anything conclusive. In this sceptical age, the glorious assurance of the mid-Victorians would find no echo."

All the same, the theme which the Executive Committee worked out that summer of 1948 had a fairly sonorous ring when Barry announced it to the press in October. It was to demonstrate Britain's contribution to civilisation, by way of showing "what the Land has made of the People, and what the People have made of themselves." "We envisage this as the people's show," said Barry, "not organised arbitrarily for them to enjoy, but put on largely by them, by us all, as an expression of a way of life in which we believe." It is the true voice of the forties speaking; not even the most Herbivorous of men, in our age of more highly sophisticated class consciousness and guilt, could stand up in public and announce that a committee consisting of a former newspaper editor, two senior civil servants, an architect, a theatre-manager, a cinéaste, a palaeontologist, a public relations officer, and Huw Wheldon, was the People. 1951 was also to be a year of "fun, fantasy, and colour," of "the fun and games which the bitter circumstances of the last few years have denied us," a year in which "we can, while soberly surveying our great past and our promising future, for once let ourselves go, and in which the myth that we take our pleasures sadly will finally be disproved."

These were the first details to be published; but the criticism which was to be a running accompaniment to the whole project for the next three years had already begun. When Morrison had first announced in the

Commons, in December 1947, that he was examining the possibility of some sort of national exhibition in 1951, the Opposition had offered its full support for the project. Not a voice was raised in protest anywhere in the House – or anywhere in the country – despite the fact that the announcement coincided with the news that Britain was just beginning to spend the last £400 millions of the American loan.

Now the Carnivores fell upon it, led by the Beaverbrook Press. Exactly why Beaverbrook took so violently against the Festival it is not easy to say. Anything with such a Herbivorous tone would naturally be antipathetic to him – yet the prospect of patriotic exultation in the achievements of British industry, with fun and fantasy thrown in, is one which might easily have struck him as being almost as admirable as the *Daily Express* Boat Show. A bookmaker might well have offered evens on whether Beaverbrook would put the Festival in the same category as the Boat Show or as the heinous British Council.

Anyway, at the beginning of August 1949, Beaverbrook's *Evening Standard* opened fire on "Mr. Morrison's multi-million-pound baby." The initial shots were two articles by Charles Wintour, complaining principally about the probable cost; though their effect was somewhat offset by Low's cartoon in the *Standard* a day or two later, which showed Barry explaining to the press: "We've now cut expenses down to twenty-five quid – and we hope to knock off another ten by not having gates so that visitors can't get in." From then on the *Express* and the *Standard* kept plugging away at it. They called it "Mr. Morrison's Monument," "Morrison's Folly," and "This gigantic waxworks cum circus cum carnival," and sniped at it day after day with stories bearing headlines like "Resort-Guide Paper Taken For Festival," "Up Up Up Go Hotel Prices," "Festival Badges Muddle," "Up Go the Costs of the Festival." Considering what a wide range of novel undertakings the Festival involved, and the speed with which they had to be pushed through, it is remarkable how little effective material the Beaverbrook papers were able to dig up. When, at the opening of the Festival, the *Evening Standard* reporter was reduced to writing: "In one corner stood an object which may be thought symbolical of Mr. Morrison and his planners. It was a brand-new twopenny slot machine. The shelves were bare. And on the machine was boldly draped a label reading NOT WORKING" – it was clear that Beaverbrook's plans, like Barry's, were being held up by a certain shortage of raw materials.

The campaign was, anyway, showing signs of wilting towards the end. Again one can only speculate on the reason. In January 1951, when the

Express, like other papers, was wondering whether the situation in Korea would lead to a world war that year, it invited readers to submit postcards explaining either "Why They Should Go Ahead With The Festival" or "Why They Should Call It Off." None was ever published. But a fortnight later the *Express* ran a leader on the Festival, saying: "What should be the public attitude towards it? It should be one of support. It is too late to say that £11,000,000 of public money has been needlessly spent. It is too late to say that the men and materials could have been better used building houses instead of a monument to Mr. Morrison." Had the *Express* discovered that it was not carrying its readers with it in its opposition to the Festival? (A Gallup Poll taken at about the same time found 58 per cent in favour of proceeding with the Festival, 28 per cent in favour of postponing it.) The Beaverbrook campaign tailed off still further in the spring – perhaps because by this time Morrison had become Foreign Secretary, and was taking a firm line, of which the *Express* approved, on Persian oil nationalisation.

The rest of the Conservative press stayed closer to the line followed by the party in the House, which was to give its general support, but to exercise its constitutional privilege of making political capital out of it whenever the chance arose. At Question Time certain of the more ancient pieces of ordnance entrenched in the rear of the Opposition would regularly discharge themselves against the whole enterprise. Now and again the Opposition in general was struck by the natural suspicion that the Festival might be used to advertise the record of the Labour Government. Morrison handled them with great tact in the House, and took considerable pains to avoid overt party propaganda in the Festival. One of the only two occasions when he intervened in the actual planning of the Festival was to remove all mention of free school meals from the Schools Pavilion. (The other occasion was when the *Sunday Pictorial* alleged that Mitzi Cunliffe's projected group of statuary, representing the Origins of the Land and the People, was obscene, and Morrison sent Barry up to Manchester, to walk solemnly round the maquette with Mrs. Cunliffe, and pronounce it decent viewed from every possible angle.)

A much heavier monkey on the Festival's back was the antipathy of the senior Carnivores, for whom Evelyn Waugh spoke. Something of the savagery of the resentment felt against the Labour Government and all its doings, of the rage to bring the nation down in their own fall, is reflected in a letter to the *Spectator*, written in 1950 by one J. Dupont, of Kittery Point, Maine, at a time when Britain's need to earn dollars was desperate. "Private letters from Britain," he wrote, "urge American friends not to

come to Britain during the Festival. . . . Many Americans who made tentative plans to visit England next year have changed their minds for two reasons, one being the possibility of a general war, and the other being the dismay and distaste with which they regard the Festival." (Two weeks later another member of the *Spectator*-subscribing community at Kittery Point wrote to say that she found the Festival advertising "essentially un-British." Americans, she said, "want England to be the same, battle-scarred but beautiful.")

Professor Albert Richardson, the Georgian-type architect, declared that the South Bank site was too small, and predicted a terrible catastrophe as thousands of visitors were pushed into the Thames by later arrivals. Sir Thomas Beecham described the Festival as a "monumental piece of imbecility and iniquity." Cyril Osborne, the Conservative M.P., declared himself against holding the Festival, on the grounds that the divorce courts were choked and the prisons were crowded. The Russians were against it, too; they thought it was a disguise for war preparations.

The Government did its best to square the Establishment by empanelling a representative selection of them on the Festival Council, along with R. A. Butler and Colonel Walter Elliot, the hostages from the Opposition. There were Sir Kenneth Clark, T. S. Eliot, John Gielgud, Sir William Haley, and Sir Malcolm Sargent; a general, an earl, and a few lords. The Council was put under the chairmanship of General Lord Ismay, Churchill's war-time Chief of Staff. An authority initially less enthusiastic about its task can rarely have been constituted. "I think we all started this job in rather a lukewarm way," said Sir Alan Herbert, one of the Council members, later. It was an understatement. Lord Ismay later told Barry that he had accepted the post partly out of relief that it had not turned out to be, as he half feared when he was summoned to Number Ten, "a more distasteful offer." Barry stirred their interest by having huge imaginary visualisations of the still unvisualised Festival drawn and hung up around the Council's walls. "The Council warmed to its task gradually," he wrote, "passing – dare one say? – from a state of reserved scepticism on the part of some of its members, through various degrees of conversion, to final unanimous conviction." After all, as Sir Alan Herbert pointed out, surviving "five years of war and five years of His Majesty's Government" was certainly something to celebrate. Members of the Council, though, came under considerable pressure from their friends, and, at awkward junctures, as late as 1950, some of them were privately of the opinion that the whole thing ought to be called off. But open criticism of the Festival among the Establishment was dampened down still further when the King and Queen became patrons in March 1950.

All in all, the Festival might have had rougher handling. The critics seem to have suffered all along from the uncomfortable suspicion that they were on the losing side. The criticism was certainly mild in comparison with the torrent of abuse and ridicule which was rained down upon the 1851 Exhibition, when its opponents predicted divine retribution for the presumption of the enterprise, a disastrous influx of Papists bent on ruining the country with idolatry and schism, the turning of Bayswater into one giant brothel, an epidemic of venereal disease, and the return of the Black Death.

Meanwhile, the Design Group was trying to give the Festival some concrete shape. The group, which was led by Hugh Casson, consisted of two display designers, James Holland and James Gardner, and three architects, Casson, Ralph Tubbs, and Misha Black. For a start they used to meet in the footman's bedroom of one of the massive red-brick houses behind Harrods, wearing overcoats on account of the shortcomings of the heating system, and taking Bisodol to keep at bay the dyspepsia to which exhibition designers are said to be martyrs. Here they sat and thought, with the despairing blankness that comes before one has actually got anything down on paper, about the South Bank site – a derelict slum, low-lying, marshy, and heavily blitzed, bisected by the arches carrying the busy main line out of Charing Cross. And when their brains were beaten dry they went to Waterloo and walked the site, often at night when everything was still, picking their way among the hopeless heaps of rubble.

Early in 1949 they had a master-plan ready, and began to appoint architects for the individual buildings. The men they chose were mostly Casson's contemporaries. Casson (another true Herbivore – the son of an Indian Civil Servant, educated at Cambridge, with a spell in the Ministry of Town and Country Planning under William Holford) was then thirty-nine. The climax of the period that had formed them all was the Paris Exhibition of 1937, and after a decade of nothingness, given the chance to work with like-minded colleagues on a project whose temporary nature encouraged them to risk boldness, they took up architecture again where it had been left twelve years before. But the fundamental decision, which affected the characteristic appearance of the Festival more than anything else, had already been taken by Casson. For it was Casson who had decided that the South Bank was not going to be laid out in the formal avenues and vistas of earlier exhibitions, but as a modest and informal complex of interlocking neighbourhoods, each with its own character – like the piazzas of Venice, or the courts of Cambridge – and peculiarly appropriate as a microcosm of life in an overcrowded island.

It was a terrible time to build an exhibition. When they started work steel was in short supply, and they were urged to use wood wherever possible, but by the time their plans were ready steel was plentiful, and it was timber that had to be avoided. To allow for these and other fluctuations in the supply of materials, plans had constantly to be re-drawn. And when the designs began to come in, in the summer of 1949, the consulting engineers declared they were too novel and too complex to be built in the time available, and all but two had to be either scrapped or modified.

The Festival authorities set up home in the forecourt of the Savoy Hotel, in offices formerly occupied by the Free French. Here, as the pace grew hotter and the exotic oddments collected for the Festival piled up, there grew what Barry called "an irresistible mood of sharrawaggy and slightly unhinged romance." A complex organisation extracted, filtered, and bottled the outstanding achievements in every department of life. A "Lion and Unicorn Pavilion" was planned, to demonstrate the glories and whimsicalities of what, on these occasions, is taken to be the British character, and, on the truly Herbivorous grounds that someone who is used to the pithy intensity of poetry would be the right man to serve the state by writing captions, Laurie Lee was appointed chief caption-writer. He appealed for oddities, and was overwhelmed with collapsible rubber buses and smoke-grinding machines. A certain melancholy British whimsy crept in elsewhere uninvited. The Ministry of Pensions asked that room should be found for "a modest display of artificial limbs." A Midlands firm wondered if space could be found for some shrouds and coffin fittings. Another manufacturer sought permission to exhibit a model of the South Bank made out of toilet rolls.

The South Bank, of course, was not the only manifestation planned for 1951. There was to be a Land Travelling Exhibition stumping the provinces inland, and another exhibition was to tour the seaports aboard the *Campania*, a mongrel ship laid down as a merchantman, and converted to an aircraft-carrier while it was still on the stocks. Towns and cities all over the country were to hold festivals of their own – madrigals on the river at Cambridge, lectures on Non-Shakespearean Comedy at Oxford, Rudyard Kipling's relics at Rottingdean, a netball display at Colchester, and pageants of local history practically everywhere. Nor was this all.

Spontaneous expressions of citizenship," said the Festival guide in positively Soviet tones, "will flower in the smallest communities as in the greatest." And the countryside duly sprouted rose shows and road safety weeks, new paint and fresh whitewash, memorial bus-shelters, memorial street-lighting, even memorial repairs to the local war-memorial.

And there were the Pleasure Gardens and Funfair in Battersea Park. It was ironical that these, which were in a way the least Herbivorous item of the whole programme, should have proved its most vulnerable point. They were entangled in dispute from the very beginning. It was during the debate on the Bill which provided for them, in November 1949, that the Opposition first cut up rough about the Festival. Spending the taxpayers' money on doing the taxpayers good was suspect; spending it on entertaining them was a jar to Conservative propriety which was much harder to explain away—though at that stage the money involved was little enough, an estimated loss of £100,000 to be shared between the Government and the L.C.C.

The Gardens were intended to recall the glories and fantasies of the eighteenth-century pleasure gardens of Vauxhall, Ranelagh, and Cremorne; a shakily nostalgic basis compared with the rest of the Festival. They were to be run by the Government and L.C.C. jointly, through a company in which they were the sole shareholders, called Festival Gardens Limited. It was intended originally to spend £1.9 millions, and recover it by keeping the Gardens open for five years. But, in the summer of 1949, Chelsea and Battersea councils made it clear that they were not prepared to have them open for more than one year, and considerable alterations had to be made to the plans to bring the gross expenditure down to £770,000. The following year there was a bitter debate about whether the amusement section should be allowed to remain open on Sundays. The Advisory Committee of Christian Churches for the Festival was vigorously opposed to Sunday amusement in the amusement park, though it had no objection to Sunday pleasure in the pleasure gardens. In the end, it was put to a free vote in the Commons, and, by a large majority, the people's representatives voted to keep the amusement out of Sunday pleasure—so helping to nourish and increase the loss, cherishing it no doubt as a topic of discussion for later sessions.

On the site at Battersea the difficulties accumulated. The work was hindered by an unending series of strikes, go-slows, and work-to-rules. The site flooded after the heavy rains of November 1950. The first five months of 1951 were the wettest since 1815, and the park was churned into a sea of mud that resembled the battlefields of Flanders rather than the pleasure-gardens of Vauxhall. Finally Richard Stokes, the Minister of Works, went down to Battersea and harangued the construction-workers himself.

But by this stage it was clear that the Gardens were not going to open on time. It was also clear that they were heavily over-spent. By the end of 1950 the estimated gross expenditure had leapt from £1,100,000 to £1,600,000. By March 1951 it had reached £2,400,000. In April the chairman and managing director of Festival Gardens Limited resigned. Stokes had two firms of chartered accountants appointed to investigate both Festival Gardens Limited and the work of the site contractors, and their report, which was published as a White Paper, put a considerable share of the blame on the Festival Gardens board for the way in which they had managed the work. In the end the Pleasure Gardens opened three weeks late, and in June Stokes had to ask the House to authorise the loan of another million pounds, and to hear Harold Macmillan grind the humiliation home with the over-rehearsed debating club locutions which the future Prime Minister affected at that time—"a little gem of mis-management, a cameo of incompetence, a perfect little miniature of muddle." Princess Margaret cancelled the visit she was supposed to make to Battersea at the end of the season, telling Morrison that she refused to come and get involved in his maladministration.

While Pleasure was brought forth in Pain at Battersea, there was plenty of agony elsewhere. In the summer of 1949 the Government's gross expenditure on the Festival (excluding the Pleasure Gardens, a grant of £2 millions to the L.C.C. towards the Royal Festival Hall, and various charges to fall on the votes of other departments) was estimated at £12 millions, of which £2 millions would be recouped from entrance money. That September, however, the Government devalued the pound, and in the ensuing round of economies the Festival's budget was cut back by a million pounds. The following summer, when the Korean War broke out, the question was raised as to whether the Festival should be held at all. It could clearly not have been abandoned at this late stage without writing off the whole investment, but there were even members of the Festival Council who had cold feet. By the beginning of 1951 itself, after the great United Nations withdrawals in Korea, the Press was full of gloomy speculations about the possibility of world war before the year was out, and the abandonment of the Festival was discussed once more. It was not only the *Daily Express* that raised the question. "The country, which formerly gave unanimous approval to the enterprise," wrote Rainald Wells in the *Daily Telegraph* on January 19th, with masterly over-simplification, "is now divided in its views. More and more people, indeed, are asking whether it should not be postponed, or even cancelled. . . . The overriding question is whether or not the Festival will tend to aid or to hinder us in what is now our primary task—that is, the strengthening of our defences."

A gay start to Festival year. By this stage, too, the prospects on the South Bank looked extraordinarily depressing. The plans were late. The materials were late. The phenomenal rainfall, as at Battersea, played havoc, and after the rains it froze. There was a series of strikes, and at the end of January work came to a complete standstill for a fortnight. For fifteen whole days the desperate rush to get the exhibition ready in time was halted, and the only sign of activity in the whole of that suddenly paralysed leviathan was the strikers playing football on the fairway.

The delay on the South Bank was made up— "A good time-and-a-half was had by all," said Casson. But the political background against which the celebrations were to be held went from bad to worse. In May 1951 the papers were still publishing the casualty lists from the Gloucesters' stand on the Imjin River. The saddest irony of all was that, by the time the Festival opened, the age of the Herbivores who made it was in its last and dimmest days. The General Election on February 23rd, 1950, had left the Labour Party with an overall majority of six, and they dragged themselves through their last painful months in the spring and summer of 1951 like an old, wounded animal, biting at its own injuries. On April 14th Bevin died. On April 21st Bevan resigned, to be followed by Harold Wilson and John Freeman, over the proposal to make a charge for National Health Service teeth and spectacles. Francis Boyd, the Political Correspondent of the *Manchester Guardian*, described the Commons debate on the "teeth-and-spectacles" clause as "a picture of a Government suffering severe internal haemorrhage and likely to bleed to death at any moment. For the greater part of three and a half hours Labour members got up one after the other to attack each other. The Opposition might not have been part of the House of Commons." And at the end of May, to add to the Government's embarrassments, Guy Burgess and Donald Maclean disappeared.

Still, on May 3rd the King and Queen went to St. Paul's for a Service of Dedication, and from the top of the steps in front of the great portico, with a fanfare from the trumpeters of the Household Cavalry, the King declared the Festival open. Barry had wanted the King to perform the ceremony on Tower Hill, and proceed to the South Bank by state barge, but the King had refused, saying that Tower Hill had too many bloody associations, and that anyway the state barge leaked. There was a sense of holiday in the air, and, after careful observation of the crowds lining the streets to see the Royal Family, *The Times* gave its verdict – "People in Joyous Mood." At the South Bank they worked all that day – and all that night – and as the guests began to come through the front gates for the private view on the morning of May 4th, so the rearguard of the army of workers retreated before them across the city they had built and withdrew through the back gates. The South Bank, or at any rate, ninety-five per cent of it, was ready on schedule. By the time the official visitors had left and the first handful of the general public had been let in, it was pouring with rain. The visitors splashed dismally round, offering no visible evidence of enjoyment. It was the gloomy baptism without which no British summer festival could be considered properly launched.

But the sense of anti-climax did not last. It quickly became clear that the South Bank, conceived in austerity and shaped by expediency, was a knockout. For two or three evenings the police had to close the streets round the Embankment to traffic, as the crowds poured down to gaze at the floodlit dream-world breathing music on the other side of the river. "People making for the South Bank," reported the London Correspondent of the *Manchester Guardian*, "begin to smile as they come close to it." The *Guardian* suggested that "on bright sunny days it seems likely that a trip across the Thames to the South Bank will be as invigorating as a trip across the Channel, for in its final form the scene is quite as unfamiliar as any foreign seaside resort." It certainly was. The crowds came in, and wandered round in a state of somnambulism, forming queues with such abstracted readiness that the attendants found difficulty in preventing the accumulation of queues that led nowhere at all. No one had ever seen anything like it before. Apart from the New Towns, it was one of the first concerted attempts at modern architecture in Britain in this century, a brilliant microcosm in which every single object had been designed for its job. For a few hours people stepped out of the squalid compromises of the everyday urban scene into a world where everything was made to please. There was music on the loudspeakers to walk round to. There were plenty of cafés to sit down at (though the chips-and-peas type food provided by the catering firms failed signally to rise to the occasion). There were the two distinctive shapes by which cartoons and souvenirs of the Festival were instantly identifiable – the great closed scallop shell of Ralph Tubbs's Dome of Discovery and the Skylon, the luminous exclamation mark with which the young engineers Powell and Moya had won the competition for a vertical feature. Round every corner there was a new delight – a catwalk to look down from, or the superb water mobile by Richard Huws, which imitated the regular sequence of small and great waves on the shore. There was the river to look at. And, on the other side of the river, the magnificent sombre building line of the north bank, revealed for the first time as a back curtain to the colourful and extravagant outlines of the Festival architecture.

Barry was duly knighted. The team of huskies in the Polar Theatre melted a million fusible hearts. The Red Cross treated sixteen people who fell, presumably bemused, into the fountains. Later in the season balloonists took off from the South Bank and drifted with the wind, in the leisurely way of Edwardian high summer, to the open country outside the city. Charles Elleano crossed the river on a tight-rope. And twice a week, when darkness fell, there was open-air dancing among the twinkling lights that studded the Fairway.

Someone, unfairly, described the South Bank exhibition as "all Heal let loose." Afterwards, the fashions it set in architecture and design were quickly copied, became clichés, and eventually looked vulgar against the growing affluence of the fifties. But now that the whole painful process of outgrowing an out-of-date fashion has been completed, we can look back and appreciate just what a box of delights the South Bank really was. Though, as with any box of delights, the most delightful thing was the packaging, and the air of surprise and excitement it gave to the contents. The contents themselves were a little more mundane. The exhibition was supposed to show Britain's contribution to civilisation. This, of course, is the sort of thing that museums are about anyway, and the Festival could only do it in the same way that a museum would, with samples of fossils and steam-engines, and pictures of more fossils and more steam-engines, garnished with the hearty Herbivorous display in the Lion and Unicorn Pavilion. But what else can you have a national exhibition about? Still, the splendour of their housing carried the exhibits; and the radar screens, the craftsmen making cricket-bats, and the three-dimensional representations of the integral calculus gave point and a sense of importance to their surroundings. The best thing of all about the South Bank was just being there.

That year the Whit-Monday Fair at Hampstead was abandoned in favour of Battersea. There were queues at the Pleasure Gardens for nylons and Festival rock – and prosecutions for traders who sold the rock without points. But, after the South Bank, the Pleasure Gardens were disappointing. There was something too insistently whimsical about the Guinness Clock and the Emmet Railway, and something even worse about the orange-girls, dressed up as replica Nell Gwyns, articulating "Come, gentle people, buy," in sub-Roedean accents, like air-hostesses at a fancy-dress ball.

Over eight million people went to the Pleasure Gardens, and nearly eight and a half million visited the South Bank. But there can have been few people in Britain whose lives remained completely untouched by the Festival. The Festival symbol devised by Abram Games (its original stark nudity draped in bunting by the Festival Council) was ubiquitous. So was the word "Festival". The great programme of poetry readings, serenade concerts, firework displays, and children's sports rolled across Britain relentlessly, and, though the local Festival Rose Show may have been remote in spirit from the pre-stressed concrete *élan* of the South Bank, it brought with it some suggestion of national identity and consciousness. The B.B.C. – the most thoroughbred Herbivores of all – hammered the Festival into the national cortex with 2,700 programmes on the subject. Even the Druids made a Festival of Britain pilgrimage to Stonehenge.

At the end of September the Festival closed. On Saturday the 29th, large numbers of people fainted in the dense crowd that packed the Fairway on the South Bank, waiting for Gracie Fields in the farewell cabaret. At midnight the crowd still surged and boiled, sliced by the violet-edged beams from the television arc lights, and full of that strange nostalgic excitement which marks end-of-term ceremonies. In the Royal Pavilion champagne corks popped among the official guests, and Ministers stood listening impassively to everyone's ideas on how to dispose of the corpse of the South Bank. On the Sunday night, with a slight air of anti-climax, the Brigade of Guards beat the retreat, the crowd sang "Abide with Me," the National Anthem, and "Auld Lang Syne," and the Festival flag was hauled down. The King should have been present, but he was ill – dying, as it turned out. The curious summer was over; a way of life was ending, too.

What is one to think of the Festival? It was not quite the roaring popular success of the Great Exhibition, which was seen by six million people – a third of the population at that time. Nor did it generate the intense national enthusiasm of a piece of routine royal pageantry like the Coronation. Rainald Wells, who at the beginning of the year had suggested abandoning it, gave in the *Daily Telegraph* a grudging but not crushing verdict on behalf of the Carnivores: "It may perhaps be likened to a moderately successful party, but one held on the wrong day and at far too great a cost. We are none the sadder for it, but we might have been wiser to have kept the money in our pockets." Far too great a cost? The total net expenditure, apart from the loans for the Festival Gardens, was just over eight million pounds – comfortably within the estimate, and working out at something over three shillings a head of the population. Not quite so satisfactory as the 1851 Exhibition, which made profits big enough to finance the building of the Victoria and Albert Museum (though to do it the organisers resorted to some pretty curious means, like leaving deliberately wide cracks between the floorboards, and letting out a concession to a private firm to keep whatever fell through; so much did that it paid for the whole floor) but cheap by modern standards of Government expenditure, and not unduly expensive by the standards of major exhibitions; Paris 1937 and New York 1939 both lost around £4 millions. Foreign visitors to Britain, moreover, for whatever reason they came, and even if they did not include some of the citizens of Kittery Point, Maine, spent eighteen million pounds more than they did in 1950.

In the summer of 1951 the Gallup Poll asked people what their impression of the South Bank was, from what they had seen and heard. 58 per cent said they had a favourable impression, 15 per cent an unfavourable one. More of the young were favourably impressed than of the older age groups; more of the averagely well-off than the very or less well-off; more Liberal voters than Socialists or Tories. By a not overwhelming majority, in other words, the country liked the Festival – the Herbivores, naturally, most of all. But the South Bank and Battersea were also paid a more striking compliment. The acid democratic test of housing estates and similar undertakings is whether or not they are smashed up by that section of the community which has no other redress for being treated with contempt or condescension; and at the end of the season the police were struck by the absence of hooliganism and other crime in both places. It was quite a tribute.

The Festival certainly absorbed building materials at a time when many were homeless. But it did provide some of the "fun, fantasy, and colour" that Barry had promised at a time when the nation was parched for lack of them, and the intense concern with design, function, and appearance which pervaded the South Bank has survived. It did not, as Barry had also suggested, exactly disprove the myth that the British take their pleasures sadly. Some nights at the open-air dancing on the Fairway couples went doggedly dancing on in heavy rain. Perhaps we took the pleasures of 1951 not so much sadly as desperately.

The Festival was a rainbow – a brilliant sign riding the tail of the storm and promising fairer weather. It marked the ending of the hungry forties, and the beginning of an altogether easier decade. But it was not, as its critics had feared, to mark the consolidation of the Herbivorous forces which had made it. To adapt Rainald Wells's verdict, it may perhaps be likened to a gay and enjoyable birthday party, but one at which the host presided from his death-bed.

What was to become of the South Bank? The Executive Committee wanted to run it for a second year. William Zeckendorf, a New York estate agent, offered to spend up to a million dollars on freight charges to get the Dome of Discovery and the Skylon to New York. The Marquess of Bath said he was interested in putting the Skylon up at Longleat, to add to the charms of that stately home. None of these plans came to anything. At the General Election at the end of October the sad remnants of the once triumphant post-war Labour Government were swept away, and a Conservative Government came in, eager to prove its freshness and efficiency. With almost guilty haste they turned on the remains of the Festival. David Eccles, the new Minister of Works, took Barry on a brisk tour of the site, indicating the buildings to be torn down, like a dictator's henchman picking out prisoners for execution. With the exception of the Festival Hall itself, a café beneath Waterloo Bridge, the Telekinema, and the verandahs slung like the gondolas of a balloon high out over the Thames, the whole 27 acres was efficiently stripped down to ground level.

And there, with what one would have thought was intolerable symbolism, it remained for a decade; 27 acres, in the very heart of one of the world's great capitals, totally derelict and unused. Until at last the ground was ready to put forth a second crop, and where the Festival had once stood there grew one of the largest and ugliest commercial office blocks in Western Europe. And a car park for 700 cars.

INDEX

INDEX